Samuel L. Southard

Samuel L. Southard (1787–1842). Reproduced with permission (including permission to publish) from Special Collections Department, Firestone Library, Princeton University.

Samuel L. Southard

Jeffersonian Whig

Michael Birkner

Rutherford • Madison • Teaneck
Fairleigh Dickinson University Press
London and Toronto: Associated University Presses

© 1984 by Associated University Presses, Inc.

Associated University Presses
440 Forsgate Drive
Cranbury, NJ 08512

Associated University Presses
25 Sicilian Avenue
London WC1A 2QH, England

Associated University Presses
2133 Royal Windsor Drive
Unit 1
Mississauga, Ontario
Canada L5J 1K5

Library of Congress Cataloging in Publication Data

Birkner, Michael J., 1950–
  Samuel L. Southard : Jeffersonian Whig.

  Bibliography: p.
  Includes index.
  1. Southard, Samuel L. (Samuel Lewis), 1787–1842.
2. United States—Politics and government—1815–1861.
3. New Jersey—Politics and government—1775–1865.
4. Legislators—United States—Biography. 5. United
States. Congress. Senate—Biography. 6. New Jersey—
Governors—Biography. I. Title.
E340.S68B57 1983   974.9′03′0924 [B]   82-48517
ISBN 0-8386-3160-6

Printed in the United States of America

For My Parents

Contents

Preface

Over the span of a full and varied, if not always satisfying life, Samuel Lewis Southard played a significant and frequently controversial role in American politics, law, and enterprise. As an influential New Jersey politician from 1812 through 1842, he had few peers. He held major office in all three branches of government, including service as a justice of the state supreme court, assemblyman, attorney general, and governor. Moreover, he was the most influential anti-Jacksonian politician in New Jersey for more than a decade, and contributed significantly to the success of the Whig party in state election campaigns.

Southard was also a consequential figure in national politics. He served as navy secretary and adviser of two presidents from 1823 to 1829, and throughout his public career labored tirelessly on behalf of a modern navy. During his twelve years in the United States Senate, Southard fought with, and against, the greatest political personalities of his times—Van Buren, Calhoun, Webster, Clay, Benton, and Rives, to name several of the most outstanding. As a senator, Southard spoke forcefully against the economic policies of two Democratic administrations, and worked closely with his friend, Henry Clay, in plotting a national Whig strategy against the Jacksonians. From his political base in Washington, Southard directed Whig operations in his home state, and as president pro tem of the Senate in 1841 and 1842 he stood one heartbeat from the first office of the land.

Despite his achievements, perhaps the overriding theme in Southard's life was disappointment, both in politics and in his private life. Though he held many important public trusts and discharged his responsibilities with credit, he was rarely fulfilled and never satisfied. Some other lucrative, prestigious, or important post always remained beyond reach. So, too, with his quest for financial security and financial repose. Though he made an excellent living as an attorney and public servant, Southard kept barely one step ahead of bill collectors and bank agents—when, indeed, he could stay ahead at all. His major adventure in business, as president of the Morris Canal and Banking Company, was a constant vexation, and his many speculations, primarily in land, failed to realize their projected profits. To compound these disappointments, Southard's marriage was a study in aggravation, conflict, and pain. A life begun with promise ended in bitterness.

9

Both Southard's successes and frustrations in a life replete with each may best be grasped against the backdrop of a fast-changing social and economic order. Born in 1787 in a prosperous but unpretentious agricultural community, Southard matured in a culture that believed in the values of "republican simplicity," values exemplified by his father, Henry, in a long and useful life. Like many of his countrymen, Southard bespoke the virtues of "republican simplicity" even as he adopted the values of a new and dynamic age. By the 1820's, as a colleague of John Quincy Adams and Henry Clay and, later, as a Whig leader, Southard embraced a more modern Jeffersonian creed, which included support for positive state action to encourage and sustain enterprise throughout America. Such a policy, he believed, would foster economic prosperity, the spread of abundance, and increased harmony in a diversifying society. Not all politicians agreed with this perspective, and the disagreement over means underlay the political debates of the Jacksonian era. How Southard came to the views he espoused and fought for, and how, in important respects, his embrace of ambition and a "go-ahead" mentality proved to be his ticket to frustration and bitterness, are central concerns of this book.

Acknowledgments

Parts of this work have previously appeared, in somewhat altered form, in the *Princeton University Library Chronicle, The American Neptune,* and *The Tennessee Historical Quarterly.* I am grateful to their editors for permission to reprint those articles here. Manuscript materials are used through the courtesy of the respective manuscript depositories.

I have been exceptionally fortunate during the years since this study was conceived to have had the encouragement and assistance of several institutions and dozens of individuals who, each in their own fashion, have left an imprint on me and on this book. Properly to acknowledge them all would be an impossible task. I am pleased, however, to pay a fraction of the debt I owe by mentioning the contributions of a few.

Professor Michael F. Holt of the University of Virginia, who guided this work as a dissertation, offered a mix of encouragement, gentle prodding, and constructive criticism that was not simply salutary but essential to its completion. To him must go much credit for whatever is valuable in this biography.

Professors James Sterling Young, Charles McCurdy, and Edward Ayres of the University of Virginia also read the manuscript in its entirety and offered trenchant appraisals both of my approach to Southard's career generally and of specific arguments within the respective chapters. Though I have not always followed their suggestions, the final version of this work nonetheless benefited considerably from what they had to say.

Edward J. Baskerville of Gettysburg College, teacher and friend, has for the past decade offered helpful advice on a wide range of matters. Though I lament that he has not quite succeeded in teaching me the fundamentals of fine English prose style, his example as a writer and his commitment to literacy have left a deep impress on my own work. Professors Lance Banning, Mary Wilma Hargreaves, and Robert Seager of the University of Kentucky each read, criticized, and thereby improved portions of several draft chapters. My friend, Dan Smith, also of the University of Kentucky, read none of the manuscript, but he merits appreciation nonetheless for aid and advice on many occasions and, not least, for tolerating my ramblings about Samuel Southard for more years than he perhaps would care to remember. Dr. Charles M. Wiltse, editor-in-chief of the Daniel Webster Papers at Dartmouth College, offered a timely suggestion regarding the title of this book. My colleague at the Webster Papers, Ken Stevens, provided equally timely editorial advice in the final stages of preparing the manuscript for press.

I am grateful to my teachers and fellow students in the graduate school at the University of Virginia, who made the study of American History a special challenge and pleasure. The Thomas Jefferson Memorial Foundation made that education possible. Another institution, the New Jersey Historical Commission, provided a grant-in-aid at a crucial juncture in the gestation of this work. To the staff of the commission, where I had the good fortune to work for a better part of a year, I owe a great debt.

Dr. William C. Wright, Director of New Jersey's Division of Archives and Records Management, contributed to this biography at every stage, in the line of duty and beyond. His generous gift of time, energy, and expertise exemplifies an ideal in the community of learning. The same may be said for the many librarians who greatly facilitated the process of getting the documents I needed as well as the printed materials that enabled me to interpret them. I cannot list all those who graciously put up with my seemingly endless requests, but I offer special thanks to Don Skemer of The New Jersey Historical Society and Edward Skipworth of Rutgers University's special-collections department.

Finally, there are the animating forces behind my scholarship. This brief mention cannot nearly repay my parents, John and Mildred Birkner, who sacrificed that I might get an education that was unavailable to them, and who never complained (too violently) that I was procrastinating in completing it. The dedication of this work seeks, in a small way, to express my gratitude to them, for everything. The last word is for my wife, Robin Wagner-Birkner. She learned to put up with Samuel Southard as well as with me, provided perspective on the place of scholarly work in the spectrum of life, assisted at many junctures in the course of my labors and, above all, in more ways than can be enumerated, made the enterprise worthwhile.

Samuel L. Southard

1

"Republican Simplicity"

It was one of the most dramatic confrontations in American history. Slightly more than half a century after the creation of a republic in which consensus rather than conflict was expected to characterize national policy-making, the body politic was bitterly divided. On one side stood a strong and unyielding president, Andrew Jackson, who viewed the second Bank of the United States as an unconstitutional and corrupt enemy of American freedoms and Americans' economic opportunity. On the other stood a coalition of opponents who were as steadfastly convinced that Jackson's veto of the bank's recharter was uninformed, mean-spirited, economically ruinous, constitutionally illicit, and threatening to the balanced system established in 1787.

At the nerve center of the opposition to "King Andrew" was a handful of anti-Jacksonian (soon to take on the name "Whig") senators, who were determined to demonstrate to the public that the bank was essential and the president wrong, men warily hopeful of saving the bank or, at the least, bloodying Jackson and his party. Henry Clay, Daniel Webster, and Samuel L. Southard were the acknowledged leaders of the pro-bank group. Their plan, as Congress convened in December 1833, was to press for resolutions requiring the public deposits to be restored to the bank.

On December 26, commencing an extended and emotional oration, Clay brought the issue before the Senate. Three days later, he concluded his argument by demanding that his colleagues formally censure the chief executive. The issue, for Clay, was not simply politics, not simply economics, but the stability of American institutions. Jackson, he said, was trying to destroy the "pure republican character of the Government," and put all power "in the hands of one man."[1]

Clay was followed by Jackson's most forceful supporter in the Senate, Thomas Hart Benton of Missouri, who refuted the Kentuckian point by point, and passionately defended the president. Then, on January 8, 1834, the junior senator from New Jersey, Samuel L. Southard, rose to make what would be the longest and most important speech of his political career. Recently returned to the Senate after an absence of ten years, Southard was familiar enough with the proceedings and so strongly op-

posed to the president's policy that he felt little trepidation. His purpose
was to follow Clay's sweeping attack on Jackson with a close examination of
the mechanics of Jacksonian economic policy. His speech never reached
the heights of Clay's eloquence, but its close and forceful argument won
Southard plaudits from anti-Jacksonians across America. Southard's argument at bottom was simple: Jackson was wrong. But his speech did more
than proclaim good versus evil. It sought to convince fellow legislators and
the public that the bank was a necessary element of American economic
life, the world, too complex to undertake fiscal experiments. To this end he
spoke for the better part of three days.[2]

Southard's was far from the final word during the "Bank War," as it was
called. He was followed by a parade of senators who answered, riposted,
and elaborated on the themes raised by the first three speakers of the
session. The New Jersey senator's influence was not decisive; in this instance, the denouement of the drama was practically assured before act
two—the removals controversy—took center stage. The Bank War was to
be Jackson's political triumph and a bitter disappointment to the Whigs.

The Bank War was important for more than national political maneuverings. It was a testing period and a milestone in the life of a number of
American politicians, among whom Samuel Southard was an example.
Southard grew up in a world congenial to that for which his Jacksonian
opponents spoke as they defended their president's bank veto. In his opposition role, and as spokesman for the largest special interest of his day,
Southard had traveled a great distance from the world of his youth.

The pastoral vision of American life in the late eighteenth century,
idealized by Hector St. John Crèvecoeur and Thomas Jefferson, had more
than a slight basis in fact. Although there is little likelihood that the inhabitants of Somerset County, New Jersey, much thought about the matter,
their lives in many respects were indicative of the possibilities offered by
freedom and honest toil on the land. The rolling countryside in Somerset
was exceedingly hospitable to farming, and particularly to the cultivation of
wheat, which Somerset's residents harvested and milled in great quantities
and transported down the Raritan River to New Brunswick.[3]

Nestled in north central New Jersey east of the Musconetcong Valley,
Somerset County was first settled by emigrants from Long Island, New
York, in the 1720s and 1730s. Several waves of immigration, primarily
though not exclusively from New York, occurred thereafter. Most of those
who moved to New Jersey were Dutchmen seeking the opportunity to farm
their own land without owing loyalty or taxes to the great patroons who
dominated eastern New York. Because of its proximity, northern New
Jersey became the main focus for Dutch farmers' aspirations and the primary beneficiary of their perseverance and skill in transforming wilderness
into an attractive and productive array of arcadian communities.[4]

Abraham Southard was typical of those who migrated to New Jersey. Of mixed Dutch and English stock, he was born in 1705 in Hempstead, Long Island, and for forty-five years lived an unexceptionable life there, farming the land. He married Cornelia Barnes in 1738, and for the next twelve years the Southards resided on property in Hempstead that Abraham had inherited from an unmarried uncle. By mid-1750, however, Abraham Southard was prepared for a change. Taking his wife and children with him to New Jersey and boarding them with relatives in the Raritan Valley, Southard examined and purchased land in the vicinity, in the new county of Somerset. Within twelve months the Southards were settled in Bernard Township in the northernmost part of the county, about a quarter-mile east of the present Basking Ridge.[5]

Although there are few extant evidences of Abraham Southard's life in Bernard Township, it must not have been too disagreeable. He stayed. Southard was surrounded (though hardly crowded) by neighbors much like himself, men who elected him an elder in the flourishing Presbyterian church there. His livelihood offered few opportunities for indulgence; but he and his wife provided adequately for their eight children, of whom one, Henry, would not merely exemplify the tenets of Jeffersonian ideology, but sustain them politically over a long and productive life.[6] Born in Long Island in 1747, Henry Southard was a child when his parents settled in Somerset County, and as a boy was educated briefly in Bernard's village school. Like his father, Henry was raised to work the land. As a youth, he toiled on his father's farm and, according to local histories, saved enough money to purchase his own property by laboring as a hired man for meager wages.[7]

Having earned enough money to win his independence, in 1771 Henry Southard married Sarah Lewis, a fifteen-year-old neighbor, whose father had migrated to Basking Ridge from Wales in 1732. Over a period of twenty-five years Henry Southard farmed his land and Sarah Southard bore his thirteen children, only six of whom lived beyond the age of eleven. There was further heartache for the Southards; their two eldest sons, Lott and Stephen, were mentally impaired—the latter so much so that he remained a ward of his family for his entire life.[8]

Henry Southard made no special mark on his community during his first quarter-century in Basking Ridge, but with the onset of the American Revolution, his life took a new turn. Shortly after American independence was declared in 1776, Henry enlisted as a private in the Somerset County militia. Serving four terms of duty, he saw action at the battles of Ash Swamp, Short Hills, and Red Bank—each of them within fifty miles of his home. Henry was made a wagoner in 1777 and did private carting for the army as well.[9]

With the war's end, Southard returned to his farm and steadily increasing family in Bernard Township. Now in his early forties, Southard was at last ready to serve his community. In 1786 he was elected a Somerset County freeholder. That same year he was named a justice of the peace and local legend says that out of thousands of cases that came before him in that post, he was overruled only four times.[10]

Henry Southard's first public service coincided with the second stage of America's experiment in independence, and also with the birth of his sixth child, Samuel Lewis. This son was to play a significant role in the affairs of his state and nation for much of the next half-century. Samuel Lewis Southard entered the world June 9, 1787, without a silver spoon in his mouth but with signal opportunities to leave the family farm and perhaps abandon farming entirely for different challenges. His father was determined he should have the best available education, and by this time had the means to afford it. Samuel spent his earliest years at home working and playing, but by the age of twelve he was enrolled in a newly established classical school in Basking Ridge, operated by the local Presbyterian pastor, Robert Finley.[11]

This was a crucial and fortunate event in Samuel's life, for Robert Finley was both a fine scholar and a remarkable man. The son of a successful Scottish businessman who had emigrated to America at the strong urging of Princeton's President John Witherspoon, Robert Finley attended Witherspoon's College, from which he graduated in 1788. After a brief and peripatetic career teaching school in New Jersey and South Carolina, Finley returned to Princeton to study theology with President Witherspoon as his first step to the ministry. Ordained as a Presbyterian minister in 1794, Finley preached for several months in New Brunswick before receiving a call from the Basking Ridge Presbyterian Church in 1795. There, Finley began instructing boys, at first in his own home, then in a school erected with village funds. According to his biographer, Finley's goal was "to make sound classical scholars, and to implant on the pupils' minds principles and habits of subordination and good scholarship."[12] As a tutor, Finley displayed a remarkable combination of discipline and affection for his students. Stern in the classroom, he was nonetheless much loved by his charges, whom he often taught individually, while hiking in the Somerset Hills. His technique not only encouraged scholarship, but it won him the devotion of a generation of schoolboys, of whom Southard was only one of the most notable.[13]

Following in his elder brother Isaac's footsteps, Samuel entered Finley's school at Basking Ridge in the fall of 1799. There he began the study of Latin under Finley together with Jacob Kirkpatrick, whose family lived in town and attended Finley's church. They were soon joined by Philip Lindsley and Theodore Frelinghuysen. These four boys were the nucleus of Finley's new academy. They graduated together in 1802 and entered the junior class at The College of New Jersey (Princeton) in September of that year.[14]

At the turn of the nineteenth century Princeton College was a modest but lively institution. Established in 1746 as one of the legacies of the Great Awakening, Princeton had become by its semicentennial anniversary a school noted for producing both ministers and statesman. Under the happy influence of John Witherspoon, president from 1768 to 1794, Princeton attained the first rank among American colleges. Always committed to advancing the cause of religion, the college under Witherspoon had turned out in increasing numbers young men who would be doctors, lawyers, and public servants at every level of American life. One of its graduates, James Madison, was secretary of state during Samuel Southard's time at Princeton, and the son of an early Princeton president, Aaron Burr, was vice-president of the United States.[15]

Unfortunately for the contingent from the Reverend Finley's school, the Princeton they entered in the autumn of 1802 was not the institution they had no doubt been primed to expect. On March 6, 1802, a tragedy had struck the college. Its main building, Nassau Hall, which served as a dormitory, recitation center, and library, was set on fire and within hours utterly destroyed save for the walls.[16]

The blaze had several immediate effects. Apart from leaving the college without a solid library or dormitory rooms for its students, the fire triggered an impulse in President Smith that was to make college life considerably less pleasant for those who attended. Convinced that lax discipline had encouraged students to set fire to their own "house," Smith determined not only to punish the alleged perpetrators but to crack down on all the others as well. "This is the progress of vice and irreligion," Smith was heard to exclaim after witnessing the result of the blaze at Nassau Hall.[17]

Although a trustee committee charged with the task of investigating the incident could not prove the guilt of any students, two students were suspended and a new regime was imposed. On the stated premise that the youth of the students required it, the trustees directed that discipline at Princeton follow the standard pattern of a grammar school. Students were to be required to pledge their "entire obedience" to the administration and to commit themselves never to frequent "a tavern or any other house or place where liquors pastery or groceries of any kind are sold for the purpose of eating or drinking without leave obtained from the authority of the college." Students were forbidden to eat or drink in their rooms, or to gamble, and prohibited from using firearms, "in or near the precincts of the College."[18]

This stringent behavior code was coupled at Princeton with a demanding, if not exceedingly broad, curriculum. From early morning till nine at night, the young scholars were kept busy with lectures, visitations, scientific demonstrations, and homework, all closely supervised by President Smith and his small faculty. Mathematics, chemistry, natural history, Old and

New Testament studies, Greek and Latin were staples of the curriculum. The president himself instructed the junior and senior classes in belles lettres, criticism, composition, and moral philosophy, logic, geography, history, and "the evidences and principles of Revealed Religion."[19]

This was a demanding regimen, but it left time for some extra curricular activities, including, most notably, participation in one of the two college literary and debating societies. Southard was a "Clio" and undoubtedly made his public-speaking debut in that society's regular confrontations with the Whigs; his experience in the Cliosophic Society may well have been the single most significant activity during his time at the college. We do not, however, know any particulars of Southard's personal experiences at Princeton in the classroom or out. Nonetheless, his devotion to Princeton in his later life, including service for twenty years as a trustee of the college, suggests that he had a deep affection for his alma mater. For its part, the college thought well of Southard. Although he entered Princeton with a deficiency in his knowledge of Roman antiquities (a deficiency he shared with his friends who had attended Finley's academy), he graduated with honors in 1802, gave the Theological Oration at commencement, and was awarded an honorary A.M. degree in 1807.[20] If Southard met no single figure at Princeton who rivaled Robert Finley as a role model, it nonetheless remains a fair conjecture that he took from Princeton its most precious offering: the basis of a liberal education and a keen sense of the virtues of public service.

Southard had been exceptionally fortunate in his opportunity to attend the College of New Jersey, since this was a time when only two out of every thousand youths had the opportunity to gain a college education. The question Southard faced in the autumn of 1804 was what he would do with such an education. Just seventeen years old, he was not quick to decide. To buy some time, Southard followed the advice of his Basking Ridge mentor, Finley, and got a teaching position in a village school in neighboring Mendham, in Morris County. (Finley, who maintained a keen interest in Southard until his death in 1817, may well have obtained the position for his protégé.) In Mendham, Southard built upon a friendship begun at Princeton with David Thompson, Jr., who became an intimate political ally and sometime adviser for approximately two decades. The year and a half Southard spent teaching in Mendham remains largely a blank. That it influenced his values or future is doubtful. It was primarily an opportunity for him to live semi-independently, to mature a bit, and to see how he liked teaching.[21]

In April 1806, Southard received an opportunity, one made possible by his father Henry's career in politics, which took him from New Jersey for the better part of five years. During Samuel's boyhood, Henry Southard had begun to rise in the political world. In 1791 he ran for the House of Assembly from Somerset County and in the course of an assembly career that saw him win reelection eight times, he helped found the Jeffersonian party in New Jersey. Jeffersonian Republicanism in New Jersey was comparatively late in organizing as a political force, but by the time of John Adams's administration it had become an effective opposition in the state. In 1798 Henry Southard joined William Pennington, a leading figure in the nascent party, in moving that the legislature notice, if not actually adopt, the Virginia Resolutions, which had been penned anonymously by James Madison in response to the Alien and Sedition Laws enacted by the Congress that year. Because Federalists controlled the legislature, the motion was not successful, but it earned the Jeffersonians good publicity in the state.[22]

Henry Southard went to the United States House of Representatives in 1801, where he served eight (not entirely consecutive) terms. There Southard met a young Virginia congressman named John Taliaferro, a man of considerable wealth and status but also a strong Jeffersonian. Taliaferro did not return to Congress in 1803, but he remained friendly with Henry Southard, and in 1806 invited Henry's son Samuel to become part of the Taliaferro household in King George County, Virginia, as a tutor to his children and nephews. This invitation Samuel quickly accepted.[23]

The move to eastern Virginia in 1806 must have brought some kind of culture shock to Southard. One assumes this because of the marked differences between the milieus from which he came and to which he went. In contrast to the relatively small farms in Somerset County, populated by individuals very like Southard's father, Henry, the Northern Neck of Virginia was a land of large plantations whose masters dominated the politics and culture of the region. Southard had seen large farms before, of course, and even slaves—but nothing compared to the dimensions of Taliaferro's holdings. John Taliaferro was owner of thousands of acres of land worked by dozens of slaves, part of a plantation, Hagley, that would be Southard's home for the next five years. Although the Northern Neck was in this period already experiencing a decline, there is no evidence that its grandeur was markedly diminished during the time Samuel lived there.[24]

To judge by a diary he kept irregularly for approximately two years, Samuel's regimen at Hagley could not have been very severe. Ostensibly a tutor, he made not a single mention of his responsibilities in the thirty-three entries from June 1807 to February, 1810. What the diary does reflect is considerable opportunity for reading, reflection, and partying. Samuel's reading was varied, if desultory, ranging from travel writings (e.g., an account of Switzerland) to adventure stories to Tom Paine's works and the writings of Gibbon, both of which he disliked for their antireligious outlook. Nor did Southard prefer Edmund Burke. He tried three times to read Burke's *Reflections of the French Revolution,* and failed all three times—though he did enjoy Burke's speeches on the American Revolution.[25]

On political matters he was more dedicated and emphatic. Reading Chief

Justice John Marshall's opinion on a subpoena for President Jefferson in the treason trial of Aaron Burr, Southard concluded that the opinion was partisan and unjudicial. As a politician, he wrote of Marshall, "I detest him. Candor and integrity are wanting to [sic] his character." Specifically, Southard intimated that Marshall was a turncoat Republican, who had deserted his party with the signing of the Jay Treaty, because he had a financial claim dependent on good relations with England. Southard's disgust for John Marshall was matched by his feelings for England. Writing in the wake of the Chesapeake affair, in July 1807, Southard wrote "I hate the English nation—tis a mass of corruption and crime—Its government has engendered and nourished more political evils than any other which history records . . . war is my wish—I should like to stand before the walls of Quebec." By contrast, Southard viewed Napoleon as "the saviour of Europe, a friend to my country."[26] All of this was standard Jeffersonian doctrine.

These diary entries suggest a number of things about Southard's character and attitudes, not only at the age of twenty but throughout his life. He was, first and always, quick to express emphatic opinions, even though he frequently found that thinking before talking would have been the prudent course. Second, he was consistently a strong partisan. Once Southard had chosen his course—usually without any great agonizing—he stuck to it and invested his sense of justice in it. In brief, he viewed himself as the champion of republican truth that not all men saw so clearly as he.

In this case, he was wildly patriotic and anti-British, and no wonder. Southard grew up in a household in which Thomas Jefferson was practically an icon. Henry Southard had supported the Jeffersonian position in the assembly in the late 1790s, helped to found the party of Jefferson in New Jersey, run for Congress as a Jeffersonian Republican, and in Congress during the Virginian's eight years as president voted consistently for the Jeffersonian program. Samuel's sponsor in Virginia, John Taliaferro, was equally ardent in the president's cause. As a freshman congressman (1801–3), Taliaferro joined Henry Southard and their Republican colleagues in repealing such Federalist legislation as the alien law and the Judiciary Act of 1801, and passing a Jeffersonian program geared to streamlining government and paying off the national debt.[27] Though defeated for reelection, Taliaferro remained committed to the Jeffersonian cause in the Northern Neck, along with such friends as Francis Taliaferro Brooke and John S. Wellford—contemporaries who would themselves become close friends of Samuel Southard. These influences could not fail to shape his political attitudes.

During his sojourn in Virginia, Samuel's political values, though deeply felt, were not the focus of his life. When not tutoring the Taliaferro boys, he was trying to define his life's aims. Southard's lack of career goals as he entered his twenty-first year is evinced in a diary entry he made in Virginia in 1807. Reflecting on his professional options, Southard indicated he did "not wish to study any profession." The ministry he rejected on the ground that he was not sincerely pious enough; medicine was brushed off because he was neither interested in it nor fit for it. Law he pondered with some misgivings because it was supposed to have a bad effect on morals. At bottom, Southard feared he lacked the three elements he saw as essential to professional success: memory, judgment, and imagination. Despite his education and his degree with honors from Princeton, Southard was convinced he was a poor leader and a poor student, perhaps not fit for any profession.[28]

Yet having committed this bleak self-portrait to paper, Southard proceeded to steer his reflections in another direction. "Few men," he wrote in the same diary entry, "have ever felt more strongly the workings of ambition in their bosoms. I am ambitious of serving my country and of being loved and praised by my friends." Law, he finally decided, would be the best means to this end. Hence, in 1807 he embarked on legal studies under the tutelage of Judge Williams in Fredericksburg, poring over James Wilson's lectures on law, and the standard Coke and Blackstone. The actual regimen Southard followed in his studies is unknown, although it was probably comparable to that endured by such contemporaries as Nathaniel Beverly Tucker, Chapman Johnson, and Joseph Cabell, Virginians all, who learned the law under the demanding tutelage of the noted jurist, Henry St. George Tucker. Even as intellectually oriented a youth as Beverly Tucker found his required reading for the bar arduous and disagreeable, and took frequent breaks from it.[29] So apparently did Southard; his diary suggests that he took weeks off to visit his family in New Jersey, or simply to read desultorily and to attend parties at various Virginia plantations, including that of a future president, James Monroe, in neighboring Loudon County. At one of these affairs, a barbecue in August 1807, Southard was introduced to Rebecca Harrow, a young woman whose conduct Southard remarked on as "so pure, so truly feminine."[30]

Rebecca Harrow was the daughter of a deceased Episcopal clergyman, and before long, she was taken in as a ward of the Taliaferros. Southard's initial impressions of Miss Harrow were sustained as he gained a deeper acquaintance. By 1811, in fact, he had completely forgotten his youthful attraction (while living in Mendham) to Reverend Amzi Armstrong's ward "Fanny" and was actively courting Rebecca. All of the Taliaferros, in writing to Samuel during his periodic trips home to Basking Ridge in 1811, mentioned "Becca's" health and activities. At the age of twenty-four, Southard was preparing to marry.[31] The question was, where would he and his bride settle? His Princeton friend Josiah Simpson repeatedly urged Southard to join him in going west, but could never get him to do more than express interest in the proposal. When Simpson, a year older than South-ard, finally did move west, to Mississippi, in 1812, Samuel remained in New Jersey.[32]

In March 1809, after nearly two years of intermittent study, and observa-tion of courtroom procedures in Fredricksburg, Southard received the last signature necessary to practice law in King George and Stafford Counties. It was there that he gained his first experiences in court and earned his first legal fees, and there that he first analyzed his opportunities for making a living at the bar. He continued to reside with the Taliaferros, but this arrangement would necessarily have soon to end.[33] Deeply in love with Rebecca Harrow, desirous of making a name and a "fortune," Samuel was ready to strike out on his own. In choosing a residence, he was undoubtedly influenced by the likely difficulty of finding a prominent place at the Vir-ginia bar, given the increased competition among newly minted attorneys there.[34] Moreover, as he wrote to an old Princeton colleague, William Max-well, in 1810, "my inclination would lead me where I could be near my early acquaintance and college companions."[35] Once convinced that Flemington, New Jersey, offered the opportunity to find a place to make a good living, Southard prepared to abandon Virginia. In December 1810, he made the long trip home to Somerset County. He would not return to Virginia again save as a visitor.

2

Politician on the Rise

The decade extending from Southard's return to New Jersey as an attorney in January 1811 to his departure for Washington in February 1821 as a United States senator witnessed his maturation as a man, a lawyer, and a politician. During this decade Southard embarked on a career at the bar in New Jersey that would extend, with breaks, to his death in 1842; he married and began to raise a family; and he entered politics, moving quickly to a position of influence and, somewhat less quickly, to statewide prominence.

I

Among the advantages Southard enjoyed in moving back to his native state was his name. His father, Henry, was an institution in the Jeffersonian party, a man whose simplicity, integrity, and warmth were widely known and appreciated and whose firm commitment to the tenets of his party was unshakable. Henry Southard was an unusual figure not only because he spent so long a time in Washington in an era when swift turnover in office was the norm, but also because he was never jaded, nor much changed in any way, by his political experiences. He viewed himself, both at the beginning and the end of his long political life, as a citizen in politics, not a politician, and his record bore this notion out. In many respects Henry Southard represented the Jeffersonian ideal of the virtuous farmer who cared about his community, and served that community with no thought of personal gain. In the halls of Congress and on his farm in Basking Ridge, Henry Southard adhered to a strict Jeffersonian creed. As a congressman, he supported three Virginia presidents in their efforts to reduce the government to a strict minimum. He consistently opposed the increased circulation of bank notes, opposed an increase in the compensation of congressmen in 1816, opposed payment of pensions to Revolutionary War veterans (though this would benefit him directly) on grounds that many veterans did not need government assistance, and he argued that economic depression was the result of laxness and luxury, and hence should not be treated by tinkering with the economy. Beyond the stark facts of a voting record, Henry Southard demonstrated the kind of personal modesty and probity that few of his colleagues could match. When, in 1816, he was urged to run for the United States Senate, he refused to countenance such talk on grounds that few politicians of his or a later era would permit to impede them: simple impropriety. "It would be very improper to appoint a member of Congress elect, to that office," he told his son. And that was the end of the matter.[1]

Henry Southard's unpretentious ways were admired by virtually all who knew him, and in large measure they explain his impressive vote-getting record from 1791 to 1818. He was out of office for only three years from 1791 to 1821, and his retirement from public life in 1820 was dictated not by the voters of his district, but rather by his advancing age. This was a man worthy of admiration and emulation. And it is evident that his son Samuel both respected and loved his father greatly, not simply for what he had accomplished, or what he represented in politics, but for what he was. "He is," Samuel wrote to Rebecca Harrow in March, 1812, "a *good* and a *great man*—and he is a plain man but *you* will love him. I know of no man more beloved."[2] Henry Southard's name would be a marked asset to Samuel in the younger Southard's first forays in Jersey law and politics.

Yet if Samuel banked on his father's reputation to win clients and per- haps public office, he did not simply sit back and let events take their course. In what would be characteristic of him for his entire life, Samuel aggressively sought positions that he felt were necessary to give him financial security. By the time of his move to New Jersey early in 1811, Southard was thinking about marriage to Rebecca Harrow, and perhaps worried a bit about the income he could derive from private practice. He threw himself vigorously not only into study for his bar examination in New Jersey, but also into a quest for a surrogacy in Hunterdon County, where he was temporarily boarding until he found a permanent place to live. In February 1811, one of Southard's old Mendham friends, Daniel Dod, mentioned that he had spoken with Governor Joseph Bloomfield about a possible appointment for Samuel. "He requested me to inform you, that on account of your having just come into the county, it would be so very unpopular a thing that he could not think of appointing you to the office of surrogate."[3] Yet within a month, the governor had begun to weaken in his opposition, despite his alleged apprehension that Southard's appointment, because of his age and inexperience, would be "very un- popular."[4]

In his new position Samuel was an officer of the Chancery Court, re- quired to assist the judge in his home county. There he would examine cases, take testimony, compute damages, and report his findings to the court in a form that would render a decision easier to reach. In addition to these duties, Samuel was studying for the bar and planning his future. He had to decide where to set up his home and legal practice, and to make wedding plans. Also, he was introducing himself to the community in other ways. For example, on July 4, 1811, Southard gave a well-received oration as part of the commemoration of the holiday in Flemington. The leading newspaper editor of the state, James J. Wilson, took note of the speech in the Trenton *True American,* observing that "the sentiments were correct, liberal and dignified," and that "it was delivered with spirit and in a style that commanded the applause of the audience."[5] Moreover, publication of this speech did not mark Samuel's debut in print. Earlier in the year he had contributed several political articles for a new Republican newspaper, the New Brunswick *Fredonian.* These were the first of what would be many anonymous contributions to the press during his political career.[6]

The year 1811, in fact, was a propitious time for an aspiring New Jersey politician. Competition between Federalists and Jeffersonians, largely quiet during the middle years of Thomas Jefferson's two terms as president, revived with the foreign-policy tribulations of Jefferson's last years in office and the growing rift between America and Great Britain during the presidency of James Madison.[7]

The New Jersey legislative elections of 1811 were the first in which Southard took an active role, though just what part he played is not clear. His father, who had been defeated for reelection to the House in 1810, agreed to stand for the assembly in 1811 and was the only Republican to win election in Somerset County. The Republicans, however, carried the state decisively, and in joint meeting replaced Federalist Attorney General Aaron Woodruff. Woodruff's successor as attorney general, Andrew S. Hunter, proceeded to name Samuel Southard as deputy attorney general (i.e., prosecutor) for Sussex and Morris Counties.[8]

Referring to his new duties in a letter to Rebecca Harrow, Samuel called them "painful and arduous," but he quite evidently looked forward to both the challenge and the remuneration. The first time he had to argue in Morris County, however, Southard felt some butterflies: repairing to his old stomping grounds, he observed that "when I begin to act on the prosecution of crimes they will watch me with a scrutiny sharpened by old recollections—And if I blunder, as blunder I no doubt shall, they will notice my errors more particularly than strangers."[9]

On balance, his was not an unenviable life. Except for a brief trip to Virginia to marry Rebecca Harrow in June 1812, Southard remained active in study and at court and, increasingly in the fall of 1812, engaged in politics. His father was once again a candidate for Congress, and Samuel worked for his election in his free time. But 1812 but was not a good year for Republicans in New Jersey. The Federalists capitalized on dissent within the Republican party on the wisdom of going to war with England and, dubbing themselves the "Friends of Peace," won a narrow victory in the October legislative elections. Then the Federalists quickly changed the election law to put the choice of presidential electors in their own hands and also to gerrymander congressional districts. Henry Southard was placed in a safe Federalist district and, like three of the other five Republican candidates, lost his bid for office.[10] In control of state appointments, the Federalists reinstated Aaron Woodruff as attorney general, and Southard as prosecutor was deprived of one of his circuits, in Morris County. Why he was permitted to remain in the other post is unclear, but it is evident he was bitter about losing one source of income and about Federalist actions generally.[11]

The war gave New Jersey Federalists a new lease on life, as they capitalized on voter discontent with the apparently feckless policies of the Madison administration. Federalism in New Jersey was not, however, a monolithic force against the war. Federalist Governor Aaron Ogden agreed to take defense measures and other leading Federalists—notably Southard's colleague at the bar, Garret D. Wall—took conspicuous places in the state militia. In general, however, New Jersey Federalism, as reflected in the press, the legislature, and the state's congressional representation, was hostile to a vigorous conduct of the war with England. To ardent administration supporters such as Southard, who believed the war just and right, Federalist complaints, footdragging, and criticisms about the war effort bordered on treason. If Southard, for one, was involved in politics because of his desire for office, which is no doubt true, it remains true also that the war energized him and was to him a Republican crusade.[12]

None of his own letters for this period survives, but those of his friends suggest the tenor of Republican thought. The Federalists, in this correspondence, are viewed as "monsters," "Tories," and "Treason mongers." As one of Southard's Republican friends, Josiah Simpson, put it, "They dread nothing so much as a successful conduct, and an honorable termination of this war. It would be a death blow to their party; and sooner than suffer such a blow to be given, they are willing to give the death blow to their country."[13] Southard's friend John Taliaferro, back in Virginia, put the matter less virulently but equally forcefully—"Your [Federalists in New Jersey] assume the epithetic [sic] of the friends of peace. . . . We are for peace but prefer war to a peace involving sacrifice of essential rights."[14]

During the war, Southard worked to overturn Federalist authority in his state by attending and organizing Republican meetings, writing for the press, and seeking political office himself. He served also in the state militia as judge advocate of the Hunterdon Brigade.[15] In addition, Southard was active in more mundane political chores, serving as conduit for patronage. His correspondence for the years 1812–15 frequently related to requests for the use of his influence in gaining appointments in the armed services or minor government patronage positions. In at least one case, he wrote directly to President Madison on behalf of a Hunterdon County citizen, Nathaniel Price, who sought appointment as collector of internal duties for the third district of New Jersey. Price got the position. Clearly, Southard was building a political base for himself with such favors, and stockpiling political credits for future use.[16]

However passionately Southard viewed the war and the Republican political cause, his life during these years was not completely focused on public affairs. Almost exactly coincident with his twenty-fifth birthday he journeyed to Virginia and married Rebecca Harrow, in June 1812, at Hagley. His correspondence with Rebecca following his return to New Jersey to seek lodgings for them suggests that the rhythms of life for Southard at this time remained relatively gentle. A diary he sent to his wife recording his activities during a July week in 1812 shows that physical labor (stockpiling hay, for example), picking fruit, intermittent legal work, and occasional duties as a Hunterdon County Freeholder (he reported his examination of a bridge in the country and his order that it be repaired), casual conversation, and reading were his prime occupations.[17] None of the pressures of business, personal finances, and family responsibilities that would become so much a part of his life, and quite soon, were yet evident. The summer of 1812 was quite likely Samuel Southard's last idyll.

When Rebecca journeyed north, Southard's life took on a new texture. He needed to find a house for himself and his bride, and to arrange for Negro servants for a wife who was accustomed to such help. These matters required a means of support and the increase in his private legal practice in 1813 is a reflection of his new financial needs. Moreover, by the winter of 1813 Rebecca Southard was pregnant, and in May of that year she was delivered of a son, John, named after John Taliaferro.[18]

With the financial help of his father, Samuel purchased a house for his family in Flemington, Hunterdon County. From this base he practiced law, pursued politics, and raised his family, which grew with the birth of a daughter, Virginia, in 1815.[19] The growing family necessitated increased income, and Southard's almost obsessive quest for public offices over the next decade surely reflects his anxiety over support of this family as much as his genuine interest in public affairs. Further, Southard had to face the reality of his wife's hypochondria, a condition complicated by the fact that Rebecca Southard was often pregnant and frequently genuinely ill. Her almost incessant complaints and illnesses, however, cannot be traced simply to the upset of moving to New Jersey and embarking on married life, or to her pregnancies. She had often been ill while living with the Taliaferros, and her unstable health remained to burden her—and her husband— throughout the years of their life together.[20]

At all events Samuel had to contend with large medical bills, compounded especially by the treatments necessary for his first son, John, who, it became apparent within several years of his birth in 1813, was both mildly retarded and severely epileptic. Southard's correspondence from 1815 is filled with mentions of his son's "affliction," his wife's "indisposition," as well as with the happier mentions of the birth of other, healthy children.[21] In order to pay his bills Samuel engaged in an extensive legal practice that frequently took him from home to follow the various state court circuits. Most of his early legal cases related to estates, debts, and land-title cases; few of them were very lucrative. As a public prosecutor, Southard's fees tended to run from ten to fifteen dollars per case. In private practice he could earn considerably more per case, and did so increasingly by 1814 and 1815, but such additional income was the exception rather than the rule.[22]

The unremunerative nature of his law practice led Southard increasingly to seek public office as a source of financial sustenance and as a basis for increasing his legal business. In August 1815 his friend David Thompson wrote Southard advising him to run for the assembly, suggesting that "you will be able by that means to extend your practice, both as regards the number and importance of the causes which will be given to you to manage. So that as a mere pecuniary matter, my opinion is that you had better accept the office if it is offered [by the Hunterdon County Republican Convention]."[23]

The decision to run for the assembly in 1815 set a pattern. Ever plagued by debts, restless in the offices he was able to acquire (though he was by no means always successful in his aims), Southard constantly sought new preferments: supreme court justice, attorney general, governor, federal claims commissioner, United States senator, United States attorney general, judge on the United States Supreme Court. Southard's political opponents, envious of his quick rise to political prominence and annoyed by his unwillingness to settle for any particular position, derided him privately and occasionally vented their feelings in the public prints—sentiments Southard did not take lightly.[24] Nor did he cease job seeking.

Prior to his successful race for the state assembly in 1815, Southard had legitimately established a name for himself as an effective and at times eloquent counselor at law. In large measure, his reputation derived from arguments he made in a case that became a legal benchmark when it was decided in 1824 by the United States Supreme Court: *Gibbons* v. *Ogden*. The case had its origins in 1798, when the New York legislature repealed a monopoly privilege to run steamboats on state waters that it had conferred on John Fitch, a pioneer in steamboat design, construction, and navigation. The legislature transferred this monopoly privilege to the state's chancellor, Robert R. Livingston, a man with some inkling that steamboats might prove to be an exceedingly profitable investment.[25]

At issue in 1815 was John R. Livingston's challenge (in 1813 he had purchased his brother's interest in the venture) to a New Jersey statute conferring similar monopoly privileges on former governor and Federalist party leader Aaron Ogden. Well aware that Livingston and his partner,

Robert Fulton, were reaping considerable financial benefits from their steamboat enterprise and seeing no valid reason he should not share the thriving business, Ogden began operating a passenger steamboat in 1813. His *Sea Horse*, as it was called, made daily trips from Elizabethtown Point to New York City and back.

Ogden's business was soon stymied, however, when the Livingston-Fulton interest demanded that New York officials enforce their exclusive privilege to traffic across the Hudson River. Unable to persuade the New York legislature to repeal a law he believed manifestly unfair, Ogden used his considerable influence in Trenton, where Federalists controlled the state legislature, to obtain a countervailing monopoly for steam navigation touching New Jersey ports.[26]

For the New Yorkers, a rival monopoly was simply unacceptable. At first, they confined their protests to plaintive correspondence with New Jersey Republican influential and supreme court justice Mahlon Dickerson, in which Livingston in particular reminded Dickerson that he had invested considerable capital in the steamboat venture when no one else could or would do so. If the New Jersey law of November 1813 stood, Livingston said, he would be out a good deal of money. Given his initial risk and his conviction that Ogden's partner, Daniel Dod, had made no material improvement on Fulton's steamboat design, Livingston considered the situation to be patently unfair. Implored by Livingston to explain New Jersey's position to Fulton, Dickerson responded that the New Jersey law was aimed less at individuals than at New York State, which, he noted, was claiming jurisdiction over all waters between the two states and, moreover, granting an unwarranted monopoly to New York entrepreneurs. Both acts denied New Jersey's fair rights. "What they [the New Jersey legislators] have done," Dickerson observed, "is to counteract a law of your state, which they deemed illiberal and unjust as it respects the citizens of this state." Should New York relent on its claims, Dickerson suggested, so would New Jersey.[27]

Dickerson's temperate analysis did not much soothe the New York partners. Frustrated at losing the income from their vessel's operation, Livingston and Fulton awaited the results of the 1814 legislative election in New Jersey and, once that campaign concluded with a Republican triumph, decided to take their case before a legislature dominated by Aaron Ogden's political foes. A hearing scheduled for late January 1815 permitted each side to assign advocates to argue its case. It was at this point that Aaron Ogden played a risky card. On January 12, 1815, Ogden wrote a brief letter to Samuel Southard, his bitter enemy in the recent campaign, requesting Southard's "professional aid in a hearing before the Legislature, which I expect will take place on Tuesday next." Observing that he had the relevant documents organized so that Southard could get quickly acquainted with the facts of the matter at issue, Ogden added that "the cause will be entertaining and interesting, and as to compensation, you will please to name your own sum."[28]

On first appearance, Ogden's invitation to Southard made little sense. Southard had practiced in New Jersey for less than four years, and though he had won a modest reputation for skill and eloquence, his youth (he was twenty-seven at the time) and meager experience in major cases militated against his selection in a hearing of this magnitude. On the other hand, Southard had an important asset that Ogden no doubt recognized. Jersey-ans knew Southard as a staunch Republican, the son of one of the founders of the Jeffersonian Republican party in New Jersey, and a rising man in the ranks of New Jersey Jeffersonians as well. In 1814 he had worked inten-sively and quite successfully to keep Ogden and the Federalists from re-gaining power in New Jersey. Given Ogden's awareness that Jeffersonian legislators might make an unsympathetic audience for his case, Southard might have been his ploy for a fairer hearing. Of course, if Southard could not meet the challenge of arguing against the well-known New York attor-ney Thomas Addis Emmet, this calculation would be worthless, even harm-ful, to Ogden's cause.

Why Southard agreed to argue Aaron Ogden's case while feeling repug-nance for Ogden's political friends and, moreover, knowing that members of his own party were unfavorable to Ogden's interests, is impossible to know for certain. Yet in the context of Southard's financial circumstances, and his admitted ambition, the decision to represent Ogden is not difficult to fathom. The blank check Ogden offered regarding a fee was undoubt-edly tempting (particularly at a time when medical bills for his wife and son were pressing), and the opportunity to speak before a prestigious forum no doubt appealed to his vanity and provided an irresistible challenge. Hence, Southard did accept his erstwhile opponent's appeal, and quickly began to prepare his brief in the case.

On Friday afternoon, January 26, 1815, before a "vast assembly of peo-ple, which continually increased until it very much exceeded anything which you ever witnessed in Trenton," as one contemporary put it, South-ard was put to the test.[29] The third speaker, he followed Thomas Emmet, who put the case for Livingston and Fulton, and Aaron Ogden himself, who introduced evidence and argued that Robert Fulton was not the origi-nal inventor of the steamboat. In his remarks, Emmet emphasized the importance of protecting those who risked capital on behalf of the public interest. Unless the New Jersey legislature agreed to repeal the Ogden monopoly, Emmet said, "you will become infamous for the invasion of the rights of private property, of genius and invention. Repeal this law, or you will become infamous as the abettors of villainy—you will make your state an asylum of thieves and robbers." In the course of his well-crafted per-formance, Emmet went on to attack the New Jersey law because it granted a monopoly. As one witness, Lucius H. Stockton, reported, "He said that monopolies had ever been considered odious in law and justice, and that they ought to be particularly discountenanced in free countries."[30] This on behalf of two men who had repeatedly employed injunctions to repulse challengers to their own monopoly in New York!

Following Emmet's discourse and a break for lunch, Southard rose to reply. His argument before the assembled legislators took up nearly a full day (Friday afternoon and Saturday morning), and he delivered it in the manner of the time, full of flourishes and asides. Yet its kernel reduced to several points.[31] First, Southard argued, one cannot understand the law being defended—Ogden's monopoly grant—without considering "each and every step which preceded it both in our own state and the state of N[ew] Y[ork]." He pointed to the 1808 New York law granting Robert R. Livingston and Robert Fulton "exclusive right" (i.e., monopoly privilege) to the waters of New York. This grant Southard called, with some exaggeration, the most extensive monopoly ever given two individuals by a government, a monopoly "destructive to the interests of her citizens and dangerous even to the regular movements of the Gov[ernmen]t itself."

New Jersey had no complaint about this grant, Southard observed, except in the context of New York's concurrent claim to *all* waters between the two states, to the "high water mark on the Jersey shore." Under New York law, Fulton and Robert R. Livingston (and later John R. Livingston) had the right to seize any New Jersey vessels coming into New York—an act that prevented Aaron Ogden from conducting a business between Elizabethtown and New York City.

What happened next, Southard explained, was perfectly understandable. "When the Legis[lature] perceived that N[ew] Y[ork] had granted the use of her waters for certain purposes to two of her citizens and that under it the citizens of New Jersey were injured, she naturally inquired[,] is this right—shall I suffer my citizens to be injured—and offer no redress?" Quoting the legal authority Vattel, Southard argued that citizens of one jurisdiction have a right not merely to the middle of waters but "over the whole River." Without this right "the purposes of navigation and mutual intercourse would be destroyed." Given New York's violation of Vattel's precept and her injury to New Jersey commerce, the question became, how could New Jersey best protect its own rights? The answer lay in the passage of a law "countervailing" the New York monopoly.

On behalf of his clients, Thomas Emmet had charged that the New Jersey law was mere "retaliation" and hence odious. But Southard insisted "retaliation" could operate only against an innocent person. What New Jersey had passed was a "countervailing or retorting system," not a retaliatory one. Aware that his audience might perceive this as a distinction without a difference, Southard quickly moved on, reminding it that no New Jersey citizen had complained about the grant to Aaron Ogden. Rather, it was the "great monopolists of N[ew] Y[ork]," who "placing the interests of

their own f[ellow] c[itizens] under their feet prepared to trample without remorse on the right of yours." Hence, the attack on Ogden and Dod
and the effort to induce New Jersey to repudiate its grant to them. Ogden,
Southard said, was not a monopolist. He merely sought an exclusive grant
as a tool "to induce N[ew] Y[ork] to retract, or to place our citizens on an
equality" with New York. At bottom, Southard said, Ogden wanted merely
"to be permitted to approach New York unmolested"—that is, to be part of
a free and open steamboat traffic between the two states. Southard, in
brief, was defending New Jersey's monopoly grant to Aaron Ogden as a
measure intended to *open* commerce and encourage steamboat travel. Because of his position as an advocate for the New Jersey monopoly, Southard could not employ the legal arguments that Daniel Webster would
advance before the Marshall Court in 1824.

Having made his main points, Southard, in the charged atmosphere of
the legislative hall, ended his argument with an appeal to New Jersey pride
and an insistence on the smaller state's dignity and equality in dealings with
its sister. "Does she [New York] permit your citizens to approach but not to
touch her shores?" Southard asked. "[Now] mete out to her the very same
measure—yield not to her one single inch of your unquestionable jurisdiction." New Jersey, he concluded, was willing to be reasonable and flexible if
New York would treat her as she deserved to be treated—as an equal,
sovereign state. "But if she tenders benefits as to an inferior reject them
with disdain—if she grants your rights under the threat of power, retort
them with the indignation which becomes Jerseymen." This peroration,
and the argument as a whole, had great impact. "At the conclusion of his
[Southard's] speech," Lucius Stockton reported, "a universal testimony of
applause issued from a crowded auditory, manifested by the clapping of
hands, which was with great difficulty suppressed by the presiding officer,
and exceeded anything of the kind which I ever witnessed in New Jersey."[32]

Southard's speech, Stockton observed in a burst of enthusiasm, would be
remembered, "while the love of brilliant genius, real eloquence, profound
erudition, and manly patriotism remain in the minds of Jerseymen." The
hearing, however, had not ended. Both Joseph Hopkinson, for the Ogden-
Dod interest, and Thomas Emmet, in rebuttal, spoke at length, arguing
many of the issues Southard had dealt with. Hopkinson focused in particular on the matter of Robert Fulton's patent rights as "inventor" of the
steamboat, forcefully arguing that "the merits of Mr. F[ulton] were those of
a successful and enterprising capitalist, practically bringing into public operation the labours of others," not those of an "original inventor" of the
steamboat.[33]

Following the lawyers' presentations, the legislature, in a committee of
the whole, debated the proposed repeal of the 1813 law favoring Ogden
and Dod. That the perfervid and often learned oratory the legislators had

heard influenced their ultimate judgments in the case is doubtful: their votes ran almost exclusively along party lines. In fact, every Federalist voted to sustain Ogden and the 1813 law. Every Republican save two, David Thompson and Nicholas Mandeville of Morris County, voted for repeal. Hence by a margin of 21–18 in the Assembly, and 7–6 in Council, the legislature voted for repeal.[34] Politics, not law, had influenced the decision. Ogden's tactical gamble on Samuel Southard as his chance to win Republican votes was, in this context, shrewd, but not quite enough for victory.

Despite his defeat in the legislative hearing, Southard benefited significantly from his participation in the case. Although the New Jersey press reported his argument rather less effusively than had Lucius H. Stockton, in a widely circulated pamphlet on the case, Southard's reputation as an advocate was made.[35] Capitalizing on the recognition he gained from the steamboat case, as well as on his father's name and his own efforts on behalf of the Republican cause in several previous elections, Southard sought and received the nomination and went on to win election to the state legislature in the autumn of 1815. Less than a month later, when Mahlon Dickerson resigned his position on the state supreme court following his election to the governorship, Southard, then twenty-eight years old, was named to replace him.[36] It is difficult to believe that he could have gained such preferment without having first demonstrated his legal skills in Trenton the previous January.

Southard's elevation to the bench from the assembly post he had held for less than a month was unusual only as it respects his youth. It was common practice for politicians to become judges, and it was common also for judicial officers to remain active in partisan politics following their accession to the bench. Southard's two colleagues on the court, Chief Justice Andrew Kirkpatrick and Associate Justice William Rossell, reflect this reality. Kirkpatrick had been a prominent Middlesex County Federalist in the 1790s and had even run for governor once on a union ticket with Republicans. In 1820, Kirkpatrick won and held a seat in the legislative council. Rossell, from a prominent Burlington County Republican family, never ran for any elective office save judge, but was active in Republican politics while on the bench. In fact, his Republican connections proved decisive in winning him a district judgeship in 1826 in an episode that would cause political headaches for Southard specifically and the Adams administration generally.[37]

Southard had no intention of abandoning political activity while on the bench. Nor did he do so. Yet in his new post, his primary attention had, of course, to be paid to the law, and judging from the law reports on Southard's five-year service as a supreme court justice, he was an able and literate jurist.[38] Not surprisingly, his presence on the court was felt less during his first few months there, when he was studying precedents and, moreover, was also forced to refrain from participating in cases that he had argued at a lower level, than later in his term. Southard wrote opinions more and more often for the court, but not infrequently in dissent.

The cases before his juridiction varied greatly. Few were of more than local significance: contract cases, procedural challenges (for example, regarding admission of improper evidence at lower levels), trials relating to sexual transgressions, neglect of duties (as in the case of *Sanford v. Colfax*, 1818, regarding a constable's responsibilities), and most especially, debt cases.[39] Some of the cases were bizarre and fascinating because of the facts, legal issues aside. In the case of *State v. Aaron* (September term, 1818), for example, the court was asked to hear arguments regarding the alleged murder of an infant by an eleven-year-old black slave. The case hinged on whether the boy would be fairly tried under the circumstances employed at the lower level in impaneling a jury, and gaining a confession from the boy. In this case, the court granted the defense a new trial.[40] In *Decon v. Allen*, Southard rendered the court's verdict in a fornication case. In his decision, denying an appeal against the damages ($500) granted by a lower court for defilement of the defendant's daughter by an acquaintance, he wrote that the father "was entitled to damages; he deserved remuneration; and the court does not think the jury have erred so far as to justify an interference with their decision."[41]

Several cases brought before the court related to the antagonists in *Gibbons v. Ogden*. Thomas Gibbons and Aaron Ogden, who had formed a partnership in the steamboat business before Ogden's accomodation after 1815 with Livingston-Fulton interest, remained partners only briefly. Almost immediately following the case in which Southard had represented Ogden, Gibbons determined to run a steamboat business from New Jersey to New York on his own, and by October 1818, Ogden was in New York's Chancery Court seeking an injunction against this traffic.[42]

The conflict between the former partners did not relate simply to business. Earlier, in July 1816, Gibbons had challenged Ogden to a personal duel because he was angry with Ogden for purchasing a note without his knowledge, a note that Gibbons did not pay and that provoked his arrest in New York City. Underlying *this* dispute was Gibbons's anger that Ogden had given friendly advice to Gibbons's daughter and son-in-law in a running battle between Gibbons and them. Because dueling was a crime in New Jersey, Ogden pressed charges against Thomas Gibbons.[43] Thus, the issue before the state supreme court in February 1818 term was whether in fact an official challenge to duel had been made and received. Arguing for the prosecution, William Chetwood said that the various threatening letters Gibbons had sent to Ogden, including one demanding a duel, were evidence enough of Gibbons's criminal intent. The court, however, disagreed, ruling that the indictment against Gibbons for his unfriendly correspondence with Ogden be quashed. The indictment, in Justice Southard's view, merely stated, in substance, that "the defendent wrote the paper set forth in it, intending it to be a challenge, and that he sent and offered it as such." There was no crime actually committed—no duel took place; and for the indictment to stand, evidence for a challenge had to be direct. However, Southard said, there was no hard evidence that the letters to Ogden had ever been received. In an obiter dicta, he suggested that the 1796 legislation against dueling had been defectively drawn.

> They [the legislators] probably intended to punish a deliberate effort to commit murder, and did not mean that the guilt or innocence of the accused should depend upon the accidental circumstance of the challenge being received or rejected, a circumstance in no way connected with his moral turpitude, nor in many cases at all depending upon his will. But if so, the phraseology is unhappily selected; and the plain and obvious meaning of the words is a much safer guide to us than any conjectures about their intention.[44]

Hence, in Southard's view the indictment had to be quashed.

Cases such as this no doubt prevented Southard's tenure on the bench from being too tedious, but on the whole, the cases he heard involved technicalities and a repetition of similar themes that likely made Southard's restless spirit rather more restless. The fact was that the court was not a real challenge. Nor was it the best base for political maneuvering, since there were limits to the partisanship a sitting judge could express. Things might have been different had Southard's pay been more substantial, but $1,000 a year, plus perhaps $400 to $500 more in various fees, did not stretch very far.[45] Within a year from the time of his elevation to the bench, Southard was again looking to other offices.

II

Service on the state supreme court did not prevent Southard from maneuvering behind the scenes—and occasionally out in the open—in politics. He had taken a seat on the bench not as a means of extricating himself from political life, but rather to achieve statewide recognition, and to a lesser extent because of the stable income the job provided. It was, after all, common practice for politicians to move in and out of judicial posts. Mahlon Dickerson had served on the state bench from 1813 to 1815 and had gained election to the governorship in October 1815, when the then chief executive, William Pennington, resigned to take a lucrative (and undemanding) seat as a federal judge for the New Jersey District. It was Dickerson's resignation in order to succeed Pennington as governor that opened up the seat on the bench to which Southard was elected by a joint meeting of the legislature in October 1815.[46]

   This movement of Republican politicians from office to office was indicative of the political situation in New Jersey at the close of the War of 1812.
Although Republicans had controlled state politics and government since
1801, with the exception of 1812–13, Federalists had been an active and
periodically effectual opposition until 1815. Owing in large part to antiwar
sentiments in New Jersey and a gerrymander engineered by the Federalist-
controlled legislature in 1812, Federalists captured four of the state's six
congressional seats that year. Two years later Republicans regained these
lost seats, and with the conclusion of the war on terms acceptable to the
American public, Federalism in New Jersey disintegrated as a statewide
party. Federalists did not contest congressional elections after 1814, regularly supported the Republicans' choice for assembly speaker, and failed to
use particular issues facing the legislature (such as imprisonment for debt,
abolition of which was more popular among the populace than the Republican leadership) as fodder for political cannons.[47]
   As a consequence, Republican politicians and the Republican organization could afford to relax their efforts. Without the threat of a Federalist
alternative to Republican control of the state government, Republican leaders focused their attention increasingly on obtaining lucrative and prestigious offices. Factionalism was the inevitable result. Men who had ignored or
brushed aside personal antagonisms on behalf of the transcendent cause of
the party or the national welfare now allowed their personal ambitions to
run free. This meant intraparty collisions, frequent deals with individual
Federalists, and considerable anguish for those, such as Trenton *True
American* editor James Wilson and New Brunswick *Fredonian* editors David
and James Fitz Randolph, who saw their beloved party splintering and
squabbling.[48]
   As a jurist, Southard was not oblivious of the breakdown of Republican
party cohesion; rather, he was an active participant in the flanking movements undertaken by the different factions in the party. These factions
were rarely openly acknowledged, and they frequently shifted when it was
in the participants' interests to change allegiance, but in general, there were
two leading configurations within the Republican party at the state level.
The first of these factions developed around Mahlon Dickerson, an aristo-
cratic iron-mine operator from Morris County. Dickerson had cut his political teeth in Philadelphia politics in the 1790s, and upon moving to New
Jersey in 1810, he immediately gained influence within Republican circles
and made political plans for himself. He served variously as assemblyman,
justice of the state supreme court, and governor, and early in 1817 was
elected to the United State Senate.[49] Until 1817, Dickerson was valued by
Southard as a political ally against a faction led by James J. Wilson, a
Trentonian whose power base was his newspaper, the *True American*. An
abrasive and ambitious man, Wilson was also an effective editor and a
successful office seeker, but he was never very popular with the politicians

with whom he dealt on a day-to-day basis. In 1814 Wilson gained election to the United States Senate, but only after a long and bruising contest with Dickerson. Dickerson and William Pennington, a Republican party leader from Newark, were generally recognized as Wilson's chief rivals for control of the state organization.[50]

Because of his youth, Southard was not at the time of his appointment to the judgeship in a position to challenge either Dickerson or Wilson's control of patronage. However, he was himself frequently applied to for assistance by seekers of state and federal positions, and in writing letters on their behalf he accumulated debts that he would, when the time came, call due.[51] By late autumn 1816, Southard was already interested in cashing in some of these political chips. Mahlon Dickerson was preparing to resign the governorship for a Senate seat, and Southard considered running for governor. He spoke with Republican party stalwarts William Rossell and Joseph McIlvaine, both of whom indicated they were not interested in running for the office. With this understanding, Southard told Mahlon Dickerson on January 1, 1817, that, while he was "not anxious to leave my present office," he would willingly "yield to any plan which the legislature shall think best."[52]

Dickerson's reply was noncommittal, but this did not discourage Southard from organizing on his own behalf.[53] In particular, he had the assistance of an old friend from the College of New Jersey and his days as a teacher in Mendham, David Thompson, Jr., who was assembly speaker. Thompson spoke to a number of Republican legislators on Southard's behalf and assemblymen Silas Condit and William Jeffers did also.[54]

Southard himself lobbied privately with various legislators. The effort, however, resulted not merely in defeat for Southard, but in embarrassment. Arguments against him on account of his youth and his constant changing of offices proved too strong for personal campaigning to overcome. In a three-way contest, ex-Federalist Isaac Williamson of Elizabethtown and Joseph McIlvaine of Burlington ran well ahead of Southard on the first ballot. On the second, Southard's five supporters threw their votes to Williamson, providing his margin of victory.[55]

Southard's dismal showing in the governor's race marked his first serious setback as a politician, and he did not take it lightly. Rumors that Mahlon Dickerson had secretly been working for Williamson only compounded Southard's chagrin, which festered in his mind until he sat down in April and penned a letter to Dickerson. "I have received such information," he wrote,

> as has excited my curiosity and induced me to enquire of you, whether it be true that you exerted your influence most *strenuously while* in Trenton to prevent my election as Governor? And that you had since your return home frequently remarked and seemed anxious to *extend* the idea "that I had done the *job* for myself by *presuming* to stand a candidate and that it

would be many years before I could regain my standing in public estimation." I make inquiries as a matter of curiosity and because your opinion upon the subject must be valuable to me, in consequence of your means of information.[56]

Southard did not in fact send this letter, and his relations with Dickerson remained correct, if cool. But Southard would never again confide in or trust Mahlon Dickerson, and it was only a matter of time before they would openly express their rivalry. There is no firm evidence, in fact, that Dickerson had maneuvered against Southard. David Thompson, the chief purveyor of such rumors, conceded to Southard that his own remarks about Dickerson, which probably planted the idea of Dickerson's enmity in Southard's mind, were at least in part "occasioned" by "a little personal resentment."[57] Nonetheless, it was evident that Dickerson had nothing to gain from Southard's advancement in party circles, and that he felt somewhat threatened by the younger man.[57] For their part, Thompson and Southard continued to believe Dickerson was interested only in his own power. Late in 1817 Thompson charged that Dickerson, along with Jonathan Dayton and William Pennington, wanted "to rule the state" and were using the politically naive Williamson as their tool.[58]

Decisive defeat in his bid for the governorship and disenchantment with Mahlon Dickerson did not result in Southard's quiet return to the bench. A combination of circumstances was working on Southard to pull his attention to other offices. His work as supreme court justice did not pay well, for one thing, and though Southard supplemented his income with work as reporter for the court, at $120 per year, and commissions as an agent of the Bank of the United States, he was often pressed for cash.[60] In truth, Southard's income was inadequate to support a growing family, a wife who was constantly ill, and a move to Trenton, where in 1817 he rented a house. Southard's doctor bills in 1816 and 1817 were particularly severe, a consequence of the seizures suffered by his little boy, John, whose life was threatened by several epileptic attacks.[61] Need for a better livelihood, combined with boredom on the bench and a desire to gain more public influence and reputation, encouraged Southard by the summer of 1817 to plan a race for attorney general when that office came up for appointment in the autumn joint meeting of the legislature. He wrote to Theodore Frelinghuysen, his old roommate at Princeton and a prominent Federalist lawyer and politician from Newark, asking whether Frelinghuysen was planning to run for the post. When his quondam friend told Southard he was not interested in the attorney generalship and assured him that talk about Southard's switching positions too frequently was not a substantial obstacle to his election ("Boys will change their minds sometimes," he observed), Southard proceeded with his own plans.[62]

Unfortunately for Southard's aims, Frelinghuysen did "run" for attorney general. Several of the Essex County man's Federalist friends, aware of

latent hostility to Southard among Eastern Republicans because of Southard's rapid rise to prominence in their party, determined that Frelinghuysen could defeat Southard in a head-to-head race. By bringing out the
Federalist vote in the legislature and combining it with the votes of the
large Republican delegation from Essex County, Frelinghuysen could—
and ultimately did—defeat Southard, though with no votes to spare. It was
a stunning upset and a mortifying defeat for the Republican candidate.[63]

Southard was greatly embittered by his failure to capture the prize he
sought, and particularly by the Federalists' agency in his defeat. Publicly
and privately for several years he castigated the party, charging it with
hypocrisy and treachery. Writing as "Observer" in the New Brunswick
Fredonian in February 1818, Southard vented some of his frustrations in a
blast at a writer in the Trenton *Federalist* who had asserted that Southard
had deserved to lose the attorney generalship. Moreover, the anonymous
author had also denied charges in the *Fredonian* and the Trenton *True
American* (perhaps penned by Southard) that Federalists were always
motivated by party gain rather than public spirit, and that "party" in New
Jersey, despite Federalist disavowals, was very much alive. While Southard
must have known, hard as it was for him to acknowledge, that Frelinghuysen had no personal agency in the maneuvering for the attorney generalship, he could not help but assail the "party" that occasioned his mortifying
defeat.[64]

The theme of Federalist treachery was picked up by the Republican
press in 1818, perhaps most notably in the *Sentinel of Freedom*. That paper
had responded to Frelinghuysen's election with a series of articles written
by "Sidney," attacking Federalism and the notion that "party" in New
Jersey was at an end. "Sidney," who Trenton *Federalist* editor George Sherman surmised was District Judge William Pennington, also attacked the
Essex County delegation for its failure to support Southard in the recent
contest with Theodore Frelinghuysen. Several other writers responded to
"Sidney," with a focus on the action of the Essex Republicans' role in
Southard's defeat.[65]

Southard's failed bid for attorney general and the intraparty squabbling
that attended it were symptomatic of the problems of a dominant party in a
period of political drift. Lacking a threatening political opposition, Republicans became increasingly motivated by a concern for advancing their self
interests.[67] Party no longer dictated policy, even when substantial public
issues arose. Across the board on the major public concerns of the day—
transportation improvements, imprisonment for debt, economic downturn
in 1818 and thereafter, and even such explosive issues as the admission of
Missouri to the Union as a slave state, there was little evidence of partisan
posturing or party differences.[67]

The Missouri issue is particularly illuminating in this context, for it might
well have stimulated a Federalist revival in New Jersey and elsewhere in the

North. Indeed, many Republicans feared precisely this possibility. Leading party editors such as the Randolphs of New Brunswick charged in their pages that anti-Missouri agitation in Burlington County in 1819 was really a Federalist plot, a last-gasp attempt to revive a discredited party. Yet the Randolphs and others who made such charges vastly (and in some cases deliberately) underestimated the Missouri question as a *moral* issue that transcended party politics. All evidence suggests that in 1819 and 1820, antislavery feeling in New Jersey was widespread and in some places— notably the Quaker counties—quite intense. It is true that Federalists took the lead in agitating against Missouri's admission as a slave state, but it is also true that New Jersey Republicans quickly picked up the refrain. The Republican-dominated legislature passed a resolution urging the state's Congressmen to oppose any compromise on Missouri, an action that was widely applauded in New Jersey's newspapers. Moreover, when three of the state's six congressmen voted *for* the compromise despite their "instructions" to the contrary, they were severely censured by the citizenry and dropped from the Republican ticket in the next election.[68]

Southard's own position on the Missouri question was unrelated to partisan loyalties. Doubtless influenced in his views by five years' residence in Virginia and a continued connection with such politically influential Virginians as John Taliaferro and Francis T. Brooke, he concluded that Missourians should be free to draw up their own constitution as they pleased, without restrictions imposed by the federal government. Such views were unexceptionable, if not necessarily popular in New Jersey at this time. In this context, the virulence of Southard's antagonism toward Federalists and Federalism appears excessive, even granting the widespread perception, which he shared, that Rufus King and other Federalists sought to use the Missouri issue as a springboard back to power, if not as Federalists per se, than in a new coalition of Northerners against the South.

Moreover, Southard himself was not above the kinds of factional intrigue that contributed to poor discipline and morale within Republican ranks. Prior to his unsuccessful race for governor, he had been informally allied with Mahlon Dickerson against James Wilson. Southard's belief that Dickerson had helped to subvert his gubernatorial hopes soured him on the Morris County man. Yet Southard was unwilling to ally himself with Wilson, the state's other United States senator, whom he had long viewed with a combination of envy for his success in gaining office and political power, scorn for his lack of scruple, and distaste because Wilson was a notably heavy drinker who, by 1818, was lapsing into chronic alcoholism.[69]

For about six months after his October 1817 defeat for attorney general, Southard retreated to a world of self-pity and spent his time castigating those who, in his view, were gaining political perquisites he considered rightfully his. After receiving a particularly dispirited letter in this vein, his friend and confidant David Thompson, Jr., brought Southard up short. "I think," he replied,

> the deceptions which have been practiced upon you are tending to produce an unfavorable effect upon your disposition. You are becoming too suspicious for your own comfort. What were the Gov. & c. doing at [Garret] Wall's? Why probably they were playing a game of *whist*. Or trying to flatter the chief into a support of the District Judiciary Bill. Rely upon it, they had no deep political maneovres in hand. You give the Federal gentry more credit for plans and controversies than they merit. The Judiciary bill you think was contrived for the purpose of aiding federalism—and lessening the consequence of the Supreme Court.[70]

Observing that he assumed that the Federalists supported a change in the judiciary law because it benefited the public, Thompson went on to urge Southard to stop envying and criticizing those with influence in the state. If Southard continued to act "mortified" by the successes of his rivals, Thompson added, he would get a reputation of always being "influenced by feelings of personal disappointment," rather than by a fairer estimation based on his own talents.[71]

There is evidence that Southard followed Thompson's sound advice. He began to cultivate Governor Williamson and returned to his role as a patronage broker in the state party.[72] At the same time, Southard continued to look beyond the New Jersey Supreme Court to other career opportunities. At various times he pressed friends on his behalf for a United States district judgeship, the U.S. Attorney Generalship, and a seat on the United States Supreme Court. He also pondered leaving the bench in New Jersey for a return to the bar.[73] None of the appointive positions materialized, and apparently Southard was not so unhappy as a judge to leave his position without having some assured regular source of income.[74] That he had no intentions of long remaining on the bench, however, he could not hide.

Not long after his thirty-third birthday, in June 1820, Southard wrote a revealing letter to his friend David Thompson, examining his current situation and future goals. "I am not much discontented with my present sphere of action," he said, respecting his service on the state supreme court. "The duties are generally pleasant—and they are, no doubt, the more pleasant, because I have persuaded myself to believe, that I *generally* perform them in an acceptable manner." Yet immediately after writing these words Southard conceded to having "no small itching, to have a place in the eye of the nation, as well as of my state."[75] In brief, a seat in either house of Congress or, better yet, a place on the United States Supreme Court was his objective.

Southard's situation, however, was complicated as usual by his family and financial obligations. "I am very poor—I never could *add* well in money matters—and no family in the state would so much need money, if I were taken from them. To make money then is extremely desirable." In this accounting to Thompson Southard was not exaggerating. His income as a justice remained modest, even when supplemented by small fees and by the monies he gained as law reporter and on sales of published volumes of Supreme Court reports. This income did not make for an opulent life-style in the best of circumstances. And Southard's circumstances were far from ideal. His growing family numbered three sons and a daughter at the moment of his confession to Thompson. His wife, Rebecca, was frequently ailing, and his eldest son John's epilepsy showed no sign of abatement. The bills that Southard faced in 1820, though not so serious as in 1817 the year when John's disease first flared and in which Southard himself was frequently ill, were substantial, and Southard drew the logical conclusion from them: he needed a larger income.[76]

Southard's concern about sustenance is understandable given his abnormal burden of expenses. Indeed, his incessant efforts to obtain one or another state office from 1812 to 1820 can in large measure be ascribed to financial exigency. One must, of course, take account of Southard's admitted ambition and his desire for a measure of fame, but it seems fair to conclude that the primary motivator in his quest for office was his need for financial security. In Southard's case, the exigencies of life did more than force him to scramble for sources of income that would mean steady and ample support for his family; they would, in a sense, mold his character as he moved toward middle age. Although he suffered temporary setbacks, some exceedingly mortifying, in his quests for office, Southard was remarkably successful on the whole in getting what he wanted: more power, more fame, more income. This was the pattern of his adult life. Yet Southard's ambivalence about his situation in 1820 was not dissimilar to his situation at various other junctures in his life. Always he could express a reasonable degree of satisfaction in what he was currently doing—whether serving as navy secretary, state attorney general, governor of New Jersey, or United States senator—while remaining desirous of something more in the interests of publicity and security. While on the Jersey bench, he sought a Senate seat or a federal judgeship; while navy secretary, he not infrequently envied the more lucrative and prestigious post held by his friend Attorney General William Wirt; while attorney general of New Jersey, he plotted variously for appointment to the United States Supreme Court, nomination to the vice-presidency, and finally election to the U.S. Senate.

In this restlessness Southard was probably different less in kind than in degree from his contemporaries. As Tocqueville and others have emphasized, Southard lived in an age of constant motion, or "go-ahead," of endless search for the security and happiness that ever lay just beyond one's grasp. This was indeed a different world from that which his father had known and to which Henry Southard continued to give his allegiance and pay his respects. Henry Southard had known the soil and hard physical labor in a way his son never did and never would. Henry's experiences on the farm shaped his outlook as a political man and sustained his commitment to the old verities regarding family, society, and economy. Henry Southard was an old republican in the tradition that such writers as Douglass Adair, Lance Banning, and J. G. A. Pocock have acutely limned. He had become active in state politics precisely because of his allegiance to the political economy for which Thomas Jefferson stood, and he resisted temptations to advance further than he himself felt justified given his abilities. Financially, Henry was not without his own burdens. But his compass, his point of departure, was always his land.

For Henry's son, life was a different proposition entirely. Henry Southard had matured in a world that remained intellectually committed to "community" and the Puritan ethic; Samuel was raised in a world that at best paid verbal obeisance to these things. Samuel's was a more secular, individualistic, and money-oriented world, a world in which men found their sense of security and self-worth less in their communities or on their property than in their work and careers, and in the financial rewards that accrued from these. Money, as Robert Remini has observed, brought not merely financial security, but important intangibles: "Social standing, recognition that one was engaged in useful pursuits, [and] a judgment from society that one's life was a 'success.' "[77] To define Samuel Southard in these terms is not to compare him invidiously with his father, but to underscore the changes in American society and culture during this era. Nearly thirty years of age when the Revolution began, Henry Southard was too set in his ways to participate significantly in the value shift that was manifest during America's emergence as an independent nation, the shift from classical republicanism to the age of commerce.[78] Samuel, born fifty years after his father, in entirely different circumstances, is not a case study in transition, but an exemplar of a democratic culture's new values. He was the insistent go-getter, the restless office seeker, the willing and ever-optimistic investor, the aggressive attorney. It is ironic, if appealing, to recall that both Southards were staunch "Whigs." But their Whiggery encompassed sets of mind that could hardly communicate.

III

Given his personal ambitions, financial needs, and growing dissatisfaction with his work in Trenton, it is not surprising that Southard would seek a change. Despite his protestations that his judicial responsibilities were "pleasant," Southard quite clearly was not much challenged by the routine cases before him. He envisioned a more exciting future for himself. Specifically, in the autumn of 1820, he set his eyes on the United States Senate seat held by James J. Wilson.

Wilson's influence had been in decline for several years. In part this stemmed from the breakdown of party regularity in New Jersey, and the consequent loss of central authority exercised by power brokers such as Wilson. No less important was Wilson's irregular but often quite fierce bouts with John Barleycorn. In early 1819 Henry Southard reported from Washington in a letter to Samuel that the state's senior senator had simply ceased to perform his duties. "Wilson lies in his bed, eats little or nothing— Drinks (it is said) more than a quart of Brandy a day—Declines seeing anybody, as much as he can—If he does not reform soon—he will never see Trenton again."[79]

Wilson's lack of temperance had not endeared him to many leading Republicans in New Jersey, who believed he was an embarrassment to the state. Given this fact, and the numerous enemies Wilson had made during his long career, Southard believed that an effort to succeed the editor-politician could succeed. He was right. After considerable maneuvering, the Republican caucus expressed its support of Southard in October 1820, and in the joint meeting of the legislature that followed in November, Southard was elected by a vote of 30–24 over his incumbent (and recumbent) opponent.[80]

Southard's election to the Senate, achieved with remarkable ease, marked the conclusion of a decade's quest for influence, status, and financial advancement. As a senator, he would be free to practice law, and given his growing reputation as an attorney and jurist, as well as his newly established political base, he could be viewed as having realized his deepest ambitions. This is the logical view, but not the reality. As his future life would show, content was not the operative term for Southard. Ambition rarely rests because an immediate objective has been attained. In a world where "republican simplicity" was giving way to competitive individualism, materialism, and eventually, acceptance of the legitimacy and desirability of party competition, Southard would always find new goals to attain, new opportunities to pursue, new enemies who had to be overcome before *his* world would be well. The twenty-one years remaining to Southard would be replete with opportunities, challenges, and disappointments. Free from the myth of the garden (and from the prosaic rhythms of the rural life), Southard fixed a course that could bring material comfort undreamed of in his youth, as well as great political influence, but fulfillment always lay in the future.[81]

3

"A Touch of Ambition"

Despite his rapid advance in New Jersey politics and his five years' service on the state's highest court, Samuel Southard remained in the shadow of his greatly respected father, who in 1820 was completing his eighth term in Congress. At age seventy, however, Henry Southard was slowing down and preparing to retire to his Basking Ridge farm. Two months before Samuel's campaign for James Wilson's Senate seat began in earnest, Henry Southard announced through the press that he would not be a candidate for reelection. Until Henry Southard took this step, Samuel was generally viewed by contemporaries as his father's son. He would now have an opportunity to step out of that shadow.[1]

In some respects, of course, Samuel *was* his father's son. Both men were convinced and ardent Jeffersonian Republicans; both felt a commitment to public service. Yet Samuel was unlike his father in other ways: in his ambition for fame and influence; in his willingness to assume a leadership role in state politics; in his materialism; and, eventually, in his interpretation of the Jeffersonian creed in the light of the dynamic conditions of early nineteenth-century America. Where Henry Southard's views and actions were shaped by and reflected a simpler world, Samuel's eyes were focused firmly on the main chance that lay ahead. Both the ideal and the reality of Republican simplicity were giving way to competitive individualism, and no better index of the change can be offered than the contrast between the two Southards, father and son.[2]

I

Immediately following his election to the Senate, Samuel resigned his seat on the state supreme court. Although he would not officially enter the Senate until March 1821, in the meantime he could and did plunge into legal practice, taking full advantage of lucrative opportunities at the bar. He found his services much in demand, and soon realized considerably better support as an attorney than he had as a judge.[3]

While Southard rode circuits with the men who had for several years been arguing cases before him—Theodore Frelinghuysen, Garret D. Wall, George Wood, William Jeffers, Lucius H. Stockton, and Peter D. Vroom, to name several of the most prominent—he was following the debate in Congress on the persistently vexing Missouri Question and on the Bankruptcy Bill, which had gained increasing support as a consequence of the economic dislocations engendered by the Panic of 1819. Missouri was particularly difficult matter for Southard. In discussing with his father and such friends as John Taliaferro the issue of possible restrictions on Missouri's entry into the union, Southard had emphatically rejected congressional authority to abolish slavery in Missouri as a prerequisite for its admission as a state. Later, he would be equally adamant regarding congressional power to compel Missouri's constitution writers to withdraw provisions prohibiting the entry of free blacks across its borders.[4] Yet such restrictions were precisely what a majority of Northern Congressmen intended to demand, and what most of Southard's fellow Jerseymen strongly favored. Indeed, New Jersey opinion was so emphatically opposed to the extension of what was widely believed to be an immoral institution that the New Jersey legislature overwhelmingly voted to send instructions to the state's congressmen to oppose *any* measures that endorsed Missouri's admission as a slave state. When three New Jersey representatives—Joseph Bloomfield, Bernard Smith, and Charles Kinsey—ignored these instructions, and voted for the various parts of the compromise package of 1820, their political fates were sealed. "A Republican Voter," writing in the Newark *Sentinel of Freedom,* pronounced them "politically . . . dead as a door nail," and was soon proved correct.[5] At the Republican party caucus in 1820, none of the three pro-compromise congressmen even gained renomination, and in the ensuing general election campaign, politicians of all persuasions were firm in denouncing compromise measures.[6]

Southard's views on the subject undoubtedly caused him some discomfort. Convinced that the public at large was not thinking constitutionally, he had to consider the virtues and the dangers of refusing to follow the majority view. It was a question that would confront—one might even say plague—Southard at other junctures in his public career. For the moment, Southard remained publicly noncommittal on the Missouri issue. He probably hoped that with luck, the matter of Missouri's recalcitrance about admitting free blacks would be resolved while he was still a senator-elect. Such calculations were upset by James J. Wilson. Despondent over his recent election defeat, gripped again by alcoholism, Wilson impulsively resigned his Senate seat in January 1821.

In a letter to his longtime friend, former Congressman William Darlington of Pennsylvania, Wilson conceded the irrationality of resigning from the Senate at a time of national crisis. "I could neither sleep nor rest, nor enjoy society and solitude," he lamely explained, and in this context, resignation seemed to him to be his only recourse.[7] Whether irrational or inescapable, Wilson's resignation left a vacancy in the Senate for the final two months of the Sixteenth Congress, and Samuel Southard was the logical choice to replace him. Accordingly, New Jersey Governor Isaac Williamson wrote to Southard on January 3, 1821, informing him of his intention to appoint Southard to the vacancy. For his part, Southard was reluctant to accept. In two replies to Williamson, he explained that, while he appreciated the governor's intentions, his professional engagements would prevent his immediate departure for Washington. If this meant loss of the interim appointment, Southard would not complain.[8]

Southard clearly did not want to confront the renewed Missouri issue. After working so long and maneuvering so effectively for elevation to the United States Senate, he did not want to have to cast a vote that would either injure his own principles or irritate his constituents. It was not an enviable choice, and the situation was exacerbated by the fact that Southard had not anticipated making it. Southard's quandary was resolved only after his father and closest friends insisted that he had to serve, and hence to choose. So Southard acquiesced, wound down his legal business early in February 1821, and journeyed to Washington to enter the maneuvering on Missouri.[9]

Southard arrived in Washington at a particularly critical point in the debate. For months, Northerners had been insisting that Missouri could not exclude free Negroes, because such an action ran contrary to the Constitution and the spirit of American republicanism, which provided for freedom of movement for all citizens. Southerners viewed the issue differently. As Southard's old friend John Taliaferro remarked, with some passion:

> What, because Missouri is disposed to exclude from her population a few free Negroes, is she to be deprived of all or any of the privileges of an independent state? If indeed free Negroes were bona fide citizens of any state in the Union at the adoption of the federal government, some ground might be assumed for the late contest. So far from it, no state in the Union even at this day allows to them the full rank of a citizen. It is clear to me that the clause in the Constitution of Miss[ouri] objected to, does not conflict with the Constitution of the U.S. If so what is to become of the laws or constitution of nearly every state in the Union on this very topic. That the very existence of the Union should be tested by such a question, that the welfare of millions . . . should be sacrificed for the speculative, uncertain, accommodation of a few Negroes is too bad to think on.[10]

In this dissection of the constitutional issue and in the complaint about Northern hypocrisy on the treatment of black people, Taliaferro and his Southern brethren were able to score debating points, and also to persuade strict constructionists and Southern sympathizers in the North—people such as Southard. In reality, however, the Missouri issue involved far more than debating points: it was a contest for political power, a focus for the articulation of deeply felt sectional resentments, and a forum for the pronouncement of principle. North and south of the Mason-Dixon line, sectional opinion was asserting itself. In the North, for example, as attested by New Jersey's position on the issue, there was a rising tide of opinion against further concessions to the South and to slave interests, regardless of Northern states' treatment of blacks.[11]

In this emotional conflict, Southard could not avoid some statement, could not avoid taking a position. He was not choosing in a vacuum or from a detached perspective. He had lived in the South, on a large plantation, for five years, and he had imbibed the strict-construction Jeffersonian doctrines espoused by his friends and associates in the Northern Neck of Virginia. Returning to his native state to begin a legal career and raise a family, Southard sustained his youthful perspective. His ownership of several slaves testified to his views on the morality of the "peculiar institution."[12] Neither in 1821 nor at any other juncture in his career did Southard express any belief in the equality of black Americans with white Americans or the desirability of their equal treatment in this country; his solution to the slavery issue was to leave Southerners alone with the problem. As for free blacks, Southard, like many political figures of the time, was firmly committed to colonization.[13]

At the same time, Southard faced real political pressures. He was aware of the fate that had befallen the three congressmen who had voted for compromise in 1820. He knew that New Jersey was watching his vote. He did not want to begin his career in the Senate on the wrong foot. But he had to choose.

Southard was sworn on February 16, 1821; he recorded his first votes on the nineteenth, voting in favor of a congressional compensation bill, and then a Senate bill to establish a uniform system of bankruptcy, which passed the Senate by a close margin.[14] But on the twenty-first he had to face the Missouri issue for the first time. Pennsylvania Senator Jonathan Roberts's resolution on the matter was read, and there was extended debate, in which Southard took no part. After some procedural maneuvering, the resolution proper, favorable to Missouri's views, was voted on, but failed. Southard's colleague Mahlon Dickerson had followed the sentiments of New Jersey voters and voted nay. Southard voted in favor of the resolution.[15]

For the next several days, as tensions built, Southard participated in the routine business before the Senate. Then, on February 24, the House of Representatives relayed a message, through Speaker Henry Clay, recommending the appointment of a joint committee to consider the still unresolved Missouri imbroglio. Southard joined a substantial majority of senators in favor of this measure. Moreover, he found himself among the seven senators appointed to the committee. By a coincidence, his father,

Henry, closing out thirty years in politics, was one of the House conferees. The negotiations proceeded in secrecy and with considerable emotion; but, spurred by the efforts of Henry Clay, a tenuous agreement was hammered out. Under the terms of Clay's compromise, Congress would insist that Missouri pass no law contrary to the United States Constitution. But Congress did not explicitly strike down the Missouri constitution's provision prohibiting the admission of free blacks. Silence in this instance could translate as assent.[16] This compromise was acceptable to Southard, and when the joint committee's resolutions came before the upper house, he voted in favor; Dickerson voted no. The bill passed both houses, and Missouri entered the Union on August 10, 1821.[17]

As he expected, Southard's vote on the Missouri issue won him few accolades in New Jersey. His old friends, the Randolphs, applauded him in the New Brunswick *Fredonian,* but no other New Jersey newspaper mentioned his vote in a favorable light.[18] John Taliaferro consoled Southard that his stance on the Missouri Question "will eventually add to your popularity at home even—abroad it has done so—when the excitement of the moment has passed."[19] Fortunately, the matter had been brought to a relatively quick conclusion, and Southard could turn to other concerns, such as his burgeoning legal practice.

In New Jersey from March through November 1821, Southard rode the circuits, talked politics with his colleagues at the bar, and ministered to a lively, if often afflicted, family. Considering the financial obligations with which he had to contend, one can appreciate Southard's unceasing concern with money and security. His family was large, growing larger, and frequently ailing. Between 1813 and 1821 Rebecca Southard bore at least four children. The eldest son, John, required constant medical attention.[20] So did Rebecca, for her natural susceptibility to illness during and immediately following pregnancy was exacerbated by persistent aches and illnesses that, judging from the evidence over the span of the Southards' life together, were as much the product of emotional disturbance as somatic disease.[21] Nonetheless, Southard's life in Trenton was not unrelievedly solemn or financially hard pressed. Family life did much to reinvigorate Southard's spirits and direct his energies. Despite his wife's frequent illnesses and her more frequent irritableness, he was a devoted husband, and he enjoyed her company most of the time. As a father, Southard was guide, playmate, taskmaster, and adviser to his growing offspring. On one hand, he encouraged their childlike tendencies and delighted in surprising them with treats and gifts; on the other, he demanded diligence in their schoolwork, a regular routine of writing (even from a very early age) when he was away, and expression of interest in the world beyond Trenton. This combination of affection and discipline bore fruit. The three children who reached maturity—Virginia, Henry, and Samuel—sustained and deepened their love for Southard over the years; beyond this, each pursued a life in which their father could take satisfaction: Virginia married a prominent New York attorney and Whig politician, Ogden Hoffman; engineering, then law, attracted Henry; and Samuel, after a legal apprenticeship, went on to become a clergyman. But all this lay in the future. For the moment, Southard presided over a household comprised of active youngsters, servants, his wife and her sister, Margaret Harrow, who provided company for Rebecca.[22]

Despite the continuing epilepsy of young John Southard, the year 1821 was not a severe trial for the family.[23] Success at the bar eased Southard's financial anxieties to some degree, and the family took on the accoutrements of good living by hiring additional staff for their State Street home. Southard was at home in Trenton for much of the year, and when he was away riding circuits, he was always within reasonable reach.

This legal work served more purpose than putting food on the Southard family table; it also enabled Southard to maintain a finger on the state's political pulse. Because he traveled so extensively, he remained closely attuned to the factional alignments within the New Jersey Republican party, and increasingly Southard employed his leverage on patronage matters to broaden his contacts and enhance his power base in the state.[24] Among his most intimate friends Southard counted about a half dozen men from different regions of New Jersey. His old party allies, the Randolphs, kept Southard in touch with political movements in Middlesex County. David Thompson, Jr., speaker of the state assembly, charted the activities of his Morris County rival, Mahlon Dickerson, and plotted with Southard about the possibility, which did not prove realistic, of blocking Dickerson's bid for reelection to the United States Senate in 1822. Lucius Q. C. Elmer, from Cumberland County, kept Southard posted on political currents in southwest New Jersey. When Southard was out of Trenton on business, his colleague at the bar and increasingly close friend, Charles Ewing, regularly wrote regarding legal, political, and family developments. Finally, Southard relied for information about his old bailiwick, Somerset County, on his brother Isaac, a farmer and sometime shopkeeper who, aided by his younger brother's influence, gained a variety of appointive positions in New Jersey at various levels of government. To these men Southard would turn when he had or sought political news of local, state, or national significance, or when he wanted advice on issues before the Senate. His confidants served Southard well by their regular reports and Southard in turn provided favors, notably appointments for friends or relatives to different government positions.[25]

II

On February 14, 1821, nearly two weeks before the resolution of the Missouri issue, James Monroe was officially reelected president of the

United States, capturing all but one of the electoral votes counted before a joint meeting of Congress. The widespread support for Monroe's bid for a second term seems incongruous in view of the ominous noises emanating from Washington and much of the nation at the time. Yet in spite of the intense emotions ignited by the Missouri issue and the economic malaise that had now gripped the nation since 1819, Monroe's easy reelection was not surprising. The last member of the Virginia dynasty, Monroe managed to remain moderate and collected in the most explosive situations, and though he was no political genius, his quiet leadership provoked few complaints. If few Americans were especially enthusiastic about Monroe in 1820, many fewer were prepared to support an alternative. His election that year was accomplished, George Dangerfield has written, by "an act of unanimous indifference."[26]

Dangerfield's remark about the lack of interest in Monroe's reelection is apt, if one restricts its application to the public at large. Aspiring politicians, by contrast, were unwilling to challenge the incumbent not so much because of indifference to his stewardship as because he seemed unbeatable. Their sights were already being set on the succession. In fact, even as Congress hammered out the final compromises on Missouri, and decided to leave well enough alone on the economic front, speculation about and planning for the presidential election of 1824 was underway.

Presidential talk centered primarily on five men: Henry Clay, the perennial Speaker of the House of Representatives, then temporarily in "retirement" at Ashland in Lexington, Kentucky; William H. Crawford, Monroe's able secretary of the treasury and his closest competitor for the presidency in 1816; John Quincy Adams, the acerbic, plodding, and immensely skilled secretary of state; John C. Calhoun, articulate, intense, and attractive, currently secretary of war; and Andrew Jackson, the "Hero of New Orleans," who had been briefly governor of the Florida Territory in 1821 before returning to private life in his native Tennessee. All five men were avowed Republicans.[27]

Henry Clay had already taken positions on foreign and economic policy that distanced him from the administration's course on these matters. Playing upon American sympathies for the opponents to Spain's colonial rule in South America, Clay had argued in Congress for a more forceful and dramatic policy by our government with respect to the revolutions then in progress. Specifically, he called for speedier recognition of the rebel states. The administration, more sensitive to the demands of negotiations with Spain over territory in Florida, and with Great Britain's looming shadow, moved more slowly albeit ultimately in the direction Clay desired. Clay's posturing on the subject may not have brought recognition any faster, but it earned him the privately expressed jeers of Secretary Adams and public criticism from administration supporters around the nation.[28]

Clay at least criticized from without; by contrast, President Monroe also had to deal with the increasingly independent and controversial maneuverings of Treasury Secretary Crawford. That Crawford aspired to succeed Monroe was not in itself problematic. Virtually the entire cabinet nursed presidential ambitions of some seriousness. What caused awkwardness and anger was Crawford's identification with a faction in Congress that consistently criticized the administration's executive operations. In particular, the congressional critics, called "Radicals" by their opponents, focused on the need for economy in an allegedly bloated government bureaucracy, and they made the War Department, headed by John C. Calhoun, their particular *bête noir*. In reality, Calhoun's administration of the department was vigorous and efficient, but this did not stop the "Radicals" from insisting on budget cuts, nor did it prevent enactment in 1821 of legislation markedly reducing the size of the army. Crawford exacerbated matters by making known his support for the cuts recommended by Congress and suggesting none too discreetly in private that Calhoun's administration of the department was not all that it should be.[29]

From the beginning of his first full Senate session in December 1821, Southard was more than mildly attentive to the growing controversy over administration policy and the heightened interest in presidential politics. For one thing, he felt a more than passing goodwill for the president and his administration. While living in Virginia from 1806 to 1810, Southard had known Monroe. Their mutual friends John Taliaferro and John Wellford were among the president's most enthusiastic supporters in Virginia. Moreover, Southard's views on economics and even the slavery issue were essentially the views of the president and his allies. Personal friendship and ideological agreement worked together to identify Southard with the administration. Southard's loyalty to the Virginia president was cemented by his ambitions. Aware that Monroe was the fount of political patronage, Southard was reasonably confident that the president would not neglect his desires if he expressed them. He had not been in the Senate for more than a few months before he began to talk with friends about a possible appointment to the cabinet, or perhaps to the next vacancy on the Supreme Court. To be sure, Southard had failed to gain the attorney generalship in 1817, despite the best efforts of Taliaferro, but that was understandable. The man to whom Monroe awarded that potentially lucrative post, William Wirt, was considerably more mature, experienced, and well known than Southard. Wirt, moreover, had the backing of various influential politicans.[30] By 1822, however, conditions for an appointment appeared more propitious. As a federal office holder, Southard had the opportunity to demonstrate his abilities on a national stage, and at age thirty-five, he could no longer be dismissed as too young and inexperienced for federal office. These factors, combined with whatever skills of advocacy he might demonstrate in the Senate, would undoubtedly have a good effect on his chances for advancement.

In the Senate, Southard did not promote himself too quickly. His professed objective was to remain a low-key supporter of administration policy save when his personal conscience or New Jersey's interests dictated a different stance. Neither of these eventualities was common, and Southard was able to bear down on the routine business facing the Senate during the Seventeenth Congress. He voted on various land-grant bills, presented petitions for pensions, supported a change in the ratio of population to representation in the House of Representatives, cast a vote against a move to prohibit the slave trade in Florida (his colleague, Dickerson, voted for the prohibition), opposed a preemption bill for Louisiana and served as a diligent member of the Judiciary and District of Columbia committees.[31]

The major anxiety afflicting Southard during the early months of the session was breaking the ice on the Senate floor and offering a maiden speech. Despite his legal background and his modest reputation as an orator, Southard had always been nervous about public speaking, and in such a forum as the United States Senate he was practically paralyzed. Opportunities to speak out on various minor issues abounded, but Southard could not bring himself to rise. December and January passed, and still he had not taken the floor. Friends, newspaper editors, and even his father, began to wonder aloud whether he would ever make his speaking debut. Finally in early February, Southard resolved to rise during a secret session of the Senate, when he would not have to face a gallery of interested onlookers. But even though he had points he wanted to make during that session, his paralysis continued to grip him, and he did not rise. "As I sat in my room at night reflecting on the business of the day," he later confessed to his wife, "I felt mortified at my own folly, in not daring to speak when my duty seemed to require it." Hence, he braced himself to speak at the next possible moment, to break the grip his fears had on him.[32]

On February 8, 1822, the Senate began a debate on a bill to confirm the title of the Marquis de Maison Rouge to a tract of land claimed under a Spanish grant. This was a typical minor concern of the Senate, and hardly a glamorous issue on which to launch one's speaking career. Nonetheless, the Marquis's claim provoked a number of senators to speak out, and Southard decided that the time was right for him to join in. As John Holmes of Maine was declaiming against the bill, Southard sought recognition to respond. He recounted the situation to his wife: "While he [Holmes] was speaking I suffered intensely—the Senate was full and spectators numerous. When I rose I shook horribly—my voice indicated a little but not much agitation— after a few minutes I became self possessed and spoke about half an hour, I suppose." Standing before the Senate, Southard was the picture not simply of nervousness, but earnestness. At the age of thirty-four, he showed all the signs of his elevated status. Good clothes and a well-kept appearance were only part of it. Slender and rather foppish as a young man, Southard's frame had begun to fill out and take on a new dignity. He enjoyed the delights of the dinner table. Within a decade, this predilection would take its physical toll, for he grew increasingly corpulent, gouty, and arthritic. But in 1822, as he addressed his colleagues and the gallery in the Senate, Southard simply looked prosperous. Short but erect, with a prominent Roman nose and the beginnings of gray at the temples, he was the very picture of a senator, and he spoke in an almost professorial tenor. The text of Southard's remarks that day was not recorded, but the congressional reporter captured the essentials. Southard, it was reported, spoke "to obviate the objections made to the claim, and to show that it was genuine, was legal, was unimpaired, and ought to be confirmed by the United States." Southard recalled that "I was not a little flattered by the silence and attention of the Senate—it was as great as I could have desired—and the compliments paid me were (I am sure) beyond my desserts." Perhaps so. But this did not stop Southard from relaying to his wife the most effusive praise bestowed upon him. Yet he also conceded that he continued to dislike speechmaking and observed that he would not rise again "until I feel compelled—I have now broken the ice and know that I can speak if I please, and I will not tire those who have to listen to me by talking all the time."[33]

Southard was, in fact, as good as his word; he spoke only rarely during his two-and-a-half-year tenure in the Senate when he did indeed feel "compelled." One such occasion arose in April 1822, during debate on a bill introduced by his colleague, Dickerson, regarding the settlement of controversies between states, such as the boundary dispute that troubled relations between New York and New Jersey. The larger state had long claimed jurisdiction to waters between the two states up to the high-water mark on the Jersey shore, a claim that New Jersey strenuously rejected, but from which New York would not recede. On this issue Southard and Dickerson joined forces and debated vigorously with New York's two senators, Rufus King and Martin Van Buren. Since the remainder of the Senate was not particular interested in this neighborly argument, Dickerson agreed to make the bill at issue specific, one embracing only disputes between New York and New Jersey, and New Jersey and Delaware. Still the Senate declined to act, the matter was dropped, and the issue was ultimately adjudicated between the states themselves after New Jersey took the case, in large measure thanks to Southard's efforts, to the United States Supreme Court.[34]

Legislative work of this kind doubtless invigorated Southard, and gave him a sense of worth. Overall, however, his duties in the Senate were routine, and his influence among his colleagues was small. Such pride as he felt resulted not from his achievement during these years, but from his close relations with President Monroe. The president regularly invited Southard to White House diplomatic dinners, formal affairs in which Southard dressed up in the old fashioned pantaloons preferred by the chief executive. Monroe, further, was wont to take walks with Southard through the streets of the capital city, confiding views on policy to him and giving Southard every indication that he would be remembered when an interesting and appropriate position in the federal bureaucracy opened up. "I know he respects and loves me," Southard reported to Rebecca in March 1822, "for he gives me daily proofs of it—and he would be willing to gratify me in any thing reasonable."[35]

Clearly proud of his association with the president, Southard was unwilling openly to press for a specific post, yet prepared to accept the right favor if offered to him. He was confident that he could have a ministry, either in South America or Europe, if he sought one, but his wife's strong opposition forced him to abandon such thoughts. Southard briefly pondered moving to Baltimore to fill the vacuum at the bar left there in 1822 by the death of William Pinkney; at other moments he calculated his chances for appointment to replace the frequently ill William Wirt as attorney general.[36]

No firm conclusions emerged from these musings, but Southard was certain that he did not wish to remain in the Senate for an extended period. "Eight dollars a day and absence [from home] for 4 or 5 months at a time," he told his wife, Rebecca, "will not answer for me."[37] Southard's unease in the Senate was likely compounded by his anxiety about speaking out in a national forum and his worries that he did not measure up to his colleagues. Given his youth (he was thirty-three when he took his seat) and the judicial environment from which he had come, his discomfort was understandable. Perhaps sensitive to the fact that he had changed positions frequently during the previous decade and unwilling openly to speak with the president about his interests in changing his station, Southard could at least *hint* that he was not averse to a change. In mid-1822 he found an opening for such a hint. Taking advantage of Monroe's written defense of his Cumberland Road veto, a copy of which he sent on to Southard, the Jerseyan responded in a letter by praising the president's arguments and observing that they "are calculated to do good—and will lead many minds to a safe opinion." Southard then discussed several other matters, ranging from his and his family's health to executive appointments of various kinds. He also conveyed good wishes from "my old father." Southard closed by remarking, probably deliberately cryptically, that

> some dissatisfaction exists with the state of things in N.J. and present appearances indicate that I shall be much solicited to change my present station—but attention to my profession as a permanent situation, is so necessary that I can consent to nothing which cannot be reconciled to one or both.[38]

The exact purpose of these remarks was probably lost on the president, but the kernel of the thought may have taken hold; Southard needed a dependable income and this meant a cabinet post. At the moment, however, that body was fixed. Despite his increasing unhappiness with William

Crawford, Monroe was not inclined to remove the popular treasury secretary, nor was Southard a likely replacement were Crawford to go. Southard
had recently admitted to his friend David Thompson that he "never could
add" well in money matters.[39] Rather, Southard's hopes were focused on
the attorney generalship. Unfortunately, William Wirt, despite erratic
health, was making a good living in his private practice in addition to his
government salary, and he was not inclined to resign. Southard remained
stymied.

He had little choice but to make the best of his situation and to consider
how very well off he in truth really was. Southard's law practice continued
to thrive, and as a senator, he could bask in a considerable degree of
prestige and also exercise significant political influence in New Jersey. By
1822, no one in the state save Mahlon Dickerson rivaled Southard as a
power broker, and Dickerson was aligned less with President Monroe than
with the partisans of William Crawford.[40]

Dickerson's and Southard's personal differences had led them to divergent political alliances. Oddly enough, however, the two New Jersey
senators both linked their fortunes to Southerners. While Dickerson
operated behind the scenes for William H. Crawford, Southard was becoming identified with the Monroe administration's most embattled member,
War Secretary John C. Calhoun. Precisely when Southard made Calhoun's
acquaintance is uncertain; it is conceivable that he had been introduced
briefly to Calhoun during one of his several visits to Washington before
1820. Evidence suggests, however, that substantive intercourse between the
two men did not begin until Southard arrived in Washington as a senator,
and Calhoun became aware of his ties to Monroe and his support for the
administration.[41]

Apparently Southard was impressed by Calhoun, whose obvious vigor
and effectiveness in conducting the War Department gave credibility to his
nascent presidential candidacy, credibility that he might otherwise have
lacked because of his relative youth. A Calhoun organ in Washington, the
Washington Republican, had announced the South Carolinian's intentions in
December 1821. Within a month, Trenton *True American* editor James J.
Wilson was suggesting in print that Southard could be counted in Calhoun's camp. This commentary, which soon reached Southard in Washington, provoked from him a fervid disavowal in a private letter to his wife:

> Mr. Wilson nor any other has no right to say that I am in favor of Mr.
> Calhoun for the Presidency. I have yet said to no man who I preferred—
> nor do I mean to do it—the election is two or three years off and I am not
> satisfied that I shall then prefer the one I should now.[42]

Throughout his political career, Southard preferred to hold his cards as
close to his chest as possible. He did like Calhoun, but he was not yet sure
whether Calhoun was a serious candidate. Calhoun, for his part, evidently

understood Southard's reticence to move openly on his behalf. Needing support in the middle states, he adopted a strategy of gently "stroking" Southard's ego. Late in March 1822, Calhoun wrote to Southard (then back in New Jersey for a visit with his family), informing him of the House of Representatives' likely support for administration military preparedness measures. "Your presence (when the Senate takes up the matter) will be of great importance," he told Southard. "I have met with no one, who so thoroughly understands it as yourself, and no one, I am satisfied, will have a more decided influence over the deliberations of the Senate in relation to it."[43] Southard acknowledged Calhoun's letter on April 2, reporting that, because of the continued ill health of his wife and son John, he would not be able to join the Senate's deliberations for several more days.[44]

Calhoun continued to treat Southard in a way calculated to play on the latter's susceptibility to flattery. In September 1822, responding to a letter from Southard that noted that New Jersey "is clearly on the side of the administration on those points which agitate us in Washington," Calhoun expressed satisfaction with the state of opinion. He added, rather theatrically, that

> I do not doubt that we are on the eve of a political struggle, for which we ought to prepare in time to meet. An opposition *originating where the present does* must soon bring a crisis which, I think, must take place before the termination of the next session. With prudence and vigor the result need not be feared. The people are sound and the opposition has nothing to stand on.[45]

Southard's position in the presidential contest was one of watchful waiting coupled with low-key support for Calhoun in New Jersey, if only to test the waters a bit. Because the election was still two years distant, Southard could afford to focus on the movements of the congressional Radicals, rather than openly trumpet Calhoun's merits as a presidential contender. This was evidenced in his correspondence with friends such as Judge Francis T. Brooke of Virginia, whose close ties with Henry Clay put him, in presidential politics if nothing else, on a different course from Southard's.[46] Few of Southard's political friends took Calhoun's candidacy seriously at first, largely because he was only forty years old in 1822, and there was no precedent for a president so young. But with Southard's insistence that merits, not age, should count, and given the course of developments in Washington, his political allies in New Jersey slowly reached Southard's conclusion: Calhoun might well be the man for New Jersey and the nation.

By early 1823 Southard was organizing a Calhoun campaign in New Jersey, working closely with an ambitious attorney and office seeker, Garret D. Wall. While Wall did the necessary legwork in New Jersey, Southard kept in periodic touch with the candidate and his operatives in the middle states.[47] In his contacts with Southard, Calhoun emphasized the

importance of New Jersey for his ultimate success, and suggested that
Southard's political "weight" would be decisive in delivering the state to
him, and hence to "the cause of the country." Too, he urged Southard to
place "short but judicious articles in your leading Republican papers," advice that Southard followed.[48] Increasingly throughout the summer and fall
of 1823, Calhoun's candidacy made advances in New Jersey, thanks to
Southard's efforts and Wall's, and those of such lieutenants in the state as
James Cook, Lucius Q. C. Elmer, James Westcott, David Thompson, Jr.,
and the young editor of the Trenton *Emporium,* Stacy G. Potts.[49]

As the second session of the Seventeenth Congress took its course,
Southard, no longer a novice in the Senate, began to assert himself more.
In particular, he researched, wrote, and delivered a major speech on the
issue of imprisonment for debt. The issue was more complex than it appeared to be on the surface, and good arguments could be mustered for
either sustaining or abandoning the practice. Opponents argued that the
traditional practice of imprisonment for debt was senseless, inexpedient,
and, as one New Jersey newspaper put it, a "relic of ancient barbarism."[50]
After all, a debtor who was clapped in jail was in no position to pay back
anything to anyone. Yet those who felt that sanctity of contracts was a
crucial element of the socio-economic order were not anxious to see the
practice dropped, and they opposed the bill introduced in Congress and
championed by Senator Richard Johnson of Kentucky that would prohibit
the imprisonment of debtors. Imprisonment for debt, the editor of the
influential New Brunswick *Fredonian* argued, was essential to law enforce-
ment, and to the credit system generally.

> Do away with coercion in this way, and hundreds would laugh at their
> creditors and defy their power. Take away the terrors which the laws
> now possess, and prudent men would be obliged to decline to give credit.
> What then? The poor man must be denied a loaf of bread or any of the
> necessities of life, unless the money be paid down. The whole system, by
> which the common business of life is transacted, must be broken in upon,
> and a new one devised and practiced upon; or the poor man would
> suffer more for want of credit, than he now does by the occasional abuse
> of the power of imprisonment.[51]

Logical as this argument may have seemed and may actually have been, it
ran distinctly against the current of the times, which favored a less stringent approach to the problem. New Jersey, for instance, had passed a
modified anti-imprisonment law in 1823, and other states were doing the
same.[52] In the Congress, many members followed a similar line and agreed
with Richard Johnson's argument that depriving a man of his "personal
liberty" was unjust and contrary to the "spirit of the constitution." In his
impassioned address before the Senate in January 1823, Johnson invoked
the ancients, insisted he was not a champion of fraud, and emphasized the

simple inhumanity of imprisonment for debt. "When you arrest the unfortunate and honest man, and cast him into prison," Johnson observed, "his prospects are blasted, and his hopes are withered."[53]

Johnson's impressive oratory was followed by nothing more than rather desultory debate and several substitute motions for various sections of the original bill, until January 20, 1823. When the Senate began its proceedings that day, Southard quickly took the floor and launched into a major speech, his first really substantive effort. Offering his own substitute for the Johnson bill, Southard suggested that he had no expectation that a majority of the Senate would support it, but that he believed its introduction might help move the Congress toward an acceptable bill.

An acceptable law on debt, Southard believed, had to be evenhanded in its treatment of debtors and creditors. One could not assume, he observed, that debtors were all honest and creditors "unfeeling or inhuman." "Their principles and motives of action are the same, and common to human nature." In Southard's view, the creditor and debtor were engaged in a transaction that required the good faith of both. The debtor had received something (money or a service), and was obligated to repay.

> If he refuses while he has the means, he is not innocent. The want of means never can exist, while he possesses property which can be devoted to the object, and no law can intervene between him and the joint claim of his creditors, so long as the power to satisfy that claim lasts. On the contrary, the authority of society ought to compel him to discharge it, by appropriating to that purpose what he possesses. One great object in the formation of society, is to ensure the discharge of the obligations which one citizen owes to another. Upon these principles the amendment rests.

The burden of Southard's position was that considerations of humanity did justify some moderation of the statutes establishing imprisonment for debt, but that moderation did not mean ending the threat of imprisonment, the "stick" by which potential defaultors might be kept in line. Specifically, Southard proposed that any debtor unable to pay a debt, though he had surrendered all his property to his creditors, would not be liable to imprisonment. But those debtors who declined this action should be liable to the federal court system. The creditor could sue and, if he won and the debtor still did not meet his obligations, prison was the debtor's just destination. What Southard objected to in Richard Johnson's bill was the immunity it provided all debtors. There was none of the desirable discrimination between honest and conniving debtors. His bill, he argued, was a viable *via media* between traditional sternness and potential lenience toward debtors. No honest man, he emphasized, need be imprisoned. To go further than this in freeing debtors from the obligations they had incurred was, Southard believed, unwarranted and unjust: "You permit without rebuke, the violation of contracts—the neglect of obligations—the prostration of the very elements of which civil society is composed."[54]

It was a solid, if not particularly enthralling, speech, and it won for Southard the plaudits of even those who opposed his views.[55] In the Trenton *Federalist*, editor George Sherman commented on Southard's speech that "the doctrine advanced is wholesome and sound." In the Senate, Southard's substitute bill was printed, and the bill laid on the table, and the next day, along with other amendments, referred to a select committee of seven, which included Southard. Although a new bill emerged from the committee on February 4, there was no serious debate on it, and the bill was tabled just prior to adjournment of the Congress, without definite action.[56]

Several days after the Congress concluded its labors, a piece of nonpolitical news revived Southard's long-flickering hopes for a federal appointment of weight and sufficient income to support his family comfortably. Supreme Court Justice Henry Brockholst Livingston died on March 18, 1823, opening a vacancy Southard hoped to fill. With Southard's consent, his good friend, New Jersey Congressman Lewis Condict, wrote to President Monroe urging the appointment of Southard to Livingston's vacated seat on the grounds of Southard's high standing at the bar and the satisfaction the appointment would give to New Jersey, which had had no representation on the court since William Paterson had graced it. Condict followed this by writing to Southard to suggest that Southard secure the backing of John C. Calhoun, influential New Jersey Congressman George Holcombe, and "our other friends." Southard replied that he appreciated Condict's efforts and believed that the New Jersey delegation in Congress would enthusiastically support him for the judgeship. As for his own role in soliciting the position, "I should be rejoiced to receive it—but I am too proud to beg for it."[57]

A refusal to beg, apparently, did not mean an unwillingness to press a bit for the office. Writing to Calhoun in late March 1823, Southard asked the secretary of war how he calculated his chances for the appointment. On his own behalf he argued that his home state was contiguous to the district that Livingston had served on circuit and emphasized that New Jersey had received not a single major federal appointment since Jefferson's accession to the presidency in 1801. "Is that fair?" he asked, and went on to request that Calhoun "remind" Monroe of his availability.[58]

Once again Southard was destined for disappointment. Despite the efforts of his friends in Washington and Monroe's real solicitude for him, Southard was not offered the post. Instead, Monroe proferred the judgeship to a member of his cabinet, Navy Secretary Smith Thompson, whose political ambitions and influence helped persuade Monroe that he should have first refusal.[59] Southard's disappointment was assuaged by the realization that, if Thompson declined the president's offer, he might have a second chance. Even more likely, if Thompson accepted, a cabinet post would come open, and at that time Thompson was the only cabinet officer from the middle states. Southard was kept in a state of suspense for nearly six months as Thompson, "in the grip of a severe case of Presidential fever," weighed his decision. All Southard could do was follow the rumors, practice his profession, calculate his chances—and wait.[60]

Responding in late March to one friend's suggestion that he was certain to be named navy secretary, Southard replied that the situation was too fluid to warrant any predictions. Some people, he observed, were saying that

> N. York strongly demands that Thompson remain where he is, and that another of her citizens be appointed judge—and N.Y. you know is strong—Jersey is weak. . . . Such has been my situation and the state of things that I have scarcely reflected a moment about it and if the Secretaryship were offered to me, I am not prepared to say whether I should accept it. There are obstacles which none but myself know or feel—and I have neither inspected closely, nor measured adequately enough, the difficulties of the office, to be prompt in encountering them. On the other hand, there are strong allurements—the future pride, glory and safety of the nation depend greatly on that arm of our defense, and I could not honestly profess indifference to the idea, of seeking a reputation and being useful in connection with it. You know I have a little touch of *ambition* in my constitution.[61]

In reality Southard was strongly interested in the navy post. His major anxiety about the position, understandably enough, was the uncertainty of tenure. Even if Thompson acted quickly to accept the judgeship, which he was not inclined to do, and Southard were immediately named to succeed him, he would have less than two years on the job before a new administration took office—with no guarantees he would be part of that new administration.

During the period of watchful waiting Southard consulted with friends such as Calhoun, Congressman Ephraim Bateman, Judge William A. Dade of Virginia, and his old counsellor, Francis T. Brooke. At the same time, he stepped up his efforts on behalf of Calhoun's presidential candidacy.[62] Finally, on August 15, 1823, Thompson ended the agony and told the president he would accept the judgeship. At a cabinet meeting that day, attended by Calhoun, Adams, Crawford, and Thompson, Monroe announced Thompson's acceptance of the judgeship and then indicated his own inclination to appoint Southard as Thompson's successor in the Navy Department. He observed that Southard was "a man of abilities" and noted that New Jersey had never been represented in the cabinet. Monroe invited comment from those present; nothing was offered. John Quincy Adams recorded the scene in his diary and added that Southard "is said to be a devoted partisan of Calhoun."[63]

Monroe broke the good news to Southard in a letter of August 16. His decision, the president explained, was "prompted by a respect for your merit, and a belief that you will discharge the duties of the office, with advantage to your country and credit to yourself." He added that he hoped Southard would commence his work in the department "when Mr. Thompson retires from it."[64] Southard withheld immediate acceptance, probably unwilling to appear too eager and also desirous of at least consulting with friends. Over the next week he dashed off more than a dozen letters to friends and acquaintances in New Jersey and Virginia, and personally spoke with many others. He even wrote to Smith Thompson, requesting a meeting to discuss the navy secretary's role and to seek advice (at least pro forma) on whether to accept the post. Claiming rather disingenuously that he was "unprepared" for the president's offer, Southard added that "a conversation with you, will influence me very much, not only in coming to a decision, but in my conduct on many points, should I accept it."[65] To the president, Southard wrote twice begging time to reflect on the offer. In the longer of these letters, Southard explained:

> I am in more difficulty than you may suppose in resolving to accept the offer you have made me. Of the value which I set on that offer, and on the feelings by which it was induced I need not speak to you. You know that I estimate both highly—and that if I hesitate, it arises from causes of a different yet powerful kind. I am *poor*—have a sickly family—am in an honorable station and enjoy professional profits, sufficient to my comfortable support. To accept the office and remove my family under such circumstances, would be justified only by strong motives—some of these motives I surely have.

After emphasizing his support for the policies of the administration and his real interest in the navy post, Southard explained that he simply had to be practical. There was no certainty he would have a job come March 1825, and the consequences of such a possibility required serious reflection.[66]

Southard's request for thinking time, while probably discomforting to an executive who had waited half a year for Smith Thompson to make up *his* mind, proved not to be a problem. In less than a week Southard sent on his formal acceptance of the navy secretaryship. Having decided to leave his family in Trenton for the present, Southard packed his bags and, in the second week of September 1823, departed for Washington as Mr. Secretary Southard.[67]

4

A Political Secretary

Secretary of the Navy Southard had three chief roles to play. As a department head, he was responsible for the day-to-day coordination of naval activities, supervision of personnel, and development of policies rendering the navy more efficient in carrying out its tasks. As a cabinet officer, Southard was charged with advising the president, not simply on naval affairs, but on overall administration initiatives.[1] Finally, as a political appointee, Southard's mandate, if only implicitly, was to work on behalf of the administration's political fortunes. He played each of these roles to the fullest, and it may well be that his nearly six years as navy secretary were the most fulfilling of his life. Certainly they were the most demanding on his energies, and the most exhilarating in terms of the status he enjoyed and the influence he wielded. Secretary Southard was an activist on all fronts, and his tenure in office, though it left him with a number of political scars, satisfied his instinct for exercising executive authority. He survived.

I

Southard's ostensible reluctance to accept President Monore's offer to join the cabinet was predicated on the realization that Monroe was a lame duck. At most Southard could count on eighteen months as navy secretary: his future after March 1825 was entirely unclear. Hence, Southard found himself, in September 1823, not simply joining an administration, but seeking to hitch his wagon to a likely successor.

In the maneuvering over the "succession," Southard was identified, as we have seen, with John C. Calhoun. As a cabinet officer, Southard reinforced his ties to the secretary of war. This is not to say that Southard and Calhoun were constantly closeted, gossiping about politics and plotting Calhoun's political future. The demands of departmental work, particularly for Southard, were too great to allow for much on-the-job politicking. Moreover, though they talked the same political language in 1823 and 1824, Southard and Calhoun were never intimate. But for the moment they were allies, and Southard's future in the cabinet after March 1825 was

65

closely tied to Calhoun's political success. As a consequence, despite the immense demands navy administration made on Southard's time and energies, he stepped up his work on Calhoun's behalf in New Jersey, writing to operatives in various counties and encouraging publication of pro-Calhoun propaganda in the press.[2]

By autumn 1823, only weeks after Southard departed for Washington, newspaper articles favoring Calhoun were appearing in influential papers, and New Jersey voters, while not deeply committed as yet to a particular presidential hopeful, were receptive to arguments favoring Calhoun. One editor wrote to Southard that "I do not believe there can be a question but that Mr. Calhoun has been gaining ground rapidly among us for a few months." His main worry was that a budding movement on behalf of De-Witt Clinton might take root and spread. The editor, Stacy G. Potts, promised to do all he could on Calhoun's behalf, and requested from Southard "leading facts, with references to authentic documents, or other credible sources" that would strengthen the case for Calhoun. Further, Potts explained, a visit by Southard to New Jersey would "do more good than all the newspaper writing in the state."[3]

The suggestion that Potts left with Southard was that Calhoun's prospects in New Jersey were encouraging, but that much needed to be done before the state could be counted on. Potts's worry that Calhoun's support was soft was prescient; the Trenton *Emporium* editor, however, pointed to the wrong sources of danger. DeWitt Clinton's candidacy never passed beyond the trial-balloon stage and a brief surge of support in canal-hungry Morris County. The hitherto low-key campaign for Andrew Jackson, by contrast, emerged in early 1824 as a genuine people's movement.[4]

The first intimation of this came from South Jersey. In early January a group of Salem County residents called a Jackson meeting to see what response they would get. Their hopes were more than realized. At a well-attended meeting, those who gathered in the county seat, Salem, expressed their "entire confidence in the virtues, talents, and integrity of General Andrew Jackson as a patriot, a soldier and a stateman, as a uniform and long tried republican, as a friend of universal suffrage and the inestimable principles that gave birth to our revolution." They spoke out against the congressional caucus as "repugnant to the spirit of our constitution and subversive to the right of suffrage," and formulated plans to publicize their views.[5]

One of Southard's operatives in neighboring Cumberland County, U.S. District Attorney Lucius Q. C. Elmer, recognized a popular movement in the making. Writing to Southard on January 19, 1824, seeking advice on ways to advance Calhoun's interests in the state, Elmer observed that, if ballots were counted at that time, "my impression is that a popular vote would be decidedly for Jackson."[6] Once launched, the Jackson effort in

New Jersey was given impetus by events that occurred outside the state. Political gatherings in Philadelphia and Harrisburg, conceived to advance John C. Calhoun's candidacy, electrified the public when Jackson rather than Calhoun was enthusiastically endorsed. Jackson's status as the "Hero of New Orleans" and his reputation as a man of will and independence had been the key to his success in Pennsylvania. He was championed by the Harrisburg delegates as a leader for all America. As the convention address put it: "A contest must shortly take place that may severely test the durability of our free institutions, one that may shake the union to the center."[7] The obvious need was for a strong leader, a unifier. That man, the Pennsylvanians believed, was Jackson.

Andrew Jackson's surprise endorsement in the Keystone State received considerable notice in New Jersey. It took on special significance in view of Crawford's poor showing, some weeks earlier, in the congressional caucus held in Washington. The Jersey press had never favored Crawford, and the recent news from the capital was good news indeed to New Jersey editors. As the Newark *Eagle,* an Adams organ, reported respecting the caucus: "Whole number of members present, sixty-six; absent, ONE HUNDRED AND NINETY FIVE!!!" And further: "When the vote for Mr. Crawford was declared, some applause was attempted by the gallery. But it was soon drowned by hisses. During the meeting the spectators were silent as death."[8]

Other papers noted that only one New Jersey representative, Senator Mahlon Dickerson, had attended the Crawford caucus—a sign that the Georgian had little support in New Jersey. The caucus did not destroy Crawford's candidacy as the Harrisburg convention had eliminated Calhoun, but it obviously did not help him.[9] Crawford's health problems and his weak showing at the caucus notwithstanding, he remained in contention, in some measure thanks to the unflagging efforts of Southard's old nemesis, Dickerson.[10]

For Southard, Crawford's political problems were encouraging, since he had long resented the Georgian's lack of loyalty to the administration and its policies. Calhoun's stunning defeat in Pennsylvania, however, was another matter entirely, since it pulled the rug out from under Southard's efforts in New Jersey. Calhoun's candidacy in New Jersey was hitting its stride just as the thunderbolt from Harrisburg struck. Now that campaign was in pieces, and the Calhoun organization reassembled on behalf of other candidates, notably Andrew Jackson. Pondering his own options, usually in context of his chances for retention as navy secretary in a new administration, Southard found himself with no clear path. Crawford he could never support. Jackson he believed unqualified, though publicly he dared say nothing to this effect. Southard knew Clay's chances, particularly in New Jersey, were minimal, and for Adams he could at the moment muster no great enthusiasm. He therefore resolved to maintain a benign neutrality, to work for his friend Calhoun's election to the vice-presidency, and to keep his political antennae in good working order.[11]

Part of Southard's adjustment to the new political circumstances included a concern to learn John Quincy Adams's views on political issues in general and, more obliquely, on retaining him in the cabinet should the Adams campaign succeed and capture the White House. Several days after the Harrisburg convention dropped its bombshell, Southard dropped in on Adams at the State Department, ostensibly on routine business, but actually to sound out his colleague's political views. Southard, Adams recalled in his diary, "talked with me largely upon election prospects, and was apparently desirous of ascertaining my sentiments concerning Calhoun and Jackson. I gave them to him without reserve."[12]

For the remainder of the election year Southard was in the anomalous position of bystander. Removing himself from the political contest in New Jersey, he absorbed himself in Navy Department work, which, given his obsession with detail, was not difficult to do. Nevertheless, he kept up with the campaign currents in New Jersey, and in his cabinet service grew increasingly respectful toward and friendly with John Quincy Adams. But intimacy between Southard and Adams was slow to develop for understandable reasons.

Southard had been nurtured in a Jeffersonian environment, and a Southern environment at that. His first political advancement was less smooth than it might have been had Federalists not acted in concert against him. Southard had a long memory of such things. And he knew Adams, if only by reputation, as his father's son—the kind of man, as Henry Adams would later recall after a childhood visit to Mount Vernon, who would equate bad Southern roads with "bad morals."[13] Temperamentally, however, Southard and Adams were kin. Both were deeply passionate and lacked diplomacy; both were willing to be candid in company to the point of rudeness; both were unwilling to say one thing, if they believed another. Neither man, of course, was immune from the little deceptions and disingenuous talk that politicians (and virtually everyone else) sometimes practice. Southard was rarely willing to show his cards politically, for example, unless he had to. Adams, similarly, was ambitious for the presidency in 1824, but unwilling to seem more than casually interested in the position. "If chance will make me king, chance will crown me," he told several friends who were undertaking political propaganda on his behalf and sought his active support.[14]

On substantive matters Southard, perhaps to his own surprise, found that he and the secretary of state had few disagreements, at least on the issues facing the nation in 1824. Southard followed Adams's reasoning in foreign affairs, which was understandable given the skill with which the secretary formulated and prosecuted the nation's foreign policy, and the degree to which Adams's views were accepted and articulated by the president. On domestic issues, discretion tended to be the better part of discussion. Although still attached emotionally to the Virginia of his youth, Southard recognized that in most respects his political fortunes depended on following public opinion in New Jersey. And public opinion there, as in Massachusetts, was exceedingly friendly to tariffs and national internal improvements. Self-interest, then, was moving Southard toward Henry Clay's American System. Adams's own steps in that direction were as tentative as Southard's (he kept his views on domestic policy muted in 1824 in order to alienate as few voters as possible), though, as he would demonstrate in the presidency, once his full attention was paid to such matters as national development, Adams took second place to no man in his espousal of economic nationalism.[15]

As the presidential campaign of 1824 progressed, Southard and Adams maintained correct but not close personal ties. Unwilling to place all his hopes for reappointment to the navy secretaryship in Adams by publicly endorsing him in the general election, Southard remained resolutely neutral. Friends who said their allegiance would depend on which of the candidates was committed to retaining Southard in the cabinet were given ambiguous replies.[16] But privately, Southard was moving toward support for Adams. Shortly after the fall returns mandated election by the House of Representatives, Southard wrote to his old friend, Francis T. Brooke of Virginia, and to former Navy Secretary Benjamin Crowninshield of Massachusetts revealing his fears that Virginia was preparing to take up Henry Clay for vice-president in an effort to throw that contest into the Senate, while various unnamed Northern states were also preparing to abandon Calhoun out of dissatisfaction traceable to his failure publicly to endorse Adams for president. This prospect Southard deplored as bad for the country in general, and bad for Calhoun and Adams in particular. "You know I did not wish for Mr. Calhoun to be V.P.," he told Crowninshield,

> but as matters are now situated, if he be not voted for by the Eastern states, the rejection of him will be so marked, as to offend his friends and they will be less disposed to vote for Mr. A. in the House—besides his being a Southern man and V.P. will be an inducement with many members to vote for Mr. A. as a Northern for Prest. If he is not elected by the electors, the Senate must choose—an opponent of Mr. A will probably be chosen by them, and then, having the power in their hands, they will not be so likely to yield, as if Mr. C. were the V.P.—indeed, I consider his being in that place, as the surest means of securing Mr. A's election by the House.[17]

Such private expressions were as far as Southard would go on behalf of John Quincy Adams in 1824–25. Southard evidently gave some consideration to lobbying New Jersey's congressmen on Adams's behalf, but such a blatant effort to overturn the will of the citizenry there (Jackson had come out of New Jersey with a 1,000-vote plurality over Adams) was not likely to be well received, and the notion was dropped. Southard, in fact, was pressed to support Jackson, a course he declined to take. By any token, Southard's position was uncomfortable. He could be, and was accused of being, a tool of Calhoun's, and a secret opponent of the secretary of state.[18] Seeking to alienate no candidate, Southard had taken a course that identified him with no one. It would have been perfectly understandable had the new president given Southard his walking papers. As events proved, however, Southard was fortunate that the president-elect was not a conventional politician. Secretary of State Adams had observed Southard's work and deemed it satisfactory. He believed he had no grounds to replace him in the Navy Department. Adams, moreover, was concerned to maintain continuity insofar as possible with the outgoing administration, a concern he carried so far as to invite William Crawford to remain in the treasury secretaryship! Thus, on January 18, Adams told Southard in confidence that, if the House elected him president, he would ask Southard to remain at the Navy Department. Once formally elected on February 9, Adams was as good as his word, adhering to his private pledge to Southard despite warnings from political friends that Southard was unreliable and from political advisers that Southard lacked "weight."[19] For the next four years, Southard's career was intimately tied to the fortunes of John Quincy Adams.

II

"My great object will be to break up the remnant of old party distinctions and bring the whole people together in sentiment as much as possible." So John Quincy Adams defined his purpose as he prepared to assume the office few presidents have been equally well equipped to take. His ideal was to be a nonpartisan president who followed the path of his predecessors and who guided the nation toward an unprecedented period of growth, prosperity, and domestic tranquillity.[20]

As a presidential candidate, Adams had been discreetly, almost disingenuously, quiet about his intent, doubtless recognizing just how delicate his position was. He spoke out on few issues of the day and stood, as Samuel Flagg Bemis has noted, on "no platform."[21] As a consequence, during the first months of his administration, with Congress still to assemble, there was much uncertainty about Adams's proposed course. Southerners feared the worst, though most were prepared to give Adams some time to orient himself, particularly in view of his assurances that he would follow in the footsteps of the Virginia dynasty. Cabinet officers such as Southard, Henry Clay, and James Barbour, with strong Virginia ties, sought to diminish their friends' anxieties. In February 1825, for example,

Southard had assured his old mentor, Francis T. Brooke, that there was no danger to the South from an Adams administration, and later in the year he responded to John C. Calhoun's observation that the new administration was weak in the South by explaining that "I think Mr. A. will act prudently—that principles especially as you understand it [sic] will be found . . . in his adm[inistratio]n of the Govt. . . . He [Adams] has my entire confidence."[22]

The principles that Southard felt that Calhoun would "understand" were the principles of Jeffersonianism reoriented by the experiences of war and the disintegration of a Federalist opposition. In the wake of America's "second war for independence" against England, the Republican party had reexamined its program, and gingerly attempted to adapt Hamiltonian means to Jeffersonian ends. Hence, under Presidents Madison and Monroe, Republicans had (with some in-house dissent) supported federally sponsored internal improvements, tariff protection, and national banking. None of this involved a repudiation of states' rights or democratic republicanism. It was this program which John Quincy Adams intended to follow and extend, and this program which Southard pointed to in assuring friends such as Brooke that Adams "will consider the line of duty marked out by Mr. Monroe as the one in which it is his duty to walk. The policy of the Government will be unchanged."[23]

Southard's soothing words, doubtless sincerely meant, may have helped buy some time for the new administration, time in which Southard could devote himself to the details of his department's business and to making new friends in the cabinet—notably James Barbour of Virginia, the new secretary of war, and Henry Clay, the president's choice to run the Department of State.[24] William Wirt, who had been attorney general since 1817, Southard knew well and admired. He would come to know the new treasury secretary, Richard Rush, almost as well and like him almost as much. Working for Adams and with a superior group of department heads, Southard would and did feel very much at home.

The president contributed to a congenial atmosphere by relying heavily on his cabinet for advice and by playing no favorites. Adams's cabinet officers, a short walk from the executive office in the White House, met regularly with him. Southard, for example, was in the White House nearly every day on some official business, and often remained to chat informally with the president about policy, politics, and personalities. The two men worked well together and, more broadly, the entire cabinet proved to be a remarkably cohesive and effective body. Diverse in views, varied in political interests and influence, the individual cabinet members nonetheless played a team game. As events would have it, however, their individual work within the departments rather than any collective administration program would constitute the major positive legacy of the Adams years. This was not the expectation. Neither Adams nor his lieutenants grasped the depth of

Jacksonians' convictions that their leader had been betrayed by the results of the House of Representatives' deliberations in February 1825, particularly in light of the subsequent appointment of Henry Clay (who had engineered Adams's election over Jackson) to the Department of State. Early portents of future political alignments were evidenced in public debate over the David Porter affair, and over the controversy that began to brew in the fall of 1825 over Georgia Governor George Troup's dealings with the Creek Indians.[25] Yet as late as November, there remained no obvious, fruitful basis for a formal opposition to the administration. The publication of President Adams's first message to the Congress changed everything.

III

John Quincy Adams's message to the Congress in December 1825 is one of the more celebrated documents in American history. It has widely been viewed as the basis for an organized opposition to the administration, and for an extended and frequently bitter political debate over Jeffersonian principles. That this would be the case was far from John Quincy Adams's mind when, after a refreshing vacation in New England in late summer and early fall 1825, he returned to Washington to write his message. By late November Adams had penned a rough draft, which he presented to his cabinet for discussion on November 23. In terms of specific proposals, there was little in it that was new or startling. It was the very breadth of the proposed program, and the boldness of the language justifying it, that brought several of the president's counsellors up short. Clay and Barbour, sensitive to Southern fears about a too active and puissant federal government, objected to the president''s proposals for a national astronomical laboratory and a national university. Other issues were debated, and the meeting adjourned. For two days more the cabinet met and discussed the president's paper, with Barbour and Clay continuing to make the most suggestions for alterations, and Richard Rush most strongly in support of the president's thrust and language. Southard interposed comments on naval affairs and relations with France, but in general was silent. All told, the cabinet members made enough suggestions for changes and deletions at these sessions that the president observed at one of them that he felt like "the man with two wives. One is plucking out his white hairs, the other the black, & none are left."[26]

Despite his good-natured protestations, Adams kept his program essentially intact. Warnings from Barbour and Clay, and, later, William Wirt (who had been absent on legal business during the cabinet meetings concerning the message), that the nationalistic tenor of the program would not sell in the South, did not dissuade Adams. "The perilous experiment is to be made," he noted in his diary. "let me make it with full deliberation, and be prepared for the consequences."[27]

Adams had spoken truly: it was a perilous experiment. When the president's message reached the Nineteenth Congress on December 6, 1825, it provoked something close to hysteria among the Southern members. Many old Jeffersonians in Congress and throughout the nation recoiled when they read the president's words. In the message Adams had argued that the central government, in its responsibility for the "general welfare" of the citizenry, had the right, the power, and the obligation to promote

> the improvement of agriculture, commerce, and manufactures, the cultivation and encouragement of the mechanic and of the elegant arts, the advancement of literature and the progress of the sciences, ornamental and profound. . . . While foreign nations less blessed with the freedom which is power are advancing with gigantic strides in the career of public improvement, were we to slumber in indolence or fold up our arms and proclaim to the world that we are palsied by the will of our constituents, would it not be to cast away the bounties of Providence and doom ourselves to perpetual inferiority.[28]

These words, combined with such specific recommendations as road building and scientific expeditions funded by the central government (not to mention a national university and an astronomical laboratory) utterly appalled many Americans, who were accustomed to a government that kept its hands off their affairs and the affairs traditionally delegated to the states. That a minority president could warn Congress not to be "palsied" by the will of its constituents was, as George Dangerfield has remarked, tactless in the first degree. Yet "it was not tactlessness of which Mr. Adams was to be accused; it was tyranny."[29]

From Jefferson and Calhoun to Jackson and Van Buren, American statesmen of different persuasions saw Adams as seeking a restoration of Federalism, perhaps even monarchy, in America. This was dangerous to the Union and to the republic; indeed, as Calhoun saw matters, Adams's avowed program was the greatest danger to republicanism in America since the crisis of 1798.[30] At the same time, the message was a convenient device to transform purely personal opposition to Adams into a crusade of principle. Politicians such as Van Buren, for example, whose political consistency left something to the imagination prior to 1824, now could convince themselves that their opposition to the administration was justifiable and necessary if the nation were to be safe.

Such a response to the president's 1825 state paper was probably predictable and inevitable, given the boldness with which Adams presented his views, the continuing resonance of the strand of Jeffersonianism that emphasized strict construction of the Constitution, and the politically fluid environment nationally in the wake of a hotly contested presidential election. Politicians, by nature, need issues to run on, and with his message of

December 1825, John Quincy Adams had not merely staked his supporters to a cause, but handed his opponents a compelling issue: the specter of a revived Hamiltonianism.[31] In truth, no issue dominated American life and politics more during the period between the Revolution and the Civil War than the matter of remaining true to the republican vision and virtues embodied within the "country mentality" so perceptively explored and analyzed in recent years.[32] On first glance, Andrew Jackson's partisans, with their fears that economic development would undermine the "republican simplicity" of an agrarian world, and their commitment to states' rights and limited participation of the federal government in encouraging business expansion, would seem to have been the logical heirs of the Jeffersonian Republican impulse. But Jeffersonianism could never be so neatly packaged, and certainly not by the 1820s. By the time John Quincy Adams took the oath of office "arcadian simplicity" was no longer the essence of republicanism. Far from sustaining the dream of a "Christian Sparta" articulated widely in the Revolutionary era, independence opened new avenues for American enterprise. Americans were, as Gordon Wood has aptly suggested, a people in transit from "virtue" to "commerce" and not even the political ascendancy of Thomas Jefferson himself could stay the advance of individualism, materialism, and capitalism in America.[33]

John Quincy Adams's vision, predicated on the conviction that "liberty" in America was a given, held that the government's great task was to encourage "improvement" in all spheres of national life.[34] Adams's republicanism accepted and hailed the diversification of the national economy, and entailed the replacement of "virtue" (simplicity and independence) with the more encompassing Renaissance concept of *virtù*. We could, apparently, survive and prosper as a nation of farmers and shopkeepers, tillers of the soil and agents of industry. J. G. A. Pocock captures this transition in American thought when he writes that "what the American is in search of by the early nineteenth century is not the nature to be contemplated in Arcadian scenery—though this option is never fully closed off—but his own nature as a man, which is civic, military, commercial and in a word active."[35] The virtuous yeoman had not yet lost his appeal in a society that remained, in Samuel Southard's time, predominantly agricultural, but the locus of virtue was in transit, with emphasis on the virtuousness of all enterprise and hard work, so long as it was honest and constructive. The path was even opening to the glorification of the entrepreneur and the industrious factory worker, albeit a worker who had ambitions to become, as Abraham Lincoln would stress, an independent enterpreneur himself.[36]

Adams's 1825 message encapsulated, in the starkest form, this dynamic conception of republicanism. It pointed accurately to the future. What it did not do, in part because of its brusque wording, in part because of its very comprehensiveness, was win the hearts of citizenry less willing and able than he to redefine republican objectives.

For those disposed to oppose the administration, Adams's message could be characterized as a portent of revived Federalism. For those such as Samuel Southard, who had been weaned on a pastoral republicanism, but who in their daily lives better reflected the newer republican vision, Adams was a leader and a spokesman. Because there was a manifestly Jeffersonian strain in the president's program, and because he was privy to the persuasive powers of the president, Southard did not find it difficult to stand with the message. If, as Samuel Flagg Bemis had observed, Henry Clay could argue with Adams over specific initiatives but recognize that at bottom Adams was talking his language, Southard was surely a related case—a man, sensitive to the allurements and benefits of improvements who could persuade himself that this was no break in substance with what had previously served as Jeffersonian political philosophy. Southard's conviction that Adams was a genuine republican, committed to improvement without infringing upon Americans' liberties, made the adoption of a stronger nationalist position easier to accept. *He* knew Adams was no secret monarchist, and he believed that opposition to the administration was founded on political opportunism, not principles. So he had few doubts about his own course—few doubts, at least, that he spoke out loud. "My first duty," he wrote in 1826 to Joel R. Poinsett, the current minister to Mexico, "I feel I owe to the Adm[inistratio]n of which I am a member—and while I approve of its acts, I shall not be found in opposition to it. When I do not approve of its acts, I will cease to be a part of the Cabinet which advises."[37] Not exactly a ringing endorsement of Adams's principles, but nonetheless a commitment to stand with them, as expressed in the message. Southard's ideological commitment to nationalism never really matured to that evinced by Adams, Clay, or Rush. But standing somewhere between these men on one side, and Wirt and Barbour on the other, Southard could find grounds for principled defense of the Adams regime. Whether he and his colleagues could organize effectively and drum up sufficient support to reelect the president who had their allegiance was another matter entirely. For the president's message, if not quite the administration's death knell, as some historians have it, was a spur to the kind of relentless and debilitating opposition the administration would face in Congress for its entire term.[38]

IV

As a cabinet officer and as a politician interested in survival and security, Southard had a self-interested responsibility to advance the political prospects of the administration. Like most of his colleagues, he worked to win the support of waverers and to strengthen the morale of supporters by regular attention to patronage. In his case, as navy secretary, he was particularly solicitous of administration friends in dispensing midshipmen's appointments and professional and clerical positions in the deparment, and in recommending individuals for more prominent and lucrative positions—collectorships and district judgeships, for example. Southard regularly received letters from political acquaintances and confidants in Virginia, Pennsylvania, New York, and especially New Jersey recommending individuals for jobs of one kind or another. Many concluded, as did Robert Arnold's letter recommending Aaron Ogden for a federal district judgeship in New Jersey, by suggesting that the appointment would "give strength to the friends of the Administration in this state."[39] In such cases, Southard weighed the political benefits of the appointment, keeping in mind where the prospective job holder had stood in the past and, more importantly, what he could do for the cause in the future. On this basis, decisions were made.

In the realm of patronage the administration trod an ambiguous path that was complicated by the stubbornness of the president. It stood to reason that, if this were an Adams administration, men loyal to the president and his program, men committed to advancing his and their future, should replace those who were not. Yet Adams had premised this administration on continuity with Monroe's and insisted further that competence rather than personal or political loyalty should determine a man's status in office. Breaking one of the cardinal principles of partisan politics, Adams declined to remove civil servants who opposed him so long as they were effective in their assigned duties. Postmaster General John McLean of Ohio, a Monroe administration holdover, was a case in point. A friend of Calhoun's and a bitter foe of Henry Clay, McLean worked increasingly closely with the emerging opposition to the administration he represented, and yet held on to his job even though the president himself was aware of McLean's treachery.[40]

The McLean situation was only the tip of the iceberg. In case after case cabinet officers and other political friends reminded the president of the need to reward allies and remove enemies within the bureacracy. The president was studiously indifferent to their claims, and such changes as were made tended to be accomplished without his oversight. Southard, Clay, and Barbour, with many positions at their disposal, worked diligently to satisfy administration supporters at the grass roots. But there were never enough commissions and offices to satisfy all who wanted them, or to undo the harm caused by Adams's well publicized unwillingness to distribute the political "loaves and fishes."[41]

In some instances the president was caught between Scylla and Charybdis on appointments he had an obligation to make. Of these, perhaps the most celebrated was a case in which Samuel Southard had considerable influence and that ultimately sparked a rupture in the New Jersey administration party. The controversy arose over the appointment of a federal district judge for New Jersey. To understand the New Jersey imbroglio, one must recall that, as a presidential candidate, John Quincy Adams had promised to make appointments without reference to party background, a commitment designed in part to win support for his candidacy from former Federalists long standing in the political cold.[42] Adams's repeated insistence that no segment of the American polity would be blackballed simply because of political pedigree was music to the ears of old Federalists such as the Stocktons of New Jersey. On the basis of their hopes for office, the Stocktons strongly supported Adams in the election of 1824 and backed pro-administration candidates in local and county elections thereafter. The head of this political family, Richard Stockton of Princeton, joined with his son Robert to finance a newspaper, the *New Jersey Patriot,* dedicated to the fortunes of the administration party in the state. Robert Field Stockton made the paper an effective vehicle for propagating the nationalist views of the president and for assailing the nascent opposition in New Jersey. The junior Stockton, moreover, was extremely active behind the scenes on behalf of the cause and was encouraged in these efforts by Samuel Southard. "I think we shall be able to carry the autumnal election in favor of the administration," he told Southard in July of 1826, in one of his periodic reports from the field. "I have been in Somerville to see your Brother and others, in Middlesex and Monmouth."[43]

In the county elections that fall, Robert Stockton was seemingly omnipresent on behalf of the administration tickets, and he could reasonably take considerable credit for the smashing victory won by the Adams men in the face of vigorous opposition. The New Jersey election was in fact one of the few bright spots for Adams in an otherwise dismal election year.[44] Thus it was not long before the Stocktons saw an opportunity to cash in some of the political credits they believed they had amassed. During the campaign, District Judge William Pennington had died, leaving open the lucrative, prestigious, and undemanding position he had long held. And who seemed more deserving than the venerable Richard Stockton, who for nearly thirty years had been a leader at the New Jersey bar?

Immediately following the state elections the Stocktons reminded the administration, and particularly Southard, that a debt was due payment.[45] Testimonials to Richard Stockton's virtue and the desirability of his appointment were directed to Southard in Washington and passed on to the president. Under normal circumstances, the debt would have been paid and Stockton would have gained the post he sought. But the circumstances were not entirely "normal." Other interests also had claim on the position. Richard Stockton was not a popular man. Most of the New Jersey Republicans who had enlisted with the Adams administration in 1825 and 1826 continued to resent and, in some cases, despise the old Hamiltonian who now made claim to one of the juiciest patronage plums at the president's disposal. Almost to a man, they supported the candidacy of a longtime Republican party workhorse, William Rossell, who was an associate justice on the state supreme court and who sought advancement to the better-paying, less-taxing, post. More than a dozen letters poured into Southard's office on behalf of Rossell and these, too, were duly passed on to the president.[46]

Southard, quite obviously, would have something to say in the matter, but to whom should he throw his support? Though the Stocktons were old political enemies, they were now effective partisans on behalf of the president and would undoubtedly be a useful aegis in 1828. Further, Richard Stockton was entirely qualified for the position of district judge, and his son had done yeoman service for the administration cause. And yet the matter was not simple at all. To satisfy the Stocktons would embitter many old Republicans, offer the Jacksonians a stick with which to beat the administration, and identify the Adams party in New Jersey with discredited Federalism. All this Southard's correspondents from New Jersey made quite clear.[47]

On the horns of this dilemma, Southard presented the options to the president in early November 1826, and quietly suggested that Rossell was the more sensible choice. Better temporarily to deny the Stocktons the office they sought than to risk the solid Republican underpinnings of the Adams organization in New Jersey. The president agreed, and in the face of stern objections by leading political advisers, including George Sullivan, Charles King, and Joseph Blunt of New York, he named Rossell to the post. To reward the Stocktons simply because they had worked and spent money on his behalf, Adams told these men, "would be repugnant to every feeling of my soul."[48]

The Stockton case caused a furor in New Jersey and much discomfort for Southard, who was the administration's most visible native son. Furious with the president's decision and not at all mollified by Southard's long and rather lame explanation that the appointment of Richard Stockton was not politically feasible, the Stocktons abandoned the administration cause and threw in with the opposition.[49] In taking this step, they were able to carry other former Federalists with them and, by early 1827, most of New Jersey's ambitious Federalist politicians took a stand for Andrew Jackson and with the Jacksonian state organization. The Stockton controversy itself gradually subsided, though in 1828 it was briefly revived, with new intensity, amidst the presidential campaign.[50]

V

Personally painful and politically damaging as the Stockton affair proved to be, it did nothing to stop Southard from directing administration forces in New Jersey to the degree that his time permitted. Although he lacked the funds to maintain two residences during his tenure in the Navy Department, through his family connections Southard maintained a base in his home state. His father, Henry, approaching his eightieth year, still farmed his land in Basking Ridge with assistance from grandchildren. More significantly, Southard's older brother Isaac, now settled with a burgeoning family in Somerville, kept his brother posted on developments in the state. Loyal to Samuel's interests and aware that his own fortunes were tied to them, Isaac worked intensely as an administration partisan in Somerset County and did not fail to take credit when election successes followed his exertions.[51]

Besides his brother, Southard had other sources of political intelligence. His fellow Princeton alumni and longtime friends, Charles Ewing and David Thompson, Jr., provided insights into affairs in Morris and Hunterdon counties, with Thompson charting the movements of Senator Mahlon Dickerson and Ewing explicating the workings of the state legislature in Trenton. These men and others insured that Southard would receive the latest word on developments in New Jersey, and they served also as conduits for Southard's strategies and suggestions. Lucius Elmer of Cumberland County, appointed federal district attorney for New Jersey with Southard's support, periodically wrote to Washington with specific requests and suggestions about patronage. "You will remember that last year I wrote to you on the subject of appointing the "Whig and Observer" man, printer of the laws," Elmer told Southard in 1827. "It will be right now to change back again—if the administration please."[52]

Because his daily responsibilities in Washington tied him to his desk for at least ten months of every year (with a few exceptions), Southard could not return frequently to assess the situation personally or act directly to strengthen the resolve of his lieutenants. Nonetheless, he yearly made a "progress" through the state, occasionally to attend a dinner in his honor, more often in conjunction with visits to his parents and his brother. What he learned on these journeys and through his heavy correspondence was on the whole encouraging. New Jersey may have voted for Jackson in 1824, but both sides generally conceded that a true expression of strength had not been made. By 1825, as the alignments essayed in 1824 reassembled (but generally held in place), the Adams men demonstrated that they were strong everywhere save in rural Warren, Sussex, and Hunterdon counties, which were decidedly pro-Jackson.[53]

The 1825 election was not a fair test of parties in the state, because national battle lines had not yet been drawn, and also because in some counties, such as Bergen, local considerations (in this instance, religious divisions) predominated. By 1826 editors on each side agreed that a straightforward contest was in the works. The issue of Jackson versus Adams was raised early, and each side made its best case, rehearsing arguments that would be repeated ad infinitum for the ensuing two years. Both sides were organized to the utmost. Pamphlets, handbills, and broadsides were printed; committees appointed, candidates screened and newspapers such as the Stocktons' *New Jersey Patriot* established. In the realm of issues, the administration seemed to have the stronger argument, if only because the incumbent was born on the right side of the Mason-Dixon line. Pro-administration newspapers pressed home the point that at last the North had a president and that he should be sustained against the backbiting of disgruntled Southerners. "Sidney," a regular contributor to the staunchly pro-administration Newark *Sentinel of Freedom,* strongly suggested that a vote for Jacksonian candidates was a vote for increase in the power of the slaveholding states:

> They oppose the bankrupt law and the judiciary law—they have op-posed the tariff—they oppose manufacturers—they oppose internal im-provements—They are opposed to every leading measure in which as Jerseymen we are interested—and who are the leaders of these patriotic and consistent politicians? McDuffie, Calhoun, and Randolph—men who have done more to disgrace their country than any three men of modern times—This is the party and these the men to whom our Jackson men would have us bow our necks.[54]

Such arguments, combined with a fuller turnout than occurred in 1824, contributed to a complete administration triumph in both the county and the congressional returns. The results, in a small measure a vindication of Southard's own efforts, strengthened his standing in the administration and encouraged hopes that a reelection for Adams was attainable.[55] They also spurred him to political efforts beyond New Jersey. In the wake of the 1826 election, Southard stepped up his lively correspondence with political friends in several states and he worked especially hard to shore up support for the president in Virginia, which to some observers was shaping up as a key battleground in the coming presidential contest. Southard kept in regular contact with his and Clay's good friend, Francis Brooke, and also with his old employer John Taliaferro, of King George County, who was presently serving in the Congress. Taliaferro and Southard played on the sympathies of former President James Monroe, seeking by whatever means to win his public endorsement of the administration's political course. Aside from his visits with and letters to the former president, Southard followed the Virginia press and occasionally inserted pro-administration pieces in the columns of a Fredericksburg paper operated by his brother-in-law, James D. Harrow.[56]

These movements were not unnoticed by the opposition, any more than were the efforts of his cabinet colleagues. In a speech before the House of Representatives early in 1827, Sam Houston of Tennessee assailed the administration's policies; in particular he took biting notice of the political activities of the department secretaries. For Southard, his scorn was unab-ashed:

As to the Head of the Navy Department, I shall not say much. I believe, however, the honorable Secretary happened, by mere chance, to make a visit to New Jersey a short time ago, previous to, or during the last Congressional election, and if the newspapers are entitled to any degree of credit, he was not inactive in the passing events. I do not say, Sir, that he was engaged in a crusade against a certain "Military Chieftain." How far he therein discharged his *official duties* I shall not take the trouble to determine. Perhaps, in illustrating the character of this gentleman, it will be best done by saying of him—*nothing,nothing,*—Sir.[57]

It was no coincidence that Sam Houston should strongly assail the administration. He was at this time a close adviser to General Jackson, who was then deeply engaged in organizing a challenge to President Adams's reelection. What was coincidental, however, was that Houston should have been personally involved in a complicated and rather ludicrous affair between the general and the secretary that, had events taken a slightly different course, might well have dampened Jackson's political prospects.

VI

Sam Houston's acerbic remarks on the floor of the House of Representatives, directed as they were at the transparently political nature of the various department secretaries' tours, suggested that these activities were having some impact. If the president himself opposed partisan politics and would do little to advance his own fortunes, then his closest advisers would have to take the lead. Hence Clay, Southard, and Barbour in particular went on the hustings, traveling as frequently as they could to attend pro-administration dinners and meetings and collaborating with leaders at the grass roots to establish newspapers and print propaganda favorable to their cause. Eventually the cabinet triumvirate, together with such politicians as Daniel Webster, John Sergeant, Peter B. Porter, John Pleasants, and Levi Lincoln, put together a national organization that was active everywhere save in the deep South.[58]

Important as it was, this work of party building can be overestimated. Zeal and organization were much more the hallmarks of the opposition than of the administration forces. The emerging Jacksonian coalition—the planters of the South with the plain republicans of the North—rapidly and effectively designed a network of committees that were a marvel of political sophistication in a supposedly antiparty age. On every front, in almost every state, the Jacksonians outhustled and outorganized their opposition.[59] The efforts of Southard, Clay, and other leaders of "National Republicanism" were in large measure a response to the opposition's initiatives, and all too frequently pale imitations thereof. And how could it be otherwise? Their president was rarely helpful on patronage matters and, more important, Barbour, Southard, and Clay were tied to their desks most of the time.[60]

Despite the limitations imposed on his political activities by navy-business responsibilities, Southard made it a point to visit old friends in Virginia whenever his schedule allowed. These visits were partly for relaxation and partly an opportunity to chart the political waters in a crucial state. One of these visits, however, caused Southard a good deal of personal pain, for words casually uttered in a private conversation put him in a direct confrontation with General Jackson.

Southard's run-in with the opposition presidential candidate was an interesting episode, one that ultimately would have important implications for the relationship between Jackson and his then ally, Vice President John C. Calhoun. It all began in late June 1826, when Southard took his family to Fredericksburg for a few days' visit with the Taliaferros and other friends. Early in July Southard had dinner at the home of his old friend, Dr. John S. Wellford, a dinner also attended by ex-President Monroe and their mutual friend, Francis Brooke. The day following this pleasant evening spent in reminiscing with this company, Southard was again invited to Wellford's home for more conversation—this time over after-dinner wine. Southard attended the soirée, where he was joined by a half-dozen of Wellford's neighbors. Talk was brisk and informal, and the wine flowed. In the course of the evening politics inevitably came up. One of Wellford's guests, Dr. John W. Wallace, vigorously contended that Andrew Jackson's performance at the Battle of New Orleans was in itself proof that he was fit for the presidency. With this remark others around that table, including Southard, took issue.[61] Jackson merited applause for the victory over the British, Southard agreed, but he had not lacked assistance. Not enough credit for the defense of New Orleans in 1814 had ever been given to James Monroe, then serving as secretary of war. Monroe, Southard argued, had made all the arrangements for the city's defense, and he had warned General Jackson of the British approach to Louisiana. Had Monroe not been so diligent as he was, Jackson would have faced immeasurably greater difficulties at New Orleans. These comments, fueled by Southard's warm affections for Monroe, and probably heated a bit by the wine he had been sipping, were fairly innocuous—essentially a sentimental if insistent defense of a man he greatly admired, and a mild debunking of a political adversary. Stretched a bit, however, the remarks could be taken as an insult to General Jackson.

Stretched they were. Wallace, a Jacksonian partisan, offered to friends his own account of the after dinner discussion, putting the worst possible face on Southard's comments. This interpretation was soon carried off to Andrew Jackson in Tennessee, where it had the same effect, as John Quincy Adams later recalled, as throwing a "scarlet blanket upon a tiger." Never one to treat insults lightly, particularly when they touched his military reputation, Jackson declined to accept remarks like Southard's, regardless of the context in which they were made. In his anger Jackson went to his table and penned an acid letter to Southard—a letter that, to say the least, was hastily and intemperately drawn. Jackson demanded that Southard explain himself; if no satisfaction were offered, there would be serious consequences.[62] The letter never reached Southard; however, Jackson had first sent it unsealed to his friend Sam Houston, who was to carry it on to Secretary Southard in Washington. When Houston read the letter he recognized that, given its subject and language (not to mention Jackson's inimitable spelling!), it was potentially explosive. Consulting with Jacksonian operatives in the capital, Houston decided to hold on to the letter and to write the general advising a milder, less contentious missive, and perhaps even delay in sending that.[63]

Houston's attempts to calm his friend were shrewd but not completely successful. As the new year, 1826, approached, Jackson's patience wore thin. He wrote to Southard on January 5, repeating what Wallace had told him about Southard's remarks and suggested that "a charge of so serious a nature" could not "pass without some notice." He requested Southard's grounds for his remarks about Jackson's alleged desire to leave New Orleans prior to the battle, and Monroe's "peremptory order to return to that place." But this letter, too, went first to Houston, who again thought it too tart and who consequently held it. Jackson was insistent, however, and he prodded Houston into delivering the letter to Southard on February 3. By this time, the letter was hardly a surprise to Southard since political gossip traveled quickly in Washington, and Southard had learned of the original Jackson protest letter by mid-December.[64] Faced at last with a demand for an explanation of his comments the previous July, Southard immediately consulted his political friends and prepared a defense. The subject would consume a good deal of his time and energy for the next few months.[65]

This clash between the general and the Secretary was unnecessary. Southard's comments had not been flattering to Jackson, but they had been casually and privately expressed and they had not included a suggestion that Jackson wished to avoid a fight with the British at New Orleans. Far worse things than Southard's attempt to minimize Jackson's organizational talents had been made on the stump or in the press. Yet Jackson, ever sensitive to honor, particularly regarding an important episode in his career, insisted on carrying the issue forward. For his part, Southard insisted on answering Jackson's letter in a similar frame of mind, if not in exactly the same tone. Southard's response, dated February 9, 1827, explained the circumstances behind the remarks at Dr. Wellford's and specifically denied that he ever "charged you with neglect or desertion of your military duties—nor denied to you the merit and glory of fighting the battle of New Orleans." His object in the conversation, Southard insisted, was "to vindicate Mr. Monroe," not "to deprecate your military exploits.

They form a part of our national glory which I have no inclination to tarnish."[66]

Jackson was not appeased. On March 6 he responded to this explanation by insisting that his information was accurate and asserting that Southard's reply was less than "frank and candid." Jackson's letter, dripping with sarcasm, went on to a lengthy recollection of the events of 1814, which, to his mind, proved that Monroe's assistance in the defense of New Orleans was, at best, peripheral. "I have therefore to request," Jackson concluded "when on your electioneering tours, or at your wine drinkings hereafter, you will not fail to recollect these historical facts which indeed you ought long since to have known." With this injunction, Jackson announced that the correspondence was at a "close."[67]

This letter reached Southard on April 2 through Major John Eaton, Jackson's Tennessee friend, currently a member of the Senate. Uncertain how to proceed in such a circumstance—Jackson, after all, had declared that their correspondence was concluded—Southard boiled. He was dismayed at the prospect of an unqualified military chieftain gaining the presidency, disgusted by the misinformation conveyed by Wallace, and appalled by the style and tone of Jackson's letters to him. In this frame of mind Southard sat at his desk and penned a thirty-one-page memorandum to himself that summarized the affair. He was particularly aggravated at this time that Jackson's third letter (the one declaring the correspondence over) was published in Duff Green's virulently anti-administration journal, the *United States Telegraph*. A private slur was one thing; public humiliation was ten times worse. As he sat at his desk, Southard vented some of his frustrations.

Aside from the atrocious style of writing, Southard observed in his "Remarks on the Correspondence," Jackson's exposition lacked every semblance of decency and fairness. Jackson had queried and Southard had given a candid response. Was this insufficient? If by a "chivalric" answer Jackson had meant a "blustery, gasconading, insulting, duel seeking" one, "I freely confess that I had no disposition to give such a one and never have given to any means." Southard professed hope and confidence that Jackson would not be so foolish as to demand a duel. On and on he wrote, as a matter of reference for himself and preparation, perhaps for further exchanges on the subject. From the perspective of 150 years, that a cabinet officer should expend such energy over so palpably absurd an affair seems ridiculous. Yet in Southard's mind, who could know what would eventuate? Jackson seemed just unpredictable enough to demand a duel with the navy secretary. Certainly Jackson had a good record on the dueling field! In the end, Southard was determined to hold his ground—to deny what he had *not* said, but also to demur in pronouncing "the eulogy which the General demands of me."[68]

To Southard there appeared to be one potential silver thread in the cloud of Jackson's churlish assault: the possibility of enlisting former President Monroe as a political ally of the administration. By 1826 Southard had come to the conclusion that, if President Adams were to carry Virginia (and the election nationally) two years hence, the endorsement of his predecessor would be almost essential. Southard was aware that Monroe and Jackson had never been friendly, and he continued to believe that President Adams was carrying on in the tradition of President Monroe. Once Jackson began to recollect the events leading to New Orleans in a fashion unflattering to Monroe, and once Jackson's lieutenants picked up the refrain in their speeches and in print, the way was open to winning Monroe's endorsement for the administration—or so it seemed.

Southard's brainstorm was not entirely unrealistic. Monroe was hostile to Jackson, and he was sympathetic to Southard. The former president was willing to provide Southard with access to his personal papers in support of Southard's recollections about the Battle of New Orleans. But there was a hitch. Monroe wanted to remain out of the controversy insofar as possible and begged Southard not to bring the issue before the public. Monroe's motives here were altruistic and selfish in turn. On one hand, he felt it would be unseemly for an ex-president to be involved in a bitter personal and political quarrel. More important, however, was an immediate financial concern. Monroe at this time was pressing a large claim before the government for services rendered earlier in his public career, and he knew that without the support of Jacksonian congressmen, his claims would have no chance of success. Hence the fervid request that Southard not publish anything that might prejudice his case—which meant, in effect, no publication. Southard agreed to comply, and for the time being, Monroe was not directly involved.[69]

The Jackson-Southard affair was not quite over. In an effort to tantalize gossip-hungry Washington and perhaps to put Southard on edge, Washington *Telegraph* editor Duff Green had been hinting about Southard's enormities and their implications since the spring. Some of these items were picked up in newspapers across the country, and Southard was not infrequently asked by correspondents just when his "duel" with Jackson was going to take place—a suggestion that he quickly dampened.[70] In late June, 1827, Green finally bruited the issue directly in an editorial titled "GEN JACKSON AND MR SOUTHARD." In this article Green recapitulated the substance of the issue between the secretary and the general from a perspective sympathetic to Jackson but professedly ignorant of the specifics of most of the correspondence. In a followup, responding to a defense of Southard that appeared in several pro-administration papers, Green charged that Southard was the "convicted slanderer" of General Jackson, a man unwilling or unable to tell the truth. In neither of these editorials, nor in a third, published on 11 July, did Green publish any of the correspondence—probably because he knew that publication would not redound to the general's benefit.[71] For his part Southard, who would have liked to exhibit the Jacksonian literary style for an interested public, was prevented from doing so because of his pledge to Monroe.[72] The Jackson-Southard duel never happened and the issue faded as political Washington turned to such matters as the tariff, Governor Troup's continued truculence regarding the Creek Indians in Georgia, and the president's penchant for billiard playing.

For Southard, the incident was a harrowing, ugly, but in the end strangely edifying experience. He had for months been talking privately about Jackson's unfitness for the presidency. Now he had personal knowledge that what he had been saying was all too true. Southard's experience convinced him more than ever that Jackson had to be defeated in the election of 1828. As he wrote to an old friend at the bar, John Wurts, who by 1827 was emerging as a Jacksonian leader in Philadelphia: "The more I see and hear of Genl J. and his disregard of all obligations which impede the course of his passions, the more I dread his ascent to the Presidency."[73]

Aside from its "educational" value, the fracas had opened the possibility of playing the Monroe "card" in the coming election. If Southard could not draw Monroe into direct confrontation with Jackson on the events at issue in the wine drinking controversy, perhaps Monroe could be brought into the Adams camp another way. One night in Fredericksburg in the fall of 1827 Southard hatched a scheme with his friend Taliaferro, whereby each would approach Monroe about running for vice-president with Adams in 1828. In one stroke the course of the current administration would be vindicated by one of the "last of the cocked hats," and Virginia could be brought into the national Republican camp. It sounded perfect when Taliaferro and Southard conversed together; they determined to make the effort. Within weeks, each man wrote confidentially to Monroe, making the suggestion to him. "In looking around for a candidate for the vice presidency, to be run with President Adams," Southard began his confidential missive,

> it seems to be generally thought that Virginia ought to furnish the man & that in selecting him, she owes it to her character & fame to let him be the first & best. . . . In reflecting about it, it has occurred to us, that you might, with propriety, be put into the situation. And if you were named, a unanimous approbation of the act would follow.

What good reasons could be given for accepting such a nomination? Southard listed several, the strongest being defense of Monroe's "Principles & policy" as president and, not least, the opportunity for "a pleasant employment" for four years, with "a handsome yearly income"—something Southard well knew Monroe needed and wanted.[74]

Despite these arguments, and similar ones offered by Taliaferro in his own secret letter, Monroe did not rise to the bait. He immediately wrote to

Southard politely but firmly declining the offer on the grounds that he had pledged himself, early and often, to "observe a perfect neutrality" between Adams and Jackson. "If I were to suffer myself to be brought forward, in the present instance, after what has passed, or being brot forward, was not to decline the trust . . . it would do to my character, an irreparable injury, since it would be concluded, by an impartial public, that I had abandoned a ground which I had adopted on principle, by the allur[e]ment of office."[75] Weeks later, Monroe also rejected efforts to place him on an electoral ticket in Virginia that was favorable to Adams. Like his old friend James Madison, who was similarly approached, Monroe had warm feelings for Adams, but was emphatic in a determination not to interfere in the election.[76]

Failure to win the public support of the two former presidents doomed the administration to defeat in Virginia, though partisans such as Southard were slow to accept the fact. Throughout 1827 Southard had been particularly solicitous, when it came time to dispense midshipmen's warrants, of Virginia supporters of the administration. His proclivities did not change in the election year of 1828. Meanwhile, in his native state, Southard was equally favorable to jobseekers who could do something to advance the administration's cause. Further, he encouraged a complicated plan designed to win over the leading ex-Federalist in Jacksonian ranks, Garret D. Wall. Wall and Southard had ridden circuits together for years, and the Trenton man had argued before Southard during the latter's service on the state supreme court. Kindred souls in many ways, they differed mainly in their political pedigree—and now, during Adams's administration, in political loyalties. Because the two men were basically friendly, and because Southard knew that Wall was desperate to gain some lucrative public position, Southard authorized an administration stalwart in Trenton, William Prall of the *True American,* to strike a deal with Wall. The administration party would support Wall for attorney general, once the current incumbent, Theodore Frelinghuysen, resigned the post to assume William Rossell's now vacant seat on the state supreme court. In exchange, Wall would back off his organizational efforts on behalf of Jackson, and perhaps even move toward an endorsement of the administration. The deal was struck and, as Wall himself later conceded, the pro-administration legislators were prepared to vote for him to consummate it. Unfortunately, Frelinghuysen declined to accept the proferred judgeship, and Wall was left out of the job he most wanted.[77] Following the collapse of the plan, Southard wrote to Wall, expressing regret that it had not matured. Still, he hoped Wall would see things in a new way. "Dont rely on what you read in the Telegraph," he implored. "You will be misled if you do." If only Wall "could be behind the scenes a little," Southard concluded, he would be "cured" of his Jacksonian tendencies.[78]

Southard's efforts with Wall were as unavailing as those with the former president. Within months Wall was back in action organizing Democratic committees and establishing pro-Jackson newspapers. Politics oftentimes proved to be a frustrating business. But it made no sense to quit in the middle of a fight. Southard pressed on in his spare moments, writing to his regular coterie of coadjutors in states from Kentucky to New York, with the bulk of his attention devoted, as always, to New Jersey. When he was able to visit his home turf, Southard wasted relatively little time chatting with relatives and old friends. He gave impromptu speeches, usually to the effect that the safety of the Union was dependent on the continuation of the present administration. His repertoire included sharp attacks on Andrew Jackson's character, and as specific evidence for the general's lack of judgment, references to Jackson's role in the executions of the six militia men were often made.[79]

Southard's stake in the outcome of the election of 1828 encouraged such sallies and encouraged a kind of wishful thinking about election prospects. This may explain his increasing closeness to the Pollyannaish Peter B. Porter, who had replaced the politics-weary James Barbour in the War Department early in 1828. The fact was that Southard had an emotional and financial stake in the administration. He knew that, if Adams lost the election, he was out of a job. This was not a comforting thought for a man who had held the navy secretaryship longer than he had held any other position in his life, and who liked his position, his status, and his influence. Moreover, after all his progress in politics, he remained financially pressed, partly because of the medical expenses incurred by his unusually sickly family, partly because of his unwillingness to cut corners in day-to-day living.

Beyond this, Southard was increasingly committed, intellectually, to the program of improvement the president had set as his agenda for American development. Advances in manufacturing, a higher tariff, internal improvements at all levels, better educational facilities, a concern for the cultural life of the nation—all of these things Southard believed good for America and compatible with Jeffersonian vision he had always embraced. Each of these aspects of the Adams program would be important to the emergent Whig philosophy.

Adams stood for the American System that history identifies with Henry Clay. So did, and so would, Samuel Southard. By contrast, Jackson and his followers appeared to Southard to be simply naysayers, men who could not construct a workable national policy. Under Jackson's direction Southard felt he could expect, at best, a do-nothing government. At worst, he foresaw a government entirely in the hands of proslavery politicians determined to thwart economic development in the north, a government opposed to just Indian land claims in the Southwest, and a government lacking prudence or good judgment at the top.

The combination of principle and expediency intensified Southard's commitments in 1828. Through the first eight months of the election year

Southard worked on virtually every front to reelect the president. He pressed forward the patronage claims of administration partisans, notably in Philadelphia, New York City, Richmond, and Trenton; he inserted essays in the press on behalf of the administration and found funds to support anti-Jacksonian organs; he secretly and successfully urged his predecessor in the Navy Department, Supreme Court Justice Smith Thompson, to run for the governorship in New York to bolster the administration ticket there; he spoke on the administration's behalf in his travels; and finally, he advised, personally and through his correspondence, with grass roots politicians.[80]

These efforts were essential because New Jersey's Jacksonians, under the direction of Garret Wall and Samuel Swartwout, were also zealous and particularly good organizers. Despite warnings from the perspicacious Lucius Elmer that Jackson had a strong appeal for the mass of citizens, and that his appeal "like a snowball will by every turn . . . increase," Southard remained optimistic.[81] He preferred the hopeful projections of Thomas Harris and John Sergeant to the warnings of a Lucius Elmer and the despair of a Francis Brooke.[82]

By late September, the pace of his efforts in the campaign combined with the unceasing burden of Navy Department business took its toll. Southard was struck by fatigue, then a fever; for nearly three full months in the late summer and autumn of 1828 he was confined to bed.[83] It probably made no difference. Whatever could be done had been done; Adams supporters would now have to rely on providence.[84] No miracle occurred, however, and Jackson swept the election, carrying the South, the West, and the middle states, save New Jersey and a fraction of New York. It was, as Samuel Flagg Bemis notes, an "earth-shaking" triumph for the Jacksonians, and a repudiation of "the perilous experiment."[85]

Southard, on his sickbed, could take some small solace in suggestions from friends such as A. S. Hooe of Spotsylvania County, Virginia, that President Adams had triumphed there primarily because of the navy secretary's exertions.[86] New Jersey's endorsement of the administration was also a happy event, though overshadowed by the Jacksonian mandate nationwide. Within weeks, Southard would be up and back at his desk, and he began to take his mind off the crushing setback suffered by his chief. Prospects for remaining in Washington under other auspices would have to be pursued. There was life after the cabinet.

5

The Navy Years: Administration

Stewardship of the Navy Department was probably the most demanding and satisfying responsibility of Samuel Southard's long public career. Beginning his tenure in the department under James Monroe almost totally innocent of administrative procedure and naval operations, Southard quickly emerged as an effective administrator, thoughful planner, and respected spokesman for naval improvement. His accomplishments as navy secretary were not spectacular because he ran the department at a time when costly programs were unpopular, however meritorious, and when political currents discouraged adventurous policies. Despite such restraints Southard achieved most of his goals, and in the process won the respect of his subordinates as well as the friendship of leading career officers. Southard was proud of his record and of his naval connections, and he endeavored throughout his public career to substantiate his reputation as a firm friend to the American navy.

I

If previous experience with naval affairs or executive office had been a requisite for appointment to head the Navy Department, Samuel Southard could hardly have been less well fitted for the position he would hold from September 1823 through February 1829. One of his friends, responding to a hurried request for advice about whether to accept the appointment tendered by President James Monroe told him bluntly to "stick to your law and to politics, about which you know something; but let alone the navy, about which you know nothing."[1] His former colleague on the New Jersey Supreme Court, Andrew Kirkpatrick, is reported to have asked Southard, "Can you honestly assert that you know the bow from the stern of a frigate?"[2] Outside of New Jersey, where public opinion was strongly favorable to the appointment on grounds of state pride, comment on Southard's nomination was generally tepid. The Washington *National Intelligencer,* for example, tersely and a bit ungenerously observed that Southard was named navy secretary not for any particular talent he had evinced but because New Jersey had not "for many years furnished any officer to the general government."[3] Only Southard's performance could belie the doubts that his elevation owed as much to his merit as his connections.

In truth, inexperience with nautical affairs did not daunt Southard much, for he was keenly ambitious, and confident that he could handle whatever administrative burden lay in store for him. He was, moreover, eager to share in the making of policy at the highest levels, eager to see and be seen with Washington's great men, eager himself to gain a national reputation. He was, at age thirty-six, a relatively young man, and if he performed his duties well, the future might hold even more important assignments.

Southard's initiation to his new responsibilities afforded him little leisure to sort out the condition of the American navy or systematically to set priorities in running the department. During the month-long interregnum between his appointment in August and his arrival in Washington in mid-September 1823, malaria had broken out at a navy base on Thompson's Island at Key West, Florida. The outbreak, understandable enough given the unfortunate location of the base, threatened not merely the lives of scores of sailors, including the West Indian Squadron's commander, Captain David Porter, but also the squadron's mission to quash piracy in the Caribbean. The first papers thrust into Southard's hands in his new office related to the emergency situation on Thompson's Island, and thus provided him with his first test. Confronted with this crisis, Southard did not hesitate. He quickly ordered five doctors to the island and commanded the veteran Captain John Rodgers to relieve the distressed Porter and assume temporary responsibility for the squadron. This proved to be a timely decision; not only did David Porter's furlough save his life, but the West Indian antipiracy campaign, languishing when Southard arrived in Washington, was salvaged and revivified thanks to the infusion of fresh personnel ordered by the navy secretary.[4]

As a consequence of his fast and firm response to the situation in south Florida, Southard won the applause of the nation's presses, which had been following the progress of the campaign against piracy with more than mild interest. Even the previously sour *National Intelligencer* congratulated Southard for "the promptitude which, after entering upon the duties of his office, he had acted upon this subject."[5] Other papers took up the refrain, while the captain's friends in Washington personally expressed their appreciation to Southard. For his own part, the new secretary viewed his actions not as heroism but, rather, simply as performance of duty. "Would I have discharged my duty had I failed to furnish the best aid in my power?" he observed.[6]

More consequential in the broader perspective than the rescue of sick sailors was the salvage of the navy's mission in the West Indies. In preparing his first annual report as navy secreary in November 1823, Southard could tell President Monroe that the long-festering piracy problem was under control, a conclusion the president reported to a grateful nation on December 2.[7] An epoch in American maritime history seemed near its close, and the new man in the cabinet could, as the new year approached, take some pride in his debut. Little could Southard anticipate that his relations with Captain Porter, at the moment on the friendliest basis, would sour dramatically within a year and cause Southard and the administration he served a great deal of distress.

II

In the 1820s the Navy Department was an important but underfunded arm of the government. Americans still spoke with pride and nostalgia about the exploits of American sailors during the War of 1812, but they were loath, in peacetime, to support a large military establishment. The ideal of republican simplicity had little place for standing armies and little more for large naval fleets. This persuasion was reinforced by the economic depression of 1819–21, which suggested to many Americans that the citizenry at large had become addicted to luxury, speculation,and loose construction of government's mandate, and that this would have to change. During the depression years and immediately thereafter, calls for retrenchment were commonly and emphatically made, and the Navy and War Departments were two major targets for significant budgetary cutbacks. In January 1821, for example, a proposal was made in the Congress to retire half the naval force still on active service, and to spread over a longer period the appropriations necessary to complete ships already under construction. Representatives from states with no direct borders on the Atlantic Ocean were particularly insistent on reshaping the navy's responsibilities and cutting its expenditures, and they had the votes to reduce the annual outlay for new ship construction by half—from $1,000,000 to $500,000 in 1821—despite the strong protests of the department. During President Monroe's second term of office, including the eighteen months Samuel Southard directed naval affairs, the department's appropriations shrank, on average, nearly a million dollars from the standard during 1817–21. Throughout his tenure in office, in fact, Samuel Southard was plagued by the public's penchant for "economy" and its indifference to the many important if unglamorous tasks the peacetime navy was charged with performing.[8]

What were these responsibilities? During the 1820s, and beyond, the republic's navy was responsible for four main tasks: the protection of American commerce, on our shores and beyond; the suppression of piracy, particularly in the West Indies, where it has been a periodic source of irritation since the early years of the republic, but also off the coasts of

Latin America and in the Mediterrenean; policing the slave trade; and the defense of American national security. Of its responsibilities the navy was probably most successful with the first and least equipped for the last. Had Great Britain, for example, sought to invade American ports, it could have done so virtually with impunity. The American navy was never, during these years, a formidable fighting force.[9] Fortunately the nation enjoyed peace, and the scale of American naval operations was modest. Confident that the world's leading naval power had a stake in supporting rather than contradicting us, American policymakers could afford the luxury of economies in the realm of defense. The calculations surrounding the promulgation of the Monroe Doctrine in late 1823 suggested as much.[10]

The immediate task facing Samuel Southard as navy secretary, aside from lobbying the Congress to abjure devastating cuts in his department's already pinched operating budget, was to reorient naval administration. Southard's predecessor as navy secretary, Smith Thompson of New York, had been bored by the day-to-day details of administration, and was given to spending weeks, even months, at a time away from Washington. For most of the spring and summer in any given year, the department was run by its chief clerk in cooperation with a board of veteran naval officers that had been established in 1815 to take some of the administrative load off the cabinet secretary.[11] Given the fact that the board of navy commissioners was geared to such matters as procurement, not policymaking, and in view of the minuscule size of the support staff, the casual manner in which Thompson conducted the department had left its morale low, its civilian personnel weary, and its direction uncertain.[12] As secretary of the navy, Samuel Southard intended to reverse this drift, and all naval historians who have studied his performance give him high marks for achieving this and more.[13]

Providing direction to the navy and oversight of its operations was and would remain Southard's chief concern from 1823 to his departure from Washington in March 1829. Beyond this, his energies were devoted to initiating programs that would strengthen the navy and its personnel; joining other cabinet members in shaping national policy; and, under John Quincy Adams, working on behalf of the administration's political fortunes. In each of these realms he made significant, if not necessarily dramatic, contributions.

Policy formulation was a weighty if secondary responsibility for Southard under Presidents Monroe and Adams. This was understandable, particularly during the eighteen months he served in Monroe's cabinet. Southard was young and relatively inexperienced in national affairs at the time of his appointment. He was surrounded by colleagues of national reputation: Calhoun, in the War Department, Crawford at Treasury, Wirt as the nation's chief legal officer, and Adams at State. Each was a formidable figure, articulate, forceful, ambitious. All save Wirt were contenders for the succession. Each had years of experience in cabinet conclaves.[14] Though he lacked nothing in the realm of intelligence and ambitions, Southard was realistic enough to recognize that his role in such a cabinet would be that of supporting player, not star.

Despite his youth and inexperience, there is nonetheless every indication that Southard was treated with respect by his colleagues and that from the outset he played a constructive, if supportive role in shaping policy. That he was able to do as much as he did may have been less a product of his innate ingenuity or forcefulness than the fact that under Monroe and John Quincy Adams the cabinet was an intimate, frequently convened, and, by any standard, influential body in the policymaking process. To this process Southard was soon initiated. He had been in office for less than two months when the cabinet convened on November 7, 1823, to consider several confidential proposals made by the British secretary of state, George Canning, to American Minister Richard Rush that had portentous implications for American relations with the European powers and, specifically, the Holy Alliance. In August 1823, Canning had broached to Rush the possibility of joint action by the United States and Great Britain against any potential interference by France or other European nations in the former Spanish colonies of Latin America. Whether such joint action was in America's interests and whether it was feasible would be the subjects for discussion when the cabinet began its deliberations in November.[15]

The details of the November cabinet sessions, beginning on November 7, out of which flowed the policy that history has identified as the Monroe Doctrine require little elaboration here. Whatever the historiographical debate about the forces shaping the president's declaration on December 2 that the American people would accept no European intervention in Latin America, there is a consensus among historians that Monroe's cabinet discussed its options at length, and that John Quincy Adams played the single most significant role in hammering out a policy. Paul A. Varg may slightly overstate the situation when he writes that "Adams captained foreign relations, and his fellow cabinet officers did not seriously challenge him," but the thrust of his assertion is sound.[16] During the 1820s Adams was the dominant force in shaping American foreign policy, not only in James Monroe's administration but also in his own.

Nonetheless, a close analysis of cabinet discussions leading to the message of December 2 reveals that Southard's and his colleagues' attendance at the sessions was not simply pro forma. Discussion was open, reasoned, and, on occasion, contentious. In the first meetings, in fact, the president and a majority of the cabinet, including Southard, supported some joint declaration with Great Britain. (They could not have known, early in November, that George Canning had, subsequent to his initial August conversations with Rush, withdrawn his offer of an alliance.) By November 15, however, it was evident that Adams's insistence on a unilateral declaration would prevail—testament to the strength of his arguments and his position as secretary of state. That Southard, along with Wirt and Calhoun, came to endorse this position was neither surprising nor in any way demeaning. They were not the experts on this question; Adams was.[17]

It may well have been, as Ernest R. May has recently argued, that cabinet debate in late 1823 over the proper response to possible European interference in Latin America was predicated in great measure on domestic political considerations. But it is not likely that this factor was very relevant to Southard's position. His role was to question and to comment, not to direct policy. To the suggestion that he took an initial position similar to Calhoun's out of political considerations, the logical response is that within two weeks he was strongly supporting the secretary of state's views.[18] National interest was and would remain throughout his tenure in the cabinet his overriding concern in the formulation of national policy.

In later years, serving under John Quincy Adams in an increasingly partisan political environment, Southard did act increasingly in a political role, primarily as an adviser and activist, and conduit and judge of public opinion on specific issues. In general, however, he seems to have been readily convinced that the Adams administration's policies—notably the controversial Panama Mission—were not merely sensible but also popular. As a political weathervane, Southard was never supremely adept. As a policymaker, he was dominant only with respect to naval affairs. Yet as an influence in the cabinet, he was, over time, increasingly a figure of weight.[19]

III

Members of the cabinet convened so frequently in some measure because of their proximity to the White House. The Navy Department building, for example, lay just west of the president's home, adjacent to the War Department, and literally a "stone's throw" from the president. Surrounding the executive mansion on the opposite side were the buildings of State and Treasury. Given this situation, it was not uncommon for Southard to visit the White House daily during his tenure in the Navy Department. Indeed, during the months when he doubled as acting secretary of the treasury or acting secretary of war Southard was often in the president's office two and three times a day. Though an exchange of small talk and political gossip was invariably a part of his contacts with Presidents Monroe and Adams, routine business dominated. During his visits Southard brought the president up to date not only on the construction of ships and the disposition of the American fleet, but also on disciplinary matters, personnel requests, and appointments. John Quincy Adams had a great tolerance for (indeed, a natural interest in) such detail, and as a consequence Southard's visits to the White House were more substantial under the New Englander than the Virginian. Under either president, however, Southard knew that he had access to the White House when he needed it. And in both administrations he threw himself deeply into all of the navy's mundane affairs, frequently working for nine and ten hours at a stretch over the never-ending stream of papers that passed his desk. Southard may not have been the most accomplished individual ever to run the Navy Department, but he surely ranks among the most diligent and durable.[20]

During his first months as navy secretary, Southard was most deeply concerned with the problem of piracy in the West Indies. This was a long festering irritation, and in assuming his post he was immediately compelled to give it attention since, as we have seen, health problems at Thompson's Island threatened the very survival of the West Indian Squadron. Southard's prompt and successful response to this crisis doubtless gave him confidence that he was equal to his responsibilities. Little could he have anticipated, late in 1823, that the piracy issue would within a year plunge him into the center of a national controversy, a political firestorm that had its beginnings in the Monroe administration but that became explosive only in the context of the partisanship during the presidency of John Quincy Adams.

Because of the reinforcement of the Thompson's Island station that Southard had ordered in September 1823, President Monroe announced publicly that the extinction of piracy in the West Indies was forseeable. This, unfortunately, was an overly rosy view of the matter. Piracy revived, particularly around Puerto Rico, in 1824, and the Spanish officials there declined to address the problem. Indeed, it was charged, and was probably true, that the local authorities colluded with the pirates. Certainly they saw no benefit in assisting the beleaguered Americans.

Because David Porter had made some dent in West Indian piracy and because the pirates feared him, clamor in the States arose for his return to duty.[21] Porter's malarial fever abated by February 1824, and with his family in tow (Southard had quickly acceded to this special request), he was back in action—but not for long. Yellow fever once again struck on Thompson's Island, Porter was again afflicted and, less than a month after his departure from the Indies, he returned once more to Washington in order to regain his health.[22] Porter's distress was so great that he returned to his Meridian Hill home without so much as requesting permission from Secretary Southard. Though they were dismayed by this breach of procedure, Monroe and Southard did not directly complain, since Porter was truly ill, but they did grow increasingly anxious about piracy, which intensified during the squadron commander's absence from his post.[23]

Southard wrote to Porter several times in the summer of 1824 reminding him of the continuing problem. Porter's subordinates were directed to cruise the troubled waters in the Gulf, awaiting their commander's return.

When Porter showed no disposition to rush back to his command, South-ard ordered him, on October 14, 1824, to do so, "that by your presence the most efficient protection may be afforded to our commerce, and you may be ready to meet any contingencies which occur."[24]

Though this directive was reasonable enough on its face, it presaged a bitter conflict between the secretary and the captain. Porter responded, as his biographer David Long has noted, with "choler and insubordination." In a letter dated October 19, 1824, he told Southard that he was unwell, that he was tired of his assignment, and finally that he felt deep frustration because of Southard's demands for explanation "at every step," which he received almost daily. He concluded his remarkable missive by requesting release from command.[25] Until this point Southard had no idea that Porter was unhappy and had nothing but praise for the work Porter had done. But the captain had to be reminded that policy was made by the executive, not by navy officers, and that civilian oversight and direction was essential. More immediately, Porter was told that, in view of increasing numbers of piracies, he must return to duty. When the secretary found it convenient he would replace him.[26]

Publicly, Southard continued to commend Porter's work in the Carib-bean, but the relations between captain and secretary were never the same, and in fact deteriorated further when Porter complained directly to the president that Southard was attempting to control his life—a reference to the department chief's steady stream of suggestions and queries about the operations of the West Indies squadron.[27] Monroe ignored Porter's com-plaints, but word of the letter reached Southard, who understandably re-sented his subordinate's attempt to undermine his standing in the administration.

The "Porter problem" in late 1824, compounded by the captain's pro-clivity for provoking conflicts with the British navy in the West Indies, and his role in calling unnecessary courtsmartial, nonetheless paled beside the larger problem of piracy in the Caribbean.[28]

During the period between the completion of his report to the president in November 1824 and Monroe's more pessimistic statement to Congress on the piracy problem in December, Southard and the cabinet as a whole discussed the issue at length. Their particular concern was to define Por-ter's mandate to pursue pirates on the Cuban or Puerto Rican mainland. The issue in question was particularly sensitive because of the United States' tender relations with the European powers regarding the autonomy of the infant Latin American republics. These relations would become still more sensitive, in part because of David Porter's activities.

At the cabinet meeting John Quincy Adams, then secretary of state, took an initial stance similar to his position on Andrew Jackson's pursuit of Seminole Indians in Florida in 1818—that is, the American commander had the right of pursuit. But Adams recalled in his diary that "the President, Mr. Calhoun, and Mr. Southard contested this fact." Southard pulled out and read to the cabinet Smith Thompson's orders of February 1, 1823, which showed that Adams was at best half-right, since Porter's permission to land on any of Spain's South American possessions was strictly "limited to the unsettled parts of the Island."[29]

This discussion proved significant and particularly unfortunate for David Porter, because several weeks earlier, and as yet unknown to the administration, he had done exactly what the president and the cabinet had concluded he has no right to do. Porter's action in the so-called Foxardo incident was a case of good intentions yielding only bitter results.[30] And Porter, though a victim to some degree of circumstances (for example, the administration's sensitivity about infringement of European sovereignties in the Western Hemisphere in wake of the Monroe Doctrine), really had no one to blame but himself.

The immediate cause of the Foxardo affair was not piracy but rather simple theft. During Porter's absence from the West Indies one of his lieutenants, Charles T. Platt, had been involved in a disagreeable and troubling incident stemming from his efforts to aid an American in distress. Platt had been informed by an American merchant (and part-time consul) in the Virgin Islands that his company's store had been entered and goods valued at roughly $5,000 taken—probably to Foxardo, Puerto Rico, where the local government was reputed to be in league with pirates. When, on request, Platt pursued the matter as a private citizen by sailing to Foxardo, he was insulted by the authorities there, taken into custody, and placed under arrest. After several hours of considerable discomfort and uncertainty as to his fate, Platt was permitted to call for his uniform and credentials as an American officer and, after further animadversions by the local officialdom, released.[31]

On November 12, David Porter had once again arrived in the Indies to resume his command, and he was in course approached by Lieutenant Platt bearing his unhappy tale. Porter listened to Platt's story with growing anger, and by the time the lieutenant had concluded, he was "boiling." Within hours, Porter put together an expedition and, on November 14, 1824, he and approximately 200 armed men debarked on Spanish soil. Upon landing, the Americans spotted several Spanish soldiers manning a small battery of guns several hundred yards inland, and Porter ordered the guns spiked. This was accomplished without incident. He then sent a small force ahead with an ultimatum that, if the local officials who had "shamefully insulted and abused" Lieutenant Platt did not immediately apologize, he would destroy the town.[32]

More guns were spiked along the way and, finally, after an enervating march in severe heat, Porter reached Foxardo. The mayor (alcalde) and his aides were there to meet him, listened to his demand for an apology, and, without hesitation, complied. All was comity. Under the circumstances there was not much more Porter could do. Having brought forward Lieutenant Platt, who expressed satisfaction at receiving an apology from the *alcalde*, Porter led his men out of town, declining any refreshments or gifts. The episode had lasted less than half a day. Porter promptly sent word of his mission to Southard, fully expecting to receive commendation for his expedition of honor. He was not prepared for the response he actually received.[33]

Precisely two weeks following the cabinet meeting that had considered the rights and responsibilities of the navy in the West Indies, the cabinet met again on the subject at Southard's request. David Porter's letter regarding the Foxardo incident was read, and several brief but inconclusive comments were offered. At this session the participants focused not on Porter but rather on various strategies for further dealing with piracy off the coast of Cuba, strategies that Southard would relay to the House of Representatives committee on naval affairs. Eight days passed before Porter's escapade won the full attention of the cabinet and president. In a "remarkable" meeting, as John Quincy Adams recalled in his diary, the president and his advisers considered what course to follow. Monroe wasted little time expressing his conviction that Porter had wantonly exceeded his instructions; he wanted the captain's recall. Southard, Crawford, and Calhoun all demurred, suggesting that an explanation of Porter's conduct would, for the moment, be sufficient. But Adams, in a complete turnabout from his long-standing latitudinarianism on such matters, forcefully supported the president's harder line, calling the Foxardo incident "one of the most high-handed acts that I had ever heard of." Despite Crawford's sharp retort that Andrew Jackson had done "ten times worse" in invading Florida, a move that had been staunchly defeated by Adams, the secretary of state remained firm and Southard was directed to consult with the president in dealing with Captain Porter.[34]

Why the fuss over Porter's expedition? Why not simply commend him for sustaining national honor generally and Lieutenant Platt's honor in particular? The answer lies in two distinct but related realms. The first of these was a concern to prevent any repetition of the kind of military action Andrew Jackson had undertaken in Florida in 1818. Jackson's movements six years earlier had brought good results, but that did not justify them in the mind of the current secretary of war, John C. Calhoun, or the future secretary of state, Henry Clay, then serving as speaker of the House of Representatives. To these men, and others, there were potentially grave consequences to giving military commanders carte blanche. Thus Clay, as secretary of state, would strongly support sharp action to counteract the "bad precedent furnished in Genl. Jackson's case." As Clay would observe at the conclusion of the Foxardo controversy, if David Porter had been commended for his unauthorized adventure on Puerto Rico, "hereafter the peace of the Country would have been in the hands of every military and naval commander of an expedition."[35]

The second and related concern was the government's desire not to violate the principles of the Monroe Doctrine. Behind this lay a fear of European intervention in Latin America in the wake of the increasing turbulence within the former Spanish colonies there, and delicate American relations with the Spanish government on this very issue. As Southard interpreted Porter's progress on the road to Foxardo, and specifically the spiking of Spanish guns at two small forts, the captain had "committed acts of war" without authority. By acting without orders to avenge a slight to an *individual,* and by his bellicose behavior on the Puerto Rican mainland, Southard believed, Porter had threatened American relations with Spain, the navy's command system, and the whole structure of international relations in the hemisphere. Porter's act simply could not be commended. And though Southard was not prejudging his subordinate, investigation was essential. As he observed to his friend Charles Ewing during the subsequent proceedings against Porter: "Had the Ex[ecutive] not made an enquiry into the facts a broken const[itution] & an offended people would have demanded a better reason than could have been given for the neglect."[36]

This was the context for the administration's willingness to proceed against David Porter. Southard, in concord with his colleagues and at the direction of the president, prepared an order to Porter that reached him at Key West early in 1825. In his letter Southard formally suspended Porter from his post and replaced him with Captain Lewis Warrington. He told Porter that he could return to Washington to explain his conduct and that he should bring witnesses, including Lieutenant Platt, with him.[37]

The political and diplomatic considerations that lay behind the cabinet decision for recall were beyond David Porter's understanding. Receipt of Southard's letter snapped something inside him. A strong-willed and extremely proud man, Porter had long resented the tight rein that Southard kept on him, as we have seen. What Southard viewed as simple diligence, Porter had interpreted as an attempt to muzzle. Hence, the letter of October 19, 1824, and the attempt to circumvent Southard's authority by writing directly to President Monroe at roughly the same time. Now, having sustained his country's honor in a minor imbroglio in Puerto Rico, Porter had to accept what to him was a slap in the face: immediate loss of command and orders to "make explanation" of his conduct.

Porter seethed, felt betrayed, determined to fight back. In his official capacity, he remained a good officer, constructively assisting Captain Lewis Warrington in the transition of command, but in all other respects Porter decided that he would make life as difficult as possible for those who had undermined his responsibility and sullied his good name. Once he had read Southard's letter recalling him, David Long has written, "Porter's policy toward the administration was not one of compliance and apology, but of massive resistance."[38]

The Porter case had political ramifications. David Porter was a national hero—not on the scale of an Andrew Jackson, but a hero nonetheless. His invasion of Foxardo was generally viewed by Americans as Jackson's incursion into Florida had been: with pride and pleasure. Finally, there were politicans who were eager to take advantage of Porter's distress to chip at the administration.[39] In the wake of the controversial presidential election of 1824–25, the Porter affair became a *cause célèbre*.

For his part, David Porter encouraged public attention by his calculated insubordination in dealings with his civilian superiors. Convinced, incorrectly as it turned out, that Southard was his chief nemesis, Porter spent his first weeks back in Washington in January and February 1825, seeking an audience with President Monroe or incoming President Adams. All Porter got from the former was a letter indicating that he would not speak with him, and reminding him that all of the orders he had received from Samuel Southard had been "given under my instruction." Adams did agree to speak with Porter, but nothing of consequence emerged from their meeting. As for Southard, the supposed source of his troubles, Porter was openly disdainful. He wrote the secretary on March 17, 1825, complaining about the slowness of proceedings in his case. And when he received a missive from Southard indicating that a court of inquiry would be called to examine his actions at Foxardo, Porter demanded that another charge—unauthorized transport of specie on navy ships—be added to the list of those to be considered. In a further letter he complained of an inability to secure evidence for his case because of his precipitate recall, an argument that Southard rebutted by mail.[40]

The court of inquiry began its deliberations on May 2, 1825, with Captain Isaac Chauncy presiding. The court's responsibility was singular: to determine whether Porter's behavior merited a full court marital or exoneration. In the week of hearings, testimony was taken on two central issues: the propriety of the Foxardo invasion; and the implications of Porter's activity carrying specie. Lieutenant Platt testified, and so did Porter, though the latter's behavior was not much calculated to advance his case. Porter alienated the court by challenging its authority to judge him, verbally abused Southard, and when told that because of his outbursts the court would accept his evidence only in writing, he stalked out. The proceedings continued, and it must be said that they yielded no crushing verdict. Porter's work combating piracy was commended, and the specie carrying charges were dismissed. But because he had invaded a "peaceful territory" without express authority, he was censured, and a court martial called to examine his actions at Foxardo.[41]

Up to this point the Porter case was national news, but not a national scandal. Courts of inquiry and courts martial were relatively common oc-currences, sometimes undertaken as much to clear an officer's good name as to punish him.[42] The Porter case was unusual, certainly, given the rank of the officer involved and the principle at stake, but what tied the case to politics stemmed less from the actual facts before a court than from Por-ter's refusal to play by the rules. Convinced that Samuel Southard was out to ruin him and sustained by a conviction that he deserved praise, not censure and trial, Porter struck at those he held responsible for his plight. Two days after the court of inquiry published its report, Porter countered with a pamphlet entitled *An Exposition of the Facts and Circumstances which Justified the Expedition to Foxardo.*[43] This 107-page document, ironically dedi-cated to President Adams, contained information regarding the West In-dian mission, correspondence between Porter and Southard, proceedings of the court of inquiry and documents pertaining to it. Publication of the pamphlet in a bid for public attention and support was obvious defiance of authority and insubordination; both the president and Southard were in-furiated by the event. David Porter would not escape their wrath on this matter, and to the list of charges before the court martial was added insub-ordination.[44]

A word here about Southard's view of the situation is in order. The navy secretary entered upon his duties with great admiration and respect for Porter, and he counted as one of his signal achievements in the department the reinforcement and nurture of Porter's West Indies squadron. Southard had passed dozens of letters with Porter on the pirate mission, all correct and cordial, without any inkling until October 1824 that the captain felt any sense of resentment about his close supervision of the command.[45] There is no evidence to sustain David Long's contention, in an otherwise thoughtful and balanced account of the Foxardo affair, that Southard lacked sensitivity to subordinates' feelings and that he was "utterly tact-less."[46] Southard's many and close friendships with navy officers and the navy department's civilian personnel—notably chief clerk Charles Hay—is well documented.[47] Indeed, Southard's ability to work harmoniously and effectively with the career officers who comprised the board of navy com-missioners stands as one of the quiet triumphs of his tenure in the depart-ment. Surely no one who was "utterly tactless" could have entered a department traditionally hostile to outsiders and, for all practical purposes, won the hearts and minds of those in it. Yet all evidence suggests that this is exactly what Southard did. Southard's personality was, to be sure, not particularly sunny, but it was hardly as "unpleasant" as Long suggests. He could be charming, at least among friends and friendly acquaintances—and at the same time icy cold to those he distrusted or disliked. This is not an uncommon trait.

The Porter affair illustrates not so much Southard's inability to relate to subordinates as his reluctance to allow direct insubordination to pass without rebuke. Southard had no animus toward Porter until the latter forced the issue. The fact that Porter publicly cited Southard as the source of his troubles naturally contributed to the rancor of the affair and raised the administration's stake in its resolution. And once Southard was convinced that Porter had "determined to make it a personal question between him and myself," he would give no quarter. But this is some distance from the charge that Southard jumped on Porter as soon as he could find the grounds to do so.[48]

John Quincy Adams's behavior in the Porter case is a bit more difficult to explain than Southard's—but only a bit. Adams had staunchly defended Jackson's unauthorized invasion of Florida in 1818, but by 1824 his diplomatic goals were different from what they had been six years earlier. In 1824 and 1825 Adams had a commitment to a foreign policy which emphasized noninterference in the internal affairs of Latin American governments, a policy that Porter's precipitate move into Puerto Rico seemed to threaten.[49] At all events, at the December 24, 1824, cabinet meeting, Adams was adamant that Porter had acted wrongly and that he would have to face the consequence of his actions. He never deviated from this position.

Overall, the Porter case was a tempest over a fundamental constitutional issue: who ultimately controls relations between nations, civilian leaders or military commanders? Many more questions stem from this basic concern. Was Captain Porter's behavior at Foxardo defensible? Had he gone beyond his authority? Had he breached international law or norms of conduct so as to antagonize any foreign authority? Was Porter acting in keeping with, or in violation of, the Monroe Doctrine? In suggesting answers to these questions, politics could hardly be excluded. Jacksonians were eager to draw the logical (though erroneous) parallels to the general's activities in 1818. Administration supporters were quick to praise the president and the secretary for upholding, in an admittedly ambiguous case, the rhetoric of nonintervention. The stakes in this controversy were potentially great. The administration could lose because Porter's case might pull together an as yet unfocused coalition against it. It could and did trigger congressional demands for an investigation.[50] But as events matured, David Porter was the major victim of the Foxardo controversy. After a long and bruising trial, one of the longer courts martial on record, he was found guilty on both of the major charges against him—unauthorized landing at Foxardo and insubordination.[51]

Throughout the trial, testimony had been closely followed in the nation's newspapers, most of which were sympathetic to the beleaguered officer. The results of the court martial, however, lent little ammunition to Porter's defenders—particularly once the full proceedings were released to the public and the full measure of the captain's insubordination became clear. Anti-administration papers did, of course, assail the conviction, but with the major exception of the Washington *Daily National Intelligencer*, few neutral or pro-administration papers joined this chorus.[52] As the evidence circulated around the nation, support for Porter's case dwindled and its political possibilities receded. A few anti-administration senators, notably Southard's old foe Mahlon Dickerson, took up the captain's case in Congress, but the matter lost, rather than gained, support.[53]

The Foxardo affair and its aftermath destroyed David Porter's faith in the American system of justice. Publicly humiliated, he determined never to serve the government so long as the likes of Southard and Adams were in positions of authority. In 1826, shortly after his rather lenient sentence, six months' suspension, expired, he left the service of the United States and joined the Mexican navy, where he would remain until Andrew Jackson's accession to the presidency in 1829.[54] As for Southard, he was greatly embittered toward a man he had once admired, and personally mortified that the diligent performance of his duties should bring on him abuse and political obloquy. Whether he had behaved with perfect fairness towards Porter is a matter historians will probably never settle. The safest judgment may well be that Southard was correct, as far as David Porter was concerned, but no more correct, no more fair, than he had to be. Convinced that Porter had ignored his instructions not to invade occupied territory and that such action could upset the delicate accommodation in the Western Hemisphere between the United States and the European powers, Southard, like President Adams, was not prepared to act generously toward Porter. When the tactless officer challenged the easily irritated secretary, conflict was inevitable. That it did not prove to be politically damaging to the administration was partly a matter of good luck—Porter's egregious behavior toward his superiors—and partly a matter of the course future events took—notably public response to Adam's first annual message in December 1825. Given the circumstances of his case, David Porter could not himself spark wide scale opposition to the administration; but President Adams, as we have seen, was for his part no mean practitioner of the self-inflicted wound.

IV

Painful as the reality was to accept, Southard came to recognize, as the controversy over the Porter affair began to spread in 1825, that a highly visible member of the executive branch might well draw fire for the good-faith conduct of his office. Washington was a political community, after all, and the war of words between politicians and editors of different persuasions commonly fanned out through the nation. One consequence was that Southard gained more national notoriety in the wake of the Porter court martial than he had during his previous decade in New Jersey government and his two years of service in the United States Senate. The abuse he suffered, as his cabinet colleagues tried to remind him, went with the job. That, of course, did not make it any more easy to accept, particularly for a man as sensitive to criticism as Southard.[55]

Of all the political editors who attacked Southard in print, the man who most regularly pierced his thin skin was Major Mordecai Noah of the New York *National Advocate.* A strong Jackson partisan, Noah had opened fire from the outset of the Adams administration, charging the new president with various crimes and follies, including a corrupt bargain with Henry Clay to win the nation's first office, antirepublican tendencies, and submissiveness to Great Britain in international affairs. Aside from the president, Noah's favorite target within the administration was Samuel Southard. When the Porter case gained attention, Noah was among the leading administration critics. Porter, he argued, was "a victim of the persecutions of the Secretary of the Navy," a theme he pounded home through much of the summer of 1825.[56] By late August, as the Porter case began to fade as partisan fodder, Noah pursued another issue: the case of former naval surgeon Isaac Phillips, who had been cashiered from the navy in 1798 and, in recent months, rebuffed in efforts to regain his commission as well as back pay. Noah's polemics here were doubtless fueled, if not strengthened, by his kinship with Phillips, who was his uncle. Certainly Noah's criticisms were based on no facts that might persuade the public that Southard had wronged the officer. In fact the matter quicky died, and Noah was forced to find other sticks with which to beat his enemy.[57]

Trivial in itself, the Phillips case merits at least brief attention because it illuminates a facet of Southard's character that ran like a red thread throughout his life: his sensitivity to criticism. In response to Noah's preposterous claims regarding Lieutenant Phillips, Southard penned an eighteen-page-long response and worked behind the scenes to encourage the publication of rebuttals to Noah in pro-administration papers. Nor was this the only time during the navy years that Southard responded so vehemently to criticism, direct or implied. His correspondence during the period 1823–29 is littered with long justifications of his conduct in any instance where his judgment or conduct had been challenged and indignant letters to newspaper editors who wrote articles he found wanting accuracy. Witness, for example, his rebuke to the editor of the *Washington Gazette,* whose paper he said he would no longer receive, due to "repeated & very gross misrepresentations respecting matters connected with the Naval Establishment of which you have permitted your paper to be the vehicle—and which are calculated to deceive and mislead the public."[58] Regarding his dealings with navy personnel, which were criticized in another Washington journal, Southard wrote to the editor demanding proof of the charges leveled against him, given his own position that the editor's assertions were "absolutely false."[59] Respecting the case of Navy Chaplain Cheever Felch, a habitual drunk who was forced out of the service in 1826 and whose dismissal was assailed not only in Noah's newspaper but in others as well, including a short-lived organ that Felch himself edited, *Coram's Champion,* Southard was virtually obsessed.[60] Ignoring his friend Charles Ewing's advice to remain calm and allow the storm to blow over, Southard inserted in the press articles refuting Felch, and took the trouble himself to pen a twelve-page analysis of the errors contained in a single critical article. He even corrected peripheral errors, such as Felch's contention that he had served as a private tutor in James Monroe's home. "I never lived an hour in his house," Southard told George Sullivan, "except as a visitor for two or three days on two or three different occasions."[61]

Fortunately for Southard's blood pressure, such controversies were minor, and most blew over quickly. Most national attention focused not on the real or alleged peccadilloes of the navy secretary, but rather, on the larger issues of the time, notably the Panama Mission, Governor Troup and the Indian controversy in Georgia, and the president's ambitious domestic program. Of course, to examine Southard's correspondence during the Adams administration in isolation, one might be led to conclude that Southard himself was the major issue of his times!

The newspaper attacks on Southard were, in truth, small change. Equally important to note is the happier side of Southard's tenure of office. As navy secretary, he had the opportunity to participate in such majestic occasions as the inauguration of a president (Southard accompanied John Quincy Adams in his carriage on the route to Capitol Hill and the oath taking on March 4, 1825), in the launching of naval vessels, such as the frigate *Brandywine* and the sloop *Peacock,* and in the fanfare surrounding General Lafayette's celebrated 1825 visit to America. This last episode, which culminated in a special festive leavetaking from the shores of Virginia in September 1825, placed Southard at the center of attention—or at least at the shoulder of the central attraction, the venerable French hero of the American Revolution.[62]

Southard also enjoyed some important if less colorful perquisites of office: access to the president on a daily basis and participation in all the major policy meetings of the administration; opportunity to work with such able navy men as John Rodgers and William Bainbridge, both of whom became his good friends; the responsibility of traveling through the nation to inspect naval facilities; and inclusion on every guest list when major parties were thrown in Washington. This last aspect of his life serves as a reminder that service in the cabinet could be enjoyed in itself, and not simply as a focus for criticism from political foes. All was not labor, all was not politics in John Quincy Adams's Washington. The capital city, rude though it appeared to foreign visitors, was nonetheless a vigorous community, a place where one could live cheaply and enjoy enormous quantities of good food and drink, and participate in a continuing round of parties if one served in the government or simply knew the right people. Increasingly over the years, cabinet members and congressmen brought their wives to live in Washington, as did members of the diplomatic corps. There were regular rounds of dinners and frequent large levees at the White House, often with dancing, in addition to a less formal social life. Gambling, drinking, cardplaying, and evening teas were other popular entertainments, as were traveling carnivals, magicians, and public lectures on diverse (and sometimes exotic) subjects.[63]

Samuel Southard enjoyed a number of these diversions whenever he had the opportunity to do so. He quickly learned that the responsibilities of a cabinet officer were considerably more demanding than those he had known in the Congress. The luxury of concluding one's labors at four o'clock in the afternoon, and the freedom to leave Washington for months at a stretch, for example, were unavailable to him. Yet Southard seems not to have missed many important social events, and he evidently enjoyed the opportunities for recreation that his cabinet status opened to him.

V

Once his retention in the cabinet was assured, in February 1825, by the election of John Quincy Adams, Southard arranged to move his family from Trenton to Washington.[64] Having rented his house in New Jersey and established himself in new, larger quarters in the national capital, Southard for the next four years lived a more stable life than he was ever again to enjoy. Samuel and Rebecca Southard engaged fully in the varied social life of the capital city. They attended the round of diplomatic dinners, executive levees, and private parties that were the norm for the Washington elite. When not so entertained, they often spent their evenings quietly at home with their children. By March 1825, the Southard family included two daughters—Virginia, age ten, and Sarah (Sally), age one—as well as two sons—Henry and Samuel, Jr., who were seven and six years old, respectively. The Southards' oldest child, John, had succumbed at age eleven to an epiletic fit in December 1824, while all of the family save its patriarch resided in Trenton. Another child, an infant girl, Mary, had died unexpectedly in February 1823.[65] Those children who remained were bright and active, and kept their father, who was responsible for discipline, quite busy. The responsibility of overseeing the houshold was shared between Rebecca Southard and her unmarried sister, Margaret Harrow, who developed a deep and lasting attachment to the Southard clan. It was a great emotional wrench to Southard when his wife, for no apparent good reason, initiated a severe quarrel with her sister, a conflict that forced Margaret to leave Washington and return to live with her brother, James Harrow, a newspaper editor in Fredericksburg, Virginia.[66] But even this upset did not substantially undermine the satisfactions of life in Washington in the 1820s. Southard took a justified pride in his status, in his associations, and in the activities of his growing family.[67] His work, no less than his evening relaxations, agreed with him.

Although Southard grew increasingly close to President Adams over the years, he rarely socialized with his chief. More often than not, when the Southards entertained, or went out for the evening, they headed to the home of Henry and Lucretia Clay, or to the homestead of the Samuel Smiths. During the 1820s, Margaret Bayard Smith, the wife of former *National Intelligencer* editor Samuel Harrison Smith, was a leading social force in Washington. Given the size of the Washington community, it was inevitable that she would have come to know the Southards at least casually. That the Southards became intimate friends with the Smiths was predicated in part on Southard's friendship with Mrs. Smith's brother-in-law, Andrew Kirkpatrick, who had served with him on the New Jersey Supreme Court. More important, probably, was the chemistry between the families. Mrs. Smith enjoyed Rebecca Southard's company, enjoyed doting on the Southard children—particularly the increasingly comely Virginia—and shared a friendship with the Clay and Wirt families, with whom the Southards also regularly socialized. Mrs. Smith's letters to her sister in New Jersey remain one of the best sources for recreating the social life of the times, and also of the Southards' home life.[68]

Had the Southards not suffered repeated family tragedies during the navy years, one could readily see this as the happiest time of their life together. Unfortunately, while in Washington Mrs. Southard witnessed the deaths of her youngest daughters, Sally and Ann, both of whom were, as Charles Ewing put it, children of great "promise."[69] Born in January 1826, several months after Sally's death, Ann lighted her parents' life. When she died suddenly in February 1829 amidst preparations for a move back to New Jersey, the blow to the family was severe. Mrs. Southard's physical and mental health, precarious in the best of times, seems to have been seriously undermined by Ann's death. In fact, Rebecca Southard because increasingly reclusive and shrewish over the years and, as we shall see, nothing her husband attempted in an effort to alleviate her complaints ever fully sufficed.[70]

VI

Grateful for his opportunity to relax at home most evenings, and for his annual August sojourn at White Sulphur Springs, Virginia, Southard nonetheless knew that his life would be dominated by extensive and often tedious desk work. He did not shirk this responsibility. No bureaucrat by training or inclination, Southard nonetheless had the temperament and discipline to accept a staggering workload. If his five-and-a-half-year tenure in the Navy Department may be summarized in a phrase, "diligent and enlightened stewardship" would probably serve.

Operating during a period when any diversion from fiscal conservatism could provoke political criticisms, Southard nonetheless pushed on with a variety of unglamorous yet significant projects. Together, they constituted a remarkably diverse and ambitious program. Included on Southard's agenda for naval development were the construction of dry docks, for more expeditious repairs of naval vessels; the development of a naval criminal code, to ensure consistency and fairness in discipline matters; detailed surveys of the Southeastern Atlantic coastline; shifting the sites of navy yards; an increase in the medical department of the navy, as well as a new promotion system for medical personnel; a more reasonable pay scale for navy surgeons and officers; the funding of new naval hospitals; the recruitment of naval personnel from the inland, as well as seaport cities; the regularization of recruitment procedures; regularizing the system of promotion for deserving officers, and the establishment of a new rank, admiral, for those captains who had distinguished themselves; the creation of new permanent squadrons for the protection of American interests in he Mediterranean and off the coast of Latin America; founding a naval academy for the training of naval officers; and the exploration of Antarctica.[71]

Above and beyond these special concerns, Southard was routinely engaged in the unceasing business of directing the movements of American naval vessels on the Atlantic and Pacific Oceans as well as the Mediterranean. Working closely with his chief clerk, Charles Hay, Southard read virtually all incoming dispatches from his ship captains, and sent prompt and detailed replies. Much of his correspondence dealt with the ordinary requests of sailors and their squadron commanders, and periodic, though usually minor, crises. There were supply and pay concerns, transfers of personnel, requests for leave, discipline problems, and matters relating to the spiritual lives and formal nautical education of sailors to consider. Southard had to read the proceedings of all courts martial, and often summarized them for President Adams. All told, he was faced with "cart loads" of paperwork, as Captain William Bainbridge tersely and accurately observed, and he met this responsibility without complaint.[72]

Some of his work, though routine, was portentous, because it touched on American relations with foreign powers, relations that could be upset by an over aggressive naval policy. At the time of his accession to the naval secretaryship in 1823, Southard was responsible for the operations of three regular naval squadrons. Each of the fleets had as its primary responsibility the protection of American trade and American personnel involved both in commercial and fishing activity.[73] In the Mediterranean, the main focus of concern was the menace of Greek pirates.[74] In the Caribbean, Spanish bandits who preyed on American shipping had to be fought. On the coasts of Latin America, Southard and his officers were involved most deeply in the "defense of neutral rights."[75] There American merchants, shippers, and whalers had to be protected not merely against pirates but also against the transgressions of legitimate, quasilegitimate, and would-be governments. This last problem was especially acute on the coast of the infant republic of Peru. There real and paper blockades frequently hindered American commerce. Impressment of civilian Americans by the Peruvian (and other) navies also troubled relations.

On the "freedom of the seas" principle, Southard was consistently attentive, firm, and prudent. That he worked diligently to avoid the appearance of condoning interference in the internal affairs of the Latin American republics is reflected in his willingness to sanction a court martial of his Pacific Squadron commander, Charles Stewart, whose aggressive defense of American trade angered the Peruvians. That Southard had no intention of abandoning America's neutral rights is also reflected in the Stewart case, for once Stewart was given a clean bill of health, Southard reaffirmed the value of Stewart's work and offered him a significant new assignment.[76] That Southard's oversight of the navy was thoughtful and diligent is attested in the thousands of dispatches he wrote and, even more tellingly, in the excellent record his navy made in protecting American property and avoiding major international conflicts during the Adams years.

Given the overall frustrations of policy making under John Quincy Adams, Southard was able to point to a remarkable array of advances during his tenure of office. Coast surveys were successfully undertaken, permanent squadrons were added to the navy fleet, ships were constructed beyond what normal appropriations made possible, sources of enlistment of naval personnel were expanded, the navy and marine corps were effectively reorganized, location of navy yards changed, discipline regularized, education for midshipmen improved, and medical facilities for naval personnel increased.[77] The score on Southard's broader initiatives, which required congressional appropriations, was less impressive, though Southard's own efforts in this realm could hardly be faulted. Congress's niggardliness forced abandonment of plans for a naval academy, and the shelving of new navy hospitals. An insurance program for navy personnel, conceived and developed by Southard, had to be operated on a voluntary basis, for Congress would contribute not one penny to its support.[78]

Despite important setbacks, Southard worked well with the Congress, even during the latter years of the Adams presidency, when the Jacksonians controlled the Senate and were not disposed to encourage administration initiatives. Southard's relations with the Senate navy-committee chairman, Robert Y. Hayne, were cordial and constructive until the campaign of 1828 forced Hayne into a stance of partisan naysaying, most notably with regard to a project he otherwise supported—the proposed exploring expedition to the South Seas and Antarctica.

The exploring expedition reflected, in important respects, the frustrations of executive service during the Adams administration. As we have seen, the president staunchly supported an ambitious plan for national development, one that included scientific experimentation and exploration as a central tenet. Adams's first annual message to the Congress expressed this commitment to scientific progress, and though it provoked strong criticism, it remained the standard by which the administration conducted its business.[80]

If the president's 1825 message provided the context and justification for a large-scale exploring expedition under government auspices, the catalyst for such a venture was a public lecture given in the summer of 1826 by a youthful advocate of "hollow earth" theory, Jeremiah Reynolds. Southard attended Reynolds's lecture, and though he dismissed the theorizing, he was captivated by Reynolds's explication of the benefits of exploration, particularly in and around Antarctica. Once Reynolds learned that Southard was interested in his ideas, he bombarded the secretary with letters and, when in Washington, cajoled him personally. His advocacy of a South Seas exploring expedition bore fruit: by 1827 Samuel Southard was publicly identified as favoring a navy-sponsored exploring expedition. Working closely with Reynolds, Southard successfully lobbied the Congress for authorization of an expedition and, by May 1828, won an expression of support from the House of Representatives. Reynolds was named a special navy agent to weigh the project's needs and stimulate scientific interest in it, and Southard himself devoted many hours to planning, as well as the recruitment of personnel for the expedition.[81] Under his oversight, a naval sloop of war, the *Peacock,* was refurbished at a cost of $64,000 for the expedition and launched, with fanfare, in September 1828. A large crowd attended and cheered the launching, and the editor of the New York *Mirror* proclaimed that the venture exemplified "the spirit of the age." Indeed, it foretold "a long career of glory and usefulness for the republic."[82] Americans seemed ready to secure the blessings of science and the expansion of knowledge—a good progressive Jeffersonian theme.

Enthusiasm for the exploring expedition reached its peak in November and December 1828. The House of Representatives followed up its May 1828 resolution endorsing the expedition with a $50,000 appropriation. Appointments to the expedition were in their final stages. The president was interested and encouraging. All seemed in place. "With permission from the Department," Jeremiah Reynolds grandiloquently wrote to Southard, "the Southern Hemisphere is ours." Always more restrained, Southard contented himself, in his final annual report as navy secretary, to observe that the *Peacock* and an accompanying vessel would sail "in a few weeks."[83]

Southard was wrong. Not only did the *Peacock* not set sail within a matter of weeks, forces were at work that would prevent its sailing at all. Involved here were two concomitant negative developments. Within the department there was a resentment against Southard's and Reynolds's recruitment of dozens of non-navy personnel to perform various scientific chores. This resentment reached the surface in December when the navy board of examiners rejected several of Southard's civilian appointments. Tied in here was the tactic of delay practiced by a key figure in the expedition, Lieutenant Charles Wilkes. Also desirous to limit, and perhaps eliminate, non-navy personnel on the exploring expedition, Wilkes stalled the collection of scientific apparatus in the hope that an expedition undertaken during a Jacksonian administration would orient itself more to the interests of the career navy, and less to the abstract cause of science.[84]

That the rejection of a few appointments, or Wilkes's dilatory tactics, could have succeeded in delaying the launching until after a new administration gained power was unlikely. More ominous was the growing sentiment within the Senate that favored delay on various grounds, most of which were related to politics. Learning of the controversy within the navy about the prominence of civilian personnel in the exploring expedition, Senator Hayne and others took up the anti-civilian position. When Southard defended his practices on the grounds that the ranks of the navy could not supply all the expertise essential to a successful mission, Hayne moved on to a full-scale attack on the expedition. In a Senate speech on February 5, 1829, Hayne insisted that the exploring expedition was an unnecessary luxury in an era when so much of American terrain remained uncharted. If such an expedition as Southard espoused were to be undertaken, Hayne insisted, it should be left to private enterprise. Scientific advances, in short, were none of the government's business. Speaking like a good Southern strict constructionist, Hayne concluded that science, commerce, and agriculture all should be

> safely left to the enterprise of individuals, which, with an instinctive sagacity that puts to shame, the assumed wisdom of governments, is invariably directed to the pursuits most profitable to themselves, and most to the welfare and honor of the country.[85]

Hayne followed his remarks with a proposed resolution requesting that Southard specify and justify the expenses thus far incurred for the expedition, and he gained his point. The handwriting was on the wall. Though Southard promptly complied with the Senate's resolution and took pains to justify his work, the Senate's failure quickly to endorse the House's actions doomed the exploring expedition for 1829 at least.[86] In fact, though President Jackson supported such an expedition (conceding that Southard, though a scoundrel, had at least one good idea to his credit), it would not be until 1838 that everything was cleared and an expedition—with Samuel Southard's full support—was launched.

For Southard, as for Jeremiah Reynolds, the Senate's action was a major disappointment. Months of work were nullified. There would be no note of triumph to mark the conclusion of six years' dedication to the interest of the American navy. Instead of hearing cheers and enjoying published plaudits for his enterprise, Southard was forced to spend his last weeks in the navy laboring over mounds of paperwork, commiserating with colleagues about the state of the Union, and planning his departure from Washington. It was not an exhilarating note on which to conclude this chapter in his life.

6

On Native Ground: Politics and Law

For nearly five years Samuel Southard and his family lived in Trenton, where the children had their earliest memories. These were both challenging and eventful years for the former navy secretary. Within a matter of months he was able to establish a lucrative law practice; he built and led a strong political party in opposition to the Jacksonians; he served, in turn, as the state's chief legal officer and its chief executive; and, at the close of this period in his life, he gained a reelection to the United States Senate, wherein his ambition to leave a mark on national policy could be realized. In a broad overview, the years 1829–33 were good years for the Southards, but they were not unblemished. The family's youngest child, Ann, died just as the Southards prepared to move to New Jersey; Mrs. Southard's mental and physical health continued on an uneven course; and Southard himself was often a victim of physical ailments. Life after the cabinet had its trials as well as its triumphs, but in weighing them, Southard rarely complained.

I

Southard was stunned and depressed by the magnitude of the Jacksonian triumph in 1828. His work and that of his colleagues had not merely gone unappreciated by the nation's voters but stood, in his view, repudiated, and likely to be undone, perhaps even reversed. "Improvement" would give way to negativism, moderation would yield to the dictates of personal whim and party aggrandizement. The prospects for the republic under the leadership of a "military chieftain" appeared dim indeed.

During the gray days following the election, Southard was confined on and off to his bed, suffering a severe fever, possibly malarial. His wife and youngest child, Ann, were intermittently ill during November 1828, and in general, life took on a dark shading.[1] Nor was he sure where to make his future living. Should he remain in Washington or seek a livelihood elsewhere?

After investigating prospects at the bar in Philadelphia and finding the waters there cold, Southard resigned himself to a return to law practice in

Trenton. "I am, and always have been poor," he told Lucious Elmer, "and must look to my daily exertions for the support of my family."[2] Aware that his legal skills had a heavy layer of rust on them after nearly six years away from the law, Southard nonetheless anticipated a return to practice in his home state.

Later in November 1828, however, it occurred to Southard that there was some prospect of remaining in the nation's capital. Mahlon Dickerson's Senate seat was due to expire on March 4, 1829, and on the strength of the administration party's victory in New Jersey's 1828 legislative elections, that party would be able to replace Dickerson with someone else. Having concentrated his own energies most intently on the presidential contest, Southard was not aware that the state attorney general, Theodore Frelinghuysen of Newark, had made a strong claim to the Dickerson seat if the administration men scored a victory in New Jersey's elections. In ignorance of this fact, Southard wrote to a number of New Jersey friends, including Frelinghuysen, asking whether he could reasonably lay claim to the Senate seat Dickerson would vacate. The responses he received were not encouraging. Lucius Elmer reported that Frelinghuysen's support for the position was firm, and Frelinghuysen himself made clear to Southard that he was in the race to stay. The only positive news that Southard learned was the hint from Charles Ewing that New Jersey's other senator, Ephraim Bateman, was seriously ill and might well resign his office before many weeks passed.[3] Ewing's information was accurate. In early January 1829, the forty-nine-year-old Bateman wrote to political acquaintances, including Southard, indicating that he would probably resign his office. By January 8, 1829, he had done so.[4]

Bateman's resignation markedly improved Samuel Southard's prospects for remaining in Washington once the Adams administration concluded its term. Southard, after all, was his party's strongest figure in New Jersey, and his home base in the state lay just west of the traditional line that divided New Jersey into two regions. The West had claims on Bateman's seat, and Southard found it easy to view himself as the most appropriate candidate to answer that claim.

Sitting at his desk in Washington, Southard did not realize that all was not harmony within the New Jersey administration party. Several of his colleagues from West Jersey nursed resentments against a man who, in their minds, had monopolized virtually all the "good" offices in the state for more than fifteen years. It was time, some believed, for other men to feed off the public trough. Such feelings were directed against Southard most feverishly by Cumberland County Assemblyman Dr. William B. Ewing. When it became apparent that Senator Bateman would relinquish his office, Ewing began to promote himself for the Senate seat and became the focus of support for those who sought an alternative to Samuel Southard.[5]

A complex political game was in the making. The anti-Southard wing of the administration party coalesced with some disgruntled former party adherents, including Lucius H. Stockton, and with Jacksonians eager to bloody their old enemy's nose. Their modus operandi in this movement was an anonymous broadside, composed by Stockton and widely circulated by Ewing's supporters in Trenton less than two weeks before the election in late January 1829.[6] This document assailed Southard from various angles, but most prominently featured was one of Southard's actions while serving in the Senate eight years earlier. Lucius Stockton's polemic charged that in 1821 Southard had voted with the South on the Missouri issue, against the patently expressed wishes of his constituents. On the question of Missouri's constitutional restriction against the entry of free Negroes, and all residual questions, the broadside charged, "Mr. Southard's influence and his votes stood recorded as arrayed with the slave holding party." If reelected to the Senate, what guarantee did Jerseyans have that when questions such as the slave trade in the District of Columbia arose, "he will not adhere to his former course." The implication was clear: none.

Although Stockton's broadside encompassed other matters as well, it seemed to Southard that the issue of his views on slavery was the central concern. Once he was notified, posthaste, that the Stockton polemic was circulating, and once he gained a copy of it, Southard penned and presented to *National Journal* editor Peter Force his own broadside, published by Force as "A Short Statement of Facts Connected with the Conduct of Mr. Southard, on What is usually called the Missouri Question."[7] In this seven-page treatise Southard tried to counter the impression that he had ever worked for the extension of slavery to Missouri, noting that he had not been in the Senate during the first Missouri debate. Moreover, Southard insisted at length, he had been joined by numerous other Northern senators in his efforts to defuse a potential threat to the Union. He personally had no brief for slavery, Southard said in the "Short Statement," and always believed that colonization was the best solution to the problem of the black presence in America. Southard denied that he had ever owned a slave "for life," and challenged his "enemies" to "point to a single vote, or to a single act of his life, private or public, which can justly bring on him, the imputation of being favorable to slavery."[8]

This defense was spirited enough, but it may not have been wise enough. In striking back on the slave issue, Southard failed to recognize that his real Achilles heel in the election was personal resentment felt by West Jersey politicians such as Ewing and, more specifically, the strangely complicated question of Southard's status as a New Jersey man. Lucius Stockton's broadside had argued that Southard was not an inhabitant of New Jersey since he had sold his house in Trenton in 1824 and moved his family to Washington. It occurred to Stockton and other opponents of Southard that under the strictest construction of Article 1, Section 3, of the Constitution,

Southard could be disqualified as a Senate aspirant on the grounds that as of January 1829 he had no home in New Jersey and therefore was not an inhabitant of the state.[9]

This was not exactly a bolt from the blue. As early as November 1828, a pro-administration newspaper had suggested that Southard was probably ineligible for the Senate on this very ground.[10] But Southard had not taken the objection seriously at that time, nor did he do so in mid-January, when Stockton's polemic appeared. It was inconceivable to him that the word *inhabitant* would be interpreted literally. Southard could not, of course, know what lay in store for his candidacy when the joint meeting of the legislature convened on January 29, 1829, to elect two senators.[11]

Once the six-year seat had been disposed of, as it was quickly and decisively with Theodore Frelinghuysen's election, nominations and balloting for the Bateman vacancy began. Five candidates were nominated to complete Bateman's term of office: Southard and Dr. Ewing from the administration party, and Jacksonians Mahlon Dickerson, Garret D. Wall, and William Jeffers.[12] On the first and succeeding nine ballots, Southard won the most votes, but no majority. Jeffers's support was negligible and he was eliminated after the second ballot. Ewing's strength ranged from eight to sixteen votes, with Southard never gaining fewer than eighteen. By the ninth ballot Dickerson passed Wall, but the election remained entirely uncertain.

After a brief adjournment for lunch and caucuses by different factions, the meeting reconvened and Stacy G. Potts, a Jacksonian legislator from Hunterdon County, rose and read a motion saying that, since Southard was not an inhabitant of New Jersey at the time, he should be stricken from the list of candidates. According to Potts's recollections, his motion "fell upon the house like a clap of thunder in a clear sky—everybody seemed astonished and paralyzed." It did not take long, however, for all the anti-Southard men to recognize the thrust of Potts's move. When the roll was again called, Dr. Ewing and six of his supporters joined the Jacksonian members in voting aye on the resolution. A majority thus formed for the first time that day, and Southard's name was stricken from the list of candidates. When the balloting resumed, a dozen Southard backers, refusing to accept Dr. Ewing as an alternative because of his perfidy, joined ranks with those who voted for Mahlon Dickerson. And on the twelfth ballot enough Wall supporters switched to Dickerson to reelect a candidate who two days earlier had seemed to have virtually no chance of victory.[13]

Dickerson's reelection was a great coup for Stacy Potts and his fellow Jacksonians. Potts savored the results in a letter to Dickerson, observing that his proposed resolution had been bait for the Ewingites, which they "swallowed . . . hook and all." Aside from the surprised and gratified Dickerson, probably the happiest man in the state was Southard's bitter enemy, Robert F. Stockton, who chortled that Southard's defeat was "retributive justice" and that with the joint meeting's action, the navy secretary had "fallen like Lucifer, never to rise."[14]

For Southard, the defeat was a mortifying experience. Not only had his own party, with a clear majority in the legislature, squandered its influence, but the man who benefited at Southard's expense was his oldest political rival. Truly there seemed to be no justice in the world. His hopes for remaining in Washington smashed and his health feeble, Southard turned attention to his navy work. He continued to sign midshipmen's warrants as rapidly as he could, assisting friends and relatives by placing their children at West Point and in the navy. He also worked assiduously to get the South Seas exploring expedition off the ground. Time, however, was not on his side, and as we have seen, the effort foundered as the last days of the Adams administration wound down.[15]

The only promising development in this train of disappointment was Southard's election, in late February 1829, as New Jersey's attorney general. Theodore Frelinghuysen had left the position open when he entered the Senate, and Southard gained it as a consolation prize.[16] He would then return to New Jersey with a lucrative and challenging office. Fighting fatigue, ill health, and a sense of bitterness toward one wing of his party, Southard tendered his resignation as navy secretary and began the process of dismantling his household and planning a move north.

Arrangements were made for the sale of many household goods at a Washington auction, and agreement was reached with a political foe, Garret Wall, to rent Wall's home in Trenton. (Wall had recently remarried and moved with his wife to Burlington.) Servants were recruited, tearful goodbyes made to Washington friends, including Margaret Bayard Smith, and the Southards began their journey home.[17]

II

Southard's first year back in his native state was not entirely kind to him or his family. His youngest child, Ann, age three, succumbed to a fever just as the family was in the midst of its move, and Mrs. Southard immediately went into a deep depression from which she did not emerge for many months. Southard himself was afflicted with fevers periodically during 1829, and in the early months of the year, burdened by disappointments, and the demands of changing residence and vocation, he looked and acted much older than his forty-one years. According to one account, old friends who saw Southard in 1829 felt he was a "broken" man, with a "melancholy" air and a pronounced stoop.[18]

This depression, however, was not long-lived. Southard's understandable anxiety about his rusty skills as a lawyer were dissipated after his first

ventures on the circuit in New Jersey. To his surprise and pleasure, Southard found that his legal services were much in demand, and indeed on
many circuits he was treated as a celebrity and his arguments in court were
lavishly praised.[19] Such encomiums and a bustling business were not unde-
served. Southard had always been an extremely diligent attorney, preparing meticulously for small cases and large, and his courtroom presence was
formidable. Lucius Elmer, who by 1829 had drifted away from Southard's
inner circle of friends, conceded that the former navy secretary was "a
skillful advocate" and a "lucid" speaker. In the courtroom Southard effectively modulated his voice as circumstances demanded, ranging from polite
and pleasant presentation to powerful, sometimes high-pitched advocacy—
a technique that doubtless impressed juries, even as it irritated his opponents at the bar.[20]

By summer 1829, his health tentatively restored, Southard was extensively engaged as both a private practitioner of law and as chief legal officer
of New Jersey. His private practice emphasized estate cases and business
law, though he handled the full run of cases, including several involving
debtors. His most lucrative work, not surprisingly, was business law. Even
before leaving Washington Southard was contacted by several corporations, including the Society for Useful Manufactures of Paterson and the
Trenton Banking Company to serve on general retainer. Clearly his political influence and status did not diminish Southard's opportunities at the
bar, but rather heightened his appeal to prospective clients.[21]

Southard came to conclude that his new life was a good life. In June he
told his old chief, John Quincy Adams, that his misgivings about returning
to the bar were much eased; a month later he boasted to Henry Clay that, if
his health held firm, "I see no cause to doubt that I shall have the best
practice in the state."[22] Southard's letter to Clay referred to his private
practice; but he was also extremely active as attorney general. In that post
Southard supervised the preparation of the state's case in civil and criminal
suits, and he occasionally argued cases himself before the state supreme
court.[23] His most important effort in this realm was the prosecution, before
the United States Supreme Court, of a suit against the state of New York
regarding a long-disputed eastern boundary line between the two states.
Southard inherited the case from the predecessor, Frelinghuysen, who had
first brought New Jersey's complaint to court and who was now retained by
the state to act with Southard in argument before the U.S. Supreme
Court.[24]

The boundary suit had roots deep in the history of both New Jersey and
New York, and in the tortuous dealings between them concerning jurisdiction over the waters of the Hudson River. Southard himself, a dozen years
earlier, had played a small role in the dispute. For New Jerseyans, the
boundary controversy was an open-and-shut case. In their view, New York
had unjustly and haughtily claimed the rights to *all* waters between the two

states, and refused any serious negotiation on the matter. New York had regularly served process in legal cases on the west side of the Hudson River, passed laws preventing free concourse between the two states, and insisted on its claims as inherent in the original charter granted by King Charles II to the Duke of York in 1664.[25]

New Jersey had protested such claims for many years and had periodically attempted negotiations and retaliations that might provoke some response from New York. In the eighteenth century, more than fifty years elapsed between the initiation of negotiations and the settlement of claims regarding the western boundaries between the two parties.[26] Some Jerseyans feared the eastern dispute would take equally long to settle. Commissions established in 1807, 1818, and 1826 failed to make satisfactory settlement because New York would not retreat from her claims to all the waters of the Hudson.[27] Legislative efforts by Southard and Mahlon Dickerson in 1822, as we have seen, yielded no better results.[28] New Jersey would finally rely on its attorney general to carry to the state's claim to the courts, in wake of continuing border disputes between county officials in the two states.

To this end in the summer of 1829, Southard immersed himself in the facts and the law involved in the boundary dispute. He also solicited the aid of his old friend William Wirt as a partner in bringing the case before the Supreme Court. It was Wirt who suggested that the state appeal directly to that court for a judgment, based on the twenty-fifth section of the 1789 Judiciary Act, which provided that the court might settle jurisdictional disputes between states.[29]

The problem with this approach was that New York, perhaps recognizing the weakness and impudence of its claims, declined to cooperate. The New York authorities refused to participate in the suit, to the point of evading subpoenas served by officers of the New Jersey attorney general. When New Jersey's service was finally accomplished, New York's attorney general, Greene C. Bronson, declined to honor it on the ground that the Supreme Court had no legitimate jurisdiction in the case.[30]

Such intransigence did not deter Southard or Wirt, who believed that the larger state's defiance could spur the court to *order* New York's appearance, or, if New York remained obdurate, issue a decree *ex parte*. Southard so informed Governor Enos Throop of New York and Attorney General Bronson early in 1830.[31] The New Yorkers were not intimidated. When Southard and Wirt appeared before the assembled members of the court on March 6, 1830, they were not met by opposing counsel. Bronson had written to Chief Justice Marshall insisting that the Supreme Court should not interfere in "controversies between two or more states."[32] The matter of jurisdiction, raised by New York, was postponed until January 1831, giving the New Yorkers more time to change their course. During this period Southard and Wirt, unaware of New York's evolving position on the matter, corresponded frequently to plan for contingencies and prepare a brief. Their effort paid off in January 1831, when New York failed to participate and the court, through Justice Marshall, justified and granted an *ex parte* proceeding.[33] Despite this, New York persisted in its recalcitrance, and though the court insisted on the equity of an *ex parte* proceeding, the case was never brought to completion. In 1832 New York indicated that it was willing to settle the dispute without recourse to any court proceeding and New Jersey's Jacksonian governor, Peter D. Vroom, persuaded a weary Southard to accept the New Yorkers' belated offer to negotiate directly.[34] Commissioners were nominated and meetings held in 1833, and this time an agreement was achieved. New York yielded its most extreme claims, and New Jersey for its part finally renounced its own hopeless claim to Staten Island.[35] Reconciliation had taken 182 years. Although neither Southard nor Wirt gained the victory and vindication that they had sought, the result of their efforts was satisfying enough to their sense of justice.

III

Southard's disappointment that his extended labors in the boundary case had yielded no dramatic triumph was considerably tempered by his recognition that those labors had laid the groundwork for a mutually acceptable compromise between the contending parties. As an experienced lawyer, he well appreciated that the serious pursuit of a cause at law will often bring results without a trial and definitive verdict. His legal efforts had achieved a useful result.

Other legal work was profitable in a more direct way. Southard found himself much in demand as an attorney, particularly in the world of business law. Though still relatively backward in its acceptance of commerce and industry, especially compared with its neighbors, Pennsylvania and New York, New Jersey had in Southard's lifetime made dramatic strides in the realm of economic diversification and development.[36] Early in the century New Jersey experienced a transportation revolution, embracing roads, canals, bridges, and, by 1829, a railroad. Increasingly, manufacturing, mining, and banking enterprises emerged as staples of the state's economy, alongside agriculture, and all of the new enterprises, jangling against entrenched interests and at times one another, needed legal assistance.[37] Because Southard was one of the state's best-known lawyers as well as a politician with considerable influence, it was not surprising that he should be in great demand to serve on corporate boards and as general counsel for corporations with legal causes to try.

Southard's most lucrative legal relationships were contracted with several of the state's largest enterprises, notably the New Jersey Railroad and Transportation Company, the Morris Canal and Banking Company, and

the Society for Useful Manufactures, based in Paterson. His relations with
each of these enterprises were long-lived and did much to keep the Southard household solvent in the face of prodigious expenses in the 1830s.[38]

Southard's connection with the Society for Useful Manufactures began
before his return to New Jersey from Washington when, in January 1829,
he accepted a retainer fee from the company's president, Roswell L. Colt.
Although Colt's brother stressed in a subsequent missive that Southard's
fee was a general retainer, the company intended from the outset that
Southard should represent it in a major suit against the Morris Canal
Company, which had recently begun operations near Paterson and challenged SUM's unrestricted access to the waters of the Passaic River and
Lake Hopatcong, waters that were essential for the operation of the manu-
facturing establishments leased out by SUM.[39]

The dispute between SUM and the Morris company was extremely important to New Jerseyans generally, because if Roswell Colt had his way,
the Morris Canal's operations through northern Jersey would cease, thus
shutting off one of the most promising economic initiatives the state had
witnessed for many years. Designed originally for the transport of anthracite coal from the Morris County Hills to New York City, the Morris company had been chartered in 1825, and sections of the canal were opened
for local use in eastern New Jersey by 1829. One such section drew on
waters that SUM claimed as its own and led to the legal action that Southard would undertake.[40]

Southard spent much of the summer of 1830, when not engaged in
politics or his work as attorney general, preparing a case seeking an injunction against the Morris Canal Company, forbidding its further use of waters surrounding Paterson. A similar case had been tried in 1828 before
Chancellor Isaac Williamson, but Williamson, nodding to the just rights of
each party to the suit, declined to grant the injunction SUM sought on the
grounds that clear injury to Paterson manufacturing had not been proved
and that it remained unclear whether Lake Hopatcong would supply a
sufficient flow of water for both enterprises. "No *actual injury* had been
sustained," Williamson observed in his decision, "but only danger ap-
prehended." Hence his denial of an injunction, coupled with a warning
that, if SUM could prove injury, it would be entitled to renew its case.[41]

Roswell Colt strongly believed that in the period since Chancellor Williamson had issued his judgment, such injuries had been palpable and
severe enough to warrant a new suit. With Southard and another leading
New Jersey attorney, George Wood, preparing SUM's case in 1830, the
renewed effort to gain an injunction was heard before Chancellor Peter D.
Vroom in October Term of New Jersey's equity court. The substance of
SUM's case was that the Morris Canal had in its operations since 1828 made
such extended use of the Passaic River that manufactures in Paterson had
to be curtailed for want of water to power machinery in SUM-leased fac-

tories. Some machines, the plaintiffs said, were lying entirely idle. An injunction was needed, Wood and Southard explained to the court, because continuation of the drain on the Passaic River would injure SUM beyond the point where any fair compensation could be attained. Citing Judge Williamson's 1828 decision, Southard's colleague Wood observed that the legislature had "no power, by subsequent enactments, to interfere with prior grants." Sounding very much as Daniel Webster would sound in his notable argument in the Charles River Bridge case of 1837, Wood insisted that "a private corporation or franchise is property: it cannot be taken away on pretence that it was wanted for great public purposes. What may not be done directly, cannot be done indirectly." In his presentation, Southard insisted that the proprietors of the Morris Canal had misled New Jersey's legislators in 1825, in petitioning for their charter, by claiming that the canal would have no need for the waters of the Passaic. But reality proved different, and the Morris Canal, by its unauthorized use of the Passaic waters, was doing manifest injury to SUM. As Southard portrayed the situation, the Morris Canal lay in an impossible situation, but one for which he had no sympathy. Either it could make do with the waters of Lake Hopatcong, in which case an injunction was fair since the Morris Company was currently using Passaic River water, or it could *not* make do with the waters of the Hopatcong, in which case an injunction was still fair, since that would require the Morris Company to remove water from the Passaic "and injure us."[42]

Southard went further, contending that SUM, for all practical purposes, *owned* the waters of the Passaic. "They [the managers of SUM] purchased the *water power* at Paterson. That consists of the uninterrupted flow of water from all the fountains or streams of water in their natural courses emptying into the Passaic, combined with the descent or fall of water at Patterson, which constitutes water power."

For their part, the Morris Company's attorneys, David B. Ogden and Joseph W. Scott, disputed the plaintiff's case about the import of the water use by the canal and told the court that an injunction against the Morris Company would not only put a "stop" to a work "in which the state, and particularly the northern and eastern part, have a deep interest," but would effectively stymie other New Jersey internal improvements. Probing the law, Ogden reminded Chancellor Peter D. Vroom that an injunction could be granted only if there was certainty that damage would occur. No such certainty existed, he contended. Ogden further rejected SUM's claims to ownership of the waters of the Passaic, as argued by Samuel Southard, noting that their right was to *land*, with water rights an incidental but not a charter right. So long as SUM enjoyed use of the Passaic River's waters, and those of Lake Hopatcong, which it manifestly did enjoy, it had no just complaint.

In his verdict, Peter Vroom offered no relief to the plaintiffs. Endorsing the argument Ogden had made and rejecting Southard's contentions, Vroom denied that SUM owned the waters it used. Both parties had rights to use the waters around Paterson, Vroom said. Regarding the alleged injuries to SUM complained of in the plaintiff's presentation, Vroom concluded that evidence was contradictory, but in any event irrelevant to the case. Past injuries, even if proved, Vroom said, were no grounds for an injunction. "The effect of the injunction is preventive." As to possible future injury to SUM, Vroom concluded that Southard and Wood had not made a case strong enough to persuade him that an injunction was necessary. To decree what SUM sought would probably destroy the Morris company, and, in reviewing the facts of the case, Vroom saw no "pressing necessity, or that certainty of mischief, which would authorize an interference in a matter of such magnitude." An injunction was therefore denied.

Once again, despite his best efforts, Southard had carried off no glory from the courtroom. Nor, in this case, could he even claim a substantive victory. Nonetheless, he had performed as effectively as the evidence permitted, and Roswell Colt evinced no disappointment with Southard's efforts. Indeed, he continued to call on Southard for legal aid and worked closely with him in various political and entrepreneurial ventures for the rest of the decade.[43] Moreover, the Morris Canal Company, which had tried to retain Southard to argue their side of the suit but simply had been beaten to the punch by SUM, was enough impressed by Southard's performance to put him on general retainer for the future.[44] Ultimately the company would have to call on Southard for even more sustained service.

IV

Samuel Southard's legal practice during the early 1830s, and beyond, thrived. Demands on his time and energy were so great, in fact, that in 1832 Southard entered a partnership with James Wilson, a young Trenton attorney who happened to be the son of the man Southard had defeated in the Senate election of 1820. Business for the firm of Southard and Wilson was extremely brisk, and over the years, the junior partner handled the bulk of the routine but necessary paperwork their practice entailed.[45]

Southard's official responsibilities as attorney general in addition to his thriving private law practice occupied most of his time and took his mind, to some degree, off the political setbacks of 1828 and early 1829. They did not, however, keep him from the political arena. Southard was recognized in 1828 as the leading anti-Jacksonian politician in New Jersey, and his work over the next decade only enhanced this reputation. Throughout his years as attorney general and governor of New Jersey (1829–33) Southard actively worked to build a strong National Republican party from the nucleus of the "administration" party of 1825–26.[46] This party would advance the causes of internal improvement, fair play for the American Indian, and an integrated economy sustained by a rational banking system, causes that Southard believed to be congruent with the interests and desires of most Jerseymen.[47]

Party building was no easy matter. The anti-Jacksonians had been "dispirited" by the national Jacksonian victory in 1828, Southard reported to Henry Clay in midsummer 1829, and to make the situation worse, the party suffered from internal divisions, notably in Essex and Morris Counties, over the best means to compete with Jacksonianism in New Jersey.[48] Some anti-Jackson men sought to use Antimasonry as a vehicle to gain political power, while others, including Southard, were convinced that the best path to political success lay in the avowal of the American System and Henry Clay's presidential candidacy in 1832.[49]

Throughout 1829, Southard was periodically lectured by Pennsylvania Antimasonic leader Amos Ellmaker about the need to build an Antimasonic organization in New Jersey and nationally. Ellmaker, a thoroughgoing convert to the idea that Masonry was a devious conspiracy with designs to control the nation and subvert the Constitution, suggested in his correspondence that Southard would be the perfect candidate to head the Antimasonic ticket in 1832—despite the fact that Southard, in Ellmaker's view, had himself been "half your life . . . the unconscious dupe of masons."[50]

Despite Ellmaker's persistent queries and suggestions, Southard kept the Pennsylvanian at arm's length until December, when he told Ellmaker bluntly that he saw no future in the movement, in New Jersey or anywhere else.[51] Antimasonry would not be dismissed so easily, since many of its New Jersey proponents remained active through the election of 1832, but Southard's own course on the matter was fixed: he would do his best to encourage a merger of Antimasonic sympathizers with anti-administration forces generally. His goal was to build a broader-based opposition party committed to a constructive and tried vision of American development.

In his commitment to the American System as the foundation for National Republican appeals to the electorate, Southard believed he was adapting Jeffersonian doctrine to the needs of an expanding society and economy. Like other politicians who would ultimately declare their allegiance to the Whig party in the 1830s, Southard identified himself with the "moderate," forward-looking wing of Jeffersonian Republicanism, building on one strain in Jeffersonian thought—the commitment to "improvement" in all its facets.[52]

New Jersey Jacksonians, many of whom were as avid for economic growth as Southard and his political cohorts, and sensitive to the trends of the day, tried to downplay "improvement" versus "no improvement" as the basis for political alignments in the state.[53] But Southard and the National Republicans could claim higher ground on the issue, since they had identified themselves with John Quincy Adams and his policies, while the Jacksonians' campaign in 1828 had been devoted primarily to criticism of Adams's initiatives and *ad hominem* attacks on the sixth president. Moreover, Andrew Jackson himself was at best ambiguous on such national concerns as tariff policy and federal support for internal improvements, and after a brief period in 1829 during which Jacksonian propagandists had insisted that the new administration was as committed to development as that which it had replaced, New Jersey Jacksonians changed their tune and began to stress the dangers of implementing the American System. Stacy Potts, for example, the party's leading polemicist, argued that the program of "improvement" identified with Henry Clay was based on bad economics and the English system of "taxing the poor for the benefit of the rich—the farmer for the benefit of the capitalist—the laborer for the benefit of the lord."[54] Other Jacksonian leaders, notably Governor Peter D. Vroom, while insisting that Jacksonianism was supportive of "improvement," also reminded voters of the dangers of "associated wealth," economic privilege, and untrammeled development.[55] If it is something of an oversimplification to see the politics of the Jacksonian era in New Jersey as a "contest between the positive state democracy of the moderate-Republican-sponsored American System and the negative popularistic political democracy of the agrarian, radical, and Old Republican wing of the Jeffersonian party," as one historian has put it, nonetheless, by 1830 clear lines between the two sides were being drawn. And they were being drawn on the grounds that Southard preferred.[56]

Drawing the lines for electioneering and winning elections, however, were distinct propositions, and Southard well recognized the difficulty of building a mass party when such a party lacked a national leader with the emotional appeal of an Andrew Jackson. Beyond this, at the state level, Southard had to contend with the reality that the majority of New Jersey's most experienced and shrewdest politicians were Jacksonians, already in power. These men well knew, as Peter Levine, among others, has shown, that "the devotion of party activists to their organizations was often determined by the ability of the party to materially reward these individuals for their efforts."[57] Once installed in power in October 1829, the state's Jacksonians efficiently, indeed, ruthlessly, removed entrenched appointed officials at all levels of government, replacing them with individuals who had demonstrated loyalty to the Jacksonian cause. Their removals ranged from the apex of the state government, with the unceremonious replacement of twelve-term governor Isaac Williamson, to the lowest levels. The Jacksonians ensured that even flour inspectors were good party men.[58] The principle of rotation in office, or "Jacksonian Reform," as *Emporium* editor Stacy G. Potts styled it, was essential, the Jacksonians contended, if there were to be "a fair equalization of the burdens and powers of government." If this required a "radical change" in officeholding in the state, then, Potts insisted, such must be pursued. "The people expect, and require, [reform's] accomplishment."[59]

Whatever the merits of the Jacksonians' patronage policy, there is no doubt that it was thoroughgoing and that it was effective. In a state with parties rather evenly balanced, an effective patronage policy could be decisive in determining the results of elections, as Southard himself observed respecting his party's defeat in 1829. By 1830, he was more hopeful of victory, though he knew this could be achieved only after a "severe struggle," as he explained to Henry Clay. "The toils have been strongly laid in our state," he wrote to Clay in August 1830, "& I fear we cannot break them eno' for the next Election—but we shall try."[60]

Southard's hopes were realized in equal measure with his fears. In two hard-fought contests in the autumn of 1830, in which the "American System" was the National Republicans' overriding theme, the two parties shared the sweets of victory. The Jacksonians won a narrow victory in the state legislative elections on the strength of powerful showings in the agricultural heartland of the state. In the congressional elections that followed, conducted on a statewide, "general ticket" basis, however, the National Republican candidates swept to victory by more than 1,000 votes.[61]

Heartened by these results, Southard set himself to laying the groundwork for an effective campaign on Henry Clay's behalf in 1832.[62] He worked for and put considerable money into the establishment of an anti-Jacksonian newspaper in Trenton, one that might with effort successfully neutralize the influence of the Trenton *Emporium*. Southard investigated the credentials of a half-dozen potential editors and editorial assistants, wrote and solicited essays for the paper, the *Union*, and offered financial aid whenever its editor, Philip J. Gray, felt a pinch.[63]

Southard was also active in other ways. He shepherded through the press Theodore Frelinghuysen's notable Senate speech attacking the Jacksonians' plans for removing the Cherokees west of the Mississippi, knowing that Frelinghuysen's remarks would be warmly received among the Quakers of West Jersey.[64] During political campaigns Southard arranged for the distribution of immense numbers of pamphlets and broadsides elaborating National Republican positions and attacking the administration on every ground. "It is our intention to send you 1000 copies of the proceedings of our last meeting in this city," Joseph Blunt wrote to Southard from New York at the height of the 1830 Congressional campaign. "In what way shall we distribute them most effectively?"[65] For this and other requests for advice Southard, despite his busy professional schedule, always had time for an answer.

During the first eight months of 1830, Southard drove himself fiercely on many fronts. There were political fences to mend, speeches to make, causes to try, official duties to attend. Beyond this, Southard had family responsibilities, particularly the need to deal with his wife's insistent complaints that he was absent from home too frequently and too inattentive to her needs and those of their children. There is every indication that Southard was a thoughtful husband and attentive father, but at the same time, the demands on his time were many. He had invitations to address conventions, association meetings, educational convocations and political rallies. He could not heed his friend Lewis Condict's warnings against overexertion. "Keep not the bow always bent," Condict cautioned in late 1830.[66] Alas, this was advice Southard could not follow. There was always one more commitment to fulfill, and ultimately, a price would have to be paid.

Late in July 1830, two weeks after delivering a rousing July 4 oration to the appreciative mechanics of Newark, Southard was afflicted by a severe case of inflammatory rheumatism, which kept him confined to bed for seven weeks, without relief, at home in Trenton. After a tentative recovery with the coming of cooler weather in September, Southard was struck with a severe bilious fever. This illness fastened its grip on him for three months, keeping him out of the legislative electioneering in October and away from legal business. At several points during the fall of 1830 his life was in danger. "For many days," he told his old navy friend, John Rodgers, early in 1831, "I was considered beyond hope, and they are now a blank in my existence, so far as any memory . . . of what occurred is concerned."[67]

In this assertion Southard may have exaggerated somewhat, since his papers include drafts of letters written during the latter months of 1830, and he did participate in the Society for Useful Manufactures' suit against the Morris Canal Company in October. Nonetheless, by all accounts, he was seriously ill until the onset of winter, and the correspondence to which he was able to attend had to be dictated to his nephew, Daniel Southard. That he was able to rebound so quickly in 1831 and undertake anew a punishing schedule of work and politics is remarkable—and typical of Southard's style throughout his life.

V

For the better part of 1831 and 1832 Southard devoted much of his energy to building a strong National Republican party in New Jersey, geared toward a twofold goal: first, recapturing control of the state legislature and the governorship from the Jacksonians; and, second, carrying New Jersey for Henry Clay and his party's congressional ticket in the election of 1832.

Southard's commitment to his task was strengthened by his ambition to be Clay's running mate in the presidential contest. During their service together in John Quincy Adams's cabinet, Southard had come greatly to respect and admire Clay, and regular intercourse with Clay as well as with President Adams doubtless pushed Southard faster and further in the direction of economic nationalism that he might otherwise have been induced to go, given his intellectual roots. When the Adams administration passed into history, Clay and Southard regularly exchanged correspondence, assaying political currents in various states, discussing the best timing for the announcement of Clay's candidacy in 1832, and weighing strategies to be pursued. Southard's hopes for the vice-presidency he kept to himself, by conscious will. But in subtle ways he gave the lie to his inclinations. In a letter written in the summer of 1829, Southard, after assuring Clay that he was the party's best and most popular choice for 1832, observed that he had often been queried about his own prospects to be on the ticket with Clay and answered, bluntly, that "it [the vice-presidency] would not suit me—I am too poor, and do not desire the office—[moreover] I think it unwise to take me from so small a state [as New Jersey]."[68] Southard's avowed disinclination for the vice-presidency notwithstanding, one could argue that he was at least halfheartedly trying to plant the seed of an idea in Clay's mind, and in the minds of other politicians with whom he periodically broached the subject.[69]

Further evidence of Southard's ambition in 1831 lay in the attention he gave to the composition of the New Jersey delegation to the national convention that met in Baltimore in December to nominate a ticket for the National Republicans in 1832. By discreet management, Southard had New Jersey's convention delegation packed with men favorable to his nomination for the vice-presidency, including his brother-in-law, Samuel S. Doty, and himself. Unfortunately for his well-laid plans, Southard's health again betrayed him, forcing him to bed for most of December 1831. He would have to wait anxiously at home for news from Baltimore—and then be disappointed to learn that he had been passed over.[70]

Since Henry Clay's nomination for the presidency in Baltimore was taken for granted, and since he had left the decision on the vice-presidency to the assembled delegates, there was a great deal of speculation about who would be named to join him on the ticket. Southard's name was on many lips and, in fact, Southard was a serious contender for the nomination. Advocating this course, two delegates from New Jersey, Amzi Dodd and William Halsted, addressed the convention on Southard's behalf, emphasizing that Southard could draw Antimasonic votes to the ticket. Unfortunately, Southard had drawbacks as a candidate. His health was uncertain, he was from a state with few electoral votes, and, most significant, he was too closely identified with the late Adams administration. Many delegates rose to praise Southard, but also to point out, as J. S. Halsted observed in a letter from the convention floor, that "they feared that our opponents would make a successful use against us of the fact of your and Mr. Clay's being both members of the Cabinet of the late administration and say that it would be bringing back upon the Union the members of the family of the late dynasty."[71]

Other delegates rose on behalf of Congressman John Sergeant of Pennsylvania, a strong advocate of the Bank of the United States. The convention quickly decided that Sergeant's nomination would strengthen the ticket in a crucial state, other candidacies for the vice-presidential nomination were withdrawn, and Sergeant was duly nominated. All was "harmony and unanimity," one participant recalled, as the convention broke up and prepared to fight a presidential campaign.[72]

Since Southard had never publicly indicated he was interested in the vice-presidency, he could conceivably have shrugged off his failure to gain the prize and, instead, been gratified by the kind words mention of his name had elicited in Baltimore. The dimensions of his disappointment, however, were great enough for Southard to write a letter to an old Washington friend, former Judge Advocate General Richard S. Coxe, confessing that he was greatly depressed by the convention's decision to nominate John Sergeant rather than himself. Apparently the lure of Washington was not easily exorcised, and though Southard manfully directed the National Republicans' effort in New Jersey in 1832, he could not help lamenting his own blasted hopes for fame and a less demanding regimen.[73]

VI

The presidential campaign of 1832 was one of the most dramatic confrontations in American political history. Two popular party leaders and two different philosophies of government were presented to the electorate. Early indications suggested that the American System would be the paramount issue nationally in 1832, aside from voter fealty or hostility to Andrew Jackson. But Henry Clay was not entirely sure that Jackson could be defeated if personalities dominated the campaign or, for that matter, on the basis of a broad ideological appeal on behalf of "improvement." He needed something to distinguish himself sharply from a president who blew hot and cold on commitment to American economic growth. The issue Clay chose to emphasize would be recharter of the Bank of the United States, which since 1829 had been the target of Jacksonian criticism, despite its evident efficiency in performing its various functions, including the regulation of the nation's money supply.[74]

What Jackson planned for the bank if Congress voted recharter in 1832 was unknown. Convinced that the bank was popular (after all, it was demonstrably efficient, at least in the view of its supporters) and that the bank issue could profitably be agitated in the election, the National Republican leadership, including Clay, convinced President Nicholas Biddle in late

1831 to make application for recharter in the current session of Congress. To bring recharter forward before the election, the bank's supporters reasoned, would catch Jackson in a dilemma. He would either have to accept the recharter of an institution he openly mistrusted or face the wrath of bank supporters (notably in the crucial state of Pennsylvania, home of the bank's main branch) at the polls. With Clay's publicly favoring the bank and Congress's voting for recharter in July of 1832, the issue was placed in the president's lap.[75]

For Jackson there was little agonizing. His understanding of economics was rudimentary, to say the least, but his sensitivity to personal challenges was acute. To Jackson, the bank issue was such a challenge. He told Martin Van Buren, "The Bank, Sir, is trying to kill me! But I will kill it!" The remark was in character. Jackson had always taken such an attitude toward his enemies. In this instance the Bank of the United States had become his nemesis, the monster he would fight to the death.[76]

The bank issue, with Jackson's veto and the stinging message the president attached to it, became the ground for political division in the 1832 election. New Jersey Jacksonians finally had a national issue on which they could base a campaign. And they could argue, quite sincerely, that the president was fighting the people's fight against an entrenched aristocracy, thus identifying themselves with the tradition of republican simplicity. To Jacksonians such as Governor Peter Vroom, Jackson was not conducting a personal vendetta against the bank, but fighting for the people against a powerful institution that threatened to undermine the constitutional system that was the basis of American freedom. "I dread the results should the Bank triumph," Vroom told Democratic Congressman Ferdinand S. Schenck in the midst of the Bank War.

> Where would be our security—would we not have a fourth power in the government, superior in power I mean, to the other three? If the Bank, justly odious as it has become, can break down an administration supported by the sound head and strong popularity of Andrew Jackson—who or what set of men will dare to utter a breath against it, in future times?[77]

The Jackson party and press echoed this theme in making the bank recharter its leading issue in the campaign of 1832. Stacy G. Potts's Trenton *Emporium* hailed the president's bank-veto message as

> a document worthy of the purest days of our Republic. It brings us back nearer to the original principles which pervaded, and the spirit which animated, the fathers of our country, than any thing which has emanated from the executive since the days of Jefferson. It is the final decision of the President between the Aristocracy and the people—he stands by the People.[78]

Whether or not the people of New Jersey identified Henry Clay and the bank with aristocracy, the bank issue sparked an immense interest in the presidential election. County meetings, speeches, resolutions, and all the other elements of a political campaign abounded. Each side did its utmost to bring out its vote. Southard, for example, worked even longer hours than he had in previous years to get the National Republican message to the voters. That message was crystal clear: the president was inept, mean-spirited, narrow-minded, and, on economic matters, simply ignorant. His opposition to the bank's recharter was not merely indicative of economic illiteracy, but was a potential danger to the workings of the economy. "If the Bank is a sound institution, it ought to be preserved," the National Republican Young Men resolved at a state convention in Trenton in the spring of 1832. More than this, the delegates argued in their resolution, the bank was

> immensely important to a great commercial, manufacturing, and agricultural nation by offering a general medium of exchange from one part of the country to the other, without which much loss and great embarrassment will certainly be experienced.[79]

National Republican editors across the state, particularly in such urban centers as Paterson, Newark, and Trenton, ran scores of essays denouncing the president's economic error in vetoing recharter of the bank. Trenton *National Union* editor Philip Grey spoke for all by observing bluntly that the bank issue was "definitely *the issue* of the campaign."[80]

Southard began the election year confident of success, but the passage of time put a damper on his hopes. For one thing, Jackson's hostility to the bank as a "monster" privilege deleterious to a republic played well in the rural counties of New Jersey, including Southard's native Somerset. Still, enough sturdy yeomen conceivably could be persuaded to recognize the virtues of a balanced economic order, with agriculture as one of the key pillars of an expanding economy.[81] What really irritated and then increasingly worried Southard in 1832 was a practical political threat to anti-Jacksonian unity in New Jersey: the insistence of the Antimasons on running their own ticket in the election in an obviously futile effort that, to Southard's mind, would succeed only in draining votes from Henry Clay. Doubly frustrating for Southard was the fact that his old friend and coadjutor, William Wirt, agreed to lend his name to the third-party effort. As late as September 1831, Wirt had assured Southard he believed Antimasonic rhetoric "foolish," and the organizational effort of their former colleague and new convert to Antimasonry, Richard Rush, a "farce." By December 1831, however, Wirt was singing a different tune, emphasizing his conviction that Henry Clay could not defeat Andrew Jackson in 1832, and that he was merely a passive vehicle for the forces opposed to Jackson's reelection.[82]

Southard viewed Wirt's rationalization as claptrap, and dangerous clap-trap at that. Even before the Wirt nomination, the New Jersey National Republican leader had confided to Henry Clay that

> I say to you now, as I said to you before, there is more danger in this than all other causes. The strength of the A[nti] M[asons] as a party, is not of itself, alone sufficient to carry any one state—but they have strength eno' if withdrawn from your friends, to endanger more than one.[83]

Southard spoke more truly than he knew. With the nomination of an Antimasonic ticket, and William Wirt's refusal to disavow his selection as that party's presidential nominee, the National Republicans in New Jersey faced a doubly difficult struggle. Unable to persuade the state's Antimasons to drop their allegiance to Wirt, Southard focused his efforts, first, on merging Antimason and National Republican tickets at the state level and, second, on bringing out the fullest possible anti-Jackson vote in the separate presidential and congressional contests.[84]

Through the summer of 1832, Clay and Southard exchanged frequent, terse missives, discounting negative omens in various state elections and emphasizing their most hopeful projections. Clay was convinced in June, for example, that New York and Pennsylvania, crucial to his hopes in the fall election, looked "well—very well." Southard himself remained guard-edly optimistic through September, observing on September 8 that "our friends are confident [of success]."[85]

Returns in New Jersey's October legislative elections justified Southard's confidence. His efforts, and those of the National Republicans throughout the state, were repaid with a decisive victory for the party. Thirty-three National Republicans gained election to the state assembly, compared to seventeen Jacksonians, and eight National Republicans captured council seats, to six for the Jacksonians—giving the National Republicans an eigh-teen-vote majority in joint meeting and through this control over the gov-ernorship and scores of appointive positions in the state government.[86]

The presidential election was a different story. The luster of Andrew Jackson's military reputation remained a strong pull on voters, and this, combined with the yeoman voters' evident support of his bank veto, gave Jackson the state's electoral votes, by a bare 463-popular-vote plurality over Henry Clay. The 468 votes that William Wirt had pulled on the Antima-sonic line may have spelled the difference in the election. Gloomier news yet lay in the victory of the Jacksonian congressional ticket, which evidently benefited from the president's long coattails.[87]

Despite his party's legislative triumph, then, a triumph that propelled Southard into the governorship, Southard was greatly disheartened by the party's defeat in the national elections. "I am in deep distress at the situa-tion of our country," he lamented to the National Republican standard bearer. "I fear that the Union & Govt are gone." The defeat of the ticket in

New Jersey Southard blamed on "the overconfidence of our friends, who feared no danger—and the course of the anti-Ms," who refused to coalesce with their logical allies. The deepest frustration in the election, Southard said, was that he was convinced that there existed "a large maj[ority]" of National Republicans in the state. "But they are a class of people who will not go to the polls, unless they see an absolute necessity for it—& this they did not see—they felt secure and they must bear the consequences."[88]

Southard's comments to Henry Clay were indicative of his disappointment with the result of the national elections and his anxiety about President Jackson's willingness to act firmly against South Carolina, if that state should carry through its threats to nullify the tariff of 1832 and prevent federal customs collectors from doing their work within its borders. But these remarks should not be taken to mean that Southard was mired in gloom. The final months of 1832 were no time for repose and disillusion. Southard was occupied on too many other fronts.

VII

Not the least of Southard's concerns following the state elections in October was the reorganization of the legislature under the auspices of a National Republican majority. Out of power since 1829, the state's opposition party now looked eagerly to its first task: replacing scores of Jacksonian appointees with men of their own political stripe.

Of these appointments, the most important was the governorship, and Samuel Southard was his party's consensus choice for the position. This was an honor he did not seek and only most reluctantly accepted when the legislature formally named him to replace Peter Vroom as governor late in October 1832. Southard, in fact, had been away from Trenton on circuit during the formal proceedings of the joint meeting, and had left word with his party colleagues to seek some other man for the governorship if this was possible. He was elected nonetheless.[89]

Was Southard, a man avowedly desirous of gaining fame and wielding political influence, suddenly uninterested in these matters? Not at all. His disinclination to accept the governorship was predicated on several practical grounds. As attorney general, he had an official position congenial to his talents, one that left him free to practice law and earn a handsome income. Because the governorship was an annual appointment, hence very possibly an honor he would enjoy only briefly, and because the governor's constitutional responsibilities as chancellor of the state chancery court would force him to abandon his second livelihood, Southard was not much inclined to change his position. Moreover, he well knew that Mahlon Dickerson's Senate term was due to expire in March 1833, and, with a National

Republican majority in the legislature, he had every expectation of replacing Dickerson in that seat if he made his desires known.

Yet Southard did accept the governorship and the challenge of holding together a party of men eager to enjoy the spoils of power. He accepted, as he explained to Henry Clay, because he believed that, as the acknowledged leader of his party, he had no other choice. "I could not avoid it without serious injury to our friends & the cause," he explained. The party simply had no other available, well-known, and well-respected statewide leader. Any effort to promote another National Republican to the governorship "was likely to produce serious evils," Southard noted.[90] And as future experience proved, on this matter he spoke the simple truth.

Southard was enticed to the governorship, then, on the grounds of duty. His "enormous sacrifice," as he styled it, in giving up the private practice of law was eased by the promise of gaining Dickerson's Senate seat several months later and picking up his practice where, in October, he had to suspend it. In the meantime, Southard's attention turned to the burdensome and rarely satisfying task of dispensing patronage. National Republicans who had toiled for the cause lined up for their reward in numbers that bedeviled a man who had spent the better part of three years decrying the Jacksonians' policy of "rotation in office." Despite his own predilections for moderation on patronage, Southard presided during his four months in the governorship over a purge of Jacksonians from state, county, and local posts. The positions he filled, or made recommendations to the legislature to fill, ranged from judgeships, surrogacies, and clerkships, to several dozen lucrative posts as master and examiner in chancery court.[91]

In keeping with his conviction that too much zeal in dispensing patronage did not comport with a "moderate" political creed, Southard declined to remove some officeholders who were obviously competent and had not been overly active in the recent campaign. To Southard's dismay, this policy won him no accolades, but rather brought him grief. National Republicans in Somerset County, for example, were appalled that the governor would not remove a Jacksonian surrogate or even support a removal, and one of their number reminded the governor that being liberal on such matters was useless. "Our opponents . . . sneer at & call us pusillanimous cowards for the lenity we have shown," one party man said. Southard's brother, Isaac, a Somerset County National Republican leader, told him bluntly that party morale in the county was at a nadir as a result of his moderate course on patronage. At a recent party convention in the county, Isaac Southard explained, when the policy of moderation was mentioned, the delegates abruptly departed, so "disgruntled and disheartened" were the National Republican stalwarts who attended. Delegates to the party's precongressional election convention declined even to carry tickets into their own townships as a consequence of their disgruntlement. Continuation of this policy, Isaac insisted, was "suicide" for the party.[92]

Pressured on one side by his allies, Southard found himself criticized on the other by old friends of a different political persuasion whenever he yielded to the dictates of partisanship. None of this did much for his dispostion. When William Anderson, a moderate Jacksonian from Sussex County, gently chided Southard for allowing inferior men to be named to judgeships in that county simply so that political debts could be paid, Southard responded by reminding Anderson that the National Republicans were merely repaying Jacksonians for their "universal proscription" of National Republicans in 1829. He alluded to the abuse he had received when he tried to ignore party distinctions in making appointments and reminded Anderson that

> I have never acted illiberally towards the J[acksonian] party, yet they persecute me without relent. There is not a J[acksonian] paper issued scarcely, which does not contain some willful lie respecting me. . . . What encouragement has any man under such treatment, to be liberal?[93]

The vexations of patronage were one of the central reasons that Southard looked eagerly to the coming Senate election. But he was not yet free, even after Christmas, from the responsibilities of the governorship. In January he had to offer a "state of the state" message, with policy recommendations to the legislature. Such substantive concerns doubtless better suited his temperament.

Southard's message, delivered to a joint meeting on January 11, 1833, was a serious and able state paper, reflective of the central, if invisible, truth of New Jersey politics in the early Jacksonian era: on substantive state issues, the two parties had few differences. Southard's specific recommendations to the legislature were couched in nonpartisan language and tended to echo the themes outlined by his predecessor. Among his recommendations were an amendment to the state constitution permitting popular election of the governor (so as to make the governor more independent of legislative majorities); a similar amendment divesting the office of its judicial responsibilities, so that nonlawyers could hold the governorship; curbs on the influx of "colored persons" into the state; and alteration of the poorly functioning militia system by making services voluntary and requiring those who chose not to serve to pay a tax that could be employed for public education or some similar purpose. Each of these proposals, as well as Southard's major initiative, support for the construction of a new state prison, which would cost $150,000, had bipartisan backing. With regard to the prison, Southard observed that

> long experience has shown that our present building, and the system of discipline necessarily connected with it, can neither be reconciled with the principles of a just economy, nor with the great purposes of human punishment.[94]

In response to Southard's suggestion, a committee studied the matter and, with bipartisan support, the legislature voted funds for the project. The initiative went forward and a new prison was erected during Peter Vroom's second tenure as governor.[95]

On state issues of this time, then, one can agree with Richard P. McCormick that "the parties were relatively indistinguishable."[96] National issues were another matter. Southard was not merely convinced that Democracy and National Republicanism presented distinct choices on the great issues of the day, he was also determined to paint his party's credo clearly for the benefit of the citizenry. In the concluding section of his message, Southard spoke less as a state administrator and more as a party leader, and injected national issues into a state forum. He said he believed that state's interests, as well as the nation's, lay in "a tariff which shall protect the industry of the country"; a "sound currency"; "internal improvements"; and "the independence of the judicial power, which was intended to possess and to exercise jurisdiction on constitutional questions and controversies between states." He alluded to the failures of the Jacksonian administration in each of these areas, and paid special attention to the Jacksonians' war on the Bank of the United States—a war that Southard avowed would mean the ascendancy of unregulated state and local banks "similar to those which once scattered ruin and distress over the country and affected even the national Treasury."

As governor, of course, Southard could have little influence on the resolution of these national issues. But on the most emotional question of the moment, the nullification crisis, he had the opportunity in a special message to present his views at some length. South Carolina's irritation with federal tariff policy had been building for many years, but only in November 1832 did the Palmetto State take the climactic step of endorsing the nullification of a federal law. Given that Andrew Jackson's political philosophy was oriented toward strict construction of the Constitution and states' rights, many Americans simply did not know how he would respond to the challenge posed by a specially convened South Carolina convention that, on November 24, 1832, endorsed a nullification ordinance and directly challenged the notion of a national union, as opposed to a compact of states.[97]

Jackson's initial reply to South Carolina's bold move was mild. In his message to Congress on December 4, 1832, the president tried to minimize the tariff issued by pointing to the nation's progress in extinguishing the national debt, and suggesting the impending opportunity to reduce tariff duties substantially. Although he took note of the recent events in South Carolina, Jackson gave no hint of the stand he would take six days later when, in a special message, he issued a strongly worded rejection of South Carolina's constitutional interpretation and warned against any challenge to the supremacy of federal laws. "Those who told you that you might peacably prevent their execution, deceived you," Jackson told the South Carolinians.

> They know that a forcible opposition could alone prevent the execution of the laws, and they know that such opposition must be repelled. Their object is disunion. But be not deceived by names. Disunion by armed force is *treason.* Are you ready in incur its guilt?[98]

The president's nullification proclamation, couched, as Glyndon G. Van Deusen has observed, "in the tones of a father admonishing his children," was designed to halt nullification before it started.[99] But the proclamation did not make clear how the president would respond if his words were not heeded. Nor was it clear, at this juncture, that South Carolina was prepared to step back from the abyss.

Samuel Southard and the rest of the nation watched with intense interest as the crisis unfolded. Southard did more than observe, however, for just as he received word of the president's December 10 proclamation, he also received from South Carolina the proceedings of that state's convention, with a request that he lay its proceedings before the New Jersey legislature. Southard believed it his responsibility to heed this request and also to make some comment upon the documents he presented the legislature. He knew, moreover, that leading Democrats in New Jersey were moving quickly to build and demonstrate support for any action President Jackson might take to quell the nullification threat. Politics and patriotism were entwined, and a partisan, patriotic governor had to make some sense out of the proceedings.[100]

Southard's first response to the crisis was to contact close and trusted friends, notably Henry Clay, John Quincy Adams, and William Wirt, to solicit their opinions of the severity of the challenge to the Union and of the options available in dealing with it. To Adams, he expressed his conviction that "violence and bloodshed" were probably inescapable. He confessed that he agreed with the "principles expressed in [President Jackson's] Nullification Proclamation," but objected to "its style . . . or the tone of its threats." Could not conciliation, Southard queried, have been conjoined with firmness? Had it been so, he believed that actual force might have been avoided."[101]

Southard's choice of tense—force "might have been avoided"—was hardly warranted, given the actual course of events, but it did accurately reflect his pessimism that Jackson could or would handle nullification prudently. In his response, the former president brought a bit of realism to the matter when he observed that South Carolina would not ultimately risk defying the law. Adams agreed with Southard that the premise of nullification was invalid, and he advised Southard, when commenting to the legislature, to offer "a strong though moderate and respectful expression of censure on it, as unconstitutional, null and void." If South Carolina resisted the execution of federal law, Adams pointed out, there would be "war against the United States," requiring the chief executive to take appropriate measures and all state governors to support him to this end.[102]

This perspective was independently corroborated by William Wirt, who tartly observed of nullification, "This will never do."[103] Both letters laid the groundwork for Southard's own public utterances on the question. Busy over the Christmas holidays with preparations for his nullification address to the legislature, Southard delivered it just one day after submitting his state of the state message. Southard introduced the South Carolinians' proclamation along with antinullification resolutions from other states, and then presented his own analysis of the crisis, his most noteworthy state paper as governor.

Southard's message, which ran to eighteen pages in print, was a scholarly yet impassioned disquisition on nullification's genesis, sophistries, and potential ramifications.[104] Several themes surfaced. First, the supremacy of law and the need to adjudicate constitutional disputes through normal channels—that is, the court system. Nullification, Southard stressed, was an illegitimate attempt to circumvent those who framed the Constitution. "The provisions which have been received in the South Carolina Ordinance of Nullification," he wrote,

> are utterly repugnant to the spirit and existence of all our institutions, and to the rights and privileges under them, of the minority of the people of that state. Their enforcement would, of itself, sever the Union—break the bonds of connection between states—and render them separate powers. That which was proposed as a peaceful remedy leads, inevitably, in the end, to war.

Second, secession was both unjustified and intolerable. It was "revolution and disunion" entirely unsanctioned by the Constitution and unacceptable to the other states in the Union. Observing that President Jackson's determination to uphold the laws of the land was "the language of duty, of office, and of the constitution of the United States," Southard made it clear that New Jersey would contribute whatever might be asked of it in a clash between federal authority and South Carolina.

Partly out of long-standing personal dislike of Jackson and public opposition to Jackson's politics, Southard qualified his words of support for the president. He expressed regret that Jackson's language should be so violent as to encourage defiance by the South Carolinians. Moreover, as he would explain in another message to the legislature (January 28, 1833), he disagreed with Jackson's constitutional interpretation in a key particular. Although he reiterated his rejection of nullification, Southard insisted that the Constitution did not sanction coercion of a state; it provided that the federal government should act directly only on individuals. "Both the coercion and the right of resistance spoken of, are opposed to the theory of our institutions"—a theory upon which he elaborated at some length.

Southard's language was constitutional, but the purport of his message was in large measure political. The governor was only too happy to join in flailing the dragon of nullification, but he did not wish to be locked in embrace with his enemy of long-standing. Hence his stress on constitutional differences even as he upheld the substance of Jackson's rejection of nullification doctrine.

Such rhetorical nuances left an opening for Jacksonian attacks on Southard's failure wholeheartedly to endorse the Jackson-Webster view of nullification. Garret Wall, Southard's old antagonist and now federal attorney for the New Jersey district, sat down after reading the message and wrote to ex-governor Peter Vroom that Southard's failure to accept the coercive powers of the general government was "the essence of Calhounism, adulterated by Clayism." "With proper management" it would help, Wall suggested, to defeat Southard's claims to Mahlon Dickerson's Senate seat.[105]

In fact, the Jacksonian press picked up on precisely this point. The Newark *New Jersey Eagle* claimed that in staking out a position apart from the president's, Southard had joined forces with John C. Calhoun, for whom (recalling his old friendship with Calhoun), he "has not yet lost his partiality." Should the two men ever again meet in the Senate, the *Eagle*'s editor suggested, "both advocating the doctrine of state supremacy, over the powers of the General Government, who will venture to foretell the consequences? Let the people of New Jersey look to it." To this attack on Southard's position the National Republican press replied at length and with vigor.[106]

The controversy in New Jersey over nullification did not, however, stymie Southard's bid for the Senate. The great question had quieted when Congress, led by Henry Clay, passed a compromise tariff and South Carolina, aware of Jackson's willingness to use force if it did not back off from threats, relaxed its defiant posture.[107] Three days before the United States House of Representatives passed Clay's compromise tariff (with little support from New Jersey congressmen or Northern representatives generally), Southard was elected to the Senate, and on February 27, 1833, Southard resigned his office after securing the support of his party for a successor, Elias P. Seeley, a little-known Cumberland County councillor. In his formal letter accepting the Senate seat, Southard reiterated his well-known positions on national issues and expressed the satisfaction he felt with the opportunity to work in Washington with Theodore Frelinghuysen, whose opinions on the issues Southard shared and in whose "purity, intelligence, and faithfulness we all have entire reliance."[108]

Southard, Frelinghuysen, and their coadjutors in the anti-Jacksonian ranks would have need of all the qualities Southard mentioned in his acceptance letter. Indeed, they would need these and more, for the next four years would be among the most turbulent in New Jersey political history and the greatest challenge yet to Samuel Southard as a political leader.

7

"Where Glory Waits You"

The years 1833–36 marked the pinnacle of Samuel Southard's active involvement and influence in politics. Service in Washington as a valued member of the Whig coalition, combined with his continued ascendance as Whig leader in his home state, gave Southard considerable recognition and power—though probably not enough to satisfy him completely. He was during these years a remarkably active and influential figure, nonetheless.

The Bank War lay at the center of Southard's political activity in mid-decade, but did not set the limits of it. He was spokesman for his party in New Jersey on all current issues, acknowledged campaign manager in election years, and the party's chief pipeline for patronage from Washington. Such roles were typical of party leaders during the Jacksonian era. For Southard, and the dozens of other state leaders like him, politics was a many-sided vocation. That the vicissitudes of politics more often brought frustration than triumph did not, for this period at least, confound him. Southard continued to labor, and with the conclusion of a successful Whig presidential campaign in New Jersey in 1836, he looked ahead to a more promising political era.

I

Southard was delighted, by late February 1833, to gain release from the burdens of the governorship. The lure of a return to the lucrative practice of law he had established upon his return to New Jersey in 1829 was, apparently, too great to resist. He felt compelled, moreover, by his still intense ambition to be better known nationally, to go, as William Wirt had urged him late in 1832, "where glory waits you, and where your country most wants you."[1] Formal election to replace Mahlon Dickerson in the Senate afforded him this opportunity.

At the same time, abandonment of the state's highest executive office left his party without an obvious successor. There simply was no logical second-in-command within New Jersey National Republican ranks, no single individual who had the stature of a Southard, and the support of New Jersey

141

voters north and south of the Assanpink, the traditional dividing line between "West" and "East" New Jersey. The "safety of the state," party loyal-
ist Joseph Randolph told Southard, lay in his hands. Certainly Southard's
departure in midterm put his party in a bind. So serious was the problem of
finding an acceptable replacement that, for a time, Southard toyed with the
idea that an able Democrat, Peter Vroom, should be supported for the
governorship in exchange for Democratic concessions on certain patronage appointments. This possibility proved unpopular with those to
whom Southard broached the idea, and Vroom, counseled by Democratic
friends, was not in any case inclined to accept such an arrangement.[2]

In the end, the National Republicans settled upon a little-known Cumberland County legislator, Elias P. Seeley, for the governorship, an appointment that was greeted with derision by the Jacksonian press when it
was confirmed in late February 1833. In the state elections that fall, it was
evident that Seeley's failure to "inspire great confidence," as one historian
has put it, weakened the party's prospects of maintaining a hold on the
legislature and, with the legislature, the state's chief executive office.[3]

II

While Jacksonians and National Republicans in New Jersey traded insults and charges about the wisdom of electing Elias P. Seeley to replace
Samuel Southard in the governorship, events nationally were moving the
two major parties to a new level of conflict. At stake was the fate of the
Bank of the United States.

Andrew Jackson's decisive victory in the 1832 election had strengthened
his determination to kill the bank before its charter expired in March 1836.
Only one month after defeating Henry Clay for the presidency, Jackson
proposed in his annual message the sale of the government's stock in the
bank and requested an inquiry by Congress into the desirability of removing government deposits from the bank. The House of Representatives
rejected both recommendations, but this action did not deter the president.
He was convinced, as James C. Curtis has observed, "that the Bank had
purchased this legislative goodwill and that he was duty-bound to save the
congressmen from their own greedy impulses and the people from their
own corrupt legislators."[4] Hence, in March 1833, Jackson informed his
cabinet that he would remove all government deposits from the bank and
place them in state banks, pending the creation of a much more limited
national bank that would operate only in the District of Columbia. Jackson
intended to press this policy during the long lull between the end of the
Twenty-second Congress and the convocation of a new Congress in December 1833.[5]

There were obstacles to such a bold move, notably the opposition expressed by members of Jackson's own cabinet, including two successive secretaries of the treasury, but discord within Democratic ranks merely strengthened the president's resolve. In September, Jackson assembled the cabinet and read a paper prepared by Attorney General Roger B. Taney explaining his intention to press for the removal of deposits. Two days later, on September 20, the paper was published in the Washington *Globe*, a signal to Democrats across the nation that a new phase in the Bank War had begun. On September 23, Jackson dismissed Treasury Secretary William Duane for refusing to accept the removals policy, and immediately replaced him with Taney. Within forty-eight hours the new treasury secretary publicly announced that the policy of "removals" would proceed, effective October 1. No longer would deposits to the credit of the government be made in Nicholas Biddle's bank. They would go, instead, to seven selected private or "pet" banks, six of which were operated by businessmen friendly to the Jacksonian cause. Although the Bank of the United States would not face immediate destruction, since no specific "removals" from its vaults were authorized, the purpose of the administration's policy was clear: death, albeit by slow strangulation, to the bank. The stage was being set for a climactic national debate on the merits of this policy.[6]

In New Jersey, and every other state, political men moved quickly to identify themselves as friends or foes of the president's policy. Following publication of Jackson's statement of September 18, Stacy Potts's Trenton *Emporium* declared that "the struggle has commenced."

> Throughout our whole country, the Bank, the Aristocracy, and the office seekers, are putting forth their gold and exertions profusely, to secure dominion over a hitherto free people. . . . The democracy have from this taken the alarm.[7]

National Republicans addressed the issue with equal vigor. Referring to Jackson's replacement of two treasury secretaries in 1833 (McLane and Duane), and the order for removal of deposits, the Newark *Sentinel* asked, "Has not the will of Congress been put at defiance, the law trampled under foot, and a solemn mockery practiced, in the forms resorted to, before the country?" Another writer for the *Sentinel* likened Jackson to Louis XIV of France. "As Louis of France said, in the plenitude of his despotic glory, 'I am the state,' our Executive Officer openly proclaims, *I am the Government*."[8]

Despite the strong rhetoric provoked in the press by the president's economic initiatives, the election of 1833 in New Jersey does not seem to have been a referendum on national policy. Andrew Jackson's announcement regarding the dismissal of William Duane and the removal-of-deposits order signed by Secretary Taney reached New Jersey voters only two weeks before the legislative elections began; the rhythm of the campaign had already been set. Jacksonian rhetoric had been, and continued to be, expended on the "injustice" done the state by the National Republicans' removal of Peter Vroom from the governorship in 1832 and Samuel Southard's subsequent abandonment of the post to an alleged incompetent.[9]

Both sides exerted themselves to get their loyalists to the polls. In this effort the Jacksonians were better motivated and better organized than their opponents, in part because of National Republican apathy in counties such as Somerset, where patronage dispensation had not suited the party's rank and file, in part because the state's Jacksonians had learned a lesson from their defeat the previous year.[10] The Jacksonians' adroit and expensively mounted campaign in 1833, which included new and significant efforts to win votes in the western counties, practically insured a Democratic triumph in the state elections. The returns in 1833 were nonetheless a revelation. Put simply, the National Republicans were routed. Their contingent in the assembly was reduced from thirty-three to nine, with forty-one Jacksonians now in the majority. From a majority of eight seats to six in the council, the National Republicans were reduced to two council seats in the legislature that would sit in 1833–34. The turnaround in party fortunes in New Jersey could hardly have been more complete.[11]

The most significant aspect of the Jacksonians' sweeping victory in 1833 was the party's remarkable advances in the National Republicans' West New Jersey stronghold. From 1829 to 1832, National Republicans easily outdistanced Jacksonian opponents in populous Cumberland, Burlington, and Gloucester Counties.[12] This was not the case in 1833. Strange to say, in an election year in which national issues were widely debated, and partisan interpretations of the quality of leadership in Trenton were dominant campaign themes everywhere else in the state, in western New Jersey the political campaign hinged on a sectarian conflict that currently obsessed the Quakers of that region. This conflict, which involved a bitter theological dispute between two factions of the Society of Friends, ultimately took a political coloration that undermined the cause of National Republicanism in New Jersey for these crucial political years.

The background of the conflict lay in a divergence of doctrine among Quakers who belonged to the Philadelphia meeting, which encompassed roughly 6,000 West New Jersey Friends. For nearly a decade before 1833 an increasingly astringent debate on the fundamental doctrines of their faith had divided the members of this religious community. On one side were those who identified themselves with the more mystical Quaker impulse and who emphasized a literal interpretation of scripture and the importance of Christ's atonement. On the other were those who subscribed to a more "rational" doctrine that downplayed the atonement's significance for men's souls and emphasized, instead, Christ's human example. Those who subscribed to the latter interpretation were identified with the preaching of a Long Island farmer and itinerant minister, Elias Hicks. Although no perfect tabulation has ever been made, it is evident that a decisive majority of New Jersey Quakers took the more rational or "Hicksite" side in theological arguments.[13]

By 1827 the two sides had reached an impasse on the fundamentals of their religion, and the "Hicksites" refused to meet further with the "Orthodox" Quakers. A legal dispute arose in Burlington County, New Jersey, over the division of property within the Chesterfield meeting, a dispute that focused on monies allocated for a Friends school at Crosswicks. By 1832 this quarrel had political ramifications of potentially significant proportions, and though the Hicksites' grievances were assuaged by Southard and other National Republican leaders that year, in 1833 the Quaker issue came to the fore in West New Jersey politics. It was this issue which destroyed the National Republicans' chances to retain their political dominance in New Jersey.[14]

Why should a bitter sectarian dispute have been injected into politics? The answer lay in the participation of leading political figures in the continuing legal fight between the contending parties of the Chesterfield meeting. In the initial argument before Justices Charles Ewing and George K. Drake of the state supreme court in January 1832, Samuel Southard and Garret Wall had argued on behalf of the "Hicksites" against George Wood and Isaac Williamson for the "Orthodox" Quakers. Despite Southard's best forensic efforts, the decision rendered by the two justices in July 1832, accompanied by detailed, separate opinions, went against the Hicksites on the grounds that as "seceders" they were not entitled to regain their school-fund contributions.[15]

But matters did not rest there. The decision was appealed in 1833 to the court of last resort in New Jersey, the Court of Appeals, with Governor Seeley presiding. In the arguments before this body, which repeated and reemphasized the points made earlier, Theodore Frelinghuysen replaced Williamson as advocate for the orthodox Quakers. The other attorneys and the end result were the same. By a 7–4 vote, across party lines, the court affirmed the decision of Justices Ewing and Drake. In a statement issued with the decision, Seeley, who had voted with the majority against the Hicksites, expressed regret that such "religious controversies" should be brought into the court and urged both parties to seek some accommodation on their own.[16]

Seeley's advice did little to calm the aggrieved Hicksites, who insisted that simple justice remained to be done. They were angry, and they knew no better place to vent this anger than at the ballot box, where National Republicans were the main targets, the Jacksonians the delighted beneficiaries, of Hicksite frustration. The two immediate targets of West Jersey Quakers were Theodore Frelinghuysen and Judge George Drake. Frelinghuysen, now serving in the U.S. Senate as Samuel Southard's senior colleague, had long been a favorite of West Jersey Quakers for his forthright attacks on Jacksonian Indian policy and his staunch defense of the Bank of the United States. By identifying himself so closely with the "Orthodox" case he argued in the Court of Appeals, Frelinghuysen dissipated his bank of good will in West Jersey and became, next to Judge Drake, probably the single most despised man in the region. This did not bode well for National Republicanism for either 1833 or 1834. In the former year, Judge Drake's reappointment would come before the legislature; in the latter, Frelinghuysen's fate in the Senate would be decided. Samuel Southard well knew that the Jacksonian leadership in West Jersey, long accustomed to defeat in this bastion of antislavery and support for Indian rights and the Bank of the United States, would not hesitate to employ the Quaker issue for political purposes.[17]

He was, of course, correct in his surmise. In 1832 Southard had been able to calm Hicksite anger at Justices Ewing and Drake by assuring the sect that it would win its case on appeal, but by the autumn of 1833, the Hicksite Quakers were in no mood for assurances. Southard's best legal efforts had not been good enough to make his predictions stick, and though he remained personally popular in West Jersey, his party suffered greatly there from the fallout from the Quaker case. Specifically, during the campaign of 1833, while Southard and his fellow National Republicans had publicly to eat the promises they had made the previous year, Garret Wall could and did pledge Jacksonian support for the Hicksite position. Wall canvassed the counties of West Jersey in 1833, promising in particular that, if Hicksites would abandon their commitment to National Republicanism, Justice Drake would be removed from the state supreme court when his term expired early in 1834, and the Jacksonian party, moreover, would work to pass a law mandating an equitable division of property between the two Quaker factions. These promises were well received by the Hicksites, many of whom broke their long-standing ties to National Republicanism. As a result, the Jacksonians scored impressive gains throughout West Jersey in 1833, including a complete sweep in Gloucester County and the election of a decisive majority of Jacksonians to Burlington County's large legislative delegation.[18]

Once the legislature convened, the Jacksonians moved to redeem their campaign pledge to remove Judge Drake and, despite the efforts of Governor Vroom to defend Drake and the principle of judicial independence, the judge was replaced with a Sussex County Jacksonian attorney, Thomas C. Ryerson. No legislation regarding division of property was passed during this session, but the Jacksonians continued to promise redemption of this pledge as well. They knew they now had a foothold in a key region of the state, and they were prepared to pursue the opportunity the Hicksite controversy offered them for continued political advantage.[19]

Southard was obviously disappointed at the turn politics in New Jersey took in 1833, notably in the West, but because he personally was not affected by the Jacksonian landslide in the legislative elections, he could more readily be optimistic that when the "real" issue of the day—the mismanagement of the national government in Washington under Jacksonian auspices—was fully explained to the public, National Republican fortunes would revive and government at both the state and federal levels would be set aright.

During the autumn of 1833, Southard devoted most of his attention to his legal work and various business affairs, including several ventures in land speculation. He was busy at home overseeing the affairs of his extended family, which included not merely his wife and their three adolescent children, but several domestic servants and a gardener. Southard also began to make arrangements for a move to Washington in December when the new Congress convened. He had to decide whether to join a congressional mess, preferably in the company of such old friends as Henry Clay, or to move his family with him to the capital. Given his wife's distaste for travel, and her tendency to fall ill after even the slightest outing, he decided, for the time being, to move only himself. By November he had arranged to live in a comfortable boardinghouse near the capitol, and by Thanksgiving he was packed and on his way south.[20]

III

Samuel Southard was a vigorous man of forty-six when he reentered the United States Senate. The bilious fevers that had periodically plagued him during his years as a New Jersey official no longer troubled him. Except for occasional attacks of gout, his health was as good as it had been in a decade, and his spirits were equally good. And there was reason for this. Southard had overcome political adversity and regained a position of great weight in politics; financially, if no more secure than he had ever been, he did have encouraging prospects. Moreover, Southard was caught up, as many Americans were at this time, in the great struggle brewing between the president and a majority of United States senators. As one of this majority, Southard believed he had a responsibility to sustain American liberties against the apparent challenge posed to them by a remarkably obtuse president.

Sworn into the Senate on December 2, 1833, Southard quickly joined with the National Republican and Calhounite members in several partisan actions. He voted, for example, to strip the Senate president's power to appoint committees, and was himself elected chairman of the Naval Affairs Committee by a party-line, 25–18 vote over William C. Rives of Virginia. Southard was also named a member of the Senate's committee on roads and canals, and the District of Columbia Committee.[21] He would have much to keep him occupied during the session.

The main focus of attention in Washington that winter was not, however, committee work. Attention focused, rather, on the conflict between the president and his opposition on the disposition of the deposit credit of the United States government. Would the Congress uphold Andrew Jackson's decision to transfer government deposits to "pet banks" and thus cripple the operations of the Bank of the United States? Would the Senate endorse or reject Secretary Taney's September 26 order to this effect? Would the admittedly fragmented opposition to Jackson successfully coalesce to assert the prerogatives of Congress against the executive's encroachments? These related questions boiled down to one main issue: were Andrew Jackson's economic policies to be sustained or repudiated by the government's legislative branch?

In the maneuvering on this essential question, Henry Clay and John C. Calhoun exerted a forceful leadership among members of the Senate opposition. Thomas Hart Benton and, to a lesser extent, John Forsyth led the administration forces in that body. Samuel Southard was one of the body of secondary figures who played a supporting role in the proceedings.[22]

The president's message of December 3, 1833, followed a day later by the secretary of the treasury's reasons for removing government deposits from the bank, provided the basis for opposition arguments and proposals. The debate began on December 26, when Henry Clay rose and did what all expected of him: he took the lead in passionately denouncing Andrew Jackson's decision to remove the deposits. In a well-orchestrated three-day speech, Clay attacked Jackson for a policy that was wrong in substance and dangerous in purport. Jackson, Clay said, was foolishly threatening the fiscal stability of the country. Worse, by ordering Secretary Taney to remove government deposits in the bank before Congress had the opportunity to evaluate such a drastic change in government policy, he had assumed unconstitutional authority that jeopardized the balance of government power and the stability of republican institutions. Clay bluntly asserted that the president was trying to destroy the "pure republican character of the Government," and put all power "in the hands of one man."[23] Rather than simply declaim against policy he abhorred, Clay offered two resolutions for consideration by the Senate. The first of these pronounced Secretary Taney's stated reasons for removing government deposits from the bank to be unsatisfactory. The second, and even more controversial resolution, stated that President Jackson deserved censure for the reckless policy he had initiated. When he concluded his remarks on December 31, the sensation in the galleries, according to one historian "was so great that it could be stilled only by ejecting the visitors."[24]

Congress and the nation at large were from this point absorbed in a duel of will and guile. Both sides would have much to say before the two resolutions introduced by Henry Clay reached a vote in the Senate and before the general question of administration policy was submitted to the public in the election of 1834. Each side would argue that the republic was threatened by a malignant force. There simply was no consensus on the source of this threat. For Jacksonians, led by the president and ably seconded in the Senate by the "magnificent Missourian," Thomas Hart Benton, the malignancy in question was the "hydra-headed monster," the Bank of the United States. No institution, the Jacksonians insisted, should have such consolidated and dominant power in a society subscribing to free enterprise and democratic ideals. From this perspective, the president was merely asserting his rightful authority as defender of republican freedom, particularly freedom from the domination of giant corporations. For the National Republicans, soon to embrace the name "Whig" (a reminder of the American struggle for liberty half a century earlier), the Jacksonian case against the bank was ignorant and misbegotten. The real danger to the nation, as Clay had insisted, was the unwarranted authority assumed by the executive branch in vetoing legislation without concern for its constitutionality, in willfully ignoring the dicta of the Supreme Court, and in circumventing the Congress when undertaking such major policies as the disposition of the nation's treasure. The issue, for Whigs, could be reduced to "executive tyranny," and the nation's destiny, in their minds, depended upon the determination of the Senate to resist any and all encroachments on the true order of the nation's republican institutions.[25]

Samuel Southard was one of the leading spokesmen for this Whiggish interpretation of the deposits question. From the outset of the session, he had regularly closeted with his colleagues in the "opposition" ranks, discussing the best way to frame the issue at hand and to carry forward the fight for the bank. Southard's stature within the opposition was reflected by the decision to place him directly behind Clay in the debate, once Thomas Hart Benton had finished the first and major defense of the administration.[26]

Benton took four days to make his points, in which he justified Jackson's policy and reminded his audience that the bank was the true threat to the "property and liberty of the American people."[27] When Benton concluded, the senator from New Jersey claimed the floor. The day was January 8, 1834, and it marked the high point of Samuel Southard's public career. This was, at last, his moment in the spotlight. With this speech Southard could realize his ambition for recognition as a leading party spokesman. He intended not to fritter away this opportunity for fame, and, of equal import, the chance to revenge previous wounds visited on him by General Jackson. He had prepared his words carefully, and for three days he leveled them at the Democratic administration.

Southard's speech, though a day shorter in delivery than Benton's remarks, was in fact the wordiest in a long session devoted to the deposits question. In pamphlet form, it ran to fifty-three pages.[28] The speech was written in the style of the time, to be heard by a large Senate audience and to be read by thousands of interested citizens throughout the land. The argument, in substance, could be reduced to several main themes. First, the question of political decision-making in a balanced system. Second, the merits of the president's and the treasury secretary's defense of removals. Third, the potential disastrous economic consequences if the bank were destroyed. Explicating these three themes, Southard minced no words and spared no sensibilities.[29]

The United States, he observed in his first remarks, was founded on the proposition that balance in government is best. Three branches of government, coequal and cooperative, were the basis for freedom and progress in America. This ideal, Southard said, lay in marked contrast to the policy of the current administration. Instead of cooperation between the executive and the legislative, Southard perceived confrontation and secrecy as the dominant thrusts of one of the branches, the executive. Instead of reason, he saw willfulness. Instead of power shared and balanced, he saw "enormous" power placed in the hands of one cabinet officer, power "dangerous to the interests of the people and the liberties of the country."

Under the auspices of the charter conferred by the Congress and president in 1816, the Bank of the United States had acted efficaciously and lawfully, Southard said. Now, matters had changed. Willful men contravened the law, and the result was "favoritism and corruption." Under Jackson, the nation's treasure would be transferred from a stable and responsible central bank to politically oriented and financially reckless "pets" of the executive. And in this transfer the responsibilities of the Congress were being ignored. By the unprecedented treasury order of September 26, 1833, Southard said, Secretary Taney had "assumed the very essence of legislation—to deal with, to control, to manage the purse of the nation." This was both unethical and illegal, in Southard's view. If the nation acquiesced in the administration's initiative, it faced further such arbitrary measures, and further loss of the freedoms guaranteed by a balanced system founded on adherence to law. If the Congress did not insist on its prerogative in financial policy, Southard asserted bluntly, Americans could say goodbye to their freedom.

> What is despotism, but the existence in the hands of a single individual of the power and right to say to all subordinate agents, you are to act on my responsibility, and by my opinion? Can the Russian go further? Can the Turk? Are Senators prepared to sustain this principle?

Southard followed this line of argument by launching into a discussion of the contrast between a system of finance in which a national bank played a major role and one in which "pet" banks would hold the bulk of the public money. The Bank of the United States, Southard said, was a great boon to

America, not an awesome and tyrannical special privilege. The constitutionality of the bank Southard accepted as a given; its efficacy he believed equally evident to any reasonably intelligent, disinterested, observer.

Nearing the close of his speech, Southard reiterated his arguments, applying the rhetorical flourish common to his era.

> The executive power has plundered your treasury, and presents you such personal security as he can get, and a safety fund in its stead. And we, sir, we, on our solemn oaths, are to answer that we approve his course. For myself, never! Let Congress approve, and not only will your money be squandered, but your constitution violated, your laws condemned; and, in the room of law, you will have executive will, acting upon and controlling an army of moneyed mercenaries, and regulating a money power, which united with the sword, can jeopard[ize] your liberties whenever he pleases. The vindication of the law, at the hands of Congress, can alone arrest this result.

When he at last concluded he was exhausted but satisfied. His points were made and his standing in the Senate was strengthened. At home, Southard's speech brought heavy applause from administration foes.

The Newton *Sussex Register,* edited by the able and acerbic John Hall, congratulated Southard for his "strong, downright and upright sort of speech," while Trenton *Union* editor E. B. Adams called Southard's effort "decidedly the ablest speech that has been delivered on this question." Dozens of New Jerseyans wrote the senator complimenting him on his speech and requesting copies to distribute among the faithful. E. H. Burritt of New Britain spoke for many when he told Southard that "the receipt of your speech on the Deposit Question, at this village, has produced the most lively gratification. Every man, of almost every grade of intellect, is eager for the perusal of it."[30]

Of course, Southard had not had the last word. He was followed, over the next two months of fierce debate in the Senate, by dozens of other speakers, several of whom, such as John C. Calhoun, would echo his sentiments, albeit in a more compressed and, in Calhoun's case, trenchant form.[31] Involved here was a war of words, thousands of them. More: this was a war of will, strategy, and organization. As Southard spoke in the Senate in early January, political leaders in the localities were in motion on behalf of or in opposition to the president's policy on the bank. Memorials and petitions from villages and cities across America began to reach Washington, arriving, as Charles M. Wiltse observes, "singly at first, then in batches, and finally, in floods."[32] Most, at the outset of the struggle, opposed the removal of deposits.

New Jersey bank supporters participated actively in this effort to demonstrate where public opinion lay and in the maneuver to pressure the president to back down. National Republicans called meetings, which hundreds attended, both in the cities and in some of the state's most obscure communities. At these meetings, several local leaders would address the audience, while others drafted resolutions condemning Jacksonian policy. Memorials were circulated and signed, demonstrating popular support for the bank. These memorials were rushed to Washington, where Southard and Theodore Frelinghuysen took great pleasure in presenting them and pointing to the "respectability" and sincerity of those who now publicly rose to be counted as friends of the bank.[33]

The efforts of this party convinced Southard that public opinion would force Jackson's defeat on this great issue. He told John C. Calhoun that good information existed that Jackson was weakening in his resolve, and he encouraged businessmen to petition the president to relieve the economic crisis that seemed to be enveloping the nation in the midst of the Bank War. In fact, talk of economic depression was commonplace in early 1834, and the opponents of Andrew Jackson had no doubts who was responsible for the problems they faced. Delegations of businessmen from the various Eastern cities rode to Washington to confront the president, insisting that the recession could only be relieved if the executive changed his policy. But, like Southard, they did not reckon with Andrew Jackson's resolve. Jackson was having none of compromises. To his petitioners he had one stock response: "Go to Nicholas Biddle. We have no money here, gentlemen. Biddle has all the money. He has millions of specie in his vaults, at this moment, lying idle, and yet you come to *me* to save you from breaking."[34]

Jackson's response to the business contraction forced early in 1834 by the Bank of the United States was as shrewd as it was emphatic. The economic dislocations complained of across the Eastern seaboard had in truth been occasioned in large measure by the policies of the bank, and Jacksonians did not fail to make this point with voters. "Go to Nicholas Biddle" became the refrain of Jacksonian politicians who were implored to persuade the president to change his course. Biddle's decision to call in many loans and sharply reduce others in order to increase public displeasure with the president's policy proved to be a political blunder of major magnitude.[35]

Biddle's miscalculation was not, of course, so clearly evident at the time. Early in 1834, the results of the Bank War were still very much in doubt. Of one thing there was no doubt. The Bank War was a remarkably energizing force in the politics of the nation, infusing political conflict with a new urgency and form. Whether one focused one's love or hate on the president's policies or simply his person (and most partisans embraced or rejected both), there was clear evidence that Jackson, as one historian has put it, "made people give a damn about party politics."[36]

New Jersey offers a case study in this politics of conflict. Both sides worked feverishly to bring their views to the public and to demonstrate that the majority of voters supported or opposed Jackson's initiatives. The Bank War, in this respect, was good for the voters, since it gave them something to choose between, and good for the parties, because it gave them clear reasons for existing beyond the disposition of office and influence. Trenton *Union* editor E. B. Adams spoke truly when he told Samuel Southard in the midst of the "panic session" that "there is great excitement in every part of the state."[37]

In New Jersey, the lines of division were well formed by early 1834. Despite the fervent efforts of Princeton Jacksonian leader Robert F. Stockton to sway the party caucus against an endorsement of the removal of deposits, the rank and file rejected his arguments and condemned the bank.[38] "The Democrats of Jersey," Borden Terhune of Trenton assured Congressman Ferdinand Schenck, "stand firm as a rock against the Bank." Democratic Governor Peter Vroom told his friend Schenck that the bank issue was "the only political subject now under agitation among us," and reported that many rural farmers had "concluded to live on 'Indian dumplings' rather than submit to the Bank." Jeremiah Leaming, an anti-Jacksonian operative in Cape May County, though not so certain that the people would sustain the president, did concede Democratic unity on this issue. "Jackson is their compass, the *Globe* their chart," he told Samuel Southard.[39] But he also told Southard what Southard doubtless already knew: the state's Whigs were equally united on this issue.

Because the Democrats controlled the legislature in New Jersey, they were in a position to act early in forcing the issue of removals from the bank. Once Robert F. Stockton's self-interested temporizing on the bank issue was rebuffed, the Democratic caucus voted in January 1834 to condemn the bank, publicly to laud the president for removing deposits, and to instruct Senators Southard and Frelinghuysen to "sustain by their votes and influence" Secretary Taney's order. The caucus decision was rammed through the legislature on a party vote, and the question of instructions now faced the state's two senators.[40]

Southard and Frelinghuysen had no intention of obeying the dictates of the Jacksonian legislature. Each responded to the "instructions" by pointing to the avalanche of letters and memorials they had received from the state's voters urging them to hold fast, and by reminding their listeners that the election of 1833 had been no referendum on removals. Southard conceded privately to a friend that "the course of our Leg[islature] mortifies me." But, he quickly added, he would not yield.

> I have no *power* to take any but one course. I *must* follow my strong sense of duty, in this crisis, or leave the Councils of my country for those to join them who, I believe, would endanger her institutions & liberties.[41]

This message Southard carried with him when he returned to his home state in March to be toasted by appreciative Whigs in Trenton and elsewhere. He could heartily agree, moreover, with editorialists in the Whig press that the issue was boiling down to "law or no law," and a balanced constitution or "arbitrary power!"[42] The opposition senators, from this perspective, had to stand firm.

The fervor of the Bank War at the grass roots, exemplified in the dinners, rallies, and petitions organized and enthusiastically endorsed by New Jersey partisans, was reflected also in the intense excitement in Washington as the debate over Henry Clay's December 26 resolutions drew to a close. March 28, 1834, was a climactic moment in the Bank War. On that day Southard joined twenty-seven other senators in pronouncing Secretary Taney's reasons for removing the deposits to be "unsatisfactory and insufficient." Eighteen Jacksonians opposed. The second resolution, which censured the president for assuming powers unauthorized by the Constitution, passed by a nearly identical margin. The Whigs had carried their point in the nation's leading deliberative body and had succeeded in thoroughly infuriating President Jackson. The president responded with a strongly worded protest on April 17 castigating the Senate's censure. Since Whigs controlled the upper house at this point, Jackson's initiative was of no avail, though Democratic leader Benton promised to "expunge" the censure as soon as circumstances permitted. The House of Representatives, for its part, was narrowly controlled by the Democrats and helped to blunt the effects of Clay's resolutions by endorsing the president's war against the bank.[43] The final verdict on the bank would necessarily await the fall elections.

IV

There is regrettably little extant evidence of Samuel Southard's private perceptions as the Bank War unfolded. We know his public position as a leading Whig, and we know how hard he worked to advance his party's fortunes. But we do not know what the experience meant personally to him or how, given the many roles all politicians must play, he set his priorities.

Despite the lack of a detailed "inner record" of Southard's mind-set in the mid-1830s, it does seem safe to suggest that Samuel Southard found the political issues of the day to be real and meaningful, within the context of his notions of republicanism. For Southard and his Whig allies, the major threat to a healthy American republic was not a central bank, which to their minds effectively regulated and encouraged the economic growth of the nation, and threatened no interests save unduly speculative ones, but rather, the allegedly venal acts of a willful president. It is in the context of optimism about the nation's economic potential and fears about the breakdown of time-honored checks and balances in our political system that the politics of Whiggery and, in particular, the politics of such New Jersey Whigs as Samuel Southard can best be understood.[44]

Beyond this there was a personal dimension to the bank struggle. Southard disliked Andrew Jackson more than any man he had met in public life.

His early conviction that Jackson was unfit for the presidency had been affirmed by their exchanges during the administration of John Quincy Adams. Now, with the onset of the war Jackson waged against the Bank of the United States, Southard's personal antipathy toward the president was leavened by the conviction that important principles and national institutions needed to be sustained. Jackson, to his mind, had no conception of the realities of economics and no understanding of the potential wealth that could be generated by an activist and pragmatic political leadership working in tandem with the most resourceful enterprises of the day. To sustain his outdated vision of arcadia, Southard believed, Jackson had resorted to tactics that did not comport with America's long-standing commitment to balanced government and a strong congressional role within that balance. Hence Southard and those who felt as he did would resist the executive's encroachments on behalf not only of American liberty, but of American prosperity as well. Principles and interest dictated this course.

It must have been rewarding to Southard, as he spoke out against the administration, to know that a "Whig of '76" was firmly on his side. That old Whig was his father Henry, eighty-six years old at the outset of the bank struggle, in ill health but still vigorous in spirit and most interested in the outcome of the duel between the president and the Senate. During these exciting years, Henry Southard lived quietly on his older son Isaac's Somerville farm, close to the home he had known since the 1750s. He continued to work in the fields when he felt up to it, but mostly he stayed close to the house, chatting with his many grandchildren and neighbors, and reading the newspaper accounts of the proceedings in Washington and Trenton. Periodically Henry wrote to his famous son to remind him that he was acting well in a good cause. "I have received and read your long speech in the Senate," he told Samuel in February 1834. "I applaud the ground you have taken. Stick to it." And further, in a letter dated March 12, amidst the controversy over the Democratic legislature's instructions to New Jersey's senators: "I perceive the people begin to be alarmed at the measures pursued by the administration. I am pleased to know that the people in some counties are by their resolves sustaining our Senators, and that our Legislature[']s resolves will not sink you so deep as that Honorable body expected." Southard and his colleagues, Henry noted, must "persevere in the good cause until every tyrant . . . and swindler are brought down to the level their characters deserve."[45]

There is no evidence of Samuel Southard's thought as he read his father's exhortations. He rarely answered Henry's letters, and he did not answer these.[46] Probably he simply paused, satisfied with his father's forceful approbation of his deeds, and then went on to more pressing matters. But Henry Southard's comments suggest something worth remarking upon. The guard inevitably changes, one generation yields to the next, and in the course of such change attitudes and values also tend to change. The transition from Southard *père* to Southard *fils* in American politics is representative of such changes. The Whiggery of 1776 was not the Whiggery of 1836; Samuel Southard was his father's son, but not a politician of his father's stripe. Henry Southard had spent thirty productive years in politics with a fixed idea—republican simplicity—and he retired from politics in 1821 with his enthusiasm for that Jeffersonian ideal not one whit diminished. For Henry Southard's son, republican simplicity was outworn stock. His lot was cast not with an arcadian vision and the politics of nostalgia, but with republican enterprise and the politics of hope.[47] That his father sustained Samuel Southard's evolving version of republicanism represented not a change of heart on Henry Southard's part about the proper dimensions of a good society, but the effectiveness of the Whig appeal to other, still resonant, strands of the republican tradition. The division between Whigs and Democrats during the 1830s can in large measure be understood in terms of the old republican themes they chose to emphasize.

To assert that Samuel Southard and other politicians identified themselves with the Jeffersonian tradition may, then, provide some insight into the nature of the struggle between the parties during the Jacksonian era. It does not, of course, explain everything. Each side believed, and constantly reminded the electorate, that it differed from the other about the conduct of public affairs. Both sides elaborated these differences in public speeches, in the party presses, and through resolutions offered at the mass meetings that seemed to occur ceaselessly during this era. Politics, however, was not simply a matter of fashioning an "ideology" and emphasizing it constantly to voters. If Southard devoted a significant portion of his energies to the politics of persuasion, he labored even more intensively in the politics of organization. His role as a political leader was, inevitably, many-dimensioned. Dispensing patronage, helping allies with legal or personal problems, and expediting appointments of political friends (and *their* relatives or friends) to a service academy or the armed forces were regular and insistent chores for any party leader, as much a part of the process of politics as stump speaking or formal discourse in the Congress. A politician who styled himself a man of principle, as Southard manifestly did, might also be, and surely was, also a political operator, a figure who not only educated the people but served them, too.[48]

Sensitive to the many sides of politics, Southard was occupied during the Bank War years on many fronts. He served as a political tribune in the Senate fight against "executive tyranny"; he was stump orator to the Whig faithful back at home; he was a Whig political boss, a man whose home in Trenton was often referred to by colleagues as "party headquarters"; and he was, of course, the ambitious politician, hopeful, in 1835, of gaining the party's vice-presidential nomination.

Through it all, Southard had to deal not merely with the maneuvers of an adroit political opposition in New Jersey, but with family and business affairs, and the nonpolitical responsibilities of an eminent public figure. That he carried off each of these obligations and challenges as successfully as he did is testament not merely to his stamina, but also to his pride, patience, and ability.

V

The bank issue was the single most galvanizing force in New Jersey politics during the Jacksonian era. To be sure, President Jackson himself was controversial enough as a public figure to spark debate and division during his tenure of office; but for mass parties to organize and high levels of citizen participation in election campaigns to materialize, some meaningful issue was essential. That issue emerged in 1832. The president's veto of the bank recharter, followed by his "removal" of deposits, and the controversy over his assertions of executive authority provided the impetus for a full-fledged party system in New Jersey and most of the nation.[49]

Until the bank veto of July 1832, New Jersey's political editors commonly lamented the absence of substantial issues for the two opposing sides to debate. Men, not measures, seemed to divide the parties, and such policy differences as were articulated—notably the New Jersey Jacksonians' caution, compared with National Republicans' enthusiasm, on national internal improvements, and the expressed differences the parties had on Indian policy—were more matters of nuance than fundamental disagreement.[50]

The themes that emerged during the years 1832–36, by contrast, were colorful and pregnant with import for the nation's future. The fate of republicanism seemed at stake, and voters argued and rallied in large measure because they believed, or wanted to believe, that *their* party alone could save the country from some dreadful fate. In the Jacksonians' case, the issue was perceived to be, as Peter Vroom put it, to avoid "the withering principle that the comforts and well being, if not the existence of our nation, is dependent upon a moneyed corporation." For good Whigs such as Samuel Southard, fearing "executive usurpation," the long-hallowed constitutional balance was at stake. Taking what side he would, a partisan in the 1830s had, in New Jersey at least, portentous themes to address.[51]

Samuel Southard would sound the "executive tyranny" theme across New Jersey during the elections of 1834. He well knew that these elections in New Jersey and other states would serve as referenda on the removal of deposits and the other issues debated so fiercely and at such length in the Congress during the winter and spring of 1834. He knew, too, that the political fate of his friend and ally, Theodore Frelinghuysen, hinged on the outcome of the legislative contest in October. Knowing this, Southard worked as hard as he had ever worked in a political campaign. Beginning in July, he spoke dozens of times before appreciative Whig audiences about the "usurpations" of President Jackson; he wrote articles to be printed in the press; and he tried to deal with the Whigs' thorniest political problem: the unrest among Quakers in the western counties, where anger still simmered as a result of the Hicksite schism and the legal suit decided in 1833. If Whiggery were to rise in New Jersey and sustain not merely "constitutional principles" but the Senate seat of Theodore Frelinghuysen, fences had to be mended in the West, and Samuel Southard recognized that his popularity among Hicksites offered some hopes that the Quakers' dissatisfaction could be eased.[52]

Through the summer and early fall, as the campaign progressed, Southard devoted much of his time to travels through the western counties. He spoke at a great Whig rally in Burlington in mid-August, trying, as one partisan observed, to downplay "local disputes and private prejudices." In Gloucester, Cumberland, and Salem Counties he encouraged local Whig leaders to form tickets that would satisfy both Quaker factions by nominating candidates of both Hicksite and Orthodox persuasions. In his speeches and in party propaganda Southard also put great stress on the bank question, since he was convinced that West Jersey voters were unhappy with the president's economic policies, and that Burlington citizens in particular needed and wanted the services of a national bank.[53]

Unfortunately for Southard and his party, the New Jersey Quakers were not willing to ignore their local resentments when they cast their ballots in the fall elections. One Whig sympathizer foreshadowed the results of the October canvass when he told Southard that though the Hicksites "detest Jacksonism, they detest orthodoxy even more. In a word they consider themselves a persecuted people [and believe] that their religious liberty is in danger—which is prized much more highly by them than their civil liberty."[54] The Hicksites remained resentful of Frelinghuysen's role in their legal defeat in 1833 and well knew that Jacksonian control of the legislature would doom the state's senior senator to defeat in his bid for reelection. That a vote for Jacksonian legislative candidates as a means of punishing the Whigs contradicted their own convictions on the policy disputes between the two parties was simply ignored. As one frustrated Whig editor lamented, "It is useless to reason with a Quaker on any subject which he makes a matter of conscience. *They are as much opposed to the measures of the Administration* as any of us; yet the question in relation to the society is of paramount importance, and every other must be made subservient."[55]

Nothing Southard said or did could entirely undo the damage inflicted on Whig unity by the Quaker schism. In the face of the legal proceedings of 1832–33, the decision by the Court of Appeals in July 1833, and the shrewd and persistent efforts of New Jersey Jacksonians to play upon Hicksite resentments, the election results in the West were inevitably a great disappointment to Southard. When the returns were tabulated, the

Whigs made some gains, but their inability to carry the West decisively made possible another Jacksonian triumph statewide and also in the congressional elections that followed the legislative contest. The Whigs carried Burlington, but by about 400 votes fewer than their hopeful projections, and Gloucester County with its large legislative delegation remained in Jacksonian hands.[56] James Wilson expressed the Whigs' response to the election when he told his law partner that the returns made his heart "ache." Zachariah Rossell, a West New Jersey party workhorse, told Southard "I am sick, sick, sick & fear you will be also."[57]

Rossell's comment was not much off the mark. Southard was indeed disheartened that all his efforts had yielded so little. He was distressed, moreover, that even in a year when everything that could be said on the bank issue was said, voters had not decided the election on the great issue before them. As he told Hezekiah Niles following the congressional elections: "I am mortified—but the fault was not in me or our friends who did all that men could do. We were conquered by foreign votes & by local causes—improperly connected with general policies."[58]

Southard's explanation was a reflection of his unbending conviction that, on economic issues alone, the Whigs held a majority in New Jersey. That "local causes"—notably the Hicksites' anger against their orthodox Quaker brethren and those politicians who had supported them—should have prevailed was mortifying to this leading Whig. Yet the same man who here complained that moral and religious questions were not legitimate campaign themes was also known for many years to have played on this same group's moral concern for the plight of the American Indian, and also on many New Jerseyans' distaste for the Irish immigrants who had arrived in Newark and Paterson to work in factories there.[59]

To claim that ethnocultural issues were dominant in New Jersey politics during the Jacksonian era would be claiming too much. With the exception of the western counties in 1833, 1834, and 1835, national economic issues shaped campaigns and determined voting behavior. Nonetheless, that a bitter religious dispute, and negative-reference behavior at election time, could and sometimes did influence the election returns seems unchallengeable. Had the negative-reference grouping worked in favor of the Whigs, Southard and his allies would not likely have complained that such matters were "improperly connected with general politics."[60]

Southard was all too aware, of course, that the state's Democrats would cite the election results as a vindication of President Jackson. He did his best to put a different face on things, emphasizing the Quaker schism and the supposed pervasive bribery of voters by "Jackson gold" in the northern counties. He began, moreover, an effort to demonstrate what he believed to be a pattern of vote fraud, based not simply on outright bribery, but also on the Jacksonians' eleventh-hour efforts to naturalize aliens and persuade them to vote the Democratic ticket. In this connection he wrote more than a dozen letters to Whig operatives in the northern counties, where Irish immigrants were most densely settled, seeking evidence for his suppositions. The response to these inquiries, however, offered little grist for Southard's mill. Whigs in Hunterdon, Monmouth, Bergen, Sussex, Middlesex, and Morris Counties all told the party leader that they had some intimation of "immense" spending in the election by the Jacksonians, but few could offer more evidence than hearsay and several admitted that the Jacksonians had spent no more in treating voters than had the Whigs. On the matter of alien voting, Southard was equally disappointed. There were charges aplenty that Jacksonians had illegally naturalized dozens of Irishmen on or immediately prior to election day. But the evidence sustaining these charges was neither firm nor copious, and few of Southard's correspondents claimed that alien voting had carried the day for the Jacksonians.[61] Southard would simply have to face the fact that the Whigs had no strong case for blaming the results on vote fraud. Facing up to another reality, reluctantly conceded by his brother Isaac, would be even more difficult: the Bank of the United States and banking generally, Isaac bluntly told his brother, are "unpopular with the people."

> The U.S. Bank is made the Scape Goat upon which has been thrown every false note, and every failure of the local banks—If there is a want of money in any portion of the Union, or if in others there is too much to suit some monopolizing individuals or a depreciation in the currency of any or even a failure tis all owing to the Banks. Or if the Govt should be extravagant in its expenditures, or meet with any dif[f]iculty at home or abroad, tis all owing to that Monster Bank.

As a consequence of public ignorance about the true functioning of the bank, Isaac observed, "the least said on that subject by the minority, the better." Whigs would simply have to shape their appeals differently.[62]

Returning to Washington for the Twenty-third Congress's lame-duck session, Southard knew that the Bank was lost, and he bowed to the inevitable. His attention turned now to two main matters: first, a continued Whig assault on Jacksonian fiscal policy generally, with particular emphasis on the inexpediency of hard money as a national standard of exchange; and the "expunging" resolutions again presented to the Senate by Senator Benton. Southard and his colleague Frelinghuysen were at the center of a small firestorm on the issue. The Jacksonian legislature in New Jersey had instructed them to vote for Benton's resolution; beyond this, "citizens' meetings" were called by Democrats in Trenton and elsewhere demanding that Southard and Frelinghuysen "obey the voice of the people" as expressed in the election of 1834.[63]

The two New Jersey Whigs refused to buckle under to these pressures. In this position they found strong support from their own partisans in New Jersey. To agree that the state legislature could instruct congressmen, one

Whig petition insisted, would mean the "end of all our free institutions." The rights of representatives would be curtailed, and the balanced constitution would no longer be balanced.[64]

On February 27, 1835, Southard rose in the Senate to make such points himself. He argued that there was no precedent for instruction in New Jersey, and that instructions could in any case not be justified on practical or constitutional grounds. Legislators, he noted, were usually elected at "a time of excitement with no relation to the question [of electing senators] at all." To accept instructions, he said, would mean accepting a "dangerous consolidation of power" in the legislatures of the respective states, a change in our customs that no right-thinking American could accept. He would neither accept instructions nor resign in rejecting them. Frelinghuysen, for his part, took the same stand, though the question for him was not so pressing as for Southard, since the Newark man's Senate term would expire within weeks of receiving instructions, and he was certain to be replaced by a Democrat.[65]

The debate over instructions in New Jersey was not nearly so extended as the debate over banking and presidential power, but it was nearly as intense. Both parties argued their cases with great passion, and Senator Southard, as spokesman for the Whig position, was widely praised and condemned, depending on his audience. Whigs, of course, hailed his courage and his logic. Daniel Webster wrote from Boston that he had read Southard's speech and believed that it was "altogether unanswerable & conclusive, upon the whole subject." Henry Clay chimed in that Southard had offered the "definitive" statement on instructions.[66] The Jacksonians in New Jersey, of course, took a different tack, and, though the expunging measure failed again in 1835, it, and instructions, were revived again as issues in the next Congress.[67]

VI

Though the debate over instructions gradually faded in 1835 as a popular issue, Southard's own deep involvement in politics continued. By the conclusion of the lame-duck session of Congress in March, his activity focused less on defending the bank or himself than on four other matters. First, Southard continued to work assiduously to shore up his party in West New Jersey, particularly among the Quakers. He continued to emphasize the Whigs' commitment to a fair settlement for both sides in dispensing property that once had been jointly held by the Quaker factions, as well as the natural affinity of Quakers for the principles and values of Whiggery. Second, Southard joined his fellow Whigs in launching a strong offensive against the New Jersey Jacksonians' increasingly pronounced hard-money policies. As evidence for his argument that the Jacksonians had no adequate understanding of the economic needs of the day, Southard cited the Jacksonian legislature's measure forbidding the circulation of local bank notes of less than five-dollar denominations. He also pointed to the president's "rigidly dogmatic" pronouncements on the currency and, by July 1836, the executive order forbidding the acceptance of paper money in the purchase of federal lands. To the Whigs, such policy was manifestly irrational, and a direct threat to the orderly development of the economy in the state and nation. Such themes surfaced in 1835, and by the presidential election year would become important to the New Jersey Whig campaign.[68]

Southard's third pressing concern during this period—relations with the state's powerful transportation monopoly—was perhaps the most confused. On the surface, the Joint Companies issue, which became politically explosive in late 1835, should have been made to order for the Whigs' purposes. The Jacksonians had effectively assailed the Whigs for three years as supporters of a "Monster Bank" inimical to equal rights and fair play. Yet this same party, so ready to focus its rhetoric on "monster" institutions that denied equal rights to others, was also the main sponsor of the transportation "monster" that controlled most of the canal and railroad traffic in New Jersey—a monopoly that, by the mid-1830s, was coming under increasing public scrutiny and criticism.[69]

The first major challenge to the Joint Companies emerged in 1833 when a Philadelphia-based Philadelphia and Trenton railroad company attempted to break the Camden and Amboy railroad monopoly and build a line between Trenton and New Brunswick. The 1804 charter of the Trenton and New Brunswick Turnpike Company would be the wedge employed by the rival railroad line to break its rival's hold on New Jersey rail traffic.[70]

The ensuing contest between the two companies was long and bitter. It was not, however, a fight between champions of the people, on one hand, and greedy capitalists, on the other, but rather, a battle between two large and wealthy special interests. Each side hired the best legal talent of the day to interpret the legal questions at issue; each spent thousands of dollars on newspaper propaganda; each did a good deal of expensive lobbying in Trenton. Ultimately the New Jersey monopoly succeeded in defeating the Philadelphia and Trenton Company's challenge. To secure this victory, the Camden and Amboy company bought out a majority of the stock of its Philadelphia rival, and proceeded to build the railroad in question under its own auspices.[71]

The transportation issue could not help becoming something of a political football. Remarkably, though, it never became a significant party issue, despite the seemingly obvious potential it held for Whigs to charge the New Jersey Jacksonians with hypocrisy and cant on the monopoly issue. The reason for the political confusion regarding the Joint Companies was twofold. On one hand, many leading New Jersey Whigs, including Samuel

Southard, were in effect "coopted" by the Camden and Amboy monopoly. Southard, for example, was hired by Camden and Amboy Railroad president Robert F. Stockton to offer legal advice and opinions as necessary, and he was put on lucrative retainer by the Delaware and Raritan Canal Company as well.[72] Other leading Whigs, such as Abraham Brown and J. H. Sloan, had interests in the Joint Companies and hence strongly opposed the efforts of the Philadelphia-based transportation company to challenge the Joint Companies in West New Jersey. These Whigs and others insisted that their party must say and do nothing to injure the Joint Companies' interest in New Jersey. "I have always understood that our true policy in New Jersey was to keep down all such questions," Henry McIlvaine told Southard in 1834 when he heard that some Whig papers were taking an antimonopoly position. "I cannot at least see what is to be gained by . . . this. . . . Who feels interest enough [in N. J.] in the other co., to be influenced at this time by this consideration, in our favor?"[73] Responding to McIlvaine, Southard agreed that to make the Joint Companies a party issue "would at this time be most disastrous. It is not possible that it could do us any good—it would *most certainly* injure us."[74] His efforts would be devoted, with mixed success, to dampening the enthusiasm of New Jersey Whigs for an all-out attack on the Joint Companies.[75]

If Whig interest is one reason for the party leadership's failure to advance the monopoly issue, Democratic policy shifts also contributed to confusion on this matter. In 1831, when the railroad and canal monopolies were legally joined and their exclusive privileges extended, the state's Democrats were united and enthusiastic supporters of the measure. By 1835, for reasons of both principle and expediency, many Democrats were moving away from this enthusiasm. Many Democrats realized, as Littleton Kirkpatrick pointed out to Garret Wall in 1835, that the party's identification with the monopoly did not assist its campaign efforts, particularly in rural counties.[76] At the same time, other Jacksonians such as Governor Peter D. Vroom were moving toward a more vigorous anticorporation position in politics. Having concluded on the basis of the Joint Companies' operations that its powers had increased, were increasing, and ought to be diminished, they broke with the monopoly and in 1835 began an anticorporation campaign that did not end for nearly a decade.[77]

The result of this confluence of developments was the failure of the Joint Companies to become a major party issue during the Bank War years. For his part, Samuel Southard was not disappointed that this should have been the case. He was increasingly involved in plans for the presidential election of 1836, activity that constituted the final strand of Southard's political life during this period.

All good Whigs could sigh with relief that Andrew Jackson would not run for a third term. His popular appeal was simply too great to challenge directly. By contrast, the Jacksonian heir apparent, Martin Van Buren, appeared manifestly a less formidable foe, and so the Whigs turned their attention to finding an electable nominee to oppose him in 1836. Political correspondence among Whig leaders in 1835 usually touched on this subject. Could a candidate acceptable to all elements of an admittedly fragile coalition be found?[78]

In 1835, Southard was identified widely and fairly as a supporter of Henry Clay.[79] Clay, however, was branded by many Whigs as a certain "loser," and hence "unavailable" for the nomination in 1836. Trial ballons for other candidates were floated, with Supreme Court Justice John McLean gaining much attention through 1835. Some New Jersey Whig leaders, including Lucius Elmer of Cumberland County and Lewis Condict of Morris, were convinced that McLean was the best hope for a unified party effort in 1836. McLean was endorsed in 1835 by several New Jersey Whig papers, and he remained the party's frontrunner in the state for most of the year.[80]

By the autumn of 1835, however, many Whigs, including Clay and Southard, concluded that nationally McLean was making no headway and, further, that no consensus party choice was likely to emerge in his stead.[81] A new strategy was contemplated. General William Henry Harrison of Ohio came to the attention of party men, particularly in the Midwest and Middle States. New Jersey Whigs increasingly talked Harrison when they talked of the election of 1836. For his part, Southard was willing to endorse Harrison, despite his private conviction that of the "available" candidates Daniel Webster was most fit. The party's best hopes, he told Joseph Randolph in December 1835 lay in pursuing a three-pronged campaign: General Harrison in the West and Middle States, Hugh Lawson White in the South, and Daniel Webster in the Northeast. This was largely the arrangement that prevailed.[82]

A diffused presidential effort in Southard's view had potential benefit not only for the party, which would be advantaged by running regional favorites against a single, unglamorous, Democratic nominee, but also for himself. Southard, in late 1835, began once again to nurse national ambitions. In October he broached the matter with Henry Clay, asking advice on the appropriate course to pursue if he wanted the vice-presidency. Clay offered modest but by no means unabashed encouragement to his friend's hopes. "There is no one that I would sooner see elected," Clay told Southard, of Southard's idea. But he believed Southard should not make himself available unless he were reasonably sure of success.[83]

The key to Southard's hopes for the vice-presidency, and ultimately to his disappointment, lay in Pennsylvania. Prior to the Pennsylvania Whig convention in Harrisburg in December 1835, Southard wrote a confidential letter to an influential Whig seeking the use of this influence on his own behalf. He told John Sergeant that the party needed a candidate who would complement General Harrison and bring strength to the ticket in the Middle States. One widely mentioned possible running mate, John Tyler of Virginia, was in Southard's view not a credible candidate. "Him we *cannot* run," he told Sergeant. "It would destroy us in N. J.—and altho' she is small, yet with Penna she paralizes N. Y.—with N. Y. she adds great strength." The implication, he hoped, was dawning on Sergeant. The one candidate who could unite both Northern and Southern Whigs, and add strength to the ticket in the crucial Middle States, was—Samuel Southard.[84]

Unfortunately for Southard, neither Sergeant nor the Whigs of Pennsylvania generally saw things quite so clearly as he did. When the nominations were made, Harrison was joined on the ticket by a New York Antimason leader, Francis Granger, and that was the end of Samuel Southard's hopes. Once again, his national ambitions simply did not correlate to his party's needs or wishes at the moment.[85] He would remain a figure of weight now and for the rest of his Senate career, but the first rank of power and fame lay just beyond his grasp, as it always had.

This time, however, Southard did not permit his disappointment to show. He threw himself into the campaign of 1836 with great panache, believing that even without himself on General Harrison's ticket the Jackson express could finally be derailed, at least in New Jersey. He was right. Despite a very narrow Jacksonian triumph in the state legislative elections—the party's fourth straight success—the Whigs rebounded to carry the Harrison-Granger ticket to victory.[86] Martin Van Buren had, of course, still carried the election nationally by a comfortable margin, but Southard could take some comfort in the Whig party's decided gains. The Hicksite schism in New Jersey was finally eclipsed as a political hindrance, and the economic trends of the times boded ill for Democratic fiscal policy. It occurred to Southard that a new day in politics was dawning. Hard times in the late 1830s might bring good times for Whiggery, and for Samuel Southard as well.[87]

8

"By Silence to Suffer Less"

Throughout the 1830s, as he performed his political duties, gained stature as Whig spokesman, and campaigned vigorously for a political vision that he believed essential to American growth and prosperity, Samuel Southard also lived a full, if not always entirely happy, private life. His personal concerns, which centered around his family, radiated outwards to legal practice and business investments, associational activities and the enjoyment of good books, food, and wine. Throughout the decade and, indeed, until his death, Southard's central concern was the support of his family, and his unceasing struggle for financial security. Though rich in its variety, Southard's life was also troubled by his wife's continued ill health and her increasing asperity. Wearied by his public service and exhausting legal practice, Southard could not, unfortunately, find repose at home. He was able, however, to find some comfort in the pursuits of his children, and their evident love and concern for him.

I

Public prominence had its rewards in Jacksonian America. A society that remembered the founders of its republican institutions, and that deeply cared about the republic's future course, valued its political leaders and looked to them to explain the challenges of the times. In return for good service and the articulation of a resonant vision, the populace paid obeisance to America's leading political men. Dinners, gifts, encomiums in the public prints—these were the standard recognitions of such notables as Henry Clay, Daniel Webster, John C. Calhoun, and Thomas Hart Benton. Leaders of second rank, among whom Samuel Southard was numbered, enjoyed similar acclaim and perquisites, albeit on a somewhat smaller scale. And they naturally took this as their due. Southard, for his part, loved the dinners that ardent Whigs planned for him, loved the wines, cheeses, hams, and other items that were regularly presented to him simply because he was who he was—United States Senator Samuel Southard. He may not have equally appreciated the steady stream of officeseekers who hammered on his door, buttonholed him in the capitol corridors, and inundated his mailbox, but even this was not always an irritation. After all, an object of supplication is a personage of influence. And influence was a commodity that Samuel Southard wielded with great diligence and some skill during his long career in politics.

Public recognition was important to Southard, but it was not central to his fulfillment. Public dinners fed his ego but not his family. His capacity to support this family comfortably was always Southard's animating concern. He was throughout his life obsessed with the achievement of financial security, a goal that he found always just beyond his grasp. "I am, and always have been poor, and must look to my daily exertions for the support of my family," he had told Lucius Elmer as he prepared his move back to New Jersey in late 1828. Two years later, having established a lucrative private law practice in conjunction with his work as the state's attorney general, Southard would remind Henry Clay that "I am poor and my family are very helpless and dependent."[1]

This refrain did not change at any point in Southard's life. He made a good deal of money during the last decade of his life, and he lived well—yet he always remained only one step ahead of the bill collector and the bank loan officer. The circumstances in which he found himself were not necessarily attributable to profligacy, nor were they unusual. Daniel Webster, for example, who earned roughly $15,000 to $20,000 a year in the 1830s, a munificent income for the day, and roughly double Samuel Southard's earnings for most of these years, was often pressed as hard financially as Southard. Both men, and many others like them, had problems living within their means, however substantial those means appeared to less fortunate contemporaries.[2]

As a public man, a much-respected attorney, and a civic leader, Samuel Southard believed that he had to live in keeping with his position in society. Hence, he owned a fine house in Trenton's most fashionable district, supported a bevy of house servants, built an impressive library, and maintained a well-stocked wine cellar, good horses, and a carriage for his family. He did not stint on luxuries at home, medical treatment for his wife, education for his children, or vacations for all of the Southards. The cost of such a life-style was remarkably low by twentieth-century standards, but it was not to be brushed off. Southard wanted the best for himself, his wife, and his children, got the best—and was forced, as a consequence, to follow a punishing schedule in order to pay the bills that streamed into his house.

Income from his flourishing legal practice above and beyond what was needed for daily expenses was devoted to an array of enterprises that, Southard hoped, might make him rich. He purchased properties in New York State, Florida, Virginia, Illinois, Wisconsin, Missouri, and Arkansas. He joined his brother Isaac, among other northern New Jersey investors, in a railroad venture from Elizabethtown to Somerville. And in what from hindsight he would surely have recognized as a great error, he teamed up, beginning in the fall of 1835, with a speculator *extraordinaire* from Hoboken, Robert Swartwout, in various ambitious and ultimately abortive investment schemes.[3]

Southard's relations with Swartwout are significant not merely for what they tell us about his mind-set in the mid-1830s, but also because one of the projects he planned with the Hoboken adventurer ultimately led Southard to accept the presidency of a major New Jersey corporation, the Morris Canal and Banking Company. As best the story can be sorted out, Southard in the summer of 1836 was particularly pressed financially. Despite the fact that his law practice yielded a healthy income, he was unable easily to raise $250 for his share of the Elizabethtown and Somerville Railroad stock. Nor could he find the capital to join New York Senator Nathaniel P. Tallmadge in some land speculations near Trenton, though he knew a number of good properties to buy "if I had it."[4]

It was in this context that Robert Swartwout approached Southard in September 1836 about joining in a major land speculation in the Bergen County Meadowlands. With a minimum of investment, Swartwout told Southard, a "splendid fortune" could be realized—something on the order of $100,000 to $200,000 profit for Southard alone within a very few years.[5] What did Swartwout have in mind? He contemplated nothing less than the purchase and drainage of some 30,000 acres of marshland that could be divided up into parcels and sold at great profit. Further, Swartwout planned that he and his colleagues in the venture (Southard and New York attorney David B. Ogden) could use some of the land to farm themselves, and some to establish "a mercantile commission House which would have the capacity to do a great and better business than any one now on this continent."[6]

Given the intractability of the marshlands in question, Swartwout's proposal was preposterous, but he was a smooth talker, and Southard liked the sound of the numbers mentioned. He agreed to speak again with Swartwout after the election campaign. By late October, the Meadowlands project was still brewing, though primarily in Robert Swartwout's imagination. He promised Southard that, if the state legislature gave them the charter they needed, "your fortunes are made." A stream of letters passed between the two men, with Southard receiving the bulk of the correspondence. Swartwout always had a new idea, a new angle, and more ambitious expectations for their venture. Unfortunately, the legislature was not willing to consider the Meadowlands proposal in its first sitting in autumn 1836, and Southard grew "gloomy" about his economic prospects generally.[7]

For his part, Swartwout continued to scheme. While the Meadowlands project lay fallow, he broached another, equally ambitious project to his friend. Why not lease the Delaware and Raritan Canal from the Joint

Companies, which had, from the outset of their operations, lavished attention primarily on the railroad, which promised quicker and larger profit to the company's stockholders. Given that New Yorkers were eager for the heavy goods, such as coal, that Pennsylvania had in such abundance, could not the canal be operated in such a fashion as to capitalize on its peculiar geographical and physical advantages? Swartwout thought it could, and convinced Southard that this was a matter worth pursuing.[8]

Late in January 1837, with Robert Swartwout's encouragement, Southard pursued the idea of a leasing arrangement with one of the officers of the Joint Companies, James S. Green. He said that a consortium of investors, including himself and Swartwout, believed that both the Joint Companies and they could profit by a lease of all the operations of the Delaware and Raritan Canal, preferably for a term of fifteen to twenty-five years. Green responded confidentially on January 30, expressing the company's interest in such an arrangement. "The great and profitable works just now are the railroads," he noted, "the immense and complicated interests of which require and command nearly all the time of the executive committee." Southard's suggested arrangement, while not perfect from the companies' perspective (the length of the lease would be a point of negotiation), presented "flattering inducements" for all concerned.[9] Green's encouraging words set Southard to work, seeking financial backing for the plan and hammering out the details of the lease with the Joint Companies. In Southard's design, he would assume the directorship of the company, and, if prospects looked promising, resign his seat in the Senate. His motives for engaging in a project of such magnitude were not complicated: he was tired of the daily grind of travel, of having to badger clients to pay their fees, and of living from day to day in terms of cash on hand. "I will not deny that I should be glad to find employment more pleasant and profitable than that in which I am now suffering," he told Robert Swartwout. "As so would you—& why may we not?"[10]

Southard's quest for more "pleasant and profitable" employment was not realized in the Delaware and Raritan Canal project, despite the most serious negotiations with the highest authorities of the Joint Companies. The plan foundered, in the end, on the Southard-Swartwout consortium's inability to raise the capital that Joint Companies' President Robert F. Stockton wanted raised before the consummation of any deal. Efforts to secure the backing of Nicholas Biddle's United States Bank were unavailing.[11] In truth, the financial crunch then in progress (the spring of 1837 had witnessed the suspension of specie payments by virtually all Eastern banks, and the deep contraction of credit from England) rendered unfeasible the transformation of Southard's dream into a reality.[12] By early June, despite having signed a tentative leasing agreement with the Joint Companies, Southard recognized that the proposition was dead. "The pressure of the times," he told an acquaintance, had made the arrangement impractical.[13] Of all his joint ventures with Robert Swartwout, this had come closest to realization, but, alas, circumstances undermined even this.

Southard was not left entirely stranded by the collapse of the Delaware and Raritan Canal lease agreement. During the months of negotiations about the canal, the possibility always existed that New Jersey's other major canal might want Southard's services. President Louis McLane of the Morris Canal and Banking Company had by late 1836 concluded to leave his post for the presidency of the Baltimore and Ohio Railroad, one of the nation's leading transportation enterprises.[14] When McLane initially announced his intention to resign in January 1837, Southard was approached about succeeding him.[15] At this point the Delaware and Raritan project was still very much alive, and Southard said he was not interested in working in any administrative capacity for the Morris company. Disappointed, the directors of that company persuaded McLane to remain until the last possible moment so as to ensure an orderly succession.[16] When McLane finally insisted on release from his responsibilities with the Morris Company in early June 1837, Samuel Southard was more receptive to the overtures of the Morris directors. By the second week of June, having been assured that he would not have to resign his Senate seat in order to assume the presidency of the Morris Company, Southard accepted the position.[17] His salary was set at $6,000 per year, the same as McLane's had been, plus expenses and a house for his family in Jersey City, the Morris Company's corporate home (its banking offices were in New York City). The son of an ardent foe of engines of credit had become, *pari passu,* president of a major New York bank.

II

Chartered in 1824 by the New Jersey legislature during a period of great enthusiasm for transportation improvements, the Morris Canal and Banking Company had a checkered early history. The canal was the brainchild of a Morris County man, George McCulloch, who had visions of the economic benefits that the transport of Pennsylvania anthracite would mean for the then depressed economy of north-central New Jersey. Like other corporations, the Morris company sought and gained banking privileges that, it averred, would help engender the capital necessary for construction of the ambitiously conceived project. In fact, the Morris Company was granted liberal privileges. It was permitted not only to borrow and loan money, but also to receive and execute trusts, participate in foreign-exchange markets, engage in bond trading and, in general, perform all services customarily assigned to banks.[18]

Because the Morris Canal was constructed without any direct financial assistance from the state government, its success was heavily dependent on the financial support it received from New York capitalists, many of whom quickly subscribed to its stock and, as Wheaton Lane and others have shown, in its early years nearly drove the company to bankruptcy through less than scrupulous financial operations. Despite the notoriety the company gained with its New York associations ("curses on the Morris" was a common epithet in the early 1830s), and despite the unexpectedly heavy expenses involved in completing construction of the canal, some sections were operable by 1829 and the canal, in skeleton, was completed from Easton to Newark, a distance of 101 miles, by 1832.[19]

The opening of the Morris Canal spurred a boom throughout northern New Jersey. Old forges were revived and new ones constructed along the canal lines, localities along its perimeters, notably Dover, Rockaway, and Boonton, bustled with new business, and capitalists looked appreciatively at its potential as a vehicle for the transport of such goods as coal, ore, hides, and wood bark to Newark and New York City.[20] Unfortunately for the canal company, this boom did not translate readily into company profits. For one thing, the canal cost far more to build—in excess of $3 million— than had originally been anticipated. Further, there were numerous expensive legal suits, initiated by property and mill owners who charged that the company's diversion of waters damaged them. Some of the plaintiffs were small farmers, who requested payment of damages running from a hundred to several thousand dollars. Others were large interests, such as the Society for Useful Manufactures, which in 1829 hired Samuel Southard to litigate against the Morris Company on grounds that threatened the Morris's very existence. Despite Southard's best efforts, as we have seen, the Morris Company fended off SUM's early legal thrusts, though it continued to face litigation, some of which proved costly, from dozens of other plaintiffs. At the same time, the company labored to meet its payments on a $750,000 Dutch loan secured by a mortgage. As of 1835, it had failed to pay its investors a single dividend.[21]

Under the leadership of a new president, Louis McLane, a former secretary of the treasury in Andrew Jackson's cabinet, and Philadelphia capitalists, the company began to improve its financial standing in 1835. Banking operations became the tail that wagged the dog, as the Morris engaged in a number of stock and bond ventures that, in the short run, brought prosperity. During the two years that Louis McLane directed the company's affairs, it moved increasingly within the orbit of Philadelphia finance. Nicholas Biddle and his brother Thomas purchased hundreds of shares of the company's stock at high prices and their cousin, Edward R. Biddle, joined the Morris Company's board of directors in 1836. Meanwhile, the prospects for the canal's profitability improved as traffic increased, and a general air of optimism prevailed. This was underscored by the decision of the directors to pay the company's first dividends in 1836 and 1837, and the completion, in 1837, of an extension from Newark to Jersey City.[22] At the same time, President McLane negotiated a lease agreement with a Pennsylvania corporation, the Little Schuylkill and Susquehanna Railroad, whereby that company would have full access and rights to the canal and its water power, as well as its equipment, for five years at a cost of six percent of "the entire expenditure made and to be made, upon the canal and its appurtenances, and upon the cost of the real estate."[23] This would enable the company to devote the bulk of its attention to its banking and stock-trading operations.

It was in the context of the Morris Company's apparent good health that Samuel Southard was first approached about assuming its leadership. By the time the Delaware and Raritan Canal lease venture had become unfeasible, however, and Southard indicated his availability for the Morris presidency, the economic picture of the company—and the nation—was much less sanguine. Money markets were extremely tight, the nation's banks were operating on a specieless basis, and the Morris was once again finding it difficult to balance its books. Beyond this, the leasing agreement that McLane had engineered with the Pennsylvania railroad company was foundering on the latter's insistence that many expensive repairs along the canal be completed before any deal was consummated.[24]

Exactly what role the leading investors in the Morris Company expected Samuel Southard to play in straightening out their finances and guiding canal operations is uncertain. It is clear that Southard was not expected to oversee the day to day operations of the company, as McLane had, since he was permitted to retain his seat in the United States Senate. Nicholas Biddle's cousin, Edward Biddle, was named to the newly created post of vice-president, at the same salary that Southard received, to perform those duties, and to make policy and chair board meetings in Southard's absence. But if Southard was not sought for his administrative expertise, his work for the company as president and later as council nonetheless proved to be extensive—and taxing.[25]

Southard was president of the Morris Company for nineteen months. During this period he wrestled diligently but unsuccessfully to keep the company solvent in face of hard times and the heavy expenses of the canal operation. Southard devoted the bulk of his energies not to high finance, which, he was the first to concede, was not his forte, but rather to dealing with citizens along the canal route who complained of damages caused by the canal feeders, and also in overseeing the progress of the many canal construction projects. He was, however, regularly consulted concerning the company's financial dealings, including the ultimately disastrous purchase of Indiana and Michigan Bonds in 1838.[26]

During the summer of 1837 Southard was able to devote nearly all of his labors to the affairs of the Morris Company. But political responsibilities came first in the fall. Responding to the depressed economy, President

Martin Van Buren called a special session of Congress for September, in which he would respond to the nation's fiscal plight. Work for the Morris Company kept Southard from his seat on September 4, when the special session convened but he was present to join debate over the president's independent treasury system—a plan through which the "collection, safekeeping, transfer, and disbursement of the public money" would be taken from the hands of private banks and placed in selected government depositories. There they would lay fallow, unavailable to both conservative bankers and freewheeling speculators.[27]

Beyond Van Buren's proposal lay straightforward hard-money Democratic doctrine. According to this analysis, overbanking and overtrading, in part with the benefit of public monies, had caused the depression. Van Buren's formula would put a clamp on speculation and, the president thought, prevent future economic fluctuations of the kind that had produced the panic and depression. In the view of most Jacksonians, the independent-treasury program was a sane and sensible measure for the Democratic party and the nation as a whole. Moreover, it gave the Democrats a rallying point. Van Buren and his backers hoped the independent treasury would bear political fruit in the later years of the decade as Andrew Jackson's attack on the "Monster Bank" had done earlier. This was not to be. For one thing, anti-bankism and the independent treasury were different kinds of policy. Anti-bankism was an essentially negative doctrine that permitted people with differing ideas about the economy to unite against the bank; the independent treasury was a positive program, unattractive—indeed, unpalatable—to the business-oriented. To Whigs it was anathema.[28]

Taking his seat next to Henry Clay, with whom he plotted strategy against the independent-treasury bill, Southard spent most of September handling routine chores, including work on the Naval Affairs Committee—his only assignment that session. Democrats ostensibly controlled the Senate, though because of the party's internal bickering over the independent treasury, it was not entirely clear who would prevail on this transcendent question. Matters were, in fact, in such flux that John C. Calhoun, formerly the *bête noire* of the Democrats, emerged second only to Thomas Hart Benton among the administration's spokesmen in debate.[29]

As Senate proceedings went, the debate during the special session was brisk. By early October, it was apparent that the administration had the votes it needed to carry the independent treasury in the Senate. A hard-money amendment to a treasury-note bill was added to the independent-treasury proposal in late September, and carried by a single vote on October 3, Southard joining his fellow Whigs in opposition. The next day, prior to the final Senate balloting on the independent treasury in 1837, Southard requested and received the floor to address the issue.[30]

Examining the proposed bill in detail, Southard, according to the stenographer's report, "objected to the plan of giving the Secretary [of the Treasury] the power of ordering the public monies to be retained by any officer he pleased, and to pay it out to whomsoever he pleased. It would be a system of favoritism."[31] Southard further charged that the independent treasury would be far more expensive to operate then the government projected. Indeed, there would be no limits to the expense. "Mr. S. contended that, down to this day, such an appropriation had never been made, in all the action of this government. Jefferson would never have sanctioned such a plan." Southard continued in this vein, resurrecting points that resembled those he had made in his speech on the removal of deposits in 1834. The independent treasury, he concluded, "would establish a tremendous system of tyranny."

The words were mostly for home consumption. Within minutes after Southard's concluding remarks the bill carried the Senate 26–20, only to die in the House. The independent treasury, as program and as political football, was, of course, far from dead. For half a decade more the divorce of government and state banks served as the litmus test of party politics in America. It was an issue on which millions of words, including thousands of Samuel Southard's, would be expended.

III

When Congress adjourned on October 16, Southard hurried back to New Jersey to close out his affairs in Trenton, to house-hunt in Jersey City, and to carry out his responsibilities with the Morris Company, which was seeking a way out of the financial quagmire in which it currently was mired. Because of his preoccupation with congressional business and private affairs, Southard played little role in the legislative elections of October 1837—elections that gave the Whigs a majority for the first time in five years. Younger party leaders, including William Pennington, Jr., William L. Dayton, and Jacob Miller, assumed an increasing share of the organizational responsibilities in the election campaign. This development seems to have suited Southard, at least as long as none of them directly challenged his position as the state's leading Whig spokesman, and the preeminent figure in internal party policymaking.[32]

In truth, Southard had more responsibilities in the late 1830s than he could properly manage without injuring his health and undermining his sense of well-being. The number of commitments he made and kept remained remarkable. He was, for example, an active trustee of his alma mater, and of its sister institution, the theological seminary at Princeton. To both institutions Southard gave as much of his time and money as he could spare. He was often on the campus of the college, and served as a frequent speaker at alumni convocations, commencement, and before its literary societies. Had he spoken any more frequently, one is tempted to say, he might well have applied for faculty status! In fact, this was suggested to him in 1835, when he was invited to inaugurate a series of law lectures, an offer he declined because the cost of the lectures would make it impossible for the college to meet the salary demands of a prominent scientist, Joseph Henry, whom Southard feared Princeton might lose.[33] As a testament to the regard in which he was held, Southard was also requested to write the history of the college, a project that he lacked the leisure time to undertake.[34] Less demanding projects, such as service on fund-raising committees and occasional lectures, were more manageable. There is no doubt that Southard cared deeply about Princeton's future and, for that matter, that his alma mater thought well of him.[35]

Aside from his continuing connections in Princeton, Southard was active in a half dozen associations, ranging from seamen's aid societies to temperance, Bible, and colonization organizations. He was a director of several New Jersey corporations, including the Trenton Bank, an investor in numerous speculative enterprises, and an active member, until his move to Jersey City in late 1838, of the Trenton Presbyterian Church. A popular public speaker, Southard could be found, probably more evenings than he wished, addressing audiences interested in one or another of the myriad causes of his day. Beyond this, he was frequently tapped for a few appropriate remarks on special occasions: July 4 celebrations, college commencements, birthdays of departed statesmen, and funerals for notables with whom he had intimate ties.[36] These were unexceptional obligations and in fulfilling them, Southard evidently met the expectations of his listeners: his correspondence is littered with letters praising his forensic efforts. Southard's discourses, taken individually or in sum, were standard fare for his time. To colonizers, he articulated the need to transport the black man from America to the only home where he could live in peace and prosperity—Africa. To Bible societies, Southard spoke of the transcendent importance for human well-being in a conscientious study of the Bible. To temperance audiences, his moral was the evil of strong drink and dissipation. To students, he stressed the necessity of a balanced education grounded in the classics. The phrases he uttered were commonplace, but they were also appropriate to the occasions on which he spoke. Taken together, they offered some insight into Southard's vision for America. He was, quite clearly, no radical. America, in his view, was a good nation, offering much to those who were willing and able to take advantage of its natural bounty. All was possible in a society with "the means of internal wealth and prosperity equal to any portion of the globe," as he had reminded the Newark mechanics in 1830. Improvement was his central theme. Education, transportation advances, and a communications revolution were the central elements for progress, elements he believed would make Americans richer, wiser, and happier. "Reform," from his perspective, was less a matter of eliminating evils, since there were so few evils in American society, than a progressive realization of the potential that American society offered its citizens.[37]

What of poverty in America? Southard's speeches never touched on this subject. Slavery? Slavery was indeed a "curse," but one "fastened upon us before we became a nation." Transcendent political considerations— notably the safety of the Union—precluded any tampering with institutions already established.[38] The plight of the Indian? This Southard acknowledged as a shortcoming in society, one he deeply regretted, but exactly what white Americans owed the aboriginal inhabitants of the nation he did not in any of his orations explain.[39]

The operative themes in these discourses, particularly the July 4 orations, were good Whig themes: the need for morality, the virtues of revealed religion, the benefits of order, the sanctity of republicanism, and the potential of an energetic people in a bounteous land. Not that Southard's Jacksonian peers would have disavowed any of this. It was testimony to the fundamental consensus underlying political controversy in America that Jacksonians embraced "virtually the same definition of the good society," as Rush Welter has observed, that Whigs espoused.[40]

On the stump and in the Senate, Southard and his peers were much more partisan. The basic consensus within American society on the desirability of order, enterprise, and freedom gave way to sharply divergent views about how best to realize these good ends. Men of different political persuasions lay their emphasis differently and developed different themes. For Jacksonians, the notion of "equal rights" was a catchword, while the Whigs tended to emphasize "development" and the partnership of the government with business in building a prosperous America. These differences of emphasis, and the differences in policy that flowed from them, were a function of the need for party men to separate themselves before the voters and offer the electorate a choice. That America would ultimately achieve the same results whether governed by Democrats or Whigs did not much change the politicians' and voters' conviction that it made a difference for whom one voted.[41]

IV

During the late 1830s, in a state such as New Jersey, voters had no difficulty identifying differences between the two major parties. The Democrats emerged as the proponents of the independent treasury and a national policy of restraints on business. The Whigs identified themselves with a much more activist policy based on support for a less confined banking system, a higher tariff to protect American industry, and an infusion of monies into the states to fund internal improvements. At the state level, party men argued about, and in the legislature voted differently on, such matters as the issue of small bank notes, extension of corporate charters and privileges, and the explanation and preferred remedies for the depression that currently plagued New Jersey.[42]

Given that the Democrats held power when the depression broke out, Whigs were the logical political beneficiaries of hard times. In 1837 they replaced the Democrats as the majority in the state legislature, and elected William Pennington, Jr., as governor. For the next six years the issues and personalities remained virtually the same. Whigs and Democrats offered different prescriptions regarding the economy, the Whigs continued to carry the state, and the Whig-dominated legislature annually reelected Governor Pennington. Samuel Southard also was a direct beneficiary of the Whig success at the polls. In November 1838, he regained an easy reelection to the Senate over Mahlon Dickerson in a joint-meeting balloting.[43]

It was fortunate that the Whigs were so firmly united in opposition to the Van Buren administration's economic positions, because increasingly they were split internally on both personal and programmatic matters. Two wings of the party emerged by 1837, for example, on the question of dealing with the depression. One, centered in the eastern part of the state, advocated a relief program based on a new Bank of the United States; another, strongest in the West, favored a do-nothing policy that let events take their course and put the Jacksonians in position to take the blame for hard times. New Jersey Whigs divided further on the man who would carry the party's banner nationally in 1840. Most eastern Whigs supported Henry Clay while sentiment was strong in the West that Clay could not win. Further, there were personal conflicts within the party. Old allies of Samuel Southard were convinced that a "Pennington cabal," as one of them put it, was attempting to take over the state party and monopolize patronage within its own ranks. For his part, Southard remained formally friendly with the governor, but there was no intimacy, no real bond outside of what politics demanded, between them.[44] None of these cracks in Whig unity undermined the party's prospects during a severe depression.

Political expediency combined with agreement on campaign strategy proved sufficient cement for the New Jersey Whig party in the late 1830s. Southard supporters and Pennington men joined together to outspend, outorganize, and outpropagandize the Democrats in 1837, 1838, and 1839. During the latter two years, Southard found the time to speak in dozens of villages and towns and to organize a campaign fund that directed monies where they were especially needed.[45] He was particularly active and spent a good deal of his money in 1838, when his Senate seat was on the line. Indeed, he spent more than he wished, though not a cent more, in his judgment, than was necessary. Writing to a campaign contributor following the legislative elections, Southard observed that the money expended by the party "secured the victory & saved the whole state to our cause. I assure you, every part of it, told, in the result." In that same letter Southard told his correspondent, Dudley Selden, that though he had spent "very far more than my means & ability justified," he had no choice. He had "received calls from every part of the state," and simply could not say no.[46]

V

It was well for Samuel Southard that the Whigs prospered politically in the late 1830s, because his private life during this period could hardly have been more wearing. The Morris Company, instead of offering him a safe haven and handsome recompense, proved to be a constant headache. Southard was dealing with men whose whole lives revolved around financial manipulations and who did not blink at illegal or unethical measures if such would bring them the economic rewards they sought. Southard's colleagues at the Morris Company, moreover, were speculating in a market that they could not control. Ultimately they would reap no profit or glory from their enterprise—only bankruptcy, legal problems, and notoriety.[47]

Just how much Southard knew about the unsavory activities of his associates and how deeply he was involved with them in their investments and hypothecations are not clear. He was regularly consulted about fiscal matters regarding the Morris, of course. But often, it seemed, he was told what the company directors wanted him to hear—frequently a sanitized version of their operations while he was away. In any case, the vagaries of the times had brought to bear great pressures on the Morris, and Samuel Southard spent long hours trying to keep his company afloat. By late 1838, he concluded that he simply could no longer handle the responsibilities as president of the Morris while serving his constituents in the United States Senate. He decided to relinquish the presidency of the company, and contemplated divorcing himself from it completely. As his son Samuel explained to his other son, Henry, Southard "could not discharge all the duties that were pressing upon him, and if he could he did not wish to have the responsibility."[48]

Given, however, that the Morris Company desperately needed financial assistance from the state to sustain its debt-plagued operations, if only indirectly through an increase of its banking capital, the directors of the Morris Company urged Southard to remain where he was. They knew they needed "respectable" influence in Trenton to press their various applications, and Southard was the most respectable man associated with the company. Southard, for his part, assured the Morris Company's leading men that he supported and would do what he could on behalf of their applications, but also insisted on leaving the presidency. An arrangement was then concluded wherein he would be relieved of that burden while continuing his legal chores. For this he would receive a salary of $4,000 per year, with expense and living allowances.[49]

Such an arrangement satisfied Southard. He could leave financial operations in the hands of those who understood them better than he, and could devote more attention to his Senate work, his party responsibilities, and his arguments before the United States Supreme Court.[50] One of the directors of the Morris Company, a leading Whig politician from Paterson, Andrew Parsons, observed that the new arrangement would "please" the state's Whigs and "be to our advantage as a party." Southard's son Samuel echoed this sentiment, adding that his father could now spend more time on matters that would magnify his public reputation. It would also, though Sam, Jr., did not mention it, leave Southard with more time for his family.[51]

In truth, however, Southard found no greater satisfaction in his new circumstances. Even after leaving the Morris Company presidency, he had little time free to enjoy the delights of home and hearth on which Jacksonian society placed such great emphasis. Keeping his head above water financially was a continuing struggle. Demands on his time by his party, his clients, and his associational colleagues did not lessen. There was too much to do and too little time in which to do it.

Had Southard enjoyed a happy marriage, much of this might have been more manageable and less vexing to him. Alas, he did not. "This is the country, above all others," Boston's William Sullivan had observed in 1832, "in which pleasures . . . are to be found in domestic life. *There is no place like home,* and in this happy land, one may have the delights of home, if he be worthy of them."[52] Had he ever come across this statement, Southard would probably have offered a painful smile. "What fantasy!" he might think. The reality was that Southard, a decent human being, certainly "worthy" of the "delights of home," could not, amidst the toil and competition of the business and political world, find relief in domestic life.

The marriage of Samuel and Rebecca Southard was a study in the wearing down of one partner by the incessant complaints, demands, and psychosomatic illnesses of the other. Their marriage had been founded on affection, and there is evidence that this affection remained strong in the first two decades of Southard's life with Rebecca. He was a remarkably patient husband and an attentive, caring parent to his children. Despite frequent absences from home, Southard played an essential role in the socialization and education of his children, instilling in them habits and values that he believed would be essential to their well-being in a changing world.

Southard was not simply a stern disciplinarian or a didactic father figure.[53] He played with his children, bought them treats when he was absent from home, and listened attentively to their complaints. Beyond this, he sent all of his children to the best tutors, boarding schools, and, in the case of the boys, who attended the College of New Jersey, to the best college that he could afford.[54] His love for his children was manifest in virtually everything he did, and this love was fully returned. Indeed, the affection between father and children only deepened as the years passed, they reached adulthood, and pursued independent lives. When Southard told his son Henry in 1837 that "I live for my family more than myself," he was speaking the simple truth.[55]

Southard's relations with his children were as good as any father might wish. His offspring lavished affection on him, confided in him when they experienced personal problems, and looked always to advance his public reputation. For his part, Southard took pride in his son Henry's budding career as an engineer, and Samuel's legal studies. He was delighted when in November 1838 his daughter Virginia married a prominent New York attorney and Whig Congressman, Ogden Hoffman. By late 1839 Southard was a grandfather, and loved to dote on his namesake, Southard Hoffman, who, in 1840, was joined by a sister, Susanna. The Southard children had grown up and pursued lives that truly gratified their father, and he never failed to let them know this or to give every assistance to them that he could.[56]

If his children brought him happiness, life with his wife did not. During the 1830s Southard's relations with Rebecca were often stormy and, as time passed, increasingly distant. Though it is impossible to grasp the dynamics of their relationship fully, it does seem fair to lay most of the problems within the Southard household to the emotional instability of Rebecca Southard. This instability, evidenced in constant complaints about every conceivable physical ailment, in bad relations with relatives and servants, in demands that Southard remain more frequently at home, grew more pronounced and disconcerting with the years.[57]

During the years that Southard lived in Washington, evidence suggests that the family took Rebecca's complaints in stride. Given that she was frequently pregnant and that she watched three children succumb to illness within a three-year span, her temperamental outbursts and frequent bouts of depression were understandable and dealt with sympathetically. Once the family moved to Trenton, Rebecca's behavior is somewhat more difficult to explain, except in terms of mental illness. During the 1830s, it was a rare family letter that did not refer to her physical afflictions or personal complaints. "Mrs. Southard is as well as usual," was about the best that Southard and other family members could usually tell outsiders. Within the family there was a conspiracy of silence about "mother's" condition, based primarily on an understandable confusion about the cause of Rebecca's behavior.[58]

To lift his wife's spirits and alleviate her physical plaints, Southard resorted to virtually every available tactic. New doctors, vacations to the seashore, to Warm Springs, to family in Fredericksburg, exotic medical treatments—all were tried on many occasions. None eased Rebecca's ailments or her unhappiness. She became increasingly demanding and shrewish and by the time her children reached maturity, they were less and less willing to be patient or understanding. Their sympathies quite clearly lay with their long-suffering father, and it is interesting to see in family correspondence the children's insistence that he take a less sympathetic approach in dealing with Rebecca. "If you did [this], none would blame you," Sam, Jr., told his father. "You must be decided, perhaps severe—or you can do nothing."[59] For his part, Southard continued to attempt to make up to his wife, though increasingly their relations were estranged. In a remarkable letter to his wife written as they approached their twenty-fifth wedding anniversary, in 1837, Southard told Rebecca that he was, at long last, unwilling to jump at her every command. She could do as she pleased, but should expect no further sustenance, at least emotionally, from him. "My sufferings," he wrote,

> have been sufficient for any error. I have often been afflicted with disease from no cause but this. I have more than once been on the very brink of insanity & suicide. My children restrained me from the latter. I will hereafter by silence to suffer less—and do as you choose you shall find rebuke not from me, but only in the consequences. I think I shall meet insanity or suicide before I am forced again to open my lips in complaint. You have obtained your triumph. I fear it will prove equally a triumph over your own & your children's happiness as over the feelings of your husband.[60]

These were the words not of an ingrate or a husband impatient with some inconvenience. They were an expression of pain, a climax of more than a decade of tribulation. They were the words of a devoted family man who found the core of his family relations—his marriage—devoid of peace and satisfaction.

Divorce, of course, was out of the question. Southard never complained to acquaintances about his wife, and never completely broke away from her. Instead, as the years passed, he spent increasing amounts of time away from home, deriving what private pleasures he could in life from the activities of his children, and to some degree, from the delights of the dinner table.[61] His love for books and quest for repose would have to be shelved, by and large. Quiet evenings at home were a rarity. Always there was a speech to give, a meeting to attend, a legal brief to compose, a business opportunity to pursue, a political engagement to fulfill. Such was his life. To be constantly burdened with public, vocational, and associational responsibilities was one thing; finding such activity one's only relief from domestic misery was something else. Samuel Southard, a goodhearted man, found himself often in low spirits. Nor did his last years materially improve his circumstances or his disposition.

9

"I Cannot Bear My Present State"

Samuel Southard's last years were an ordeal. His legal labors for the Morris Company remained burdensome but not particularly remunerative. His speculations were failures. His efforts to secure payment of fees owed him for legal services as well as past debts were often unavailing. Yet expenses continued to press him heavily. Moreover, home life increased his malaise, and even the happy marriage of his daughter Virginia and the birth of two healthy grandchildren did little to relieve his increasingly testy relations with his wife.

Politics, too, contributed to Southard's travail. Despite the continued dominance of the Whig party in New Jersey in the early 1840s and the national party's decisive triumph in the elections of 1840, Southard gained little. He was incessantly importuned on patronage matters he could not control, and increasingly distant from the inner workings of his party in New Jersey. Moreover, relations with Southard's old comrade, Henry Clay, soured dramatically in late 1839, and Southard found himself quite deliberately bypassed when a new Whig administration was formed during the winter of 1840–41. President pro tem of the United States Senate during the first years of Whig ascendancy, Southard emerged not as a policymaker but, rather, a bystander. By the winter of 1841–42 Southard was a dying man, and his final months of life offered no alleviation for the private hurts and financial obligations that weighed on him. His death, in some significant respects, proved to be a release.

I

Whatever the travails of his private life, Samuel Southard as a Whig leader could, as the presidential election year of 1840 approached, take some pleasure in the prospects of a party resurgence nationally, and the replacement of a Democratic administration after a twelve-year hiatus. The panic of 1837, which presaged a deep depression, virtually ensured the success of Whiggery in the party's bid to oust President Van Buren. All agreed that the Whigs had never been so well situated to capture the White

House. Beginning in the summer of 1837, talk among party loyalists was constant and often excited about the most "available" nominee to contest Van Buren's reelection. In New Jersey opinion was, in early discussion, fairly equally divided between those who backed Henry Clay (who clearly wanted the nomination very badly) and those who supported the state's successful candidate in 1836, General William Henry Harrison.[1]

This division of opinion tended to reflect a regional bias. Southard's North Jersey friends were staunch Clay men who were confident that Southard agreed with their views and who regularly urged him to organize on Clay's behalf. John J. Chetwood of Elizabethtown, for example, was convinced that Henry Clay was the choice of "nineteen-twentieths of the party" and believed that efforts to nominate a different candidate "will be an entire failure." One Clay adherent, Thomas Alexander, believed that Clay's nomination was a foregone conclusion. "The one who should predict his [Clay's] triumphant election will hardly be entitled to the epithet of Prophet," he told Southard early in 1838. The real "agitation," Alexander thought, should be focused on the vice-presidency. Was not New Jersey, after all, "*entitled* to that honor"? On this he would get no argument from Samuel Southard.[2]

The Clay bandwagon, however, was much less fervent in western New Jersey. Whigs there could acquiesce in a Clay nomination, as they had in 1832, but were not particularly enthusiastic about a slaveholder as national standard bearer. Other Whigs, such as William P. Sherman of Trenton and Newton *Sussex Register* editor John Hall, thought that expediency must be paramount. Clay was a loser. As Hall bluntly observed in the autumn of 1838, Clay's

> unsuccessful collisions with Gen. Jackson engendered prejudices against him in the public mind which are still deeply rooted, and need but the formal presentation of his name in connection with the Chief Magistracy, to burst forth in all their original intensity.

Such observations, Hall added, were made out of no disrespect for Clay, for whom he had the greatest admiration. Pragmatism, rather, dictated his position. Clay would never be able to carry Pennsylvania or Ohio, and hence was a certain also-ran. A stronger candidate, possibly General Harrison, had to be named.[3]

Hall's refrain was a common one in 1838 and helped discourage efforts by Clay's supporters to press for a legislative resolution endorsing Harry of the West for the presidency. Even a triumphal progress that Clay made with Southard through the western counties in the spring of 1838, calculated to counter talk that Clay was "unavailable," could not break through many Whigs' reluctance to back a potential loser.[4] Aware of the climate of feeling among the state's Whigs, Southard opposed any public nomination of his friend by the legislature, calling such a move "premature." This was a reasonable position, indeed a practical one, given that Clay men lacked the votes to have their way, but it ultimately contributed to a wrenching break between Southard and the Whigs' greatest leader.[5]

Despite their failure in 1838 to gain an endorsement for Clay, and the breakdown of efforts to call a state convention in 1839 to nominate him formally, Clay's backers remained confident that at the national conclave in Harrisburg, Harry of the West would have the backing of New Jersey. They were wrong. Although a majority of New Jersey's eight-man delegation expressed public commitments to Clay, at the convention in December several members of the delegation shifted their stance and delivered the state's votes, through the unit rule, to dark-horse candidate Winfield Scott.[6] Southard's brother, Isaac, a Clay hold-out, had argued, "If we cannot succeed with [Clay], . . . we cannot succeed at all," but his protests were unavailing.[7] Ultimately the convention turned, not to Scott, but to General Harrison, and the New Jersey delegates fell readily into line. Even such a devoted, longtime Clay backer as Rahway's Adam Lee conceded to Samuel Southard, shortly after the results of the Harrisburg convention were known, that "our friends say in West Jersey Harrison has the most friends & that he will carry a large vote in the Quaker Countys [sic]." Even Isaac Southard, a Clay adherent to the bitter end, excitedly reported on December 17 that a Somerset County Whig meeting, called in response to the Harrisburg proceedings, had been a perfect success. "The best feeling prevailed. . . . The battle cry was raised 'Harrison and our Country.'"[8]

Henry Clay's friends in New Jersey could readily accept a Harrison nomination. Harry of the West himself, however, did not lightly take defeat in this most propitious of all election years. In his room at Brown's hotel in Washington when the news of Harrison's nomination arrived, Clay cursed his fate. "My friends are not worth the powder and shot it would take to kill them!" he allegedly shouted, adding:

> It is a diabolical intrigue . . . which has betrayed me. I am the most unfortunate man in the history of parties, always run by my friends when sure to be defeated, and now betrayed for the nomination when I, or anyone, would be sure of an election.[9]

Though Clay composed himself within a matter of days and assured his friends that he would support the Whig ticket enthusiastically in 1840, his bitterness ran deep. Much of his anger was directed at Thurlow Weed, the New York kingmaker who had initiated the boomlet for Winfield Scott, and also at such New Yorkers as Charles King and James A. Hamilton, who, in the balloting in Harrisburg, reneged on their commitments to Clay.[10]

Clay's conviction that sabotage had thwarted his nomination led him to attack even those innocent of any malevolent designs—notably Samuel Southard. Convinced that Southard was behind the New Jersey delegation's vote for Scott, Clay petulantly and unjustly took his wrath out on his old friend. When the two men arrived in Washington in late 1839 for the beginning of a new session of Congress, Clay, according to one witness, "abused" Southard "shamefully." Southard's honest denial that he had anything to do with the New Jersey delegation's support for Scott was abruptly dismissed, and Southard, for the next two years, was relegated, as far as Clay was concerned, to the status of outcast.[11]

Samuel Southard's unhappy confrontation with Henry Clay was surely one of the most humiliating experiences of his life. He had worked with and for Clay for more than a decade, promoting him privately and publicly as the great hope of the republic. His intimacy with Clay was a badge of honor to him. All this now lay in ruins. Humiliated by his interchange with Clay, ostracized from the inner circle of Clay's cohorts, Southard was forced to nurse his hurt in private and hope that time would heal his wound.

Publicly, Southard uttered not a word of reproach to Clay. Whig unity in 1840 was of paramount importance, and beyond this, there was always the possibility that Clay might see the truth and apologize to him. Clay, in fact, ultimately did something of the sort, but not for nearly two years, by which time Southard was gravely ill and no longer active in the political struggles of his time.[12]

II

Prepared to work to the utmost of his strength on behalf of General Harrison's bid for the White House, Samuel Southard in the early months of 1840 was active also on a variety of other fronts. There was, for example, the matter of a family home in Jersey City. When Southard assumed the presidency of the Morris Company in 1837, he had been required to move his family from Trenton to Jersey City, with the company assuming the cost of the move and the rent for a home there.

Jersey City was at this time a bustling and fast-growing community of about 2,500. The initiation of evening ferry service across the Hudson in 1834 had vastly stimulated the prospects of the New Jersey community, since it was now possible for a businessman to live in New Jersey and commute daily into New York with a minimum of trouble. The city's rapid population growth transformed it from a backwater into a bustling metropolis with a wide range of civic associations and recreation opportunities, as well as a thriving business district. It became, in brief, a desirable place to live.[13]

Unfortunately for the Southards, the growth of Jersey City made housing a scarce commodity, despite the best efforts of local builders. Failing in 1837 and again in 1838 to obtain a suitable lease on a home, Southard took up residence above the Morris Company's central office in Jersey City. Shortly after his family moved in, a hurricane destroyed the structure, and the Southards were forced across the river to a New York hotel until another Jersey City dwelling could be found. After some effort, Southard was able in late 1839 to conclude an agreement with the mayor of Jersey City, D. S. Gregory, for a home that Gregory would build to his specifications and lease at a rate of $500 a year. The house was completed by May 1840, and the Southards were finally able to settle down.[14]

During the months that his home and office were being constructed in Jersey City, Southard boarded in Washington, leaving his wife and son Samuel in New York. Mrs. Southard continued to complain of various ailments and imaginary slights committed by her husband and children and in general made herself entirely disagreeable to everyone.[15] (Virginia Hoffman and her husband, Ogden, lived in the same New York hotel—the Astor House—for much of this period.) Then, in the spring of 1840, Mrs. Southard was struck with a severe case of erysipelas, an excruciatingly painful and seriously disfiguring disease that caused intense inflammation and considerable swelling of her neck, ears, and face. There seemed, alas, to be no end to her suffering.[16]

It may well be that, given the upsets of life in the North, Southard was relieved to be in Washington, doing the public's business. During the long session of Congress that ran from December 1839 through July 1840, both parties jockeyed for post position for the forthcoming presidential contest. Despite the continued attacks and parliamentary maneuvers by Whigs, the Democrats were able finally to assert control of the Congress and pass the independent treasury bill that Martin Van Buren triumphantly signed on July 4, 1840, in what was probably the Democrats' last hurrah of that election year.[17] In the debate on this hoary issue, Southard was quiet. His silence may have been a product of preoccupation with other matters, or with the conviction that enough was enough, that he could eschew yet another speech on the independent treasury. Beyond this, Southard was aggrieved that Senate reporters never paid him enough attention when he rose on the floor, and hence garbled his speeches when they did not simply ignore them. In a sharp letter to *National Intelligencer* editor William W. Seaton early in the session, Southard made a strange promise to his old friend. Believing that Seaton's reporters had been derelict, at least so far as he was concerned, Southard said he would offer no further formal comments on the Senate floor "unless I feel assured of fair play." He was, he insisted, "too old to make speeches & let others build theirs on mine & acquire reputation thereby—while I lose."[18] Although Southard may well have thought better of this approach, and not sent the letter, it nonetheless reveals something about his vanity, and perhaps also how he sublimated some of his other frustrations. (He had, after all, only recently endured the surprise and unwarranted attack on his character by Henry Clay.) Service in the Senate did not always mean fame—a painful reality for a man such as Southard, who hungered for public recognition.

Southard did, in fact, abstain during the Twenty-sixth Congress from making any sustained presentations. He participated in debates on the assumption of state debts by the federal government, bankruptcy legislation, stay laws for banks, and military appropriations, but most of his efforts were routine.[19] Southard's major energies during the session were devoted much less to party legislation, or even work on the Naval Affairs Committee, than on routing a private land bill through the Congress in face of the strong opposition of Thomas Hart Benton.

As early as 1837 Southard had become an investor in a major speculation that encompassed a huge tract of land in Missouri and Arkansas. The Clamorgan Grant, as this land was known, was originally established by the Spanish government in 1796 and surveyed a decade later. The tract contained roughly 536,000 acres, much of it reputed to be prime land. Title to the Clamorgan Grant was claimed by a Missouri fur magnate, Pierre Chouteau, who, in February 1837, sold his rights to it for $53,699 to a syndicate that included Samuel Southard, Daniel Webster, Virgil Maxcy, several New York capitalists, former Washington Mayor William A. Bradley, and New Jersey entrepreneur Roswell L. Colt.[20]

Southard had been lured into the syndicate at precisely the moment he assumed the presidency of the Morris Company, in June 1837. His motive for joining it was similar to that of his other investments—the lure of easy wealth. The Clamorgan tract was sure, he was told, to be profitable. As one of the syndicate leaders, C. M. Thruston, remarked, the movement of the day was westward, and good land in Missouri and Arkansas would, in no time, become very dear. Their associate William Bradley told Southard bluntly that "if you do not realize a competency from that affair [Clamorgan] it will be your own fault. You can if you will."[21]

The major obstacle to the realization of a "competency" and, better than that, riches was the matter of the land title. Webster, Thomas Ewing, Abel P. Upshur, and Southard all delivered legal opinions in 1837 testifying to the validity of the Clamorgan title.[22] Senator Benton, however, the champion of western squatters, was not so readily convinced. Benton did his best in the Senate to block or, failing that, delay the passage of a bill that would enable the Clamorgan syndicate to pursue their claims in federal courts. If the syndicate's bill passed, squatters could be sued, and presumably fewer of them would attempt to stake claims to Clamorgan lands.[23]

The Clamorgan associates put great reliance on Southard to shepherd their bill through the Senate, a responsibility that Southard preferred to pass to Benton's Missouri colleague, Lewis Linn.[24] Although the *Congressional Globe* does not reveal much of the manner in which the bill moved through the Senate, it is clear that Southard played an important behind-the-scenes role in securing its passage in April 1840 over Benton's continued objections and amendments.[25]

Once the Clamorgan bill passed Congress, of course, its investors would still need to find buyers for the land, and much of Southard's time, in the remaining two years of his life, would be devoted to this task. His salesmanship, however, brought little but frustration in this, as in every other speculation in which he ever engaged. Indeed, at the time of his death Southard's accounts indicated that for all the hours he had devoted to the Clamorgan speculation—probably well into the hundreds—he was in debt some $750.[26]

III

At the same time that Southard pressed for passage of the Clamorgan legislation in the Congress, his associates at the Morris Canal and Banking Company were desperately maneuvering to gain the New Jersey legislature's assent to an ambitious plan that conceivably could pull the troubled company from the financial straits in which it was then foundering.[27] For three years the Morris Company had sought legislative aid, with no success, despite intense lobbying efforts. Bills were introduced in 1838, 1839, and again early in 1840, variously seeking a vast increase in banking capital; an agency in London to facilitate the sale of Morris stock; a $10-million loan; authority to enlarge the canal to increase its coal-carrying potential; and the right to sell water power.[28]

There were good arguments on behalf of each of these requests. The canal's success *was* important to the prosperity of the state. The company *had* incurred enormous expenses in the construction and upkeep of its canal and feeders. It had already done much to revitalize the economy of the northern counties without a cent of government support. Given these realities and the Whiggish complexion of the legislature, the company might well have expected to gain a sympathetic hearing in Trenton. This was not the case, however. Citizens from the counties through which the canal ran—notably Sussex, Warren, and Morris—were by and large hostile to the canal because they viewed the canal company as a threat to their way of life and a "souless" and greedy corporate giant that refused to deal fairly with individuals in its path.[29] According to one critic, the Morris Company directors had "shown no disposition to accommodate their operations to the interests or convenience of any individual with whom a conflict has arisen." Indeed, he accurately reported,

> the spirit of the people along the whole line of the canal so far as I am acquainted with it is adverse to any enlargement of their powers and

must remain so until they have learned to be more circumspect and discreet in the use of the powers already exercised by them. Their rule has been to take what they could and only pay when they could no longer avoid it.[30]

Because such sentiments were widespread, none of the rationalizations offered by Morris Company lobbyists, none of their pleas and, for that matter, none of their political threats could persuade a majority of legislators that the state should commit itself to the financial well-being of the Morris Company.[31]

This state of affairs vexed Southard for several reasons. He was, first, in 1840 still closely identified publicly with the canal and its operations, and remained the company's chief advocate in its major damage suits.[32] Further, Southard had a financial state in the success of the legislative applications. In 1838 the Morris Company Directors offered him a $1,500 bonus if the company gained the banking privileges it sought, an offer that was sweetened to $2,500 in 1839.[33] Third, Southard recognized that the public's identification of him with the Morris Company, and the Morris Company with Whig interests, was doing his party no good anywhere in the state, and that the political fallout from the 1840 application was potentially dangerous to the party's chances of electing William Henry Harrison and a Whig senator that year.

As a consequence, Southard tried his best to aid the company, but without too open or forceful exertions. In 1838, believing that the company could not persuade a majority of legislators to grant its request, he counseled delay, on the ground that "it is always best to err on the safe side, if there must be error."[34] In 1839 he had written letters on behalf of the company's application to show wavering legislators, but, despite intense pressures placed on him, he declined to lobby directly in Trenton.[35] In 1840, Southard finessed the issue by citing the press of Senate business.[36]

That his absence from Trenton in 1840 when the Morris application was aired and quickly rebuffed was crucial is doubtful. The public's antagonism toward the company was far too widespread and intense for northern county legislators to oppose. What is clearer is the consequence of the company's failure to gain any state support for its enterprises. Although publicly the company's president, E. R. Biddle, talked in optimistic tones, the truth was that the Morris Company was heading into bankruptcy and receivership.[37] The state's unwillingness to rescue it simply served as the final nail in the Morris Company's coffin[38]

Whatever the merits of the case for the Morris Company, it did become a political issue in 1840. Southard, for example, found to his chagrin that during the election campaign he was identified as the "leading man" of the Morris Company—a simple fantasy—and that, if the Whigs were elected, he would "palm off" the canal, and all of its debts, onto the state. Inaccu-

rate though such comments might be, they were common fodder for
Democratic candidates in the northern counties and forced Southard on
the defensive.[39]

Southard's connections with the Morris Company in 1840, then, proved
politically awkward for him. At times the relation was more than awkward—it was acutely embarrassing. The company's directors, for example,
did not candidly explain to him the extent of their financial troubles, and
encouraged him early in 1840 to persuade the New Jersey state treasurer
(who happened to be his brother Isaac) to accept promises from the company that it would pay its taxes tardily, but pay them nonetheless. Isaac
Southard agreed to bend his accounts to accommodate this request, but by
the early summer of 1840 realized that he had been misled. The company
did not pay, and admitted to him that it could not pay, whereupon the
brothers Southard were left to explain why accounts had not been properly
kept. Isaac Southard was forced to endure Democratic taunts that he was a
"lackey" of the Morris Company, and he was required to sue the company
to recover the $5,000 that it owed the state.[40] For his part, Samuel Southard
could only promise that, if the company failed to pay, he would borrow the
requisite funds to pay the tax.[41] He could hardly have been more angry at
the company for its doubledealing. All told, the Morris Canal connection
was proving to be a major albatross around his neck.

IV

Much as he feared the impact of the Morris Company's problems on
Whig fortunes in 1840, Southard refused to permit this to dampen his
enthusiasm for the cause of "Harrison and Our Country." Throughout
the year Southard was deeply involved in all facets of the Whig campaign. He kept up with many correspondents about the state of party
finances and organization, addressed scores of Whig rallies, and penned
anonymous essays for the press. As early as February 1840, Whig editor
William Sherman urged Southard to write an article about the government's employment of bloodhounds to round up Seminole Indians in
Florida—a current political controversy in Congress—which Sherman
thought could be circulated with good effect among Quaker voters. This,
Sherman said, would take the voters' minds off Democratic charges that
Harrison was "a coward, dotard, vagabond or if you please, lousy."[42] In
April, Assembly Speaker Lewis Condict told Southard that prospects for a
Whig triumph in the fall were excellent. "There never was a better spirit,
nor better symptoms of perfect union & harmony than now exist." As
evidence for this, Condict pointed to the mass rally of Young Whigs at the
state capital, two-thirds of whom, he estimated, were from western New
Jersey, where "all our former troubles have come. But for the Quaker
controversy," Condict mused, "New Jersey never would have been Jackso-

nian—& with that old sore dried up & healed over, she will never be loco foco."[43]

Encouraged by this and other signs that Whig prospects were bright, Southard traversed the state through the summer and fall, reminding audiences that the independent treasury was tyranny, that Democrats were the party of depression and "Brownsonism" (a reference to the doctrines promulgated by the prominent Democratic pamphleteer Orestes Brownson), and that only the election of General Harrison could save republicanism and return prosperity to the country. He even journeyed to Utica, New York, to attend a massive Whig convention there, where he attacked the subtreasury as "unwarranted" and a "waste" of government dollars. Southard's speech, one Whig partisan claimed, "established his reputation as one of the first orators of the nation."[44] In the hotly contested counties of Cumberland and Salem, Southard's presence was viewed as essential to the Whig cause. The people there, James Wilson told Southard early in September, insisted that the party's leading man had to address them. "The cry of the people down there is Southard—Southard—let us hear Southard— he will tell us the truth—the evil & the remedy."[45] Such pleas were common, and trying to coordinate his legal practice with campaign activities, Southard attended as many rallies as humanly possible. During the campaign, in fact, he spoke in every county except Bergen and Cape May, traveling and orating to the point of exhaustion. Whig audiences cheered and Whig editors praised his performances, which were, in turn, biting and florid. At one Sussex County rally, for example, in late October, a Whig observer recalled that Southard "tore up the pretensions of the administration to 'democracy' root and branch, and laid bare its incompetency, faithlessness, corruption and extravagence, with a master hand."[46] By contrast, one young Democratic onlooker at a Southard speech in Cumberland County, drawn to the rally by a desire to hear the senator's "famed voice," had a rather different response, doubtless dictated by his partisan leanings. Southard's speech, he recalled in his diary, was a "disappointment." "This much, however I can say," Isaac Mickle wrote: "he can lie faster than any other man I ever heard."[47]

The Democratic leadership tried to counter Southard's influence by sending its own best speakers, notably Garret Wall and Peter Vroom, into the same towns Southard had visited, and offering a different perspective on the issues of the day. Democratic newspapers defended the administration's national programs and attacked General Harrison as "totally unfit" for the presidency. In the northern part of the state, Democrats also made what they could of Southard's ties to the Morris Company, and suggested that Southard, together with Camden and Amboy Railroad president Robert Stockton (a recent Whig convert), was trying to run the state.[48]

The campaign of 1840 was one of the most remarkable in New Jersey history. Because the issues of the day were so familiar, because the Whigs were so hungry for office, spectacle rather than substance tended to dominate the proceedings. The state's partisans had never been mobilized to a greater degree than in 1840; the size of rallies was unprecedented. Torchlight parades, hickory poles, and campaign toasts (the hard cider flowed at Whig rallies) were notable aspects of the 1840 campaign.[49] Each party worked to the greatest degree to build enthusiasm for its national ticket and bring out its largest possible vote—efforts that spurred the opposition to equally fervent exertions. The great interest sparked by the campaign was reflected not only in the mass rallies that occurred almost daily and in the propaganda emanating from the press, but also in the turnout on election day. Each side brought out its normal vote in 1840, and many more; fully 80% of the state's voters went to the polls.[50]

When the votes were counted, the Whigs had won a smashing victory. The party's majority in the legislature rose from sixteen in 1839 to forty-three in 1840, and General Harrison carried the state by more than 2,300 votes (a significant margin in a very well-balanced state) out of 64,380 cast.[51] All six of the Whig candidates for Congress gained victory, avenging their narrow defeat in 1838. Never before had the Whigs so completely dominated New Jersey politics. Never again would they be in such complete control of the state. Never before, as the historian of New Jersey Whiggery has noted, had the state party organized so well or used rallies to such effect. At the same time, both parties ran issues-oriented campaigns in New Jersey, and the results of the election provided a strong endorsement of the principles that Southard and other Whig leaders had propounded throughout the summer and autumn of 1840. For better or worse, a new administration in Washington, it was expected, would change the direction of national policy.[52]

Samuel Southard was delighted by the Whig success in 1840, and properly credited with helping to forge that success. From it, however, he would gain little. The Whig victory of 1840 proved to be a temporary blessing, a brief triumph, for Whigs generally and Samuel Southard in particular. Winning elections and governing, as the Whigs soon learned, are two distinct concerns.

V

As the election returns from across the country made it apparent that the Whigs had scored a great victory, Whig newspapers in New Jersey trumpeted the good news and talked of "The Revolution of 1840." One leading party organ, the Newark *Sentinel of Freedom,* interpreted the Whig sweep as a mandate for a new kind of governance. "The cry of the nation is for CHANGE through all channels of intelligence and communication . . . the cry is CHANGE! CHANGE! Change of MEASURES, and to that end, a change of MEN."[53] That the heart of the transition in government would be a matter of accommodating a new set of officeseeking partisans was soon evident. For the first time good Whigs had access to positions ranging from cabinet appointments, clerkships, and diplomatic posts to lighthouse keepers that heretofore had been the domain of the Democrats.

As the leading patronage broker in New Jersey, the man who had, as one Whig put it, "the sole power of appointment," Southard was inundated with solicitations for aid and influence.[54] Having complained to his son Henry in the heat of the campaign that the incessant demands on his energies had "almost destroyed" him, Southard found that victory brought further, if different, burdens.[55] He was deluged with letters from loyal Whigs, recent advocates of the cause, and hangers-on, few of whom talked very much about Whig principles, and all of whom had imperative reasons why they needed the particular job in question. It was vexing business in any circumstances. Given Southard's current coldness with one of the Whig kingpins, Henry Clay, and his lack of intimacy with the other, Daniel Webster (precisely because Southard had long been identified with Clay), his situation was particularly awkward. Further, there was the matter of his own role in a new administration.

Southard clearly expected that, when General Harrison put together a cabinet, he would be invited to join it. His own preference was attorney general, a post he had sought two decades earlier and which he believed he was well fit to handle. If that post should be promised elsewhere—as indeed it was, to Henry Clay's alter ego John J. Crittenden—then the Treasury Department might suit, or perhaps his old post at the Navy Department. Prior to the elections in 1840, Washington banker William A. Bradley had told Southard in a letter that he requested be destroyed that "no man has a better claim to be a member of the new Administration than you have, nor is there one whose claims will, I think, be more readily acknowledged." Proposing that Southard accept the position of postmaster general in the new administration, Bradley suggested that "you may be if you please Gen. H's successor."[56] This last comment was, of course, simple blarney, but expectations that he join the cabinet were hardly unreasonable. Indeed, as one of only a handful of living Whigs who had had executive experience in Washington, Southard understandably believed that his place in Harrison's cabinet was virtually a foregone conclusion.

It wasn't. The maneuvering behind the appointment of cabinet officers was complex, and neither Clay nor Webster got everything his way.[57] Both men did, however, have a major hand in the appointment of cabinet officers, and it was evident as the cabinet took form that neither much thought in terms of Samuel Southard.

Although he nursed some hopes as late as the middle of January that he would be named to one of the departments, Southard began to see the handwriting on the wall. He confidentially told his son Henry on January 10 that "I expect no offer of any kind." He hinted that the capital kingmakers wanted him to play a special role in the Senate, but "in this I may disappoint them."[58] The obscurity of this latter comment suggests that Southard, in early 1841, was trying to cope with the reality that he would, indeed, be left in the Senate, unrewarded for his political efforts. It was a bitter blow, and one he did not know as yet how to face.

One thing was clear. Southard's family and friends were amazed and angry when he was not named to the cabinet. His brother Isaac bitterly noted, once the names of department heads were released in mid-February, "Are you to get nothing under the new administration for all your toil & sacrifice & labor?" William B. Kinney of Newark called the decision to leave Southard out of the cabinet and, indeed, out of the inner councils of the new administration "remarkable." That a man whose "knowledge of the country might be supposed to give value to his counsels, should not have been consulted at all . . . is passing strange. Who rules the hour?" Samuel, Jr., wrote his brother Henry that their father was the victim of "intrigue" by "some of our leading politicians" in Washington—notably Henry Clay. "Mr. Clay is doing all he can to destroy him—and, considering all that has passed in former years, he is acting like a little man and no gentlemen." Even Southard's wife, Rebecca, expressed outrage at the course of events. "You are treated badly," she wrote her husband from New Jersey, "and Clay and Webster are at the head of it. . . . I do think the sooner you leave Washington the better."[59]

Mrs. Southard wanted her husband to resign in protest over his ill treatment, but this he could not and would not do. The awkwardness of his situation would only be highlighted by a resignation at this time.[60] Besides, Southard very much needed the income that the senatorship afforded him. Instead of publicly showing his displeasure with the course of events, Southard chose to retain his Senate seat and run for the presidency of the Senate—a post he had unsuccessfully sought in a contest with William R. King in 1836, but which now lay within his grasp. Southard gained his objective, in some measure as a consolation prize. One senator who voted for him in the Whig caucus, William C. Preston, later recalled that he had voted for Southard in part because "he was continually mortified by the petulance of Clay," and in part because Southard spoke to him before anyone else had.[61] Others no doubt cast their votes for similar reasons.

Having secured a position of prestige but little real weight, Southard returned to New Jersey at the close of the twenty-sixth Congress to nurse his wounds, catch up on his private enterprises, and explain to his fellow New Jerseyans why things had eventuated as they had.

VI

If matters in Washington had taken a turn far different from Samuel Southard's expectations in early 1841, something very similar occurred on a broader scale for the Whig party. Leading Whigs had anticipated a new thrust in government, geared to the ascendancy of the Congress in its relations with the executive, repeal of the independent treasury, and the fashioning of a truly Whiggish program for America. In this the Whigs were to be disappointed, at least in part because the genial Ohioan who intended to rule as board chairman rather than chief executive died within one month of his installation.

Before the onset of his final illness, President Harrison had agreed to a special session of Congress that was the *idée fixe* of Henry Clay.[62] His death did not change this mandate, nor did it much affect Henry Clay's plans for legislation in 1841. From the Kentuckian's perspective, John Tyler might, as of April 4, be president in name, but Henry Clay would remain the de facto power in the government. American politics in 1841 hinged on this expectation, and on Henry Clay's failure to reckon with the new man in the White House. Clay knew, of course that John Tyler's Whiggery was thinly veneered, that the Virginia man had been placed on the Whig ticket primarily to win the votes of the states' rights men in the South. But Clay expected, or wanted to believe, that Tyler would follow the Whig line on the major issues of the day and, as he put it in a letter to John L. Lawrence, "interpose no obstacles to the success of the Whig measures, including a Bank of the U.S."[63]

Clay was working under a severe delusion. Though John Tyler insisted, in his early public and private statements, that he would carry on a good Whig administration, he reminded Americans that he was not sympathetic to the reconstitution of the old Bank of the United States, and that he preferred a fiscal arrangement that stood somewhere between such a bank and the independent treasury. Though anxious to work closely with Whigs in the Congress, Tyler made clear that he wanted an institution that would, as he told Clay, "avoid all constitutional objections."[64]

In the making, though few realized it as the Congress set about its business in 1841, was a major confrontation between the president and a Whig Congress. The spectacle that ensued—Tyler's vetoes of two separate bank bills that Clay had advocated with all of his strength—put Washington and the nation into a political fever. It also effectively negated the dreams of voters who believed that the results of the 1840 election would truly inspire a "revolution" of measures. Simply put, the duel between Tyler and Clay in 1841 left the Whig program in a shambles.[65]

As an experienced and respected legislator, Samuel Southard might have been expected to play a major role in the drama that unfolded in Washington in 1841, a drama culminating in September with the resignation, en masse, of the cabinet, save for Clay's longtime rival, Secretary of State Daniel Webster. But Southard did not actively participate in the shaping of the legislation that led to John Tyler's vetoes and his ostracism by the Whigs. Instead, he presided dutifully over the Senate, declined to participate in its debates, and worked in his spare moments to meet the financial obligations that pressed ever more ominously upon him. Southard's only surviving comment about the impasse between the Whigs and the president in 1841 lies in a letter he wrote on September 3 to Lewis Condict, indicating that he expected the president to veto the second bank bill laid before him, even as he retained "some very slight hopes" Tyler would sign it. "I fear we must fall," he said. "But let us do it manfully. We shall do much good—let not this one evil dispirit us."[66]

Southard's interest in the struggle between Clay and Tyler may have been sparked by some small hopes that Tyler would resign the presidency as he had resigned his Senate seat in 1834 over the issue of instructions. Such a move would have made Senator Samuel Southard into President Southard, and, perhaps, changed the course of American history. Tyler did not, however, weaken in his resolve to veto measures he disapproved and retain the reins of power. It was, rather, Henry Clay who would leave Washington, in March 1842, after pronouncing a prolonged philippic against the recalcitrant president.[67]

VII

Congress adjourned in an ugly mood in September 1841, and Southard immediately journeyed to New Jersey, where he tried to sort out his painfully stringent financial situation. Bills flew in from every direction, and income simply did not keep pace. Back in New Jersey, Southard was faced with a demand for payment of a $1,500 note owed to the American Trust Company of New York, and other large notes due from the Trenton Banking Company and a branch of the United States Bank.[68] By November, his situation was so desperate that he penned a less than friendly letter to his old acquaintance, Samuel L. Gouvernor of New York, from whom he demanded payment of legal fees in a recent case he had tried and won on Gouvernor's behalf. He was, he said, in "a situation of great pain, with a large amount of money due me, I am unable to meet my debts." "I am not," he added, "in the situation of those who can devote their time & skill to stocks—borrowing money &c. I must suffer as a private & public man unless those who owe me, will pay me." Alluding to Gouvernor's supposed wealth and his failure to pay what he owed, Southard closed with the admonition that "it is very, very wrong, & I am, you know, unable to bear such things."[69]

Southard got no satisfaction on this matter, or on others—including his effort to prod one man, P. R. Fendall (an officeholder in the Adams administration), whose debt to Southard dated back to 1829! It was, indeed, a sorry situation in which he was mired.[70] Southard's financial travail was compounded by his increasing ill health and the continued erratic behavior of his wife. He fell so ill in November 1841 that he was confined to his room in Jersey City, and "unable to attend to business," as he told Isaac Williamson.[71] He did recover sufficiently to return to his Senate post in December, but by February his illness—never precisely diagnosed, but probably some kind of uremic poisoning—again forced him to bed.[72]

Samuel Southard's life was in fact ebbing away, and the political excitements of the moment, which were soon to conclude with President Tyler's veto of a Whig tariff measure, mattered less and less to him. Perhaps the saddest aspect of Southard's situation in early 1842 was not his illness per se, but his loneliness as death approached. His children were at this time each pursuing their own lives and he was in Washington with his wife, whose presence served only to agitate him. Shortly after opening the Senate on February 17, Southard was forced to leave his chair for his room, and there he penned a note to his wife that pictures a man in extremis. His life, he wrote, was intolerable.

> I cannot bear my present state. . . . After the sacrifice of a quarter of a century of the best part of my life, for my children & in the hope of justice & happiness, to see no end to suffering is—beyond my philosophy to bear. You promised "not to give me any more trouble." How do you keep your word?[73]

Death was closing in on Southard, though he could not have known it. By early April, he returned again to his Senate chair, and introduced a number of routine reports and communications to that body.[74] Within a month, however, he was forced back to his room, and he never returned to the capitol.[75] Late in May, after a brief remission in his disease, he was taken to the house of his in-laws, in Fredericksburg, Virginia, where he had passed so many happy hours.[76] He hoped that a change in climate and the opportunity, possibly, for exercise in the open air, would do him some good. But in Virginia his health only worsened. On May 31, Southard sent a letter to the Senate resigning as president pro tem. "My indisposition," he wrote, "for the present, continues; and to prevent the possibility of either private or public interests being neglected, I feel constrained to resign."[77] Senator Willie P. Mangum of North Carolina, who had long coveted the post Southard now abdicated, was elected in his stead, and the business of the Senate continued without significant interruption. It was clear by June to most of his associates that Southard was dying. Henry Clay, for example, who had made a kind of peace with Southard before departing Washington, wrote from his Lexington home that "I am afraid that my apprehensions that Southard would die within six months will be realized. His vital organs, I fear, are irrecoverably prostrated."[78] He was right.

Four days before Samuel Southard resigned as president pro tem of the Senate, his family suffered a different, but equally sad blow. The patriarch of the Southard clan, Henry L. Southard, died in Basking Ridge at the age of ninety-five. The old man was remarkably lucid to the end, and expired with his famous son's name on his lips.[79] His death, more than that of his son, symbolized the passing of an era and a vision. Henry Southard had never been unfaithful to the republican faith in which he was bred and to which he had committed himself during the Revolution. His son, of course, could make a similar claim, for Samuel Southard was to die a committed republican and a principled Whig. But the complexion of the nation was much different in 1842 than it had been in 1776, and Henry Southard's sad comment, in his later years, that the slogan of Americans had changed from "liberty or death" to "office and money" had a basis in fact.[80] The republic was changing, and the vision of republican simplicity that sustained the Revolutionary cause was now obscured by an ethos of get-rich-quick. Good republican that he was, Samuel Lewis Southard nonetheless embodied this latter compulsion. He prized different values and set different goals than his father. Whether they were less worthy goals is not easy to say, but one can readily suggest that, whatever their worth, they were not realized nearly so well as Henry Southard's had been.

At all events Samuel L. Southard, a different kind of republican from his father, but a statesman in his own right, was soon also to close out his term. Throughout June, Southard's son Henry, who had rushed to be with his father in Fredericksburg, sent bulletins to friends in Washington and New Jersey, apprising them of his condition. These letters were published, essentially intact, in the major newspapers.[81] Throughout the month of June, Southard lay in Fredericksburg, alternately in great pain and in a coma. He experienced a brief resurgence at midmonth, when he was able to converse and be shaved, but soon he lapsed again into unconsciousness and, on June 26, died without regaining his senses. His entire family was with him at the end.

Southard's death was greeted in the Senate with sadness but no surprise. His colleague from New Jersey, Jacob Miller, announced the news on June 27, and, along with Senator William King of Alabama, offered a brief eulogy. In the House, John Maxwell (the son of Southard's old friend from Princeton days, George C. Maxwell) and his old chief, John Quincy Adams, added their own words of praise. Adams observed that Southard had proved, in six years as a colleague in the executive branch, that he was a man of high caliber. "The soundness of his judgment, the candor of his disposition, the sweetness of his temper, and the firmness of his adherence to his own sense of right were, to me, as a colleague and a confidential assistant and adviser, a treasure beyond all price."[82]

The eulogies pronounced, Southard's body lay briefly in state at the capitol, and he was interred, next to two of his children, in the congressional cemetery.[83] He had died without realizing the fame he always sought, or the blessings of a happy and comfortable private life. But he had contributed much to the nation in whose service he had spent so many years. Distinguished in its achievements if unexceptional in its values, his life served as an emblem of the passage of time and the impact of social and economic change on the ideals that guided Americans.

Notes

Chapter 1

1. The literature on the Bank War is enormous. References to the most helpful of these works may be found in chapter 7. Clay's remarks are quoted from Glyndon G. Van Deusen, *The Life of Henry Clay* (Boston: Little, Brown and Company, 1937), p. 280.

2. U.S. Congress, *Register of Debates in the Congress of the United States* (Washington, D.C.: Gales & Seaton, 1834), 23d Cong., 1st sess., pp. 143–98 (hereafter cited as *Register of Debates*).

3. *Proceedings of the New Jersey History Society*, 2nd series, 5 (1877): 88–89; Peter O. Wacker, *Land and People: A Cultural Geography of Preindustrial New Jersey: Origins and Settlement Patterns* (New Brunswick, N.J.: Rutgers University Press, 1975), p. 52; Rudolph J. Vecoli, *The People of New Jersey* (Princeton, N.J.: D. Van Nostrand Company, Inc., 1965), p. 16.

4. Peter O. Wacker, *The Musconetcong Valley of New Jersey: A Historical Georgraphy* (New Brunswick, N.J.: Rutgers University Press, 1968), p. 41; Wacker, *Land and People*, pp. 165, 169; Irving Mark, *Agrarian Conflicts in Colonial New York 1711–1775* (New York: Columbia University Press, 1940), p. 14. The decision to migrate was not a difficult one in most cases. Witness the Earl of Bellomont's report of the recollections of a New Yorker: "What man will be such a fool to become a base tenant of Mr. Dellius, Colonel Schuyler, Mr. Livingston (and so he ran through the whole role of our mighty landgraves), when, for crossing the Hudson River, that man can for a song purchase a good freehold in the Jersies?" Quoted in Vecoli, *People of New Jersey*, pp. 14–15.

5. Though not reliable in all respects, Ralph K. Potter, "Early Southards of New York and New Jersey" (New Jersey State Library, Trenton) is helpful on Southard's ancestry. The name Basking Ridge is probably derived from the local tradition that the ridge was a place for wild animals to bask in the sun. See Ludwig Schumacher, *The Somerset Hills* (New York: New Amsterdam Book Co., ca. 1900), p. 92.

6. Among the best of many works on Jeffersonian ideology are Douglass Greybill Adair, "The Intellectual Origins of Jeffersonian Democracy: Republicanism, the Class Struggle, and the Virtuous Farmer" (Ph.D. diss., Yale University, 1943); Lance Banning, *The Jefferson Persuasion: Evolution of a Party Ideology* (Ithaca, N.Y.: Cornell University Press, 1978); and J. G. A. Pocock, *The Machiavellian Moment: Florentine Political Thought and the Atlantic Republican Tradition* (Princeton, N.J.: Princeton University Press, 1975), esp. chap. 15.

7. Abraham A. Messler, *First Things in Old Somerset* (Somerville, N.J.: The Somerville Publishing Company, 1899), pp. 39–40.

8. "Earliest American Ancestors of Somerset Families," *Somerset County Historical Quarterly*, 5 (1916): 279; Potter, "Early Southards," passim. My statement regarding Henry's sons Lott and Stephen is based on miscellaneous comments in the Samuel L. Southard Papers, Princeton University Library (hereafter, PUL), and Henry Southard's will, number 2835R, New Jersey State Library, Trenton.

9. Records show that the Army Quartermaster in Morristown issued certificates to Henry Southard totalling $13,763.00 for carting—worth perhaps $400–$500 if one converts the continental currency to market value at the time. See Department of Defense, Military Records, Revolutionary War card index, New Jersey State Library, Trenton. My conversion of the monies issued to Southard for his carting services is roughly based on conversions in John Shy, *A People Numerous and Armed: Reflections on the Military Struggle for American Independence* (New York: Oxford University Press, 1976), pp. 282–83, n. 7.

10. See *Minutes of the Meetings of the Justices and Chosen Freeholders for the County of Somerset, May 13, 1772, to September 2, 1822* (Somerville, N.J.: Somerset County Historical Society, 1978), pp. 59–68, and Messler, *First Things in Old Somerset*, pp. 38–40. Tax records for Bernard Township, Somerset County, indicate a noticeable, if not dramatic, increase in Henry Southard's property holding during and after the war. The 1778 ratables show that Southard's tax was quite modest compared to most of his neighbors, and no property holdings are listed for him. By 1784, Southard had one hundred acres of improved land, roughly the average in his community, and owned three horses and seven head of cattle. His holdings did not change markedly after he went into politics, even after many years of service in the United States House of Representatives. See Ratables, Bernard Township, Somerset County, May, 1778, August, 1784, 1788, 1797, 1802, 1805, 1818, Bureau of Archives and History, New Jersey State Library, Trenton, N.J.

11. Folder on Samuel L. Southard, Alumni Records, Seeley G. Mudd Library, Princeton University.

12. "Robert Finley," in Allan Johnson and Dumas Malone, eds., *Dictionary of American Biography*, 20 vols. (New York: Charles Scribner's Sons, 1929–37), 6:391; Isaac V. Brown, *Memoirs of the Rev. Robert Finley, D.D.* (New Brunswick, N.J.: Terhune and Letson, 1819), p. 34.

13. Brown, *Finley*, esp. pp. 35–38.

14. John P. Snell, comp., *History of Hunterdon and Somerset Counties* (New York: Evarts and Peck, 1881), p. 748. After his graduation Kirkpatrick studied for the ministry and embarked on a career as a Presbyterian clergyman; Lindsley remained in academia, first at Princeton and then, 1824–50, as president of the University of Nashville. During Lindsley's years on the Princeton faculty he and Southard corresponded frequently. Theodore Frelinghuysen, Southard's roommate in college, studied law and joined the New Jersey bar. Active in philanthropy, church work, education reform and politics, he served as New Jersey's attorney general, United States senator and, 1850–62, as president of Rutgers College.

15. Thomas Jefferson Wertenbaker, *Princeton: 1746–1896* (Princeton, N.J.: Princeton University Press, 1946), chaps. 1–4.

16. John Maclean, *History of the College of New Jersey from its Origin in 1746 to the Commencement of 1854* (Philadelphia: J. B. Lippincott & Co., 1877), 2: 32; Wertenbaker, *Princeton*, p. 127; "Memoirs of George Strawbridge" transcript, Special Collections, PUL, pp. 28–29.

17. The quote is from "Memoirs of George Strawbridge," pp. 28–29. See also Wertenbaker, *Princeton*, p. 127.

18. College of New Jersey, Trustee Minutes, Seeley G. Mudd Library, Princeton, N.J., March 16, 17, 18, 19, 1802. Works which place this stern discipline within a broader context in American higher education include Wertenbaker, *Princeton*, pp. 135–43; Joseph F. Kett, *Rites of Passage: Adolescence in America, 1790 to the Present* (New York: Basic Books, 1977), pp. 52–53; and Steven J. Novak, *The Rights of Youth: American Colleges and Student Revolt 1798–1815* (Cambridge, Mass., 1977). It is worth noting that Novak believes that President Smith's response to the Nassau Hall fire was conditioned by student unrest *prior* to the incident.

19. Laws of College of New Jersey, 1802, p. 36, Seeley G. Mudd Library, Princeton, N.J.; Maclean, *Princeton* pp. 57–59; Nelson R. Burr, *Education in New Jersey, 1630–1871* (Princeton, N.J.: Princeton University Press, 1942), pp. 138–39; "Letters of James Iredell, Jr." (transcript, Special Collections, PUL). The Iredell letters provide a pungent word portrait of Princeton, from a student's eye view, for 1804 and 1805. The originals of these letters are in the Johnston Papers, North Carolina Historical Commission, Raleigh, N.C.

20. References to the deficiencies of Messrs. Southard, Lindsley, Kirkpatrick, and Frelinghuysen is in College of New Jersey Faculty Minutes, November 23, 1802, Seeley G. Mudd Library, Princeton, N.J. On April 6, 1803, the faculty pronounced itself satisfied with their progress, and declared them to be "in full standing with their classes." For college honors in 1804, see September 7, 1804, Faculty Minutes. Award of the A.M. degree to Southard is mentioned in his folder in the Seeley G. Mudd Library. For a provocative argument that the literary societies such as Southard's Clio at Princeton were probably the chief intellectual stimuli at American colleges in the early nineteenth century, see James McLachlan, "The Choice of Hercules; American Student

Societies in the Early 19th Century," in *The University in Society*, vol. 2; *Europe, Scotland, and the United States from the 16th to the 20th Century*, ed. Lawrence Stone (Princeton, N.J.: Princeton University Press, 1974), pp. 449–94.

21. On the inside cover of Southard's early commonplace book is a note in his hand: "Samuel L. Southard came to Mendham on the 8th day of October, 1804." Box 115, Southard Papers, PUL. For references to his brief tenure in Mendham, see letters from David Thompson, Jr., and Amzi Armstrong, Southard Papers, Box 1, PUL. There is evidence that Southard was invited to return to Princeton shortly after his graduation to work as a tutor at the college—an offer he declined. Notebook entry of Oct. 29, 1807, Box 115, Southard Papers, PUL. The reference to two out of one thousand American youths having the opportunity to attend college at this time is from Irving Bartlett, *Daniel Webster* (New York: W. W. Norton & Company, Inc., 1978), p. 20.

22. The rise of the Jeffersonian Republican party, and Henry Southard's role in that cause is traced in Carl E. Prince, *New Jersey's Jeffersonian Republicans: The Genesis of an Early Party Machine, 1789–1817* (Chapel Hill, N.C.: University of North Carolina Press, 1964), esp. p. 36.

23. Trenton *New-Jersey State Gazette*, June 30, 1842. Lucius Q. C. Elmer, *The Constitution and Government of the Province and State of New Jersey, with Biographical Sketches of the Governors from 1776 to 1845, and Reminiscences of the Bench and Bar, During More than Half a Century* (Newark, N.J.: M. R. Dennis, 1872), pp. 204–7.

24. Jackson Turner Main, "Sections and Politics in Virginia, 1781–1787," *William and Mary Quarterly*, 3rd ser., 12 (January 1955) 97–98; Second Census of the Inhabitants of King George County taken by Theo Hansford, Assistant to David Meade and Randolph Marshall for the District of Virginia, Virginia Historical Society, Richmond, Mss. 485895a; Main, "The Distribution of Property in Post Revolutionary Virginia," *Mississippi Valley Historical Review* 41 (September, 1954): 255–56. The decline of Tidewater Virginia in the late eighteenth century has been remarked on in numerous studies, but none has traced it in its complex detail. Among the best secondary discussions of the region's decline are Avery O.Craven, *Soil Exhaustion as a Factor in the Agricultural History of Virginia and Maryland*, 1606–1860 (Urbana, Ill.: University of Illinois Press, 1926), chap. 3; Archie D. Andrews, "Agriculture in Virginia, 1789–1820," M.A. thesis, University of Virginia, 1950); Gerald Mullin, *Flight and Rebellion: Slave Resistance in Eighteenth Century Virginia* (New York: Oxford University Press, 1972), pp. 124–27; and Robert Brugger, *Beverly Tucker: Heart Over Head in the Old South* (Baltimore: Johns Hopkins University Press, 1978), pp. 35–36. Lucius Q. C. Elmer's *Constitution and Government of New Jersey*, quoting the Rev. J. W. Alexander of Charlotte County, refers to the Northern Neck in the early nineteenth century as "a rich, fertile, region, producing great quantities of prime tobacco, and of course growing, wealthy." This statement simply cannot be accepted. By the early nineteenth century even large planters in the Northern Neck faced economic problems, and some such as John Taliaferro, seriously considered moving west. See, for example, John Taliaferro to Col. John F. Mercer, Feb. 22, 1814, Mercer Family Papers, Virginia Historical Society, Richmond, and John Taliaferro to Samuel L. Southard, Dec. 14, 1816, Southard Papers, PUL.

25. Southard began the diary on his twentieth birthday, June 9, 1807. His last entry was made in February 1810. See Box 115, Southard Papers, PUL.

26. Southard diary, entries for June 19, 20, July 4, 1807. See also J. A. Cuthbert to Southard, March 21, 1808, Southard Papers, PUL.

27. The votes of Henry Southard and John Taliaferro can be followed in U. S. Congress, Joseph Gales, comp., *The Debates and Proceedings in the Congress of the United States . . .* (Washington, D.C., 1834–56), 7th Congress, passim. (Hereafter cited as *Annals of Congress*.)

28. Southard diary, entry of June 9, 1807.

29. Brugger, *Heart over Head*, pp. 21–25.

30. Southard diary, entries dated June 9, 25, August 12, 27, 1807, May 8, 1808, March 2, 1809.

31. Details of Rebecca Harrow Southard's ancestry and early life are provided in (draft) Samuel L. Southard to Alexander McKea, December 27, 1823, Southard Papers, PUL. On

Southard's earlier infatuation with Reverend Amzi Armstrong's ward, see Armstrong to South-ard, March 15, May 10, 1809, and January 17, 1810; David Thompson Jr. to Southard, May 22, July 10, 1808, Southard Papers, PUL. On relations with and the health of Rebecca Harrow, E. A. S. Taliaferro to Samuel L. Southard, January 23, March 22, June 10, 1811; John Taliaferro to Southard, January 7, March 6, April 25, June 10, 1811; Lawrence Taliaferro to Southard, January 21, February 29, March 25, April 29, May 25, July 16, November 16, 1811, Southard Papers, PUL.

32. Southard's diary entry of October 29, 1807, indicates that he had agreed to join Simpson in traveling west to see about prospects there for a legal career. There is no evidence, however, that he actually did this. See also Josiah Simpson to Southard, November 11, December 14, 1811, Southard Papers, PUL.

33. "Financial Memos and Transactions," Box 117, Southard Papers, PUL, contains records of Southard's early practice in Virginia. Southard's license to practice law in both the inferior and superior courts of Virginia, dated May 2, 1809, is in the Samuel L. Southard Papers, Library of Congress (hereafter, LC). Also there is his license to practice in King George County, dated December 14, 1810.

34. Brugger, *Heart Over Head*, p. 265.

35. Samuel L. Southard to William Maxwell, December 20, 1810, Charles Bartles Mss., Hun-terdon County Historical Society, Flemington, N.J. See also Thomas Ryerson to Southard, Febru-ary 26, 1811 and Josiah Simpson to Southard, February 22, 1811, Southard Papers, PUL.

Chapter 2

1. On political values and practices in Washington in the early nineteenth century, see James Sterling Young, *The Washington Community, 1800–1828* (New York: Columbia University Press, 1966). Henry Southard's voting record may be traced in the *Annals*, 7th through 11th, and 14th through 16th Congresses. His personality emerges most vividly in his correspondence in the Samuel Southard Papers at Princeton University. (There is, regrettably, no Henry Southard archive.) On Henry's refusal to run for the Senate in 1816, see Henry Southard to Samuel L. Southard, December 24, 1816, Southard Papers, PUL.

2. Samuel L. Southard to Rebecca Harrow, March 9, 1812, Southard Papers, PUL.

3. Daniel Dod to Southard, February 14, 1811; John Taliaferro to Southard, January 7, February 9, March 6, 1811; Thomas Ryerson to Southard, February 26, 1811; Josiah Simpson to Southard, February 19, 22, March 13, 1811; Henry Southard to Samuel L. Southard, February 20, 1811, all Southard Papers PUL. Evidence suggests that Henry did not use his political influence to gain the surrogate post for his son.

4. Josiah Simpson to Southard, March 13, 1811, Southard Papers, PUL. In a letter to his son on May 28, 1811, Henry Southard expressed surprise that Samuel had been named surrogate, saying that he thought that Samuel, at most, would be licensed to practice law in New Jersey. Southard's appointment was announced in the Trenton *True American*, May 27, 1811.

5. Trenton *True American*, July 29, 1811. The oration was subsequently published and sold for twelve and a half cents per copy at the bookstores of James Wilson, Daniel Fenton, and James Oram in Trenton. See Trenton *True American*, August 5, 1811, and Daniel Dod to Southard, September 4, 1811, Southard Papers, PUL. Copies of the oration are extant in the Virginia Historical Society, Richmond, Va., and The New Jersey Historical Society, Newark, N.J.

6. Southard's first polemic was written under the pseudonym "Florian"; it pleased New Bruns-wick *Fredonian* editors David and James FitzRandolph enough for them to request further pro-ductions. As they observed: "We shall at all times be extremely happy in receiving communications from so valuable a correspondent, and shall at any time be willing to stand *Godfathers* to productions which accord with the one already received and inserted. Should you be

204 SAMUEL L. SOUTHARD

at leisure when this reaches you, and could favor us with some of your ideas for the next number, we should consider ourselves under many obligations." David and James FitzRandolph to Southard, April 10, 1811. Southard apparently took them up on the offer, for their assistant, Bernard Smith, wrote six weeks later acknowledging a further contribution to the *Fredonian,* and expressing hope that "Mr. S. will continue his 'useful labours in the political vineyard.'" Bernard Smith to Southard, May 30, 1811, Southard Papers, PUL.

7. Carl E. Prince, *New Jersey's Jeffersonian Republicans: The Genesis of An Early Party Machine, 1789–1817* (Chapel Hill, N.C.: The University of North Carolina Press, 1964), chap. 6; and Walter R. Fee, *The Transition From Aristocracy to Democracy in New Jersey, 1789–1829* (Somerville, N.J.: The Somerset Press, Inc., 1933), pp. 138–40, 148–60, 170–82.

8. Trenton *True American,* October 12, 28, November 4, 1811. Woodruff's removal as attorney general was assailed in the Federalist press and defended by "A New Jersey Farmer," Trenton *True American,* December 23, 1811. See also Josiah Simpson to Southard, December 14, 1811; and Bernard Smith to Southard, December 17, 1811, Southard Papers, PUL. The papers offically designating Southard as deputy attorney general are in Samuel L. Southard Papers, LC.

9. Samuel L. Southard to Rebecca Harrow, February 15, March 9, March 25, May 21, July 5, 1812, Southard Papers, PUL. By the time Southard wrote the last of these missives, Rebecca Harrow was Rebecca Harrow Southard.

10. Fee, *Transition,* p. 193; Prince, *Jeffersonian Republicans,* pp. 174–81; New Brunswick *Fredonian,* October 22, 29, 1812. Copies of neither the *Fredonian* nor the *True American* are extant for the months of December 1812 and January 1813.

11. George Maxwell to Southard, November 13, December 11, 1812; John Johnson to Southard, November 14, 1812; William Maxwell to Southard, November 12, 1812; (draft), Samuel L. Southard to Aaron Woodruff, November 12, December 7, 1812, (draft), March 29, 1813; Aaron Woodruff to Southard, November 18, 1812, February 27, 1813. The document notifying Southard of his appointment as deputy attorney general for Sussex County, dated November 18, 1812, is in Samuel L. Southard Papers, LC.

12. On the Federalists and the war effort, see Fee, *Transition,* pp. 188–92, 198–200; Elmer, *Constitution and Government,* pp. 153–54, 422; and Rudolph J. Pasler and Margaret C. Pasler, *The New Jersey Federalists* (Rutherford, N.J.: Fairleigh Dickinson University Press, 1975), pp. 147–59.

13. Josiah Simpson to Southard, January 18, 1813, Southard Papers, PUL.

14. John Taliaferro to Southard, December 14, 1812; see also Taliaferro to Southard, November 27, 1814, and Taliaferro's circular to his constituents, evidently written during the war, which is in the Southard Papers, PUL.

15. Letters on Southard's political activities include John Taliaferro to Southard, October 30, 1813, February 10, 1814, and William Pennington, Sr. to Southard, October 3, 1814. The Pennington letter alludes to a scheme Southard had suggested in order to get Republican militia men to the polls. The plan, Pennington suggested, was workable, and "if anything more can be done it will be." Southard apparently made an unsuccessful bid in 1814 for a Republican nomination to the legislature from Hunterdon County, and was placated by being named an "alternate" candidate. See Trenton *True American,* September 6, 1814. Southard's commission as judge advocate of the Hunterdon Brigade, dated February 23, 1813, is in Box 80, Southard Papers, PUL.

16. Among many letters, see especially David Thompson, Jr. to Southard, October 18, 1813; William Pennington, Sr. to Southard, November 17, 1813; Southard to James Madison, n.d., 1813 (same letter addressed to New Jersey Congressmen); Lewis Condict to Southard, January 23, 1812, August 2, 1813; George Drake to Southard, September 4, 1814; William Bonnell to Southard, December 26, 1812; Lewis Dease to Southard, December 21, 1812; John Lambert to Southard, February 25, 26, June 18, 1813, December 4, 1814, Southard Papers, PUL. Southard himself gained a minor patronage post when, on April 7, 1815, he was appointed by Joseph McIlvaine as deputy collector of revenue for Somerset and Hunterdon counties. Southard Papers, PUL.

17. Samuel L. Southard to Rebecca Harrow Southard, July 19, 1812, Southard Papers, PUL.

18. Mention of John Southard can be found in E. A. S. Taliaferro to Samuel L. Southard, October 27, 1813; Henry Southard to Samuel L. Southard, May 3, 1813; and John Taliaferro to Southard, February 10, 1814, Southard Papers, PUL. On Southard's need to secure a Negro slave for his wife, see James J. Wilson to Southard, July 20, 1812, Southard Papers, PUL.

19. Southard's financial concerns are discussed in George Maxwell to Samuel L. Southard, December 11, 1812; James D. Harrow to Southard, January 6, 1813 (misdated 1812); and Henry Southard to Samuel L. Southard, May 3, 1813. A deed on a house and lot in Flemington that Southard purchased from Alexander Bonnell on April 1, 1812, three months before his marriage to Rebecca Harrow, is in Box 80, Southard Papers, PUL.

20. See especially chapters 8 and 9 below. For evidence that her health problems were not simply physical, see two letters, written twenty years apart, by her brothers James and Charles Harrow, respectively. James D. Harrow to Southard, February 3, 1823, and Charles Harrow to Henry L. Southard, August 22, 1843, Box 156, Southard Papers, PUL.

21. Like many young marrieds, Southard and his wife had some difficult times adjusting to one another. In 1814 Southard collected and committed to paper some of his wife's more disparaging comments about him, observing, at the end: "And has it really come to this—Is this the language of my wife to me? Or am I under some mistake on the subject? Did I hear right or did I not? Have I really so far failed in my duty?" Box 80, Samuel L. Southard Papers, PUL. Medical bills are in Box 117. In 1817 Southard paid Dr. Nicholas Belleville $120 for services to the family. Though Southard's debt to Belleville never reached that peak again, it was never insignificant. Moreover, in treating his son's epilepsy, Southard contracted Dr. John Van Cleve and a Dr. Manners. For details on John Southard's illness, see John Van Cleve to Southard, March 10, 24, April 7, 1817, Southard Papers, PUL. In the last of these letters, Van Cleve offered Southard the hope that his son might be "cured" as he reached puberty.

22. A fairly complete accounting of Southard's early legal earnings may be found in account books he kept for his various circuits, which are in Box 83, Southard Papers, PUL. Although he worked regularly in Sussex, Somerset, and Morris Counties as well as Hunterdon, it is evident that his home county, Hunterdon, was his bread and butter.

23. David Thompson to Southard, August 2, 1815, Samuel L. Southard Papers, PUL.

24. Southard had a thin skin and was particularly sensitive to the whispers of political men that he had gained preferment and perquisites too quickly and too frequently for a person of his age and attainments. See, for example, the gossip Southard collected about himself in Box 80, Southard Papers, PUL. He filed this information, with intentional irony, under the rubric "Memo of Good Will."

25. For a more extended discussion of the steamboat controversy, see Michael Birkner, "Samuel L. Southard and the Origins of *Gibbons v. Ogden,*" *Princeton University Library Chronicle* 40 (Winter 1979): 171–82.

26. For Ogden's petition to the New Jersey Legislature, see Archives and History Bureau, Manuscript Collection, State Library, Trenton, N.J. Manuscripts Collection #451. See also *New Jersey Laws,* February 12, 1813, November 3, 1813; David W. Thomson, "The Great Steamboat Monopolies, Part 2: The Hudson," *The American Neptune* 16 (October 1956): 274–75; and Theodore Thayer, *As We Were: The Story of Old Elizabethtown* (Elizabeth, N.J.: The New Jersey Historical Society, 1964), p. 234.

27. See John R. Livingston to Mahlon Dickerson, November 17, December 14, 1813, and Mahlon Dickerson to Robert Fulton (draft), November 29, 1813, Mahlon Dickerson Papers, The New Jersey Historical Society. The boundary dispute over waters between New Jersey and New York had its origins deep in colonial American history, and contributed to the smaller state's anger at New York's attempt to monopolize water transportation between New York and New Jersey. On this subject, see *Report of the Commissioners on the Controversy with the State of New York Respecting the Eastern Boundary of the State of New Jersey* (Trenton: Wilson and Halsey, 1807), and *Autobiography of Aaron Ogden of Elizabethtown* (Paterson, N.J.: privately printed, 1893), pp. 16–17.

28. Aaron Ogden to Samuel L. Southard, January 12, 1815, Samuel L. Southard Papers, PUL.

29. Lucius H. Stockton, *A History of the Steamboat Case, Lately Discussed by Counsel before the*

Legislature of New Jersey, Comprised in a Letter to a Gentleman at Washington (Trenton: Privately printed, 1815), p. 10. Manuscripts Division, Princeton University Library.

30. Ibid., pp. 3–4.

31. Two major sources reconstruct Southard's presentation. The first is Lucius H. Stockton's pamphlet, *A History of the Steam Boat Case . . .* , cited above, n. 29. Historians studying *Gibbons* v. *Ogden* have rarely used this fifty-two-page document written by a loyal political ally of Ogden. Yet the Stockton pamphlet vividly presents the arguments made in Trenton from January 26 to 29, particularly those made by Southard and his coadjutor in the case, Joseph Hopkinson. And though the pamphlet is obviously biased in Aaron Ogden's favor, the Samuel Southard papers at Princeton, which contain the second source—Southard's notes on his speech—corroborate Stockton's account at virtually every point, leaving in doubt less *what* Southard said than the force and effect with which he spoke. In reconstructing Southard's argument before the legislature I have quoted directly from Southard's brief in Box 126, Southard Papers, PUL.

32. Ibid., p. 18.

33. Ibid., passim.

34. *Votes and Proceedings of the 39th General Assembly, Second Sitting* (1815), pp. 182–83.

35. Because of the wide interest in the case, a noted legal reporter, William Sampson, contracted with a New York publisher to reproduce the arguments offered in Trenton in January 1815. Southard, however, seems to have undermined this venture, since he declined to furnish Sampson with his brief despite repeated requests. See William Sampson to Southard, February 9, March 23, April 5, October 21, 1815, and Southard to Sampson (drafts), February 17, March 27, 29, May 29, November 18, 1815, Southard Papers, PUL.

36. Elmer, *Constitution and Government*, pp. 207–10. Trenton *Federalist*, October 30, 1815; and New Brunswick *Fredonian*, November 9, 1815. Ironically, the Federalist candidate whom Southard defeated in the assembly race, Charles Ewing, would within a few years become Southard's closest friend.

37. Elmer, *Constitution and Government*, pp. 306–7, 311–12. The matter of Rossell's elevation to the federal bench is discussed in chapter 4.

38. Southard was appointed reporter for the supreme court in February of 1814, attended that court session and took notes, but the judges of the court declined to furnish him with their opinions. In 1816, while serving on the bench, Southard was again appointed reporter, and he served in this position for the rest of his term, with the exception of 1817. For details on the problems Southard faced in getting out the reports, see Thomas T. Kinney to Southard, December 8, 1817; Andrew Kirkpatrick to Southard, December 18, 1817; Southard to Thomas T. Kinney, December 9, 1817; Southard to Joseph Hornblower, November 15, 1817; and printed committee report on the delay in reporting and publishing the decisions of the supreme court in Box 80, Southard Papers, PUL. Southard ultimately published two volumes of court reports.

39. There is virtually no secondary literature on the history of the New Jersey Supreme Court. Interested students may find of limited value the comments of Lucius Elmer, who began to appear before this body in 1818. *Constitution and Government*, passim.

40. *New Jersey Reports*, 4 (Southard, 1), September term, 1818.

41. Ibid., pp. 392–97.

42. See Herbert A. Johnson, "*Gibbons* v. *Ogden* Before Marshall," in Leo Hershkowitz and Milton M. Klein, eds., *Courts and Law in Early New York: Selected Essays* (Port Washington, N.,Y.: Kennikat Press, 1978), pp. 106–7, and Thayer, *Old Elizabethtown*, pp. 238–40.

43. Thayer, *Old Elizabethtown*, chap. 12; Wheaton J. Lane, *From Indian Trail to Iron Horse: Travel and Transportation in New Jersey, 1620–1860* (Princeton, N.J.: Princeton University Press, 1939), pp. 185–90.

44. "State v. Gibbons," in *New Jersey Reports*, 4 (Southard, 1): p. 63. See also "State v. Trumbull," in ibid., p. 139, a case which is colorfully recounted in Elmer, *Constitution and Government*, pp. 300–4.

45. Box 115, Southard Papers, PUL contains information about his earnings while on the bench.

46. Elmer, *Constitution and Government*, p. 151; Robert Russel Beckwith, "Mahlon Dickerson of New Jersey, 1770–1853" (Ph.D. diss., Teacher's College, Columbia University, 1964); pp. 183–84; Trenton *True American*, November 6, 1815. On the political activities of judges in this era, see Lawrence M. Friedman, *A History of American Law* (New York: Simon and Schuster, 1973), p. 121.

47. Prince, *Jeffersonian Republicans*, pp. 207–8, observes that "Federalism continued to exist locally, but political conflict after 1815 lost its sharpness and clarity." See also Fee, *Transition*, pp. 237–38, and the Paslers, *New Jersey Federalists*, chap. 7.

48. The decay of the Republican organization is effectively traced in Prince, *Jeffersonian Republicans*, chap. 7.

49. Beckwith, "Mahlon Dickerson," chap. 4.

50. Carl E. Prince, "James J. Wilson, Party Leader, 1801–1824," *Proceedings of the New Jersey Historical Society* 83 (January 1955): 24–39. Further details on the Wilson-Dickerson maneuvers for the Senate seat may be found in Edward Yard to Mahlon Dickerson, November 7, 1814, Mahlon Dickerson Papers, NJHS: and David Thompson Jr. to Samuel L. Southard, November 15, 1814, Southard Papers, PUL.

51. See, for example, A. Van Sychel to Southard, February 4, 1815; (draft), Samuel L. Southard to George Graham, January 28, 1817; (draft), Southard to President-elect James Monroe, January 28, 1817, also February 17, 1817; James Fitz Randolph to Southard, November 6, 1817; Aaron Woodruff to Southard, February 7, 1817.

52. Samuel L. Southard to Mahlon Dickerson, January 1, 1817, Mahlon Dickerson Papers, NJHS. See also William Nixon to Southard, October 24, 1816, Dickerson to Southard, October 29 November 26, 1816, Southard Papers PUL. Robert R. Beckwith's contention that Southard's correspondence with Dickerson indicated that Southard "obviously accepted Mahlon's opinions as those of the party boss" (in "Mahlon Dickerson," pp. 185–86) is not accurate, in my judgment.

53. Mahlon Dickerson to Samuel L. Southard, January 10, 1817, Southard Papers, PUL.

54. See David Thompson, Jr. to Samuel L. Southard, December 30, 1816, January ?, 1817 (misdated 1816 by Southard), January 11, 23, 29, 1817; William Jeffers to Southard, December 16, 1816; Silas Condit to Southard, February 15, 1817; and Joseph Bonnell to Southard, undated but written in February, 1817, Samuel L. Southard Papers, PUL.

55. Newark *Sentinel of Freedom*, February 18, 1817. The governorship contest was not considered significant enough for either the *True American* in Trenton or the New Brunswick *Fredonian* to report or comment on.

56. Southard to Mahlon Dickerson, April 1, 1817, not sent. Southard Papers, PUL.

57. David Thompson Jr. to Southard, April 7, 1817; see also Thompson to Southard, March 24, 1817, for details of Dickerson's supposed perfidy.

58. Dickerson's letters to his brother Philemon as well as his behavior suggest a wariness and jealousy regarding Southard's ambitions. In July 1824, Southard offered his own assessment, telling John Quincy Adams that he believed "the only key to Dickerson's thoughts and actions is personal hostility to him [Southard]—the jealousy of a younger man rising and supplanting him in political influence, power, and reputation." *Memoirs of John Quincy Adams* (Philadelphia; J. B. Lippincott & Co., 1875), entry of July 14, 1824, 6:400–1.

59. Thompson to Southard, July 19, 1817, Southard Papers, PUL. Southard apparently made the same remark to Thompson, since Thompson alludes to this statement in a letter to Southard, March 28, 1818.

60. Southard's fees as a justice and his income as law reporter are outlined in Box 117, Samuel L. Southard Papers, PUL. Notice of his service as agent for the Bank of the United States is in Trenton *Federalist*, May 20, 1816.

61. In a letter to Thomas Kinney, December 9, 1817, Southard alluded to the "unusual &

extraordinary" amount of sickness in his family that year. On Rebecca Southard's ill health, see James D. Harrow to Southard, February 19, 1815; (draft), Southard to William Sampson, May 29, 1815; Rebecca Southard to Southard, July 10, 1816, Southard Papers, PUL. For mentions of and details on John Southard's travail, see Andrew Kirkpatrick to Southard, October 7, 1816; Henry Southard to Southard, December 24, 1816; John Taliaferro to Southard, October 7, 9, December 14, 1816, January 10, March 22, June 4, 1817; Josiah Simpson to Southard, March 5, 1817; John Wurts to Southard, January 28, 1817; Dr. John Van Cleve to Southard, March 10, 24, April 7, 1817; Dr. Richard Corson to Southard, January 13, and n.d., 1818; and Henry Southard to Rebecca Southard, January 5, 1818, Southard Papers PUL.

62. Theodore Frelinghuysen to Samuel L. Southard, August 14, October 4, 1817, Samuel L. Southard Papers, PUL.

63. See David Thompson, Jr. to Southard, October 5, November 20, 1817. The New Brunswick *Fredonian*, November 6, 1817, has the balloting for attorney general. Frelinghuysen himself professed amazement at the result of the election. "You will readily believe," he told Garret D. Wall (a young Federalist politician who had written Frelinghuysen with the happy news of his election) "that I was utterly astonished at the information carryed by your letter—I hope Judge Southard will not suspect me or us of any combination—I have always held him up as the serious candidate and never in any instance even hinted that I should pretend to it—and indeed he has frequently expressed his views to me on the subject and received my encouragement—and now to place me directly in his way is, to say the least of it, unpleasant as it regards my feelings—But as I have left the *course* free and clear to him, without interposing the least wish, I trust he will be manly enough to attach no *censure* to me." Theodore Frelinghuysen to Garret D. Wall, November 1, 1817, Isaac Williamson Papers, New Jersey State Library, Trenton, N. J. Perhaps needless to say, Frelinghuysen did not spurn the position to which he had just been elected. He was to serve as attorney general for twelve years, and relinquished the post only in 1829, upon his election to the United States Senate—in an election in which he had Southard's warm support.

64. "Observer" appeared in the *Fredonian*, February 12, 1818. The week previous, the *Fredonian* editors reprinted a Trenton *True American* article, titled "Liberal Feelings," which strenuously argued that Republicans were foolish to assume that Federalism was dead or that individual Federalists were oriented to accommodation with the majority party.

65. Newark *Sentinel of Freedom*, August 25, September 1, 8, 15, 22, 29, 1818. Clearly, attacks on Federalist "perfidy" were a good Republican topic as an election approached. In the weeks prior to the election of 1818, New Jersey's Republicans circulated an "address" on behalf of the party's congressional ticket, insisting that "the cause of republicanism has not been in greater danger, than at present." The cause of this danger lay not in overt opposition by Federalists, or changes in public opinion, but rather, in the insincere promises by Federalists that "party" was at an end in New Jersey. Southard's defeat in the joint meeting in 1817 seemed proof positive to his partisans that Federalist promises were "unsupported by acts." New Brunswick *Fredonian*, October 8, 1818.

66. For a good insight on this point, see William Pennington Sr., to Samuel L. Southard, August 14, 1818, Southard Papers, PUL.

67. Elaboration on these matters may be found in Michael J. Birkner, "Politics, Law and Enterprise in Jacksonian America: The Career of Samuel Lewis Southard, 1787–1842," (Ph.D. diss., University of Virginia, 1981), pp. 75–78.

68. For background, consult Glover Moore, *The Missouri Controversy, 1819–1821* (Lexington, Ky.: University of Kentucky Press, 1952), pp. 67–73; *Votes and Proceedings, 44th General Assembly, 2nd sitting*, pp. 69–71; Newark *Sentinel of Freedom*, August 8, September 12, 26, 1820; Woodbury *Columbian Herald*, December 23, 1819, December 13, 1820. See also Henry Southard to Samuel L. Southard, September 2, 1820; James Wilson to Samuel L. Southard, January 8, 1820; and Samuel McKeechan to Samuel L. Southard, April 17, 1820, Southard Papers, PUL. Both Charles Kinsey and Bernard Smith justified their procompromise votes in Con-

gress on the grounds that the Union was in peril—an argument that evidently did not persuade their constituents. See *Annals of Congress,* 16th Cong., 1st sess., pp. 1578–1583, for Kinsey's remarks, and Trenton *Federalist,* May 22, 1820, for extracts from Bernard Smith's letter to the people of New Jersey explaining his own course.

69. Prince, "James J. Wilson, Party Leader: 1801–1824," pp. 24–39.

70. David Thompson, Jr., to Samuel L. Southard, March 28, 1818, Samuel L. Southard Papers, PUL.

71. Ibid.

72. On Southard's cultivation of Governor Williamson, see David Thompson, Jr., to Samuel L. Southard, September 7, 1818, Samuel L. Southard Papers, PUL. For Southard's increased involvement in patronage matters, see, among other letters, Nathaniel Saxton to Southard, August 1, 1818; William Penington to Southard, December 10, 1819; (draft), Southard to James Monroe, September 29, 1818; J. N. Simpson to Southard, February 23, 1819; Bernard Smith to Southard, January 3, 1819, December 29, 1820; James F. Randolph to Southard, October 21, November 9, 1820; J. M. Sherrerd to Southard, November 23, 1820; J. F. Blackwell to Southard, n.d., 1820; Henry Southard to Southard, January 15, 1820; William Ten Eyck to Southard, September 1820, Southard Papers, PUL. Even Mahlon Dickerson had cause to seek Southard's help, as witness Mahlon Dickerson to Southard, January 1, 1820, Southard Papers, PUL, requesting Southard's assistance in getting the post of clerk of Essex County for Dickerson's brother Philemon. "If you could give him a lift, without interfering with your own arrangements or plan of operations I should be gratified," Dickerson wrote. Southard's response in this matter is not recorded.

73. John Taliaferro to James Monroe, November 20, 1817, Argosy Collection, University of Virginia Manuscripts Division, Charlottesville; Taliaferro to Southard, January 8, February 6, December 24, 1819, October 24, 1820; John Wurts to Southard, December 24, 1819; David Thompson, Jr., to Southard, July 20, 1820; James W. Scott to Southard, February 14, 1819; Henry Southard to Southard, January 15, 1820, Southard Papers, PUL.

74. Samuel L. Southard to David Thompson, Jr., n.d. (probably June 1820), Southard Papers, PUL.

75. Ibid.

76. Ibid. See also Box 117, Southard Papers, PUL, for medical bills.

77. Robert V. Remini, *The Revolutionary Age of Andrew Jackson* (New York: Harper and Row, 1976), p. 7. For a penetrating examination of the evolution of American values away from classical republicanism, see Pocock, *Machiavellian Moment,* esp. chap. 15. Also helpful in this context are Gordon Wood, *The Rising Glory of America, 1760–1820* (New York: George Braziller, 1971), pp. 1–22; Michael Kammen, *A Season of Youth: The American Revolution and the Historical Imagination* (New York: Alfred A. Knopf, 1978), pp. 96–97; and Michael Paul Rogin, *Fathers and Children: Andrew Jackson and the Subjugation of the American Indian* (New York: Alfred A. Knopf, 1975), esp. chaps. 1, 8.

78. For valuable insights on this subject, particularly as they relate to generational change, see Pauline Maier, *The Old Revolutionaries: Political Lives in the Age of Samuel Adams* (New York: Alfred A. Knopf, 1980).

79. Henry Southard to Samuel L. Southard, January 6, 10, 1819; Elmer, *Constitution and Government,* p. 212.

80. New Brunswick *Fredonian,* November 16, 1820. See also David Thompson Jr., to Southard, October 14, 1820; Lewis Coryell to Southard, October 24, 1820; and Henry Southard to Southard, September 2, 1820, Southard Papers, PUL; and Elmer, *Constitution and Government,* p. 212. Southard was elected with no help from Mahlon Dickerson. As Philemon Dickerson reported to his brother after the election, "Wilson was much mortified and disappointed at the success of Southard. J. J. Kinney was at Trenton at the time Mr. Southard was appointed, and he informed Mr. Parsons that Southard had complained, publicly and bitterly against you; on acc[oun]t of your supporting Mr. Wilson in opposition to him, and obliged that you first

advised him to become a candidate." Philemon Dickerson to Mahlon Dickerson, November 18, 1820, Canfield Genealogical Papers, NJHS.

81. Marvin Meyers, *The Jacksonian Persuasion: Politics and Belief* (Stanford, Calif.: Stanford University Press, 1957), pp. 50–51, is helpful in delineating this restless striving.

Chapter 3

1. Henry Southard's letter announcing his intention not to seek reelection was typically modest. He assured his constituents that they could easily find a suitable replacement for him in Congress, but none who "attend to them with more fidelity." New Brunswick *Fredonian*, October 5, 1820. See also Henry Southard to Samuel L. Southard, September 2, 1820, which contains a rough draft of Henry's retirement letter, offered for his son's perusal and comment. Southard Papers, PUL.

2. See, generally, Wood, *Rising Glory of America*, "Introduction."

3. From November 25, 1820, to March 1, 1821, Southard earned $401 in roughly thirty-five cases as an attorney. Over the next eight months, he earned $2,000 more, in addition to his income as a senator. Clearly the year running from November 1820 to November 1821 was Southard's most remunerative by far. See his account books in Samuel L. Southard Papers, PUL, Box 117.

4. Henry Southard to Samuel Southard, January 3, 15, 1820; John Taliaferro to Southard, February 7, 1820, Southard Papers, PUL. The constitutional issue in question was considerably more ambiguous than at first glance it might appear. Article IV of the federal constitution states that "Congress shall have Power to dispose of and make all needful Rules and Regulations respecting the Territory or other property belonging to the United States." Yet it is quite possible, as George B. Forgie has recently observed, to interpret the word "territory" as simply *land*, rather than as a political community. When one considers that Congress had not prohibited slavery in any territory except the Northwest Territory (a fait accompli by 1789) and that another section of the constitution gives Congress the power to "exercise exclusive Legislation in all cases whatever" over the federal capital city—"much stronger language for a much smaller place" than Missouri, as Forgie notes—one can see that there were reasonable grounds for arguing either side of the question. See *Patricide and the House Divided*, pp. 127–28.

5. Newark *Sentinel of Freedom* August 8, 1820. *Votes and Proceedings, 44th General Assembly, 2nd sitting*, pp. 59–61. Other anticompromise sentiments may be found in the *Sentinel*, September 12, 26, 1820; and Woodbury *Columbian Herald*, December 23, 1819, December 13, 1820. Congressional debate and voting on the Missouri issue in 1820 are perceptively analyzed in Moore, *The Missouri Controversy*, chap. 4.

6. Pasler and Pasler, *New Jersey Federalists*, pp. 151–52.

7. James J. Wilson to William Darlington, January 16, 1821, William Darlington Papers, LC.

8. Isaac Williamson to Samuel Southard, January 3, 1821; (drafts), Southard to Williamson, January 8, 12, 1821, Southard Papers, PUL.

9. Henry Southard to Samuel Southard, January 11, 1821; James Fitz Randolph to Southard, January 15, 1821;David Thompson, Jr., to Southard, January 13, 1821, Southard Papers, PUL.

10. John Taliaferro to Samuel L. Southard, March 27, 1821, Southard Papers, PUL.

11. In his study, *Slavery, Race, and the American Revolution* (Cambridge, England: Cambridge University Press, 1974), p. 12, Duncan J. MacLeod suggests that until 1819, "Southern problems were viewed by most Americans with a fair degree of sympathy . . . but the Missouri crisis revealed to an unsuspecting public just how far the slaveholders' world view had developed. What had previously been regarded as 'flexible' and 'mediatory' was increasingly to be seen as

hypocrisy; and the greed of the class began to excite more comment than the social problems with which it was faced." See also Dangerfield, *Era of Good Feelings*, pp. 199–201.

12. See (typed) catalogue of Southard's slave purchases and sales, Southard Papers, PUL, Box 80. One of Southard's "servants," George, absconded to Boston in 1818, and Southard followed him there to regain custody. There is no indication whether he succeeded in this venture. See S. D. Parker to Joseph Story, August 2, 1818, copy in Southard Papers, PUL.

13. Southard's mentor, Robert Finley, was the driving force behind the American Colonization Society, and Southard himself was for many years active in the New Jersey chapter. He often spoke before colonization groups, and was himself president of the New Jersey colonization society in the late 1830s. P. J. Staudenraus, *The African Colonization Movement, 1816–1865* (New York: Columbia University Press, 1961), chaps. 2, 3; speech file, Southard Papers, PUL, Box 81; Southard to John P. Jackson, November 16, 1839, John P. Jackson Papers, NJHS.

14. *Annals*, 16th Cong., 2nd sess., 350, 359. The Senate vote was 23–19, with Southard and his New Jersey colleague, Mahlon Dickerson, in the affirmative. The bill was lost in the House. Lucius H. Stockton told Southard that his vote on the bill would "give great satisfaction to your friends and constituents." Stockton to Southard, February 25, 1821, Southard Papers, PUL. See also Charles Ewing to Southard, February 23, 1821, ibid.

15. *Annals*, p. 364. See also Perceval Perry. "The attitudes of the New Jersey Delegations in Congress on the Slavery Question, 1815–1861" (M.A. thesis, Rutgers University, 1939), chap. 2.

16. *Annals*, pp. 380–82. Several brief biographies of Southard including, most notably, the sketch offered by Lucius Q. C. Elmer, have suggested that Southard, not Henry Clay, actually authored the key compromise that concluded the controversy over free blacks in Missouri. According to Elmer, who was quoting James A. Hamilton, who purportedly got *his* story from Southard's son-in-law, Ogden Hoffman, Southard told Hoffman that he had prepared the compromise resolutions and showed them to Henry Clay, who suggested that they should be brought forward in the House of Representatives, and requested Southard's permission to follow this course. Southard acquiesced, and as a consequence, Clay received credit for ending the crisis. The major problem with this analysis is that no corroborating evidence exists. Nothing in the Southard Papers at Princeton or the Library of Congress, and nothing in Henry Clay's correspondence even hints that Southard played the role he allegedly claimed for himself. For testimony to Clay's preeminent role, see Everett Somerville Brown, ed., *The Missouri Compromises and Presidential Politics, 1820–1825: From the Letters of William Plumer, Junior* (St. Louis: Missouri Historical Society, 1926), p. 42. Elmer, *Constitution and Government*, pp. 212–14.

17. *Annals*, pp. 389–90; Dangerfield, *Era of Good Feelings*, pp. 241–42; Clement Eaton, *Henry Clay and the Art of American Politics* (Boston: Little, Brown, & Co., 1957), p. 123.

18. New Brunswick *Fredonian*, March 8, 1821. In the legislative elections of fall 1821, James Fitz Randolph was the only Republican candidate to lose in Middlesex County. It is certain that his stance on the Missouri issue contributed to his deat. *Fredonian*, October 18, 1821.

19. John Taliaferro to Samuel Southard, March 27, 1821, Southard Papers, PUL. In fact, Southard's vote for compromise on the Missouri issue was to haunt him when he ran for the United States Senate in 1829. For a full discussion of this mortifying incident in Southard's life, see chapter 6.

20. John was born in 1813, Virginia in 1815, Henry in 1818, and Samuel, Jr., in 1819. Ralph K. Potter's dating of the children's births, in "Early Southards of New York and New Jersey," p. 90, is not reliable.

21. See Southard Papers, PUL, Box 80, and family correspondence for the years 1821–23.

22. Southard Papers, PUL, family correspondence for 1821–23, plus undated correspondence, Box 78. At this time the household also included William Wellford, the young son of Samuel Southard's old Virginia friend, John S. Wellford. William was attending school in New Jersey as part of a "broadening" experience common among affluent young Southerners.

23. John Southard died on December 27, 1824, after an agonizing series of epileptic fits. See Virginia Southard to Samuel Southard, November 16, December 11, 1824; Isaac Southard to Southard, December 29, 1824; and, for most detail, Charles Ewing to Southard, December 27, 28, 29, 1824, Southard Papers, PUL.

24. Notable letters on patronage include (draft), Southard to William H.Crawford, February 23, 1821; D. Miller to Southard, February 5, 1821; (draft), Southard to James Monroe, December 12, 1821; John N. Simpson to Southard, February 9, 1821; John M. Sherrerd to Southard, June 18, 1821; Bernard Smith to Southard, November 14, 1821; David Thompson, Jr., to Southard, January 13, December 8, 1821; Richard Stockton to Southard, March 10, 1821; John Taliaferro to Southard, February 20, March 2, December 13, 1821, and various letters to and from Postmaster General Montgomery Meigs, Southard Papers, PUL.

25. Lucius Q. C. Elmer to Southard, December 21, 1821, January 21, March 2, April 17, 1822, January 30, August 13, October 10, 17, 31, November 8, 15, 22, 28, December 5, 10, 1823; Charles Ewing to Southard, February 23, December 18, 1821, January 26, 30, February 11, March 8, 26, April 10, 15, December 16, 19, 1822; of Ewing's thirty-two letters to Southard in 1823, those of November 29, December 16 are most important for politics; David Fitz Randolph to Southard, February 2, 1822; Isaac Southard to Southard, July 5, 1821, October 22, 1822, November 24, December 19, 1823; John Taliaferro to Southard, March 27, 1821, January 7, February 7, 15, 27, April 8, December 17, 1822, February 25, 1823; David Thompson, Jr., to Southard, January 13, February 13, April 7, 19, August 9, 26, 29, September 3, 8, 12, 18, 22, 25, 29, December 8, 22, 1821, January 19, March 6, 26, September 3, 1822, January 25, February 13, April 17, May 14, August 3, October 26, November 15, 1823, all in Southard Papers, PUL.

26. Dangerfield, *Era of Good Feelings*, p. 240.

27. The literature on the background to the campaign of 1824 is enormous. George Dangerfield, *The Awakening of American Nationalism, 1815–1828* (New York: Harper & Row, 1965), chap. 8, is a standard account.

28. Van Deusen, *Life of Henry Clay*, pp. 116–33. Van Deusen grants Clay's sincerity in his criticism of Monroe and Adams, but indicates that their course in dealings with Spain, not the Kentuckian's, was the sounder. For a similar assessment, see Dangerfield, *Era of Good Feelings*, pp. 270–73, and Samuel Flagg Bemis, *John Quincy Adams and the Foundations of American Foreign Policy* (New York: Alfred A. Knopf, 1950), chap. 17. For John Quincy Adams's jaundiced estimate of Clay, see Adams, ed., *Memoirs*, 6:26.

29. There is considerable scholarly testimony to Calhoun's effectiveness as war secretary. See especially Charles M. Wiltse, *John C. Calhoun: Nationalist, 1782–1828* (Indianapolis, Ind.: Bobbs-Merrill Co., Inc., 1944), chaps. 11, 12, 13; and Carlton B. Smith, "John C. Calhoun, Secretary of War, 1817–1825: The Cast Iron Man as an Administrator," in John B. Boles, ed., *America, The Middle Period: Essays in Honor of Bernard Mayo* (Charlottesville, Va.: University of Virginia Press, 1973), pp. 132–44. On the emergence of "Radical" opposition to the administration, Harry Ammon, *James Monroe: The Quest for National Identity* (New York: McGraw Hill Book Company, 1971), pp. 469–72, 493–501. Norman Risjord, *The Old Republicans: Southern Conservatives in the Age of Jefferson* (New York: Columbia University Press, 1965), pp. 231–37, puts somewhat less stress on the link between Crawford's ambitions and "Radical" criticisms of the administration. In his biography of Crawford, Chase Mooney argues that the Georgian had nothing to do with congressional attacks on Calhoun and, for that matter, that Crawford's position on the issues before the nation in the early 1820s mark him as no "Radical." *William H. Crawford, 1772–1834* (Lexington, Ky.: University of Kentucky Press, 1974), pp. 196, 288–89. Even granting this, one must recognize that Crawford's allies and his enemies readily identified him with "Radicalism," and so did much of the public. See Robert Lorish, "William H. Crawford and the Presidential Election of 1824" (M.A. thesis, University of Virginia, 1965), pp. 34–35.

30. Ammon, *Monroe*, p. 363. John Taliaferro's glowing recommendation of Southard for

the position was expressed in a letter to the president on November 20, 1817. Argosy Collection, Alderman Library, University of Virginia Special Collections.

31. *Annals,* 17th Cong., 1st sess., passim. Southard did vote, against the president's wishes, for the Cumberland Road Bill advocated by Henry Clay. After its veto, when a substitute measure was introduced, he was absent. Ibid., pp. 444, 455. On the bill to apportion representatives, see also David Thompson, Jr., to Southard, March 6, 1822; Isaac Williamson to Southard, December 19, 1822; and James J. Wilson to Southard, January 9, 1822, Samuel Southard Papers, PUL.

32. Samuel Southard to Rebecca Harrow Southard, February 14, 1822, Samuel Southard Papers, PUL. Henry Southard to Samuel Southard, February 20, 1822, noted matter-of-factly that people were asking him, "Why you don't spout?"

33. *Annals,* 17th Cong., 1st sess., p. 194. In an amusing coda to Southard's effort, his wife wrote back asking him why, if public speaking made him so nervous, he bothered to continue with it. Rebecca Harrow Southard to Samuel Southard, February 21, 1822, Southard Papers, PUL. See also Southard to Rebecca Southard, February 14, 16, 1822.

34. *Annals,* 17th Cong., 1st sess., pp. 390, 394. A copy of Dickerson's bill, introduced in the Senate on January 10, 1822, is in Samuel Southard Papers, PUL, Box 98.

35. Samuel Southard to Rebecca Harrow Southard, March 2, 9, December 22, 1822, Southard Papers, PUL.

36. On the possible appointment to a South American mission, see David Thompson, Jr., to Southard, March 6, 1822. For rumors that Southard would be named attorney general in place of the ailing William Wirt, Charles Ewing to Southard, March 26, 1822. Indications of the president's friendship for Southard are in James Monroe to Southard, February 12, March 8, December 17, 1822. Also, John Taliaferro to Southard, February 15, 1822, in which Taliaferro, trying to lift his friend's current low spirits, observed, "I am well informed that you stand on high ground at headquarters. . . . Every day brings you more into notice." Taliaferro advised Southard that proximity to the president was the key to advancement. "See him often, and converse with him freely. Nothing pleases him more." John Taliaferro to Southard, February 15, April 8, 1822, and Garret D. Wall to Southard, March 26, 1822, Southard Papers, PUL.

37. Samuel Southard to Rebecca Harrow Southard, March 2, 1822, Southard Papers, PUL.

38. Samuel Southard to James Monroe, June 8, 1822, Southard Papers, PUL.

39. (Draft), Southard to David Thompson, n.d. [1820], Southard Papers, PUL.

40. Beckwith, "Mahlon Dickerson," pp. 237–38.

41. For an indication of Calhoun's warm relations with President Monroe, see Margaret Coit, *John C. Calhoun: American Portrait* (Boston: Houghton Mifflin Company, 1950), p. 151.

42. Samuel Southard to Rebecca Harrow Southard, February 16, 1822, John Patterson to Southard, January 12, 1822 (misdated 1821), Charles Ewing to Southard, January 26, 1822, Southard Papers, PUL. See also Trenton *True American,* January 26, 1822.

43. John C. Calhoun to Samuel Southard, March 31, 1822, Southard Papers, PUL.

44. Samuel Southard to John C. Calhoun, April 2, 1822, Southard Papers, PUL.

45. Samuel Southard to John C. Calhoun, September 19, 1822; Calhoun to Southard, September 23, 1822, Southard Papers, PUL.

46. Francis T. Brooke to Samuel Southard, January 15, February 5, March 1, April 2, 23, 1822, Southard Papers, PUL.

47. John C. Calhoun to Samuel Southard, March 19, 27, April 9 (2 letters), 10, June 14, August 17, October 12, 1823; Southard to Calhoun, March 18, 31, 1823 (drafts); Richard Coxe to Southard, August 16, 1823; Ninian Edwards to Southard, March 20, 1823; (draft), Southard to Edwards, March 26, 1823, Southard Papers, PUL.

48. John C. Calhoun to Samuel Southard, March 19, 1823, Southard Papers, PUL.

49. James Cook to Samuel Southard, September 25, November 15, 1823; James Westcott to Southard, October 17,1823; David Thompson to Southard, August 3, 1823; Richard S. Coxe

to Southard, March 31, July 31, August 26, 1823; Stacy G. Potts to Southard, November 29, 1823, Samuel Southard Papers, PUL.

50. Bridgeton *Washington Whig*, February 15, 1823.

51. New Brunswick *Fredonian*, June 15, 22, 1820; August 14, 1823.

52. Lutzker, "Abolition of Imprisonment for Debt," pp. 9–12; Peter J. Coleman, *Debtors and Creditors in America: Insolvency, Imprisonment for Debt, and Bankruptcy, 1607–1900* (Madison, Wisc.: The State Historical Society of Wisconsin, 1974), passim.

53. *Annals*, 17th Cong., 2nd sess., pp. 105, 107–26, January 14, 15, 1823.

54. Ibid., pp. 113–45.

55. See, for example, comments by the editor of the Bridgeton *Washington Whig*, May 10, 1823.

56. Trenton *Federalist*, March 10, 1823. *Annals*, pp. 148, 187, 287.

57. Richard S. Coxe to Samuel Southard, March 10, 22, 1823; Lewis Condict to Southard, March 22, 1823, enclosing a copy of his letter to President Monroe, urging Southard's appointment to the vacant court post; (draft), Southard to Condict, March 24, 1823, Samuel Southard Papers, PUL.

58. (Draft), Samuel Southard to John C. Calhoun, March 23, 1823, Samuel Southard Papers, PUL.

59. Ammon, *Monroe*, pp. 513–14.

60. Ibid. For an analysis of Smith Thompson's maneuverings during this period, see Robert V. Remini, *Martin Van Buren and the Making of the Democratic Party* (New York: Columbia University Press, 1959), pp. 33–35.

61. J. H. Clarke to Southard, March 22, 1823; (draft), Southard to J. H. Clarke, March 31, 1823, Samuel Southard Papers, PUL. For similar views, see (draft), Southard to William A. Dade, June 9, 1823, Southard Papers, PUL.

62. Ephraim Bateman to Samuel Southard, April 2, 1823; John C. Calhoun to Southard, March 19, 27, April 9, 10, June 14, August 17, 1823; William A. Dade to Southard, July 29, 1823, Southard Papers, PUL. During this period Southard's name cropped up frequently in the press and in private political talk as a likely appointee to the navy secretaryship. See, for example, *Niles Weekly Register* for summer 1823, Charles Miner to Henry Clay, June 19, 1823, and Henry Clay to Charles Hammond, August 21, 1823, in James F. Hopkins, et al., eds., *The Papers of Henry Clay*, 6 vols. (Lexington, Ky.: University of Kentucky Press, 1959——), 3:435, 472.

63. Adams, ed., *Memoirs*, 6:173–75.

64. James Monroe to Samuel L. Southard, August 16, 1823, Southard Papers, PUL. John C. Calhoun followed Monroe's announcement with his own congratulations in a letter of August 17.

65. Samuel L. Southard to Smith Thompson, August 23, 1823, Ely Collection, NJHS. There is a somewhat differently worded draft of this letter in the Southard Papers at Princeton.

66. Samuel Southard to James Monroe, August 27, 1823 (private), James Monroe Papers, New York Public Library. Rough drafts of this letter, as well as his brief note of August 21, 1823, are in the Southard Papers,PUL.

67. Southard's official commission as secretary of the navy, signed by James Monroe and John Quincy Adams, and dated September 16, 1823, is in the Samuel Southard Papers, Library of Congress.

Chapter 4

1. Southard's administrative and policymaking role as navy secretary is treated in chapter 5. Inevitably there is a gray area between his advisory responsibilities, on one hand, and his

political activity, on the other: Southard's role in shaping policy with regard to the Creek Indians in Georgia and the Panama Congress are cases in point. This chapter, however, will focus primarily on the aspects of Southard's secretaryship in which he played a significant political role as an advocate, activist, or target.

2. Calhoun's outlook and activities as a presidential candidate are laid out in Charles M. Wiltse, *John C. Calhoun: Nationalist, 1782–1828* (Indianapolis, Ind.: Bobbs-Merrill Co., Inc., 1944), chaps. 18–20, 22.

3. Stacy G. Potts to Samuel L. Southard, November 29, 1823, Southard Papers, PUL. On Calhoun's rising prospects in New Jersey in late 1823, see also James Cook to Southard, September 25, 1823, James Westcott to Southard, October 17, 1823, Southard Papers, PUL: Isaac Williamson to Mahlon Dickerson, December 16, 1823, Mahlon Dickerson Papers, NJHS; and James J. Wilson to William Darlington, November 14, 1823, William Darlington Papers, Library of Congress.

4. Clinton was supported by the Morristown *Palladium of Liberty* and that was the extent of the New Yorker's press support in the state. See Newark *New Jersey Eagle*, January 3, 1824.

5. Woodbury *Columbian Herald*, January 21, 1824.

6. Lucius Q. C. Elmer to Southard, January 19, 1824, Southard Papers, PUL.

7. Quoted in Paul C. Nagel, "The Election of 1824: A Reconsideration Based on News-paper Opinion," *Journal of Southern History* 21 (August 1960): 323. On maneuvering among politicians in the Keystone State in early 1824, see Herman Hailperin, "Pro-Jackson Sentiment in Pennsylvania, 1820–1828," *Pennsylvania Magazine of History and Biography* 50 (July 1926): 206; John Spencer Bassett, *The Life of Andrew Jackson* (New York: Doubleday and Co., 1911), 1:331–34; and Kim T. Phillips, "The Pennsylvania Origins of the Jackson Movement," *Political Science Quarterly* 91 (Fall 1976): 489–508.

8. *New Jersey Eagle*, February 20, 1824.

9. Trenton *True American*, February 21, March 6, 1824; Newark *Sentinel of Freedom*, March 9, 1824; Thomas Robson Hay, "John C. Calhoun and the Presidential Campaign of 1824," *North Carolina Historical Review* 12 (January 1935): 38–40; Herbert Ershkowitz, "The Election of 1824 in New Jersey," *Proceedings of the New Jersey Historical Society* 84 (April 1966): 17–19.

10. Isaac Southard to Samuel L. Southard, March 8, 1824, Southard Papers, PUL. See also the papers of Richmond *Enquirer* coeditor C. P. Gooch, University of Virginia Special Collections, for evidence of Dickerson's deep involvement in the Crawford campaign and for several letters from Dickerson devising strategy for that campaign.

11. Samuel L. Southard to Francis T. Brooke, November 15, 1824, Lucius Q. C. Elmer to Southard, March 14, 1824, Charles Ewing to Southard, June 24, 1824, Southard papers, PUL; Southard to Jonathan Dayton, March 13, 1824, Gratz Autograph Collection, Historical Society of Pennsylvania; Adams, *Memoirs*, 6:365–68, 400–401, 470–71, 479–80.

12. Diary entry of March 11, 1824, in *Memoirs*, 6:253–54.

13. *The Education of Henry Adams* (New York: Modern Library, 1931), p. 47.

14. Quoted in Culver R. Smith, "Propaganda Technique in the Jackson campaign of 1828," *East Tennessee Historical Society Publications* 6 (1934): 44.

15. Samuel Flagg Bemis, *John Quincy Adams and the Union* (New York: Alfred A. Knopf, 1956), chap. 2. For specific references to Southard's concordance with JQA on foreign policy, see *Memoirs*, 6:178, 181, 196, 204, 225, 234, 268, 435–37, 445.

16. Lucius Q. C. Elmer to Southard, June 28, 1824, Charles Ewing to Southard, undated, 1824, marked "confidential & to be burned," Southard Papers, PUL.

17. Southard to Benjamin W. Crowninshield, November 16, 1824, two drafts, Southard Papers, PUL. See (draft), Southard to Francis T. Brooke, November 15, 1824, in which he took pains to relieve Brooke's fears that Calhoun was a Federalist in disguise.

18. Adams, *Memoirs*, 6:506–7 (February 11, 1825).

19. Ibid., 479–80. See also Brown, ed., *The Missouri Compromises and Presidential Politics*, pp. 139–42.

20. Adams, *Memoirs*, 6:474 (January 1, 1825). See also Daniel Walker Howe, *The Political*

216 SAMUEL L. SOUTHARD

Culture of the American Whigs (Chicago: University of Chicago Press, 1979), pp. 48–49.

21. Bemis, *JQA and the Union,* p. 55; Nagel, "Election of 1824," pp. 326–27.

22. (Draft), Southard to John C. Calhoun, September 12, 1825; Calhoun to Southard, October 11, 1825, expressing satisfaction with Southard's assurances, Southard Papers, PUL; Southard to Francis T. Brooke, February 27, 1825, Southard Papers, LC.

23. Southard to Brooke, February 27, 1825, Southard Papers, LC. On the reorientation of Republican thinking after the War of 1812, see Drew R. McCoy, *The Elusive Republic: Political Economy in Jeffersonian America* (Chapel Hill, N.C.: University of North Carolina Press, 1980), chap. 10, and Ralph Ketcham, *James Madison: A Biography* (New York: The Macmillan Company, 1971), pp. 604–5.

24. Southard and Clay had met one another on numerous occasions prior to 1825, but their relations were cool, primarily because Clay had opposed the Monroe administration on several important issues. Nonetheless, the two men had much in common, and they became quite close during the years they served together in the cabinet.

25. On the "Corrupt Bargain" charge, see, among many sources, Robert V. Remini, *The Election of Andrew Jackson* (Philadelphia: J. B. Lippincott Company, 1963), pp. 20–29. David Porter's controversial landing at Foxardo, Puerto Rico, is discussed in chapter 5. On Governor George Troup and the controversy over the Creek Indians, see Dangerfield, *Era of Good Feelings,* pp. 390–91.

26. Dangerfield, *Era of Good Feelings,* pp. 348-50; Bemis, *JQA and the Union,* pp. 66–69. Both assessments are based on Adams's *Memoirs,* 7:59–64. Quote is from p. 61.

27. *Memoirs,* 7:63. For a different interpretation of the outcome of the cabinet deliberations than that offered here, see Young, *Washington Community,* pp. 238–39.

28. James D. Richardson, comp., *A Compilation of the Messages and Papers of the Presidents,* 10 vols. (New York: Bureau of National Literature and Art, 1901), 2:315–16.

29. Dangerfield, *Era of Good Feelings,* p. 349.

30. *The Autobiography of Martin Van Buren,* ed., John C. Fitzpatrick (Washington, D.C.: U.S. Government Printing Office, 1920), pp. 192–98; Wiltse, *Calhoun: Nationalist,* p. 321; John C. Calhoun to Mahlon Dickerson, April 7, 1827, Mahlon Dickerson Papers, NJHS.

31. This point touches a complex and as yet unresolved historiographical "debate," of which three perspectives are most readily identifiable. One view, propounded by Samuel Flagg Bemis, holds that Adams's proposals *were* Hamiltonian ideas revived. A second view, offered by Richard E. Ellis in *The Jeffersonian Crisis: Courts and Politics in the Young Republic* (New York: Oxford University Press, 1971), suggests that there were two major Jeffersonian traditions—a "moderate" tradition, emphasizing "improvement" as its central motif, a tradition embraced by Adams, Clay, and ultimately the Whig party; and a "radical" tradition, strictly based on the "principles of '98," which served as the intellectual foundation for the Jacksonian movement. Finally there is the argument, as yet not fully developed, by Lance Banning and Drew R. McCoy, that the Hamiltonian "specter" had been confronted without any particular trauma by Republican policymakers in 1816, and that Adams's program can in large measure be seen in the context of a single Jeffersonian tradition in transit. For this view, see Banning, "The Moderate as Revolutionary: An Introduction to Madson's Life," *Quarterly Journal of the Library of Congress* 37 (Spring, 1980), p. 175, and McCoy, *The Elusive Republic,* chap. 10.

32. The major works on republican ideology are cited in chap. 1, n. 6, above. See also Fred M. Somkin, *Unquiet Eagle: Memory and Desire in the Idea of American Freedom, 1815–1860* (Ithaca, N.Y.: Cornell University Press, 1967); Michael F. Holt, *The Political Crisis of the 1850s* (New York: John Wiley & Sons, Inc., 1978); and Forgie, *Patricide in the House Divided.*

33. Wood, *Rising Glory,* introduction. On Southern opposition to these tendencies, and specifically to federal aid for economic development, see Robert E. Shalhope, "Thomas Jefferson's Republicanism and Antebellum Southern Thought," *Journal of Southern History* 42 (November 1976): 529–56.

34. Bemis, *JQA and the Union*, pp. 61–62.

35. Pocock, *Machiavellian Moment*, p. 539.

36. Rowland Berthoff, "Independence and Attachment, Virtue and Interest: From Republican Citizen to Free Enterprizer, 1787–1837," in Richard L. Bushman, et al., eds., *Uprooted Americans: Essays to Honor Oscar Handlin* (Boston: Little, Brown, and Co., 1979), pp. 97–124; Eric Foner, *Free Soil, Free Labor, Free Men: The Ideology of the Republican Party Before the Civil War* (New York: Oxford University Press, 1970), pp. 29–30.

37. Samuel L. Southard to Joel R. Poinsett, November 20, 1826, Gilpin Collection, HSP. See also Elmer, *Constitution and Government*, pp. 221–22.

38. See, generally, Mary W. Hargreaves, *The Presidency of John Quincy Adams*, University of Kansas Press, forthcoming.

39. Robert Arnold to Southard, September 18, 1826, Southard Papers, PUL.

40. George Dangerfield, *The Awakening of American Nationalism, 1815–1828* (New York: Harper Torchbooks, 1965), pp. 240–41.

41. Bemis, *JQA and the Union*, pp. 136–40; see also Hopkins and Hargreaves, eds., *The Papers of Henry Clay*, 6: 110, 320. Southard's attention to patronage is well evidenced in his papers at Princeton.

42. Adams, *Memoirs*, 6 : 312–14, 315–17. See also Daniel Webster to Henry Warfield, February 3, 1825, in Charles M. Wiltse, ed., *The Papers of Daniel Webster: Correspondence*, 5 vols. (Hanover, N.H., 1974——) 2 : 18, 21–22. There is no indication from Adams's comments or his correspondence that he had done anything more than promise to act "liberally" when making appointments. On this, see Webster to Jeremiah Mason, February 14, 1825, and Webster to Ezekial Webster, February 26, 1825, ibid., 23–24, 35.

43. Richard Stockton to Southard, March 25, 1826, Robert Field Stockton to Southard, May 6, June 5, July 1, 1826, Southard Papers, PUL. There is no adequate biography of Robert F. Stockton, but see Alfred Hoyt Bill, *A House Called Morven: Its Role in American History* (rev. ed., Constance M. Greiff; Princeton, N.J.: Princeton University Press, 1978), chap. 6.

44. Robert F. Stockton to Southard, October 19, 1826, Southard Papers, PUL; Adams, *Memoirs*, 7 : 154, 161; *New Jersey Patriot*, September 7, 14, 1826 (Box 147, Southard Papers, PUL).

45. Stockton to Southard, October 19, 1826, Southard Papers, PUL.

46. See, for example, Ephraim Bateman to Southard, November 1, 1826, Abraham Brown to Southard, October 23, 1826, William Jeffers to Southard, October 20, 1826, Southard Papers, PUL.

47. Southard's brother Isaac caught the nub of the matter by noting in a letter dated November 16, 1826, that "Stockton, though capable, is *unpopular*," Southard Papers, PUL. See also John Wilson to Southard, October 25, 1826, John Patterson to Southard, October 24, 1826, Southard Papers, PUL; Ephraim Bateman to Henry Clay, October 30, 1826, *Papers of Henry Clay*, 5 : 841.

48. Bemis, *JQA and the Union*, pp. 138–39.

49. (Draft), Southard to Robert F. Stockton, November 23, 1826, Southard Papers, PUL. Robert F. Stockton's bitterness over what he interpreted as the administration's betrayal ran deep. He poured out his resentment in 1828 to Daniel Webster, expressing "great pain" that he should be forced to oppose Webster in politics. But under the circumstances it is impossible for me to go with you—the injustice and *contempt* with which we have been treated . . . give rise to emotions not readily subdued—and by such a man as Samuel Southard—who was not in truth worthy to be esteemed by a man like my father—is enough to drive from the heart every feeling of civilization and humanity." Robert F. Stockton to Daniel Webster, July 14, 1828, in Wiltse, ed., *Correspondence of Webster*, 2 : 353–55.

50. The issue was revived in April 1828 by the editor of a Jacksonian newspaper in Buffalo, who claimed that Daniel Webster had shown Richard Stockton a letter from John Quincy Adams pledging to appoint Federalists to office, specifically in New Jersey. Despite Webster's

prompt denial that there had been any such letter, the charge circulated widely in the Jacksonian press. See Daniel Webster to Joseph Hopkinson, April 21, 1828, in Wiltse, ed., *Correspondence of Webster*, 2:336. See also Samuel Cassedy to Garret D. Wall, September 16, 1828, Garret Wall Papers, PUL, for indication of New Jersey Jacksonians' willingness to employ "The Webster Pledge" against the administration. For an account of the Stockton affair emphasizing the role of Daniel Webster, see Shaw Livermore, *The Twilight of Federalism: The Disintegration of the Federalist Party, 1815–1830* (Princeton, N.J.: Princeton University Press, 1962), pp. 174–77, 214–16.

51. Note, for example, Isaac's remark following the county elections of October 1826 that "I believe the result of Somerset is owing to Mr. Hartwick & myself. This you may consider boasting but it is *true*." Isaac Southard to Samuel L. Southard, October 18, 1826, Southard Papers, PUL.

52. Lucius Q. C. Elmer to Southard, December 20, 1827, Southard papers, PUL. (This letter has been misfiled with 1825.)

53. David Thompson, Jr., to Southard, August 27, 1826, Southard Papers, PUL; Richard P. McCormick, "Party Formation in New Jersey in the Jackson Era," *Proceedings of the New Jersey Historical Society* 83 (July 1965): 164–65; Michael J. Birkner, "Peter Vroom and the Politics of Democracy," in Paul A. Stellhorn, ed., *Jacksonian New Jersey* (Trenton, N.J.: New Jersey Historical Commission, 1979), p. 15.

54. September 26, 1826.

55. Adams, *Memoirs*, 7:154; Robert Arnold observed to Southard after the results were in in New Jersey that "this is a very important triumph in my opinion." Arnold to Southard, October 17, 1826, Southard Papers, PUL.

56. Other frequent correspondents regarding political currents included Simon Cameron of Pennsylvania, Congressman Frank Johnson of Kentucky, and Governor Joseph Kent of Maryland. For Southard's interest in newspaper propaganda in Virginia, James D. Harrow to Southard, September 11, 1827, Hugh Mercer to Southard, September 15, 1827, Southard Papers, PUL.

57. Quoted in Amelia W. Williams and Eugene C. Barker, eds., *The Writings of Sam Houston* (Austin, Tex.: University of Texas Press, 1938) 1:98.

58. Robert V. Remini, *The Election of Andrew Jackson* (Philadelphia: J. B. Lippincott and Co., 1963), pp. 125–35. On James Barbour's activity on behalf of the administration, Charles D. Lowery, "James Barbour, A Politician and Planter of Antebellum Virginia," Unpublished Ph.D diss., University of Virginia, 1966, p. 308.

59. Remini, *Election of Andrew Jackson*, pp. 47–50, 53–65, 68–71, 76–120. New Jersey, it might be noted, was an exception to the general rule.

60. Barbour and Southard occasionally traveled together, ostensibly on departmental business, but on occasion to perform political chores. See, for example, Adams, *Memoirs*, 7:156, 158, 239, 244.

61. Few standard biographies of Jackson or histories of the period mention the Jackson-Southard controversy, and none goes into much detail. Of these accounts, the most reliable is John Spencer Bassett, *The Life of Andrew Jackson* (Garden City, N.Y.: Doubleday and Company, 1911) 1:395–96. What follows is reconstructed from correspondence in the Jackson papers (published and unpublished), the Southard Papers at Princeton, and the Library of Congress, and particularly Southard's thirty-one-page memorandum, "Remarks on the Correspondence," in Southard Papers, LC.

62. Adams, ed., *Memoirs*, 7:218–19; Andrew Jackson to Sam Houston, November 23, December 15, 1826, in John Spencer Basset, ed., *The Correspondence of Andrew Jackson* (Washington, D.C.: Carnegie Institute, 1926–35) 3:318, 325.

63. Bassett, *Life of Jackson*, 1:395–96; Llerena Friend, *Sam Houston: The Great Designer* (Austin, Tex.: University of Texas Press, 1954), pp. 14–15.

64. Andrew Jackson to Samuel L. Southard, January 5, 1827, in *Correspondence*, 3:329–30;

Jackson to Sam Houston, January 5, 27, 1827, in ibid., pp. 330–33. Southard mentioned the undelivered Jackson letter to John Quincy Adams on December 23, 1826. On February 3, 1827, he told Adams that he had finally received a letter, but not the one anticipated. Requested for an opinion on how best to proceed, Adams urged Southard to take a defensive approach and, on February 9, expressed satisfaction with the course Southard was taking. *Memoirs*, 7:218–19, 220, 221, 223.

65. For example, the spate of letters to friends, requesting advice or assistance, many of which are in the Southard Papers, LC.

66. Samuel L. Southard to Andrew Jackson, February 9, 1827, in *Correspondence of Jackson* 3:342–44.

67. Andrew Jackson to Southard, March 6, 1827, in ibid., pp. 345–48. See also Jackson to John Coffee, March 16, 1827, in ibid., pp. 348–49.

68. "Remarks on the Correspondence," Southard Papers, LC.

69. Southard to James Monroe, February 4, 1827, Monroe Papers, LC microfilm; Monroe to Southard, February 9, 1827, Southard Papers, PUL. On Monroe's financial plight, and its bearing on the controversy between Southard and Jackson, see Lucius Wilmerding, Jr., *James Monroe, Public Claimant* (New Brunswick, N.J.: Rutgers University Press, 1960), pp. 88–90, 112. See also Ammon, *Monroe*, pp. 558–59.

70. See, for example, William Ten Eyck to Southard, n.d., 1827, Thomas W. White to Southard, July 4, 1827, George Holcombe to Southard, May 28, 1827, Peter J. Clarke to Southard, May 19, 1827, Southard to Peter J. Clarke, n.d., 1827, Southard to Thomas W. White, July 9, 1827, Southard Papers, PUL. The letters written by Southard were both rough drafts.

71. Washington, D.C., *United States Telegraph*, June 29, July 7, 11, 1827.

72. A further restraint on Southard's conduct was the continuing advice from President Adams to avoid, insofar as possible, being drawn further into the controversy. Adams, *Memoirs*, 7:259, 260. See also John Taliaferro to Southard, May 26, 1827, Southard Papers, PUL.

73. (Draft), Southard to John Wurts, June 27, 1827, Southard papers, LC. See also Southard to Wurts's brother, Alexander Wurts, February 1, March 1, 1828, in which Southard alludes not only to Jackson's deficiencies as a writer, but the general's commitment "to hate me without cause."

74. Southard to James Monroe, December 16, 1827, Monroe Papers, LC, microfilm. See also John Taliaferro to Monroe, December 15, 1827.

75. James Monroe to Samuel Southard, December 17, 1827, Southard Papers, PUL.

76. Ammon, *Monroe*, pp. 559–60.

77. William Prall to Southard, December 29, 1826, Garret Wall to Southard, December 29, 1826, Southard Papers, PUL.

78. Samuel Southard to Garret D. Wall, January 13, 1827, Southard papers, LC.

79. On Southard's speechmaking, William D. Waple to Southard, October 9, 1827, and David Thompson, Jr., to Southard, December 6, 1827, Southard Papers, PUL.

80. On patronage, see, among many letters, George Sullivan to Southard, April 6, November 21, n.d., 1827, Hugh Mercer to Southard, September 15, 1827, Samuel M. D. Moore to Southard, September 28, 1827, John Meyers to Southard, May 8, June 1, 1827, Thomas Newton to Southard, March 21, April 16, 23, May 1, 9, 1827, Philip Nicklin to Southard, January 11, February 3, November 13, December 24, 1827, February 2, April 11, 17, 23, May 1, 5, June 23, 28, October 18, 1828. On Southard's bid to Smith Thompson regarding the New York governorship, Southard to Thompson, July 12, 1828, Smith Thompson Papers, PUL. On materials for the pro-administration presses, Richard S. Coxe to Southard, August 10, 1828, William Prall to Southard, November 12, 1828, John Taliaferro to Southard, June 10, 1828.

81. Quoted in Elmer, *Constitution and Government*, pp. 223–25.

82. Thomas Harris wrote on August 29, 1828, from Philadelphia that "we are achieving wonders in Pennsylvania." See also John Sergeant to Southard, June 25, July 11, 1828, Southard Papers, PUL.

83. Francis T. Brooke to Southard, October 8, 27, December 14, 28, 1828, Southard to Colonel Knapp, October 1, 1828, Southard to Daniel Doty, December 14, 1828, Thomas Harris to Southard, November 2, 1828, Charles Harrow to Southard, October 25, 1828, Charles Hay to Southard, September 24, 27, 1828, copy, Southard to Robert Hayne, August 19, 1828, John McLean to Southard, September 24, 1828, James Monroe to Southard, October 2, 1828, copy, Southard to Philip H. Nicklin, October 11, 1828, Isaac Southard to Southard, October 29, 1828, Southard papers, PUL. Each of these letters refers to Southard's health problems—but not a single one specifies any ailment.

84. Francis T. Brooke to Southard, November 1, 1828. Despite such reports, Southard continued to hold out hope. Writing from a sickbed on October 30, he told his brother Isaac: "You permit these lying fellows to depress your spirits. There is no danger in Ohio—*Every Election* with the solitary exception of Penna has shewn a decided change in our favor—& I ought not to except P. for even there, the returns shew a change in our favor of more than fifty thousand since the former election. The result unquestionably turns much on N. York. As far as any calculation can be made on Elections 112 votes are *certain* for Mr. Adams—& if he can get 19 in N. York, his election is safe. Or if he gets Illinois, or Missouri, or Virginia—in all of which there is *fair* ground to hope for success—he may do with less from N.Y. The result is no doubt uncertain—but the chances & probabilities are *decidedly* in our favor. Do your duty in N Jersey—disbelieve the lies told to depress your spirits, & all will be well." Southard to Isaac Southard, October 30, 1828, Southard Additional Papers, PUL.

85. Bemis, *JQA and the Union*, p. 150.

86. A. S. Hooe to Southard, November 4, 1828, Southard Papers, PUL.

Chapter 5

1. Quoted in Elmer, *Constitution and Government*, p. 218.

2. Quoted in Charles O. Paullin, *Paullin's History of Naval Administration, 1775–1911....* (Annapolis, Md.: U.S. Naval Institute, 1968), p. 160.

3. Washington, D.C. *National Intelligencer*, September 17, 1823; Ammon, *Monroe*, pp. 364–65. For a sample of New Jersey opinion on the appointment, see Bridgeton *Washington Whig*, September 6, 1823.

4. David F. Long, *Nothing Too Daring: A Biography of Commodore David Porter, 1780–1843* (Annapolis, Md.: United States Naval Institute, 1970), pp. 213–16, offers the essentials. For further details, consult *American State Papers. Documents, Legislative and Executive....* (Washington, D.C.: Gales and Seaton, 1832–61), *Naval Affairs*, 1:1094–95, 1116–21 (hereafter cited as *ASP, Naval Affairs*).

5. Washington, D.C., *National Intelligencer*, October 1, 11, 12, 1823. (Quote is from issue of October 1.)

6. (Draft), Southard to J. S. Skinner, December 23, 1823, Southard Papers, PUL.

7. Long, *Nothing Too Daring*, pp. 216–17.

8. Leonard D. White, *The Jeffersonians: A Study in Administrative History, 1801–1829* (New York: The Free Press, 1951), pp. 120–22; Harold and Margaret Sprout, *The Rise of American Naval Power, 1776–1918* (Princeton, N.J.: Princeton University Press, 1939), p. 97.

9. Sprout and Sprout, *American Naval Power*, pp. 98–102; Paul A. Varg, *U.S. Foreign Relations, 1820–1860* (N.P.: Michigan State University Press, 1979), p. xiv.

10. This is a major premise of Ernest R. May, *The Making of the Monroe Doctrine* (Cambridge, Mass.: Harvard University Press, 1975).

11. On Thompson's laxness, see Adams, *Memoirs*, 4:310–11. See also Paullin, *History*,

p. 164. In 1819 Thompson was absent from Washington from March 28 until December 8—a period of more than eight months.

12. See Edward M. Hall, "Samuel L. Southard," in Paolo E. Coletta, *The American Secretaries of the Navy* (Annapolis, Md: U.S. Naval Institute, 1980). Professor Coletta's generosity made it possible for me to read Hall's essay in typescript.

13. The two most recent discussions of Southard's tenure in the navy department, Leonard White's *The Jeffersonians,* chapters 19, 20, and Edward Hall's essay in the Coletta volume, are essentially glosses on Charles O. Paullin's pioneering essay on the navy department in the era of the naval commissioners, 1816–42, which was originally published in June 1907 in the *United States Naval Institute Proceedings,* and subsequently republished in the volume cited in note 2 above. Paullin's analysis, in my view, remains the best single institutional study of Southard's navy department years.

14. For elaboration, consult any of the standard biographies of these figures and May, *Monroe Doctrine,* chap. 2.

15. Cabinet deliberations leading to the Monroe Doctrine have been traced helpfully in many works, including Bradford Perkins, *Castlereagh and Adams: England and the United States, 1812–1823* (Berkeley, Calif.: University of California Press, 1964), chap. 17; May, *Monroe Doctrine,* chap. 5; and Samuel Flagg Bemis, *John Quincy Adams and the Foundations of American Foreign Policy* (New York: Alfred A. Knopf, 1950), chap. 19. For Southard's participation in cabinet discussions, see Adams, *Memoirs,* 6:181, 196, 200, 204, 210.

16. Varg. *U.S. Foreign Relations,* p. 49.

17. The works cited in n. 15 all point to this conclusion.

18. Compare Southard's comments recorded in Adams, *Memoirs,* 6:181, with those recorded in idem., pp. 196, 210.

19. I base this judgment on a reading of the Adams diary for the years 1825–29 as well as the corpus of Southard correspondence for these years.

20. Adams, *Memoirs,* 6, 7:passim.

21. Porter's first efforts to exterminate pirates are carefully delineated in Long, *Nothing Too Daring,* pp. 203–16.

22. Ibid., pp. 218–19.

23. Although his evidence actually shows that President Monroe was the irritated party in Porter's unauthorized return to Washington, Porter's biographer David Long claims that this event was a "watershed in relations" between the captain and the navy secretary. "From the moment of his unauthorized return until his naval career ended, Porter found Southard's hostility toward him virulent and unrestrained." *Nothing Too Daring,* p. 219. The problem with this position is that there is no evidence prior to the Foxardo incident of November 1824 to sustain it. Doubtless Southard felt frustrated that Porter's illnesses were slowing the campaign against piracy, but his relations with Porter were correct and straightforward until the captain's controversial landing at Puerto Rico and his subsequent public efforts to exculpate himself.

24. Samuel L. Southard to David Porter, July 20, 24, October 14, 1824, Letters Sent by the Secretary of the Navy to Officers, 1798–1868 (M-149), Roll 15:321, 327, 363, Records of the Navy Department (RG 45), National Archives, hereafter cited as Letters Sent, Navy Dept. (M-149).

25. Long, *Nothing Too Daring,* p. 225. There is a copy of Porter's letter to Southard in the papers of Mahlon Dickerson at The New Jersey Historical Society.

26. Southard to David Porter, October 21, 1824, Letters Sent, Navy Dept. (M-149), Roll 15:379. Southard reminded Porter that he was not required to remain based on Thompson's Island or to lead every expedition from it. He was simply to coordinate the movement against pirates to the best of his abilities.

27. Porter's missive to Monroe is quoted in *Nothing Too Daring,* p. 226. For Southard's reaction on hearing of it, see Samuel Southard to James Monroe, February (?), 1825, Southard Papers, NYPL.

28. On the unnecessary and embarrassing court martial of Lieutenant Beverly Kennon, and the incident with the British involving Lieutenant Francis Gregory, see *Nothing Too Daring*, pp. 220–22. Southard's initial soothing comment on the court martial is in Southard to David Porter, December 31, 1823, Letters Sent, Navy Dept. (M-149), Roll 15:178. He took an icier tone in a letter of March 29, 1824, ibid., p. 258. On the need to avoid conflicts with foreign powers, such as occurred in the Gregory incident, Southard to Porter, May 31, 1824, ibid., p. 290.

29. Adams, *Memoirs*, 6:434. (Entry for December 2, 1824.) For Smith Thompson's instructions to Porter, dated February 1, 1823, see Letters Sent, Navy Dept. (M-149), Roll 14:429. David Long's analysis of the letter, in *Nothing Too Daring*, pp. 207–9, stresses its ambivalence. For Southard, and ultimately for John Quincy Adams, the instructions were quite clear on the central issue.

30. The location in question was also called Fajardo and Faxjardo.

31. Long, *Nothing Too Daring*, p. 227; Richard Wheeler, *In Pirate Waters* (New York: Thomas Y. Crowell Company, 1969), pp. 142–44.

32. *Nothing Too Daring*, pp. 228–29; *In Pirate Waters*, p. 147. For a more detailed discussion of the episode, see Michael Birkner, "The Foxardo Affair Revisited," *The American Neptune*, 42 (July 1982): 165–178.

33. Ibid.

34. Adams, *Memoirs*, 6:445, 453–54. (Entries of December 16, 24, 1824.) Recalling cabinet reaction to the Foxardo affair in a letter to former President Monroe, Southard wrote on July 22, 1825 that "in the cabinet meeting for his [Porter's] recal[l], there was no difference as to his conduct demanding enquiry—nor any as to the mode of proceeding, except that I proposed before he was recalled, that he should be written to for further & fuller information. I was alone in this opinion." James Monroe Papers, LC, microfilm. John C. Calhoun's recollection of the meeting substantially supports Southard's account save that he recalled that he initiated the suggestion about requesting a written explanation—a recollection that comports with Adams's diary account. See Calhoun to Southard, August 16, 1825, Southard Papers, PUL. There is a variant copy of this letter in the Southard Papers, LC. Both are reprinted in Clyde N. Wilson and W. Edwin Hemphill, eds., *The Papers of John C. Calhoun*, 12 vols. (Columbia, S.C.: University of South Carolina Press, 1959–   ), 10:37–39.

35. Henry Clay to James Brown, September 4, 1825, in Hopkins, ed., *Papers of Henry Clay*, 4:617–19.

36. (Draft), Samuel Southard to Charles Ewing, July 9, 1825, in Box 82, Southard Papers, PUL.

37. Long, *Nothing Too Daring*, pp. 230–31; Adams, *Memoirs*, 6:455. (Entry of December 28, 1824.)

38. Long, *Nothing Too Daring*, pp. 235–36.

39. For a politician like Mahlon Dickerson, a strong Crawford backer in 1824, an anti-administration stance on the Porter case was a convenient step toward the Jacksonian camp. Dickerson's biographer, Robert R. Beckwith, sees "the demands of political intrigue" as the basis for Dickerson's behavior during this period. "Mahlon Dickerson of New Jersey," p. 223.

40. Long, *Nothing Too Daring*, pp. 235–36.

41. *Minutes of Proceedings of the Courts of Enquiry and Court Martial in Relation to Captain David Porter* (Washington: Davis & Force, 1825). For background see Adams, *Memoirs*, 6:542–43, 544–45, 547. (Entries of May 10, 12, 14, 1825.)

42. Consider the case of Captain Charles Stewart, who had been charged by the government of Peru with smuggling along the coast of South America, and with partiality in dealings with royalists. See the brief account below and, for details, consult Edward B. Billingsley, *In Defense of Neutral Rights: The United States Navy and the Wars of Independence in Chile and Peru* (Chapel Hill, N.C.: University of North Carolina Press, 1967), pp. 148–93.

43. Washington: Davis & Force, 1825.

44. Far more than anything else Porter had said or done, the foundation for Southard's

animus toward him lay in the publication of *An Exposition.* Aside from his conviction that the publication at that time was extremely ill-advised, Southard was particularly angered by what he believed were the "omissions and misrepresentations" strewn throughout it. "Could such a publication," Southard rhetorically asked his friend Charles Ewing, "produce any effect but to deceive & mislead?" For further comments in this vein, as well as a statement of the principle involved, see Southard to Charles Ewing, July 9, 1825, a seventeen-page draft letter that Southard requested Ewing to burn after reading. The draft is in Box 82 of the Southard Papers, PUL. Ewing's responses, indicating that he had discreetly used Southard's arguments to enlighten "some gentlemen here whose first impressions were erroneous, but whose good opinion & approbation were worth having," are in Charles Ewing to Southard, July 18, September 6, 1826, Southard Papers, PUL.

45. See the dozens of letters in Letters Sent, Navy Dept. (M-149), Rolls 14–15. For Porter's side of the extensive correspondence, see Letters Received by the Secretary of the Navy: Captain's Letters, 1805–85 (M-125). Rolls 85–90. Originals of many of these letters may be examined in the David Porter Papers, LC.

46. Long, *Nothing Too Daring,* pp. 216, 231.

47. See correspondence between Southard and John Rodgers and William Bainbridge in Southard Papers, PUL. For a vignette revealing Southard's friendliness with naval personnel, see Frances Leigh Williams, *Matthew Fontaine Maury: Scientist of the Sea* (New Brunswick, N.J.: Rutgers University Press, 1963), pp. 38–39.

48. (Draft), Southard to John C. Calhoun, July 19, 1825, Southard Papers, PUL. See also Southard to Charles Ewing, July 9, 1825, insisting that the Porter case "will be found to be one not of personal bearing between himself & the executive or any branch of it, but between himself & the people of the U.S. & the constitution . . . which they have established"; also, Southard to James Monroe, July 22, 1825, Monroe Papers, LC, microfilm.

49. David Long claims that the "mystery" of why the administration was "so eager" to prosecute Porter is "compounded" by the fact that Spain made no protest about the Foxardo landing. This is incorrect. A letter from the American minister to Spain, Hugh Nelson, to Secretary of State Henry Clay on April 6, 1825, included a report on the complaint of Spanish Secretary of State Francesco de Zea Bermudez about Porter's actions at Foxardo. The Spanish government even attempted to offer testimony explaining the Foxardo alcalde's motives regarding the treatment of Lieutenant Platt, and to provide other documents regarding the incident. This testimony was rejected by the Court as "incompetent evidence." Regardless, Alexander H. Everett, the new U.S. minister to Spain, told Clay on October 16, 1825, that the result of the court martial "has made a favorable impression" on the Spanish government. On all this see Henry Clay to Samuel L. Southard, May 5, 1825, Southard to Clay, July 8, 1825, and Alexander H. Everett to Clay, October 16, 1825, in Hopkins, ed., *The Papers of Henry Clay,* 4:327, 520, 738. A précis of Nelson's letter to Clay is in ibid., p. 224.

50. *Minutes of Proceedings,* pp. 361–414; Long, *Nothing Too Daring,* pp. 241–47.

51. *Annals,* 19th Cong., 1st sess., pp. 55, 57, 59.

52. The *National Intelligencer,* which had strongly supported the "gallant" Porter through the spring of 1825 and through the various proceedings against him, was remarkably mild in responding to the guilty verdict announced in mid-August. Accepting the "conscientiousness" of the court, the editors said they "do not judge for others, however deeply we may lament their perceptions of truth and justice." August 18, 1825. Twelve days later, responding to criticism from other papers that the *Intelligencer* was too lukewarm in support of the administration on the Porter issue, Gales and Seaton suggested that, if Porter had erred, it was in "misinterpreting & exceeding his instructions"—a matter that could have been handled without recourse to a court martial. For David Long's account of national press opinion on the affair, which he concluded was "mixed" but increasingly favorable to the administration, see *Nothing Too Daring,* pp. 250–52. See also the clippings in Southard Papers, PUL, Boxes 148, 150.

53. Charles Ewing to Southard, January 23, 1826, Southard Papers, PUL. See also Charles

Hammond to Henry Clay, August 31, 1825, Clay to Hammond, September 23, 1825, and Clay to James Brown, September 4, November 14, 1825, in *Papers of Henry Clay*, 4:610–11, 618–19, 676, 823. Several weeks after the court handed down its verdict, Southard wrote former President Monroe that insofar as the controversy over Porter was concerned, "the nation is settling down right." Southard to Monroe, August 30, 1825, Monroe Papers, LC, microfilm.

54. Long, *Nothing Too Daring*, chap. 10.

55. Although it is impossible precisely to quantify such a matter, evidence suggests that, next to Henry Clay, Southard was the most common cabinet-level target for opposition attacks. Southard was not the political heavyweight Clay was, of course, and it would be misleading to view public debate over his performance as a major issue during the Adams presidency. Criticism of Southard was never so pervasive or sustained as the attack on the "corrupt bargain" or the Panama Mission. Yet Southard was often a target of abuse, most of it poorly founded, particularly in the Washington, Baltimore, New York, and Philadelphia presses. For samples of press criticism, see the clippings in Boxes 147–51, Southard Papers, PUL.

56. *New York National Advocate*, August 23, 1825. For background on Noah, see Isaac Goldberg, *Major Noah, American Jewish Pioneer* (Philadelphia: The Jewish Publication Society of America, 1936) and Jonathan D. Sarna, *Jacksonian Jew: The Two Worlds of Mordecai Noah* (New York: Holmes & Meier Publishers, Inc., 1981). Both works, however, are disappointingly thin on Noah's political journalism.

57. *New York National Advocate*, August 11, 24, 1825. For Southard's defense of his conduct relating to Dr. Phillips, probably published anonymously in a pro-administration journal, see Box 82, Southard Papers, PUL. See also Navy Department letterbook, NYPL, pp. 272–88, 386–99.

58. (Draft), Southard to J. Elliott, n.d., Box 76, Southard Papers, PUL.

59. (Draft), Southard to "Mr. Gore," n.d., Box 77, Southard Papers, PUL. See also the draft defense of his conduct as navy secretary, apparently intended for newspaper publication, in Box 82, Southard Papers, PUL.

60. Major Noah was a principal in this controversy also. Not only did he editorially assail Southard for Chaplain Felch's dismissal, but he also opened his columns to Felch's vituperative comments about Southard under the by-line "Coram." For samples, see Box 148, Southard Papers, PUL. In 1826 Felch established his own paper in New York, *Coram's Champion*, which was devoted primarily to attacks on Southard. One friend of Southard predicted that the paper's "editorial wrath must pass away as a vapour," and he was apparently correct. *Coram's Champion* lasted less than a year. On this controversy, see Robert Spence to Southard, June 4, July 13, 1826, Robert F. Stockton to Southard, August 27, 1826, James G. Brooks to Southard, July 19, 1826, George Sullivan to Southard July 17, August 3, 8, 23, 1826, and (draft), Southard to John Quincy Adams, n.d., Box 82, Southard Papers, PUL. Transcripts of official correspondence relating to Felch are in United States Navy file, 1823–25, NYPL.

61. Charles Ewing to Southard, February 8, 1826. Quote is from (draft), Southard to George Sullivan, July 24, 1826, Southard Papers, PUL. For background, see Felch's letter of October 24, 1825 to Southard and a longer one, n.d., to President Adams, in Southard Letterbook, NYPL.

62. For a colorful account of General Lafayette's ceremonious leavetaking, as orchestrated by Southard in September 1825, see Marian Klamkin, *The Return of Lafayette: 1824–1825* (New York: Charles Scribner's Sons, 1975) pp. 195–96. For details on Southard's preparations, see Adams, *Memoirs*, 7:26–27, 32–33, 36–40, 43–47, 48, 49.

63. Works which convey the flavor of Washington social life in the 1820s include Josiah Quincy, *Figures of the Past: From the Leaves of Old Journals* (Boston: Roberts Brothers, 1883), esp. pp. 265, 268, 273, 275, and Nathan I. Sargent, *Public Men and Events from the Commencement of Mr. Monroe's Administration, in 1817, to the Close of Mr. Fillmore's Administration, in 1853* (Philadelphia: J. B. Lippincott, 1875), 1:46–55.

64. See Rebecca Southard to Southard, February 8, 26, 1825, Southard papers, PUL.

65. In both instances when his children died in Trenton Southard was in Washington on government business.

66. For background on the quarrel between Rebecca and Margaret, see James D. Harrow to Southard, April 21, 22, 1825, and especially several undated letters from Margaret Harrow to Southard, Box 77, Southard Papers, PUL. On Mrs. Southard's poor relations with servants, see, for example, Sarah Smith to Southard, December 5, n.y., Box 78, Southard Papers, PUL.

67. Aside from his identification with the leading figures of his day, Southard basked in the attention accorded him by his New Jersey compatriots. On public dinners in his honor in New Jersey, see Littleton Kirkpatrick to Southard, October 6, 17, 1825 and Garret Wall to Southard, October 11, 1825, Southard Papers, PUL. Other honors accorded to him during the navy years included resident membership in the Columbian Institute. See Asbury Dickens to Southard, July 2, 1825, Southard Papers, PUL.

68. Consult Gaillard Hunt, ed., *The First Forty Years of Washington Society . . .* (New York: Frederick Ungar Publishing Co., 1965 reprint), pp. 163, 211, 212, 238, 243, 245, 246, 249, 252, 257, 258, 273.

69. Sally died early in November 1825. Her death, Charles Ewing wrote, "is indeed a sad & unexpected stroke. A child of uncommon loveliness & promise—of fine health & great sprightliness—all that could delight a parent's eye & win a parent's heart." Ewing to Southard, November 18, 1825, Southard Papers, PUL. On the death of Ann, see Southard to Henry Clay, July 23, 1829, Clay Papers, LC (microfilm).

70. On this theme, see chapters 8 and 9.

71. Southard's activities are documented in the *ASP, Naval Affairs*, vols. 1–3. His initiatives are summarized in the Paullin, White, and Hall accounts cited above.

72. Such activities may be followed in the letters sent by the secretary of the navy to ship captains, available on microfilm through the National Archives, and also in a thick letter book at NYPL. For the "cart loads" quote, see William Bainbridge to Southard, February 5, 1828, Southard Papers, PUL.

73. Sprout and Sprout, *American Naval Power*, pp. 94–95.

74. James A. Field, Jr., *America and the Mediterranean World, 1776–1882* (Princeton, N.J.: Princeton University Press, 1969), pp. 127–28.

75. For the continuing story regarding piracy in the West Indies, see Wheeler, *Pirate Waters*, chap. 11. On the navy's work off the coasts of Latin America, see Robert Erwin Johnson, *Thence Round Cape Horn: The Story of the United States Naval Forces in the Pacific Station, 1818–1923* (Annapolis, Md.: U.S. Naval Institute, 1969), chaps. 1, 2, and Billingsley, *Defense of Neutral Rights,* chaps. 8, 9.

76. Stewart was offered membership on the board of navy commissioners, but declined on account of his "family and private concerns." See (draft), Southard to John Quincy Adams, July 10, 1826, Southard Papers, PUL. On Stewart's travail in Latin America and subsequent court martial, the best account is Billingsly, *Neutral Rights,* pp. 152–93.

77. See generally, Hall's essay in Coletta, ed. *American Secretaries of the Navy.* On enlistments, see Harold D. Langley, "The Grass Roots Harvest of 1828," *United States Naval Institute Proceedings* 90 (1964): 51–59.

78. For a sympathetic account of Southard's work regarding naval hospitals, White, *Jeffersonians,* pp. 294–95. On Southard and the naval academy, *ASP, Naval Affairs,* 2:44, and Park Benjamin, *The United States Naval Academy* (N.Y.: G. P. Putnam's Sons, 1900), pp. 41–42. Southard's sensitive and persistent concern for the health and well being of midshipmen is traced in Harold D. Langley, *Social Reform in the United States Navy, 1798–1862* (Urbana, Ill: University of Illinois Press, 1967).

79. For Southard's early cordial relationship with Hayne, see their correspondence for 1825–27 in Southard Papers, PUL.

80. The connection between Adams's message and the exploring expedition is drawn in David Tyler, *The Wilkes Expedition: The First United States Exploring Expedition, 1838–1842*

(Philadelphia: American Philosophical Society, 1968), pp. 4–8.

81. For Southard's relations with Jeremiah Reynolds, and the planning for an exploring expedition to the South Seas and Antarctica, I have leaned heavily on the compelling and authoritative account in William Stanton, *The Great United States Exploring Expedition* (Berkeley, Calif.: University of California Press, 1975), pp. 1–28.

82. Quoted in Stanton, *Great Exploring Expedition*, p. 20. Southard's support for the expedition was evinced in a letter to Reynolds, July 6, 1827, Southard papers, PUL.

83. *American State Papers, Naval Affairs*, 3:211. On appointments, see correspondence in Southard Papers, PUL, and especially Thomas Ap Catesby Jones to Southard, December 26, 1828 (misfiled with 1827), Southard Papers, PUL, The Reynolds quote is in Reynolds to Southard, n.d., 1828, Box 78, Southard Papers, PUL.

84. Stanton, *Great Exploring Expedition*, pp. 23–24.

85. *Register of Debates*, 20th Cong., 2nd sess., pp. 50–52.

86. Southard's response to the Senate's resolution of inquiry is in *ASP, Naval Affairs*, 3:308–17.

Chapter 6

1. On Southard's and his family's poor health, see John Taliaferro to Southard, November 6, 1828, Isaac Southard to Southard, October 29, 1828, Dr. Thomas Harris to Southard, November 2, 1828, and (draft), Southard to Daniel Doty, December 14, 1828, Southard Papers, PUL. Margaret Bayard Smith, a family friend from Washington, observed in ealy January 1829 that "poor Judge Southard has been very ill, is still confined to his room and looks wretchedly." Smith, *The First Forty Years of Washington Society*, ed., Gaillard Hunt (reprint ed.; New York: Frederick Ungar Publishing Co., 1965), p. 259. A month later Mrs. Smith reported that, if anything, Southard's physical condition had deteriorated. Ibid., p. 273.

2. Quoted in Elmer, *Constitution and Government*, p. 226. For Southard's inquiry about practicing law in Philadelphia, and John Wurts' pessimistic response, see (draft), Southard to John Wurts, December 3, 1828, and Wurts to Southard, December 8, 1828, Southard Papers, PUL.

3. Lucius Elmer to Southard, December 1, 1828, Theodore Frelinghuysen to Southard, December (?), 1828, Charles Ewing to Southard, November 26, 1828, Southard Papers, PUL.

4. On Bateman's resignation, see Ephraim Bateman to Southard, January 6, 8, 1829, and J. N. Clawson to Southard, January 12, 1829, Southard Papers, PUL.

5. Background on resentment against Southard is offered in Michael Birkner, "Journalism and Politics in Jacksonian New Jersey: The Career of Stacy G. Potts," *New Jersey History* 97 (Fall 1979): 166–67.

6. Ibid. Stockton's broadside, titled "Reasons Why Mr. Southard ought not to be elected by the Legislature to supply the vacancy in the Senate, created by the resignation of Dr. Bateman," may be found in Alexander Library, Rutgers University, Special Collections.

7. James Fitz Randolph, a political friend of Southard's and editor of the New Brunswick *Fredonian*, sent Southard a copy of Stockton's handbill in his letter of January 19, 1829, observing that "there is no time to be lost" in counteracting it. Southard Papers, PUL. For Peter Force's role in publishing Southard's counterpolemic, see Peter Force to Southard, n.d., but undoubtedly January 1829, in Box 77, Southard Papers, PUL. Southard's "Short Statement" is in Box 116, Southard Papers. See also "Remarks on 'Reasons Why Mr. Southard ought not to be elected by the Legislature to supply the vacancy in the Senate, created by the resignation of Dr. Bateman,'" filed with undated Peter Force correspondence, Box 77, Southard Papers.

8. Southard's argument about not owning a "slave for life" was designed to minimize the fact that he had indeed owned a number of blacks during his days in Trenton.

9. Birkner, "Journalism and Politics," p. 167.

10. Newark *Sentinel of Freedom* editor William Tuttle, a friend to Southard, had noted on December 2, 1828, that Southard was not a likely candidate for the Senate given that he "is not a resident of the state, and it is questionable whether he would be constitutionally appointed, even if such a thing was in contemplation."

11. Southard told Peter Force in January 1829 that "the constitutional objection has no foundation. There is not a well informed man in Washington who does not know that it [is] without substance, & opposed to the whole action of the Govt since its establishment." Southard to Force, January 19, 1829, Southard Additional Papers, PUL. Unfortunately for Southard, opinion in Washington was not terribly relevant to the Senate election in New Jersey.

12. The Newark *Sentinel of Freedom*, February 3, 1829, contains the fullest newspaper account of the election in the joint meeting.

13. Aside from the *Sentinel*, see the vivid account of the election in Stacy Gardiner Potts, "Autobiography," Archives and History Bureau, Manuscript Collection, New Jersey State Library, Trenton, N. J. Potts's recollections generally comport with contemporary evidence, with one signal exception. Given the prior circulation of the broadside that emphasized Southard's residency in Washington, it would seem unlikely that the members of the joint meeting would have reacted as though a "thunderclap" struck them when Potts rose and made his motion to delete Southard's name from the list of candidates.

14. Stacy G. Potts to Mahlon Dickerson, January 31, 1829, Robert F. Stockton to Dickerson, January 30, 1829, Canfield Genealogical Collection, NJHS.

15. Southard's activities are traceable through his heavy correspondence from November 1828 to March 1829. See also above, chapter 5.

16. On his election as attorney general, Charles Ewing to Southard, February 19, 20, 1829, J. J. Foster to Southard, February 20, 1829, William Prall to Southard, February 20, 1829, John Wilson to Southard, n.d., February 20, 1829. Even here Southard faced the enmity of Dr. William Ewing, who, one onlooker reported, "sturck out Ag[ains]t you to the very last." William Pennington, Jr., to Southard, February 21, 1829, Southard Papers, PUL. Southard was in fact selected only after six ballots.

17. On the renting of Garret Wall's Trenton home, Charles Ewing to Southard, December 22, 29, 1828, Garret Wall to Southard, January 14, February 28, 1829, Southard Papers, PUL.

18. The death of Southard's daughter Ann is mentioned in Southard to Henry Clay, July 23, 1829, Clay Papers, LC; Charles Ewing to Southard, March 23, 1829, James Monroe to Southard, April 17, 1829, Southard Papers, PUL. On his appearance, *Forty Years of Familiar Letters to James W. Alexander,* ed., John D. Hall (2 vols.; New York: Charles Scribner, 1860), 1:128.

19. Salem *Messenger and Public Advertiser,* December 9, 1829.

20. Elmer, *Constitution and Government,* p. 232.

21. The breadth of Southard's legal practice is indicated in his notebooks for these years, Box 115, Southard Papers, PUL. On relations with New Jersey corporations, J. O. Clarke to Southard, February 10, March 5, 1829, Roswell Colt to Southard, January 23, 1829, Southard Papers, PUL.

22. (Draft), Southard to John Quincy Adams, June 6, 1829, Southard Papers, PUL; Southard to Henry Clay, July 23, 1829, Clay Papers, LC. See also William Wirt to Southard, June 21, 1829, on this subject.

23. For a typical example of Southard's routine work as attorney general, see Southard to John Smallwood, a Trenton attorney, December 26, 1831, New Jersey Letters, Alexander Library, Rutgers University Special Collections. "I forgot to request you & the sheriff to make out the best statement in your power of the persons—occupations-residence &c &c of each of the criminals who are in Phila.," Southard wrote. "I wish to send a letter to the Recorder, & see if I cannot get hold of some of them. Will you send me a copy of the Horse race indictment?" In a postscript, he added: "I also forgot to enquire what had been done in the case of (I forget

his name—the little man who had the squabble about the taverns) vs Danl McKage & William Ferguson. You issued a writ—send the memo of fees & c & tell me what you have done & what I have to do."

24. Frelinghuysen's 1828 brief in the case is printed, untitled, in a broadside in Princeton University Library.

25. For background on the dispute, from New Jersey's perspective, see Isaac Williamson's special message to the legislature in February 1828, in Box 139, Southard Papers, PUL.

26. For a full account of the eighteenth-century boundary quarrel, see Philip J. Schwarz, *The Jarring Interests: New York's Boundary Makers, 1664–1776* (Albany, N.Y.: State University of New York Press, 1979), pp. 81–88, 136–86.

27. *Report of the Commissioners on the Controversy with the State of New York Respecting the Eastern Boundary of the State of New Jersey* (Trenton, N.J.: Wilson and Halsey, 1807); *Report of the [New Jersey] Committee on the Correspondence Between Governor Clinton and Governor Williamson Touching the Arrest of a Ministerial Officer, &c* (Trenton, N.J.: William L. Prall, 1826), and the Williamson message cited in note 25 above. The Commissioners' Reports may be found in the Princeton University Library.

28. Chapter 3.

29. (Draft), Southard to William Carroll, May 22, 1829, (Draft), Southard to William Wirt, November 28, 1829, William Wirt to Southard, November 28, 1829, Southard Papers, PUL; Marvin R. Cain, "William Wirt Against Andrew Jackson: Reflections on an Era," *Mid-America* 47 (April 1965): 122–23.

30. For New York's position on the dispute, see Greene C. Bronson's official opinion, which accompanied Governor Enos Throop's message to the New York legislature, January 5, 1830, in Box 139, Southard Papers, PUL. One should also consult Southard's correspondence with Wirt and Governor Peter Vroom for the period 1830–32, and the proceedings in 3 *Peters* 461.

31. Samuel Southard to Enos Throop and Greene C. Bronson, January 12, 1830, Southard Additional Papers, PUL.

32. Cain, "William Wirt," pp. 122–23.

33. Southard's brief in the case is in Box 98, Southard Papers, PUL. See also 4 *Peters* 284, and 6 *Peters* 322.

34. Peter Vroom to Samuel Southard, March 12, 1831, June 25, 1832, Southard Papers, PUL.

35. The final folder in the Rutgers University Philhower Collection, marked "Vroom-Wall-Rhea-Trenton Militia—1st Class Miscellany," contains a draft of Peter Vroom's letter to President Jackson, March 20, 1834, enclosing a copy of the agreement between New York and New Jersey regarding territorial limits and jurisdiction between the two states See also *Acts of the 58th General Assembly of New Jersey, 1st Sitting*, pp. 118–26. For indication that New Jersey won its major points in the negotiations, compare the final agreement with the recommendations sent Southard by commissioner John Rutherford, March 7, 1830, Southard Papers, PUL.

36. See, generally, John T. Cunningham, *New Jersey: America's Main Road* (Garden City, N.Y.: Doubleday and Company, 1966), chaps. 10, 11. For the case of Newark, Susan E. Hirsch, *Roots of the American Working Class: The Industrialization of Crafts in Newark, 1800–1860* (Philadelphia: University of Pennsylvania Press, 1978), esp. chaps. 1, 2.

37. John W. Cadman, Jr., *The Corporation in New Jersey: Business and Politics, 1791–1875* (Cambridge, Mass.: Harvard University Press, 1949), chap. 2; James Willard Hurst, *The Legitimacy of the Business Corporation in the Law of the United States* (Charlottesville, Va.: University of Virginia Press, 1970), p. 18.

38. Thomas Woodruff to Southard, January 5, 1830, John Colt to Southard, March 7, 1831, Abraham Godwin to Southard, March 6, 1831, John P. Jackson to Southard, April 18, July 31, 1833. Southard Papers, PUL.

39. John Colt to Samuel Southard, April 27, 1830, Southard Papers, PUL.

40. Wheaton J. Lane, *From Indian Trail to Iron Horse: Travel and Transportation in New Jersey*,

1620–1860 (Princeton, N.J.: Princeton University Press, 1939), chap. 9; H. Jerome Cranmer, "Improvements without Public Funds: The New Jersey Canals," in Carter Goodrich, ed., *Canals and American Economic Development* (New York: Columbia University Press, 1961), 126–46.

41. *Law Opinion in the Case of the Paterson Manufacturing Society Against the Morris Canal and Banking Company* (Paterson, N.J.: B. Burnett, 1829). Quote is from p. 27. At NJHS. For the Morris Canal's public retort to SUM's attacks, see *An Answer to Mr. John L. Sullivan's Report to the Manufacturing Society in New Jersey in a Letter to the Directors of the Morris Canal Company by the President of that Company* (New York: William A. Davis, 1828), NJHS.

42. All quotes here and below are from Nathaniel Saxton, comp. *Reports of Cases Decided in the Court of Chancery of the State of New Jersey*, 142 vols. (Elizabethtown, N.J.: Edward Sanderson, 1836), 1 : 157–93.

43. Colt's heavy correspondence with Southard, in the Southard Papers, PUL, is testimony to their close working relationship. Unfortunately, the rich collection of Colt Papers at the Historical Society of Pennsylvania contains few of Southard's letters to Colt.

44. P. Gilchrist to Southard, December 16, 1829, Southard Papers, PUL.

45. The Southard-Wilson partnership can be traced in Southard's correspondence in the 1830s. That Southard still maintained a wide practice and was willing to handle small cases for modest fees is evident in his legal notebooks in Box 115, Southard Papers, PUL. See also the interesting draft, Southard to Alexander Rea, December 17, 1832, respecting a recent case Southard had argued for Rea. Southard accepted a $15 fee, which he indicated was the norm, but suggested that he deserved a better recompense in view of all the effort he had devoted to the case.

46. Hebert Ershkowitz, "New Jersey Politics During the Era of Andrew Jackson, 1820–1837" (Ph.D. diss., New York University, 1965), pp. 134–38.

47. The National Republicans' positions on national issues may best be traced in the pages of its newspapers during this period, notably the Paterson *Intelligencer* and the Newark *Sentinel of Freedom*. See also Walter R. Fallaw, Jr., "The Rise of the Whig Party in New Jersey" (Ph.D. diss., Princeton University, 1967), pp. 65–73, for a discussion of the major issues.

48. Samuel Southard to Henry Clay, July 23, 1829, Clay Papers, LC (microfilm). On National Republican divisions, Newark *Sentinel*, October 6, 13, 20, 1829.

49. On Antimasonry in New Jersey, and the failure of its adherents to compete effectively with the two major parties, Frederick M. Herrmann, "Anti-Masonry in New Jersey," *New Jersey History* 91 (Autumn 1973): 149–65. Herrmann concludes that "the early arrival of the second American party system in New Jersey left the Anti-Masons with no hope of competing with the entrenched parties" (p. 159). See also William Preston Vaughn, *The Antimasonic Party in the United States, 1826–1843* (Lexington, KY: University Press of Kentucky, 1983), pp. 166–167.

50. Amos Ellmaker to Southard, January 1, 1829, Southard Papers, PUL.

51. (Draft), Southard to Amos Ellmaker, December 29, 1829, Southard Papers, PUL.

52. See Richard E. Ellis, "The Political Economy of Thomas Jefferson," in Lally Weymouth, ed., *Thomas Jefferson: The Man, His World, His Influence* (New York: G. P. Putnam's Sons, 1973), pp. 81–95, for the "improvement" motif in Jeffersonian thought. Although its orientation is rather different, McCoy, *The Elusive Republic*, chap. 10, is suggestive on this matter.

53. See the editorials, in 1829 and early 1830, in the Trenton *Emporium*.

54. Trenton *Emporium*, July 10, 1830. The shift in Potts's rhetoric may be linked to Andrew Jackson's veto in 1830 of the Maysville Road Bill.

55. Birkner, "Vroom and the Politics of Democracy," esp. pp. 23–26.

56. Richard E. Ellis, *The Jeffersonian Crisis: Courts and Politics in the Young Republic* (New York: Oxford University Press, 1971), p. 284, most clearly draws this line of division. Although Ellis's lines of demarcation between the parties need to be qualified and elaborated in some respects—the views of entrepreneurial-minded Jacksonians and the role of former Federalists in the Jacksonian-era parties, for example, remain unclear—his argument is the

most suggestive attempt so far to connect the politics of the Jefferson-Jackson eras.

57. Peter D. Levine, *The Behavior of State Legislative Parties in the Jacksonian Era: New Jersey, 1829–1844* (Rutherford, N.J.: Fairleigh Dickinson University Press, 1977), p. 104.

58. Ershkowitz, "New Jersey Politics," pp. 125–31.

59. Trenton *Emporium,* November 7, 1829.

60. Samuel Southard to Henry Clay, August 8, 1830, Clay Papers, Lilly Library, Indiana University.

61. Herbert Ershkowitz observes that the election returns "reveal that the National Republicans succeeded only partially in using national issues to defeat the Jacksonians." "New Jersey Politics," p. 156.

62. On Southard's satisfaction with the results of the 1830 Congressional election, see Daniel Southard to his father, Isaac Southard, January 6, 1831, Isaac Southard Papers, PUL. "Uncle [Samuel]," Daniel noted, "has not stopped grinning since he learned we were safe." For his conviction that Clay was "the choice of this state," see Southard to Gustavus Scott, September 12, 1830, Nelson Collection, NJHS.

63. William Halsted to Southard, June 27, 1831, Redwood Fisher to Southard, May 20, 1831, D. Mallory to Southard, May 20, 24, 1831, Robert Lee to Southard, September 21, 1830, P. J. Gray to Southard, August 17, 1830, and various letters from Gray to Southard in Box 77, Southard Papers, PUL. In one of these latter, Gray told Southard how deeply he appreciated Southard's "many acts of kindness." For evidence that Southard occasionally wrote, anonymously, for the Trenton *Union,* see the draft of a campaign essay by "Publius" in the first folder of correspondence for 1832, Southard Papers, PUL.

64. James F. Randolph to Southard, November 29, 1830, Southard Papers, PUL.

65. Joseph Blunt to Southard, December 22, 1830, Southard Papers, PUL.

66. Lewis Condict to Southard, October 27, 1830, Southard Papers, PUL.

67. Southard to Gustavus Scott, September 12, 1830, Nelson Collection, NJHS; (draft), Southard to James Peterson, December 3, 1830, John Quincy Adams to Southard, December 6, 1830, Peter D. Vroom to Southard, December 20, 1830, and (draft), Southard to John Rodgers, January 15, 1831, Southard Papers, PUL. The Rodgers letter is filed with Southard's correspondence for 1830.

68. Southard to Henry Clay, July 23, 1829, Clay Papers, LC.

69. See, for example, Southard to James Barbour, December 17, 1829, Barbour Papers, New York Public Library, and Southard to Henry Clay, September 18, 1831, Clay Papers, Lilly Library, Indiana University.

70. Southard's health for most of the latter part of 1831, as in 1830, was poor. See (draft), Southard to John Agg, August 13, 1831, Henry Clay to Southard, December 12, 1831, Southard Papers, PUL; Southard to Henry Clay, September 18, December 10, 1831, Clay Papers, Lilly Library.

71. Job S. Halstead to Southard, December 15, 1831, and Samuel S. Doty to Southard, December 15, 1831, misfiled with 1832, Southard Papers, PUL.

72. J. Johnson to Southard, December 21, 1831, Southard Papers, PUL. See also James S. Chase, *Emergence of the Presidential Nominating Convention, 1789–1832* (Urbana, Ill.: University of Illinois Press, 1973), pp. 219–20.

73. Richard S. Coxe to Southard, January 29, 1832, Isaac Southard to Southard, January 16, 1832, Southard Papers, PUL.

74. Bray Hammond, *Banks and Politics in America: From the Revolution to the Civil War* (Princeton, N.J.; Princeton University Press, 1957), chap. 13, is helpful on the background to the recharter fight.

75. Glyndon G. Van Deusen, *The Jacksonian Era, 1828–1848* (New York: Harper and Row, 1959), pp. 64–65.

76. My understanding of Jackson has been informed by three recent biographies: Robert V. Remini, *Andrew Jackson,* 3 vols. (two volumes published to date; New York: Harper & Row, 1977–); Michael Paul Rogin, *Fathers and Children: Andrew Jackson and the Subjugation of the*

American Indian (New York:Alfred A. Knopf, 1975); and James C. Curtis, *Andrew Jackson and the Search for Vindication* (Boston: Little, Brown, 1976).

77. Peter D. Vroom to Ferdinand S. Schenck, December 25, 1833, Schenck Papers, PUL.

78. Trenton *Emporium & True American*, July 21, 1832. Three days before Jackson released his Bank veto message, *Emporium* editor Stacy G. Potts warned that, if the president caved in to the Bank, "the needs of the people are laid beneath the feet of the aristocracy." Release of the veto message on July 10 encouraged an *Emporium* crusade against the bank that did not abate for several years.

79. Trenton *New Jersey State Gazette*, April 21, 1832.

80. Trenton *National Union*, July 7, 1832.

81. See the Newton *Sussex Register*, September 17, 24, October 29, November 5, 1832, for strongly worded endorsements of the bank from one of New Jersey's most rural enclaves.

82. Wirt's evolving position in Antimasonry can be traced in William Wirt to Southard, September 30, October 19, December 9, 1831, Southard Papers, PUL.

83. Southard to Henry Clay, September 18, 1831, Clay Papers, Lilly Library, Indiana University.

84. (Draft), Southard to John Rutherford, October 1832 (no day), Rutherford to Southard, October 29, 1832, Southard Papers, PUL. Rutherford's insistence that as an Antimason he preferred a Jackson to a Clay victory since "the present masonic dynasty" then would end in four years, rather than eight, doubtless severely tried Southard's patience, and forced him to lower his expectations for the election.

85. Henry Clay to Samuel Southard, June 6, 1832, Southard Additional Papers, PUL; Clay to Southard July 21, August 27, September 11, October 23, 1832, Southard Papers, PUL; Southard to Clay, August 13, 1832, Clay Papers, Lilly Library, Indiana University.

86. Trenton *New Jersey State Gazette*, October 13, 20, 1832.

87. Fallaw, "Whig Party," pp. 129–31.

88. Southard to Henry Clay, December 1, 1832, Clay Papers, LC.

89. Trenton *New Jersey State Gazette*, October 27, 1832. See also Southard to Henry Clay, November 3, 1832, Clay papers, Lilly Library, Indiana University; Southard to Clay, December 1, 1832, Clay Papers, Library of Congress; Southard to John Quincy Adams, December 1, 1832, Adams Papers, Massachusetts Historical Society, Microfilm Reel 496.

90. Southard to Henry Clay, November 3, 1832, Clay Papers, Lilly Library, Indiana University.

91. The range of appointments on which Southard had influence is amply documented in his correspondence for 1832 and early 1833, Southard Papers, PUL.

92. J. N. Reading to Southard, January 11, 1833. Isaac Southard to Southard, November 4, 1832, Southard papers, PUL. For evidence that the Democratic leadership faced similar problems with its rank and file, see Levine, *Behavior of State Legislative Parties*, p. 104.

93. William Anderson to Southard, January 16, 1833, (draft), Southard to Anderson, March 16, 1833, Southard Papers, PUL.

94. Southard's message, in pamphlet form, is in Box 116, Southard Papers, PUL. For comparison with the legislative initiatives of his predecessor, Peter Vroom, Birkner, "Vroom and the Politics of Democracy," pp. 16–17, and Herbert Ershkowitz, "Peter D. Vroom," in Michael J. Birkner and Paul A. Stellhorn, eds., *The Governors of New Jersey* (New Jersey Historical Commission, 1982, pp. 98–101.

95. *Votes and Proceedings of the Fifty-Seventh General Assembly*, pp. 142–52. 279.

96. Richard P. McCormick, *The Second American Party System: Party Formation in the Jacksonian Era* (Chapel Hill, N.C.: University of North Carolina Press, 1966), p. 134.

97. William W. Freehling, *Prelude to Civil War: The Nullification Controversy in South Carolina, 1816–1836* (New York: Harper and Row, 1966), chap. 8, contains a detailed and trenchant account of events during the crisis months.

98. Quoted in Van Deusen, *Jacksonian Era*, p. 75.

99. Ibid., p. 74.

232   SAMUEL L. SOUTHARD

100. Southard was alerted to the Jacksonians' maneuvers by his brother, Isaac, who in a missive dated December 29, 1832, said Peter Vroom was their instigator. Southard Papers, PUL.

101. (Draft), Southard to John Quincy Adams, December 15, 1832, Southard Papers, PUL.

102. John Quincy Adams to Southard, December 19, 1832, Southard Papers, PUL.

103. William Wirt to Southard, December 6, 1832, Southard Papers, PUL.

104. Southard's message of January 11, 1833, and another, shorter paper delivered January 28, were printed and may be found in Box 116, Southard Papers, PUL.

105. Garret D. Wall to Peter Vroom, February 6, 1833, Philhower Collection, RUL.

106. Newark *New Jersey Eagle*, February 15, 1833; Trenton *New-Jersey State Gazette*, February 23, 1833. Henry Clay alluded to the newspaper attacks on Southard by urging him to "bear them with the same fortitude and philosophy which *you know* I have always exhibited under the influence of similar attacks. I think you are beyond the reach of their rage." Henry Clay to Southard, April 22, 1833, Southard Papers, PUL.

107. Freehling, *Prelude*, pp. 292–94.

108. See (draft), Southard to Elias P. Seeley and J. P. Jackson, n.d. Southard Papers, PUL. This letter was printed in the Newton *Sussex Register*, March 18, 1833.

Chapter 7

1. William Wirt to Southard, November 29, December 6, 1832, Southard Papers, PUL. (Quote is from letter of Nov. 29.)

2. Joseph Randolph to Southard, December 29, 1832, Southard Papers, PUL. See also Garret Wall to Peter Vroom, February 6, 1833, Philhower Collection, RUL, in which Wall implored Vroom not to accept the governorship if the National Republicans followed through on their initial feelers. Acceptance would make Vroom "a footstool," Wall said, "for another man to climb to office. . . . The proposal *now* would be insulting—as it would imply that you from any cause can be insensible to personal dignity & submissive to the cravings of individual ambition." For the National Republicans' perspective on the governorship, see Lucius Q. C. Elmer to Southard, February 16, 1833 (misfiled with 1832), P. J. Gray to Southard, February 16, 1833, J. H. Sloan to Southard, February 11, 24, 1833, Southard Papers, PUL.

3. Fallaw, "Rise of the Whig Party," p. 154; Michael J. Birkner, "Elias P. Seeley," in Birkner and Stellhorn, eds., *The Governors of New Jersey*, pp. 105–108. The claim of Herbert Ershkowitz, "New Jersey Politics," p. 192, that Southard's election to the Senate "did irreversible damage to National Republican chances in the October election," seems extreme.

4. Hammond, *Banks and Politics*, pp. 412–13; Curtis, *Andrew Jackson*, p. 159.

5. Ibid.

6. Hammond, *Banks and Politics*, pp. 417–19.

7. Trenton *Emporium and True American*, October 5, 1833.

8. Newark *Sentinel of Freedom*, September 26, October 4, 1833.

9. See, for example, the essay, "Things to be Remembered," Trenton *Emporium*, September 14, 1833, and the editorial in the September 21, 1833, *Emporium*.

10. On National Republican organizational problems, William L. Dayton to Southard, September 25, 1833, Isaac Southard to Southard, September 4, 1833, Southard Papers, PUL.

11. Trenton *Emporium and True American*, October 12, 19, 1833; Trenton *New-Jersey State Gazette*, October 12, 19, 1833.

12. Fallaw, "Whig Party," pp. 88–90, 94–98, offers helpful background on the western counties. See also his election maps, pp. 103–6.

13. On the number of Quakers, see Thomas F. Gordon, *A Gazeteer of the State of New Jersey, Comprehending a General View of Its Physical and Moral Condition* (Trenton, N.J.: Daniel Fenton, 1834), p. 83. On background to the schism, see, among many sources, Bliss Forbush, *Elias*

Hicks, Quaker Liberal (New York: Columbia University Press, 1956); Elbert Russell, *The History of Quakerism* (New York: The Macmillan Company, 1942), chap. 23; Howard Brinton, *Friends for 300 Years: The History and Beliefs of the Society of Friends Since George Fox Started the Quaker Movement* (New York: Harper and Brothers, 1952), pp. 187–93; and most especially, Saxton, comp., *Reports of Cases Decided in the Court of Chancery*, 1:577–685. It should be noted that the "Hicksite" Quakers of New Jersey rejected that appellation, but because the term was nonetheless universally applied to them, I have employed it throughout my discussion.

14. Details of the case are recounted in *Hendrickson v. Decow*, in Saxton, comp., *Reports of Cases*, 1:577–685. On the political ramifications, Joshua Brick to Southard, October 30, November 8, 1832, Southard Papers, PUL.

15. Judge Ewing based his ruling on narrow legal grounds. His associate, George Drake, by contrast argued in his opinion that the Hicksites had "not proved" their doctrines were closer to the original Quaker tenets than those avowed by Orthodox Quakers, and hence he ruled the Hicksites deserved no consideration from the court. Charles Ewing died of cholera just as his decision was released in July 1832. Hicksite anger thereupon focused on Judge Drake, whose reappointment to the bench in 1834 they intended to block.

16. See Birkner, "Elias P. Seeley." Samuel Southard's argument in the appeal, which included a forceful criticism of Judge Drake's reasoning and an emphasis on the injustice done to the interests of a majority of Jersey Quakers, was transcribed by Edward Hopper and published in a 279-page volume, *Argument of Samuel L. Southard in the Case of Stacy DeCow and Joseph Hendrickson versus Thomas L. Shotwell. . . .* (Philadelphia: Elijah Weaver, 1834).

17. Ershkowitz, "New Jersey Politics," pp. 197–98.

18. Fallaw, "Whig Party," pp. 138–39.

19. Peter Vroom to James Parker, January 14, 27, 1834, Parker Papers, RUL; Vroom to Ferdinand Schenck, January 24, 1834, Stacy Potts to Schenck, January 15, 1834, Schenck Papers, RUL. It should be noted that Thomas Ryerson himself opposed Judge Drake's removal, and only acquiesced in the appointment once it was a fait accompli. Ryerson to Vroom, October 30, 1833, Vroom Papers, RUL.

20. Perry M. Goldman and James S. Young, eds., *The United States Congressional Directories, 1789–1840* (New York: Columbia University Press, 1973), p. 268.

21. *Register of Debates*, 23d Cong., 1st sess., pp. 29, 42–44.

22. Robert V. Remini, *Andrew Jackson and the Bank War* (New York: W. W. Norton and Co., 1967), offers an incisive analysis of the issues and maneuvers during this period. Among many other accounts of the Senate's duel with President Jackson, none matches Charles M. Wiltse, *John C. Calhoun: Nullifier, 1829–1839* (Indianapolis, Ind.: Bobbs Merrill Company, Inc., 1949), chaps. 16–21, for depth, insight, and narrative power. Though my own discussion of the Bank War lays much less emphasis on Calhoun's leadership than does Wiltse, I am nonetheless deeply indebted to his work.

23. *Register of Debates*, 23d Cong., 1st sess., p. 59.

24. Wiltse, *Calhoun: Nullifier*, p. 214.

25. See, generally, Van Deusen, *The Jacksonian Era, 1828–1848* (New York: Harper and Row, 1959), chap. 4; and Newton *Sussex Register*, January 20, 27, February 10, March 24, April 21, June 2, August 4, 18, September 8, 22, 1834. It is interesting to observe how, as time passed, the editor of the *Register* and other anti-Jacksonian papers came to abandon support for the Bank of the United States per se, and focus all attention on the "despotism versus democracy" theme.

26. Wiltse, *Calhoun: Nullifier*, pp. 224, 228.

27. William N. Chambers, *Old Bullion Benton: Senator for the New West* (Boston: Little, Brown and Co., 1956), p. 199.

28. The pamphlet may be found in Southard's speech file, Box 116, Southard Papers, PUL.

29. The discussion here and below, including all quotes, is taken from *Register of Debates*, 23d Cong., 1st sess., pp. 143–98.

30. Newton *Sussex Register,* January 20, 1834; E. B. Adams to Southard, February 18, 1834, E. H. Burritt to Southard, January 25, 1834, Southard Papers, PUL.

31. See Wiltse, *Calhoun: Nullifier,* pp. 219–20.

32. Ibid., p. 215.

33. See, for example, Charles Kinsey to Southard, February 3, 1834, Samuel Read to Southard, February 17, March 24, 1834, William P. Sherman to Southard, March 20, 1834, Richard Howell to Southard, March 10, 1834, Thomas Sinnickson to Southard, March 27, 1834, Jeremiah Leaming to Southard, March 29, 1834, and *Register of Debates,* 23d Cong., 1st sess., pp. 339–41, 525–27, 614–15, 679, 809–10, 862–65, 1049, 1050–57. For a typical memorial, see one from the citizens of Clinton, in Box 81, Southard Papers, PUL.

34. John Sergeant to Nicholas Biddle, February 27, 1834, in Reginald C. McGrane, ed., *The Correspondence of Nicholas Biddle Dealing with National Affairs, 1807–1844* (Boston: Houghton Mifflin Company, 1919), pp. 222–24; Hammond, *Banks and Politics* pp. 429–34. Quote is from Schlesinger, Jr., *Age of Jackson,* p. 109.

35. Remini, *Jackson and the Bank War,* pp. 127–30. While denying that Biddle was primarily responsible for the economic dislocations of 1834, Hammond does agree that his course was political folly. *Banks and Politics,* pp. 433–34, 438–39.

36. Holt, *Political Crisis of the 1850s,* p. 24.

37. E. B. Adams to Southard, February 18, 1834, Southard Papers, PUL. For nearly identical language on the Jacksonian side, see H. H. Wilson to Ferdinand Schenck, January 13, 1834, Schenck Papers, RUL. Peter Vroom demonstrated a sense of humor in capturing the public's fascination with the bank issue when he told his friend Schenck that "the Removal of the Deposites . . . has got to be a new bye word. If an old woman sneezes once oftener than usual, it is set down to the removal of the deposits." Vroom to Schenck, January 24, 1834, Schenck Papers. See also Vroom to James Parker, March 15, 1834, Parker Papers, RUL.

38. Birkner, "Vroom and the Politics of Democracy," pp. 20–22.

39. Borden Terhune to Ferdinand S. Schenck, January 7, 1834, Peter Vroom to Schenck, December 31, 1833, Schenck Papers, RUL; Jeremiah Leaming to Samuel Southard, January 11, 1834, Southard Papers, PUL.

40. *Votes and Proceedings of the New Jersey General Assembly,* 58th Session (1834), p. 177; Ershkowitz, "New Jersey Politics," p. 214. For the anti-Jacksonian perspective on instructions, see E. B. Adams to Southard, February 18, 1834, Roswell Colt to Southard, January 23, 1834, William P. Sherman to Southard, February 12, 1834, Southard Papers, PUL.

41. Southard to James W. Alexander, February 15, 1834, Southard Additional Papers, PUL. For a considerably more cynical estimate of Southard's motives during the Bank War, see Peter Vroom to Ferdinand Schenck, December 25, 1833, Schenck Papers, RUL. Southard's "great object" in politics, Vroom confided to the Democratic Congressman, was "the overthrow of the dominant party and the elevation of Mr. Clay or Calhoun."

42. Isaac Southard to Southard, March 6, 1834, Southard Papers, PUL; *Paterson Intelligencer,* September 24, 1834; and editorials in the Newton *Sussex Register* cited in n. 25 above.

43. Wiltse, *Calhoun: Nullifier,* pp. 217–22.

44. Howe, *American Whigs;* Berthoff, "Independence and Attachment," in Bushman et al., eds., *Uprooted Americans,* pp. 97–124; and Edwin A. Miles, "The Whig Party and the Menace of Caesar," *Tennessee Historical Quarterly* 27 (Winter 1968): 361–79.

45. I have drawn my observations about Henry Southard's life in the 1830s from various family letters within the Southard Papers. Quotes are from Henry Southard to Southard, February 28, March 12, 1834, Southard Papers, PUL.

46. When Samuel Southard responded to a letter, he wrote "ans" on the back of it. He left no such notation on either of his father's letters quoted above.

47. At the conclusion of his superb study, *The Jeffersonian Persuasion,* Lance Banning suggests that the Republican party of the 1850s "could be characterized as men of old agrarian and even Harringtonian principles who had fallen in love with enterprise" (p. 302). This

insight could be applied equally to the Whigs, as Daniel Walker Howe, *American Whigs*, has shown. On generations and political values, see the suggestive essay by Morton Keller, "Reflections on Politics and Generations in America," *Daedalus* 107 (Fall 1978): 123–36.

48. In an otherwise useful summary of Southard's public career, Herbert Ershkowitz makes the error of confusing the amount of time Southard spent on organizational and patronage-related activities with the whole thrust of his political life. See Ershkowitz, "Samuel L. Southard: A Case Study of Whig Leadership in the Age of Jackson," *New Jersey History* 88 (Spring 1970): 5–24. Peter D. Levine seems closer to the mark when he observes that "strongly principled men who view party in Burkean terms . . . may recognize the need to build and maintain effective electoral organizations in order to achieve power. So, too, might party elites in a competitive situation see the need to manufacture and to manage issue conflict in order to secure politically advantageous positions. Nor do these choices exhaust the possibilities." *Behavior of State Legislative Parties*, pp. 17–18. Relevant here also is Daniel Howe's analysis of Abraham Lincoln in *American Whigs*, pp. 264–65.

49. Even Richard P. McCormick, in his "electoral machine"–oriented *The Second American Party System*, concedes the salience of the bank issue (p. 131).

50. See above, chap. 6. For editors' laments, see, for example, the files of the Newton *Sussex Register* for 1830–32.

51. Peter D. Vroom to Ferdinand Schenck, December 25, 1833, Schenck Papers, RUL. Southard's January 1834 speech before the Senate on the "removal" of deposits, explicated above, is a good index of anti-Jacksonian sentiment.

52. Fallaw, "Whig Party," pp. 158–59. Given his convictions about the transcendent importance of the issues debated in Washington in 1833 and 1834, the injection of an unusual, purely local dispute in an anti-Jackson stronghold must have been a particular aggravation for Southard. Convinced that a natural majority in New Jersey opposed President Jackson's *policies*, he emphatically did not want religious controversy to enter into the political arena. But over this, as he found to his frustration, he had little control.

53. Charles Ridgeway to Southard, August 19, October 1, 1834, Isaac Townshend to Southard, September 6, 1834, G. Scull to Southard, September 22, 1834. Henry McIlvaine of Burlington wrote to Southard on January 22, 1834, that his speech in the Senate on the deposits question was so powerful that even the Orthodox were "willing to forget" his advocacy on behalf of the Hicksites. All of these letters are in Southard Papers, PUL.

54. Thomas Harris to Southard, July 9, 1834, Southard Papers, PUL.

55. Newark *Sentinel of Freedom*, October 21, 1834.

56. The key to the Jacksonians' slender 36–28 margin in the joint meeting was their sweep of the five contested legislative seats in Gloucester County. Had Gloucester gone Whig, as it likely would have had the Hicksites not been so aroused against Theodore Felinghuysen, the Whigs would have narrowly carried the state. For a breakdown of the vote, and editorial comment, see Newark *Sentinel of Freedom*, October 21, 1834.

57. Newton *Sussex Register*, October 27, 1834; James Wilson to Southard, October 17, 1834, Zachariah Rossell to Southard, October 17, 1834, Southard Papers, PUL. See also R. S. Rodgers to Southard, October 10, n.d., but probably 1834, Box 78, and William P. Sherman to Southard, n.d., 1834, Box 78, Southard Papers, PUL.

58. Samuel Southard to Hezekiah Niles, December 6, 1834, Southard Papers, NYPL.

59. See, for example, George Sherman to Southard, n.d., but ca. 1835, Box 78, Southard Papers, PUL.

60. My own approach to party politics in Jacksonian New Jersey is not oriented to an ethnocultural interpretation in the vein of works by Lee Benson, Ronald Formisano, and William Shade. If one examines the ethnic-religious makeup of the state population, one can argue that Whigs were supported by a marked majority of Quakers (save under exceptional circumstances, as prevailed in 1833–35) and persons of English origin, while Democrats were strongest in areas with concentrations of persons of Dutch and German ancestry. Nonetheless,

the appeals made by politicians and editors were overwhelmingly economic appeals, oriented to national party positions on the issues of the day. Religious and ethnic appeals were rarely salient, and even where they were the basis for party divisions, as in Bergen County, the two sides talked economic issues, not religion, at campaign time. For helpful background on ethnocultural politics as a strand of partisan conflict see Richard B. Latner and Peter D. Levine, "Perspectives on Antebellum Pietistic Politics: The Salience of Ethno-Cultural Issues," *Reviews in American History* 4 (March 1976): 15–24.

61. See, among many letters, Job S. Halsted to Southard, December 17, 1834, Jacob Mann to Southard, October 17, 1834, James Nevius to Southard, December 14, 1834, William Pennington to Southard, December 12, 1834, William P. Sherman to Southard, December 20, 1834, Joseph F. Randolph to Southard, December 17, 1834, J. P. B. Maxwell to Southard, January 20, 1835, and J. C. Smallwood to Southard, February 9, 1835, Southard Papers, PUL.

62. Isaac Southard to Southard, January 1, 1835, Southard Papers, PUL. Note also the comments of James N. Reading of Hunterdon County, who, in response to Southard's request for evidence about alien voting there in the recent elections, reported that the Democratic majority in Hunterdon derived in greatest measure from anti-Jacksonians who "had become frightened of the Bank. I know a number that left us on that account and it was impossible to convince them to the contrary." Reading to Southard, December 13, 1834, Southard Papers, PUL.

63. Fallaw, "Whig Party," p. 192.

64. Ibid. See also Elias P. Seeley to Southard, March 30, 1835, Southard Papers, PUL.

65. *Register of Debates*, 23d Cong., 2nd Sess., pp. 660–89. The main subject for Southard's discourse was the expunging resolution.

66. Henry Clay to Samuel Southard, April 12, 1835, Daniel Webster to Southard, April 28, 1835, Southard Papers, PUL. Southard's speech was printed and nearly 2,000 copies circulated. See Gales and Seaton to Southard, January 18, 1835, March 29, 1835, John Shackford to Southard, April 10, 17, 1835, Southard Papers, PUL.

67. James Wilson to Southard, January 2, 1836, Southard Papers, PUL. On the ultimate passage of the expunging resolution, Wiltse, *Calhoun: Nullifier*, pp. 298–300.

68. Fallaw, "Whig Party," pp. 195–99.

69. For background on the Joint Companies, see Lane, *Indian Trail to Iron Horse,* chap. 12.

70. Robert T. Thompson, "Transportation Combines and Pressure Politics in New Jersey, 1833–1836," *Proceedings of the New Jersey Historical Society* 57 (January 1939): 1–15, 71–86.

71. See Lane and Thompson accounts for details. George L. A. Reilly, "The Camden and Amboy Railroad in New Jersey Politics, 1830–1871" (Ph.D. diss., Columbia University, 1951), regrettably, is not a useful source.

72. Southard did not simply sell his name or influence to the Joint Companies. He performed significant legal services for both and in particular argued roughly a dozen cases for the canal company. See the accounts regarding his "professional services" for the company in Box 119, Southard Papers, PUL. See also John Potter to Southard, March 26, May 19, July 1, 1835, and Richard Shippen to Southard, December 23, 1835, Southard Papers.

73. Henry McIlvaine to Southard, August 21, 1834, Southard Papers. PUL. See also J. H. Sloan to Southard, July 11, 1832 and Abraham Brown to Southard, September 12, 1832, Southard Papers, PUL.

74. (Draft), Southard to Henry McIllvaine, August 22, 1835, Southard Papers, PUL.

75. Fallaw, "Whig Party," pp. 222–23.

76. Littleton Kirkpatrick to Garret D. Wall, December 23, 1835, Wall Papers, RUL. Kirkpatrick was a New Brunswick Jacksonian who had an interest in a new company that sought to build a road from Trenton to New Brunswick.

77. Birkner, "Vroom and the Politics of Democracy," pp. 26–31.

78. See Henry Clay to Southard, July 31, 1835, Southard Papers, PUL. Two excellent accounts of the maneuvering for the Whig nomination in 1836 are Norman D. Brown, *Daniel*

Webster and the Politics of Availability (Athens, Ga.: University of Georgia Press, 1969), chap. 5; and Sydney Nathans, *Daniel Webster and Jacksonian Democracy* (Baltimore: Johns Hopkins University Press, 1973), chap. 3.

79. In August 1835, this identification was strengthened when the Princeton *Whig* began to put at the head of its columns, "Henry Clay for President, Samuel L. Southard for Vice President." See James Wilson to Southard, August 20, 1835, Southard Papers, PUL.

80. Lucius Q. C. Elmer to Southard, February 17, May 22, 1834, Lewis Condict to Southard, July 19, 1834, Southard Papers, PUL.

81. The rabidly Jacksonian editor Stacy G. Potts captured the Whigs' problem of finding an acceptable candidate by noting tartly that the Whigs "have now nearly as many candidates as voters." Trenton *Emporium and True American*, August 1, 1835.

82. (Draft), Southard to Joseph F. Randolph, December 20, 1835, Southard Papers, PUL. It should be noted that Harrison, a favorite of Antimasons, was run for president in several Northern states, and actually carried Vermont against Van Buren.

83. Henry Clay to Southard, October 12, 1835, Southard Papers, PUL.

84. Southard to John Sergeant, December 12, 1835, Southard Papers, PUL. This letter was returned by Sergeant, at Southard's request, evidently because Southard wanted no written record outside of his own hands of his ambitions for the vice-presidency.

85. Once Pennsylvania nominated Harrison and Granger, Joseph Randolph suggested that New Jersey might still nominate Southard for the vice-presidency, a notion that Southard immediately rejected. "Have you thought," he told Randolph, "of the effect *on me?*" Though disappointed with Granger's nomination, he was not "blind" to political reality, and saw "no promised benefit to myself or others" in running an independent campaign for the second place on a Harrison ticket. (Draft), Southard to Randolph, December 20, 1835, Southard Papers, PUL.

86. Fallaw, "Whig Party," pp. 224–81, offers a detailed account of the New Jersey Whig campaign in 1836 as well as an analysis of the election returns.

87. James Wilson to Southard, December 10, 1836, Southard Papers, PUL.

Chapter 8

1. Samuel Southard to Lucius Q. C. Elmer, November 1828, quoted in Elmer, *Constitution and Government*, p. 226; Southard to Henry Clay, November 14, 1830, Clay Papers, Lilly Library, Indiana University.

2. Bartlett, *Webster*, p. 204. See also Edward Pessen, *Riches, Class and Power before the Civil War* (Lexington, Mass.: D. C. Heath, 1973), pp. 17–18; and Richard N. Current, *Daniel Webster and the Rise of National Conservatism* (Boston: Little, Brown, 1955), pp. 91–93.

3. Southard's land speculations may be traced in his correspondence with John Rodgers, Peter B. Porter, Hiram Raynor, Roswell L. Colt, William Duvall, James B. Murray, William T. Carroll, John M. Robinson, and Virgil Maxcy, all in Southard Papers, PUL. See also deeds in Box 117. On his ties to the Elizabethtown and Somerville Railroad, see correspondence with Isaac Southard, 1835–40, in Southard Papers.

4. Isaac Southard to Southard, May 13, June 6, 1836; (draft), Southard to Nathaniel Tallmadge, July 18, 1836, Tallmadge to Southard, November 8, 1836, Southard Papers, PUL.

5. Robert Swartwout to Southard, October 6, 1836, Southard Papers, PUL.

6. See documents dated April and August 30, 1838, in Robert Swartwout Papers, New York Public Library.

7. Robert Swartwout to Southard, October 28, November 5, 19, 26, 28, 1836, Samuel Southard to Henry L. Southard, December 13, 1836, Southard Papers, PUL.

8. Robert Swartwout to Southard, November 19, 26, 1836, February 5, 6, 14, 20, 1837, Southard Papers, PUL.

9. James S. Green to Southard, January 30, 1837, Southard Papers, PUL. See also Green to Southard, February 27, 1837, for details on the prospects of the Delaware and Raritan Canal and the observation that "I have no doubt, that if the canal should be placed under the direction of an individual who would devote the whole of his time to its immense business . . . that its profits would augment almost beyond calculation."

10. (Draft), Southard to Robert Swartwout, February 20, 1837, Southard Papers, PUL.

11. David B. Ogden to Southard, March 10, April 6, May 5, 22, 24, June 12, 1837; (draft), Southard to David B. Ogden, June 14, 1837. Nicholas Biddle wrote to Southard on April 30, 1837, saying he was unwilling to engage in the project because the anticipated profit margin was "not sufficiently tempting." Southard Papers, PUL.

12. See, generally, Hammond, *Banks and Politics,* chap. 15.

13. (Draft), Southard to Louis McLane, June 8, 1837, Southard Papers, PUL.

14. John A. Munroe, *Louis McLane: Federalist and Jacksonian* (New Brunswick, N.J.: Rutgers University Press, 1973), p. 457.

15. John Travers to Southard, January 14, 1837, "private," Southard Papers, PUL.

16. Munroe, *McLane,* pp. 462–72.

17. (Draft), Southard to Louis McLane, June 11, 1837, Louis McLane to Southard, June 15, 1837, Southard Papers, PUL; Morris Canal and Banking Company Minutes, June 7, 15, 22, 29, 1837, Archives and History Division, New Jersey State Library, Trenton, N.J. (hereafter NJSL).

18. Lane, *Indian Trail to Iron Horse,* p. 227; for background on the importance of canals to the transport of Pennsylvania anthracite, see Alfred D. Chandler, "Anthracite Coal and the Beginnings of the Industrial Revolution in the United States," *Business History Review* 46 (Summer 1972): 141–81.

19. Lane, *Indian Trail,* pp. 228–32.

20. Hirsch, *Roots of the American Working Class,* p. 17; Cunningham, *America's Main Road,* pp. 146–47.

21. Munroe, *McLane,* pp. 434–36; Lane, *Indian Trail,* pp. 233–37.

22. Munroe, *McLane,* pp. 440–55. E. R. Biddle took his place as a director at the board meeting of December 1, 1836. See Morris Canal and Banking Company Minutes for that date.

23. Munroe, *McLane,* pp. 456–58. Quote is from McLane's report to the Morris Company's stockholders, March, 1837, p. 5, in Box 112, Southard Papers, PUL.

24. Morris Canal and Banking Company, Minutes, August 21, 1837, March 1, 1838, NJSL.

25. Morris Canal and Banking Company Minutes, June 29, 30, July 1, 1837, NJSL.

26. Wilson Knoll to Southard, July 24, 1838, Southard Papers, PUL, offers a précis of cases involving the company. See also documents in Boxes 82, 112, 113, 114, Southard Papers, PUL, and Minutes of the MCBC for 1837 and 1838. On the Indiana and Michigan Bonds, E. R. Biddle to Southard, August 26, 1838, Thomas A. Alexander to Southard, April 14, June 23, 1838, Samuel R. Brooks to Southard, February 8, 15, 1838, Southard Papers. Reginald C. McGrane, *Foreign Bondholders and American State Debts* (New York: The Macmillan Company, 1935), pp. 129–34, 144–53, offers a judicious analysis of the bonds imbroglio.

27. Van Deusen, *Jacksonian Era,* pp. 121–22.

28. Birkner, "Vroom and the Politics of Democracy," pp. 27–28, and, more generally, James C. Curtis, *The Fox at Bay: Martin Van Buren and the Presidency* (Lexington, Ky.: University of Kentucky Press, 1970).

29. Wiltse, *Calhoun: Nullifier,* pp. 355–56; *Sketches of United States' Senators, of the Session of 1837–8, by "A Looker on Here in Verona"* (Washington: William M. Morrison, 1839), pp. 40–43; *Register of Debates,* 25th Cong., 1st sess., p. 6.

30. *Register of Debates,* 25th Cong., 1st sess., pp. 496–97.

31. This and succeeding quotations are from ibid.

32. I draw these observations from scattered comments in the Southard Papers, PUL. See also Ershkowitz, "Southard," pp. 22–23.

33. On the law lectures, John Maclean to Southard, January 14, March 2, 1835; Wertenbaker, *Princeton*, pp. 229–32. On the Joseph Henry connection, see Nathan Reingold, ed., *The Papers of Joseph Henry* (Washington: The Smithsonian Institution Press, 1975), 2:424–26.

34. E. B. Adams to Southard, February 4, 1835, Southard Papers, PUL.

35. Wertenbaker, *Princeton*, pp. 216–17, 232–33. See also Southard's correspondence with such Princeton notables as James Carnahan, James W. Alexander, John Maclean, and Albert B. Dod, Southard Papers, PUL. Several Southard letters to Maclean survive in the Maclean Collection, Seeley Mudd Library, Princeton University.

36. Many of Southard's nonpolitical addresses are collected in Box 116, Southard Papers, PUL.

37. Quote is from a printed copy of the speech to the Mechanics of Newark, July 5, 1830, Box 116, Southard Papers, PUL.

38. Southard was hostile to abolitionism throughout his public life. He did reluctantly accept and present petitions from the antislavery Quakers of West Jersey, but was no champion of their cause. See, on this, the revealing (draft) letter Southard wrote to C. F. Clark of Burlington County, January 17, 1839, Southard Papers, PUL.

39. Southard's comments on slavery and Indians are in his speech to the Newark Mechanics, Box 116, Southard Papers, PUL.

40. Rush Welter, *The Mind of America, 1820–1860* (New York: Columbia University Press, 1975), p. 141. See also Edward Pessen, *Jacksonian America: Society, Personality, and Politics* (Homewood, Ill.: The Dorsey Press, 1969), pp. 205, 350, and Glyndon G. Van Deusen, "Some Aspects of Whig Thought and Theory in the Jacksonian Period," *American Historical Review* 63 (January 1958): 305–22. The major difference between Southard and a leading conservative New Jersey public figure of the eighteenth century, William Paterson, seems to have been that Southard was more accepting of majoritarianism and also more receptive to a dynamic economy, geared to speculation, development, and change. On this, see John E. O'Connor, *William Paterson: Lawyer and Statesman, 1745–1806* (New Brunswick, N.J.: Rutgers University Press, 1979), pp. 128–29, and passim.

41. See, generally, Welter, *Mind of America*, chaps. 1–9; Howe, *American Whigs*, chaps. 1, 2; and Holt, *Political Crisis of the 1850s*, chap. 2.

42. Herbert Ershkowitz and William G. Shade, "Consensus or Conflict? Political Behavior in the State Legislatures During the Jacksonian Era," *Journal of American History* 68 (December 1971): 591–621, on the basis of a sample of votes, concluded that party divisions in the legislatures extended to social issues as well as economic ones. Peter D. Levine, in *Behavior of State Legislative Parties*, is not sympathetic to this argument. Levine sees no substantial division between the parties on "social" issues such as education, social welfare, temperance, and prison reform, though he does concede that Democrats and Whigs voted consistently differently on economic issues. Chaps. 5–7. For a vivid indication of how the parties differed on the economy, see the majority and minority reports on national economic policy offered in *Votes and Proceedings, 62nd General Assembly, 2nd Sitting* (Newark: M.S. Horner, 1837), pp. 54–61, 146–52.

43. The tally in Southard's favor was 36–23. Newton *Sussex Register*, November 26, 1838. See also Andrew Parsons to Southard, November 15, 1838, Isaac Southard to Southard, October 18, November 1, 15, 1838, Southard Papers, PUL.

44. Fallaw, "Whig Party," pp. 301–4, 309–10. On the "Pennington Cabal," John J. Chetwood to Southard, October 7, 1838, Southard Papers, PUL.

45. John J. Chetwood to Southard, October 3, 7, 1838, July 31, August 5, 14, 1839, J. R. Clawson to Southard, September 20, 1838, George Green to Southard, September 6, 14, 1838, William Halsted to Southard, September 18, October 16, 1838, Job S. Halsted to Southard, September 30, 1839, John P. Jackson to Southard, September 21, 30, 1839, F. S. McCulloch to Southard, September 13, 1838, Joseph F. Randolph to Southard, October 10, 1838, J. C. Smallwood to Southard, October 4, 1838, William White to Southard, September 29, 1838,

Southard Papers, PUL.

46. (Draft), Southard to Dudley Selden, November 1, 1838, "confidential," Southard Papers, PUL.

47. See, on this, Alvin F. Harlow, *Old Towpaths: The Story of the American Canal Era* (New York: D. Appleton and Co., 1926), pp. 199–200; Cornelius C. Vermeule, Jr., *Final Report of the Consulting and Directing Engineer* (N.p., 1929), p. 58; and Lane, *Indian Trail*, pp. 237–39.

48. Samuel Southard, Jr., to Henry L. Southard, January 19, 1839, Box 160, Southard Papers, PUL. See also (draft), Southard to Theodore Frelinghuysen, February 12, 1839, and Frelinghuysen to Southard, February 15, 1839, Southard Papers, for Southard's unsuccessful effort to interest Frelinghuysen in succeeding him as president of the Morris Company.

49. Morris Canal and Banking Company Minutes, January 15, 16, 24, 1839, NJSL; E. R. Biddle to Southard, December 22, 1838, Simeon Draper to Southard, January 8, 15, 16, 1839, Southard Papers, PUL; Munroe, *McLane*, p. 463.

50. Newton *Sussex Register*, February 4, 1839. Southard's most noteworthy arguments before the United States Supreme Court took place in 1837 and 1838, in *Briscoe* v. *Bank of Kentucky* and *Rhode Island* v. *Massachusetts*, respectively. Although the court's decision in the *Briscoe* case went against him, Southard ranked it, and his argument in the *Rhode Island* case, as among his best. For his comments, see annotation at end of his brief on the *Briscoe* case in Box 87, Southard Papers, for the *Rhode Island* brief, Box 101. For secondary accounts of the two cases, see, among many sources, R. Kent Newmeyer, *The Supreme Court Under Marshall and Taney* (New York: Thomas Y. Crowell Co., 1968), pp. 100–101; Charles G. Haines and Foster H. Sherwood, *The Role of the Supreme Court in American Government and Politics* (Los Angeles: University of California Press, 1957), pp. 48–54; Carl B. Swisher, *The Oliver Wendall Holmes Devise History of the Supreme Court of the United States, 5: The Taney Period, 1836–64* (New York: Macmillan Publishing Co., Inc., 1974), pp. 107–8, 513–15; Carl Brent Swisher, *Roger B. Taney* (New York: The Macmillan Company, 1935), pp. 374–76, 529.

51. Andrew Parsons to Southard, February 1, 1839, Samuel Southard, Jr., to Southard, January 19, 1839, Southard Papers, PUL.

52. Quoted in William H. Pease and Jane H. Pease, "Paternal Dilemmas: Education, Property and Patrician Persistence in Jacksonian Boston," *New England Quarterly* 53 (June 1980): 167.

53. Although Southard hardly qualified as a "patrician," his standards and practices as a parent were markedly similar to those described in Pease and Pease, "Education, Property, and Patrician Persistence," pp. 147–67.

54. Southard's sons both graduated from the College of New Jersey in 1836. His daughter Virginia's formal education included a stint at Emma Willard's school for young women in Troy, New York.

55. Southard to Henry L. Southard, October 9, 1837, Southard Papers, PUL.

56. These remarks find ample documentation in correspondence between Southard and his children extant in the Southard Papers, PUL.

57. See the correspondence of Southard's children and his brother Isaac for the 1830s.

58. In a remarkable letter from Samuel, Jr., to Henry, written shortly after their father's death, Samuel told his brother that "I have heard lately from different sources of rumors in the world of which we suspected nothing, that her [Rebecca's] conduct has been ascribed by servants of the family to *drink & opium!* I am afraid that the latter is too true—I have feared it for some time. Can it be that our dear father was destroyed by a madness of which we could not guess the cause!" Letter of October 20, 1842, Box 160, Southard Papers, PUL.

59. Samuel Southard, Jr., to Southard, n.d., Box 78, Southard Papers, PUL.

60. Samuel Southard to Rebecca Southard, n.d. Box 78, Southard Papers, PUL. It is possible, of course, that Southard wrote this letter as an act of catharsis, and never submitted it to his wife. This possibility does not diminish the reality that at this time in his life, Southard was a deeply unhappy man.

61. On Southard's constant travels, Samuel Southard, Jr., to Henry Southard, December 29, 1838, September 1, 1839, January 25, November 5, 1840, in Box 160, Southard Papers, PUL. In *Inside the Great House: Planter Family Life in Eighteenth-Century Chesapeake Society* (Ithaca, N.Y.: Cornell University Press, 1980), chap. 4, Daniel Blake Smith notes that marital irritations and conflicts often provoked family heads to spend a good deal of time away from home. This analysis seems relevant to Southard's situation. Unable satisfactorily to resolve his wife's grievances, Southard chose a life of constant motion. That his regimen wore him down, emotionally and physically, appears certain. Witness Samuel, Jr.'s, observations, in his letter to Henry on Demember 29, 1838, that their father's "labors are too arduous and unless lessened soon may utterly destroy him." Box 160, Southard Papers, PUL.

Chapter 9

1. Fallaw, "Whig Party," pp. 365–66; Abraham Godwin to Southard, June 29, December 11, 1837, Thomas Gordon to Southard, February 2, 1838, Isaac Southard to Southard, January 26, February 12, 18, 1838, Southard Papers, PUL.

2. John J. Chetwood to Southard, February 18, 1838, Thomas A. Alexander to Southard, January 19, 1838, Southard Papers, PUL.

3. William P. Sherman to Southard, February 2, 1837, Southard Papers, PUL. Newton *Sussex Register*, October 22, 1838.

4. One staunch Clay backer, Paterson's Andrew Parsons, wrote Southard on March 19, 1838, telling him how gratified he was about Clay's New Jersey tour, and noting how "delighted" West Jersey Whigs were with Clay. "All went home with a determination to forward his interests in West Jersey with all their influence and personal exertions. Here you know we need none being all one way." Southard Papers, PUL. Unfortunately for Clay, appearances were deceiving; his support in the West was shallow.

5. David B. Ogden to Southard, January 31, 1838, (draft), Southard to David B. Ogden, n.d., but probably February 1838, Box 78, Southard Papers, PUL; James Wilson to Southard, February 10, 1838, Isaac Southard to Southard, February 18, 1838, Southard Papers, PUL.

6. Fallaw, "Whig Party," pp. 366–68. Robert Gray Gunderson, *The Log-Cabin Campaign* (Lexington, Ky.: University of Kentucky Press, 1957), chap. 5, offers a helpful account of the maneuvering in Harrisburg.

7. Isaac Southard to Southard, December 7, 1839, Southard Papers, PUL. Isaac said he told his fellow delegates that he prefered to "sink" with Clay and "our principles, professions, and practices," then to "abandon" them for the sake of expediency.

8. Adam Lee to Southard, December 15, 1839, Isaac Southard to Southard, December 17, 1839, Southard Papers, PUL. See also Newton *Sussex Register*, December 16, 23, 1839, and Newark *Daily Advertiser*, December 9, 10, 12, 1839.

9. Quoted in Robert Seager II, *And Tyler Too: A Biography of John and Julia Gardiner Tyler* (New York: McGraw-Hill Book Company, Inc., 1963), p. 134.

10. See L. Combs to Henry Clay, December 4, 1839, Clay Papers, LC (microfilm), on perfidy in the New York delegation. On Clay's endorsement of the Whig ticket, Gunderson, *Log-Cabin Campaign*, pp. 68–70, and Van Deusen, *Henry Clay*, p. 334.

11. Elmer, *Constitution and Government*, p. 231. The witness to Southard's mortifying encounter with Clay was Roswell L. Colt.

12. The beginnings of the rapprochement between Clay and Southard may be traced to efforts by a New York intermediary, Daniel Ullmann, operating on behalf of Southard's son-in-law, Ogden Hoffman. Responding to these overtures in January 1842, Clay informed Ullmann that he "should be most willing to hear anything which Mr. Hoffman might choose to say to me, in regard to the Harrisburg Convention. On that subject both he and Mr. Southard have preserved a silence, which I did not think I ought to break." Clay to Ullmann,

January 6, 1842, New York Historical Society. Typescript in M. I. King Library, University of Kentucky. By December 1841, Southard could write his—and Clay's—old friend Francis T. Brooke that things had been patched up. "I need not detail facts—many things were said & done, wounding to the pride both of myself & friends—& mortifying to my family. . . . But I attribute them to misapprehension & the malice of lying talebearers. I continued in his support, publicly & privately, until my friends regarded my conduct as a wanton sacrifice of myself. He now I think understands better & feels better. . . . You need not be uneasy. All is right." (Draft), Southard to Brooke, n.d., but ca. December 1841, Southard Papers, PUL.

13. J. Owen Grundy, *The History of Jersey City, 1609–1976* (Jersey City, N.J.: Chamber of Commerce, 1976), p. 33.

14. Henry L. Southard to Southard, May 10, 1840, Samuel Southard, Jr., to Southard, February 27, June 13, 1840, and undated correspondence in Box 78, Southard Papers, PUL. For terms of rent, see Andrew Clark to Southard, February 2, 1842, Southard Papers, PUL.

15. See the family correspondence, much of it undated but overwhelmingly for the period 1838–42, in Boxes 160, 161, Southard Papers, PUL.

16. Samuel Southard, Jr., to Southard, June 29, 30, July 8, 10, 1840, Southard Papers, PUL. After the onset of her illness Mrs. Southard was taken to Fredericksburg, Virginia, and put under the care of family friend Dr. John Wellford. That her illness further unbalanced her mind was the opinion of Virginia, expressed in a letter to her brother Henry, n.d. Box 79, Southard Papers, PUL.

17. Van Deusen, *Jacksonian Era*, p. 128.

18. (Draft), Southard to William W. Seaton, January 8, 1840, Southard Papers, PUL.

19. *Congressional Globe*, 26th Cong., 1st sess., pp. 155, 229, 358, 382, 426, 466, 471, 535–36, 543, and Appendix, pp. 114, 425, 438, 441, 856.

20. *Title Papers of the Clamorgan Grant, or 536,904 Arpents of Alluvial Land in Missouri and Arkansas* (New York: T. Snowden, 1837); Magdalen Eichert, "Daniel Webster's Western Land Investments," *Historical New Hampshire* 26 (Fall 1971): 29–30; and Wiltse, ed., *Papers of Daniel Webster*, 4: 220–22.

21. C. M. Thurston to Southard, June 6, 26, 1837, William A. Bradley to Southard, November 27, 1837, and copies of John M.Walker to Bradley, February 16, 1837, A. G. Harrison to Bradley, February 27, 1837, Joseph Kent to Virgil Maxcy, June 15, 1837, Southard Papers, PUL.

22. *Title Papers*, p. 1, 14–24.

23. See a copy of Senate Bill number 153, 25th Cong., 3rd Sess., pertaining to the Clamorgan association, filed with Richard Coxe to Southard, January 15, 1838, Southard Papers, PUL.

24. Roswell L. Colt to Southard, February 6, 15, March 28, 1840, Southard Papers, PUL.

25. *Congressional Globe*, 26th Cong., 1st sess., pp. 321, 325. William A. Bradley told Southard once the bill passed the Senate that a brief on the matter prepared by Southard for several Whig senators was "so clear & unequivocal that it removed all doubt." Bradley to Southard, April 14, 1840, Southard Papers, PUL.

26. Southard's continued and unavailing efforts as a Clamorgan associate may be traced in his correspondence for 1840–42 with Virgil Maxcy, Roswell L. Colt, James B. Murray, and William A. Bradley. On the final settling of his accounts regarding Clamorgan, see Roswell L. Colt to Henry L. Southard, December 14, 1842, Southard Papers, PUL. For further background on Clamorgan, see documents in Boxes 117, 133, Southard Papers, PUL, and Wiltse, ed., *Papers of Daniel Webster*, volumes 4 and 5, passim.

27. For specifics on the company's problems with its Indiana and Michigan bonds, see McGrane, *Foreign Bondholders*, chaps. 7, 8.

28. Important letters that give background on the company's proposals include Isaac Southard to Southard, February 8, 16, 25, 1839, Samuel R. Brooks to Southard, February 8, 1838, (draft), Southard to John J. Chetwood, n.d., but probably February 1838, Box 78,

Southard Papers, PUL; E. R. Biddle to Southard, January 1, 1839, Samuel P. Hull to South-ard, January 11, 1840, Southard Papers. See *Reasons for Granting to the Morris Canal and Banking Company an Increase of Banking Capital and the Loan of State Bonds* (New York: James Van Norden, n.d.), in NJHS, for the proposals of 1838 and 1839; Newark *Daily Advertiser*, February 18, 1840, for the 1840 bill.

29. For various memorials and newspaper pieces critical of the Morris Company applica-tions, see Box 112, Southard Papers, PUL.

30. Samuel Halsey to Lewis Condict, January 19, 1839, Southard Papers, PUL. Condict evidently passed this letter on to Southard.

31. *Votes and Proceedings of the Sixty-third General Assembly, 1st Sitting* (Newark, N.J.: M. S. Harrison & Co., 1839), pp. 399, 401, 402, 407, 431; *Votes and Proceedings, Sixty-fourth General Assembly, 1st Sitting* (Belvidere, N.J.: Wilson & Brittain, 1840), p. 303; Newark *Sentinel of Freedom*, February 18, 1840; Newark *Daily Advertiser*, February 9, 12, 13, 14, 16, 18, March 7, 1839, February 7, 13, 14, 1840.

32. Southard resigned his position as counsel to the Morris Company on August 3, 1841. A copy of the letter of resignation is in Box 80, Southard Papers, PUL. For his final tabulation of accounts with the company, listing the status of cases on which he had labored, Box 82, Southard Papers.

33. Edwin Post to Southard, January 25, 1838, February 17, 1839, E. R. Biddle to South-ard, February 1, 8, 28, 1839, Edwin Lord to Southard, February 8, 1839, Southard Papers.

34. (Draft), Southard to John J. Chetwood, n.d., but probably February 1838, Box 78, Southard Papers, PUL.

35. (Draft), Southard to E. R. Biddle and Edwin Post, February 11, 1839, Southard Papers, PUL.

36. E. R. Biddle to Southard, January 24, February 12, 1840, William P. Sherman to Southard, February 14, 1840, Southard Papers, PUL.

37. President Biddle's report to the Morris Company stockholders, December 31, 1840, is available in NJHS.

38. Lane, *Indian Trail to Iron Horse*, pp. 239–41.

39. Paterson *Guardian*, October 6, 1840.

40. E. R. Biddle to Southard, ?7, 1840, Isaac Southard to Southard, March 14, May 27, June 12, July 6, 1840, Samuel Southard, Jr., to Southard, June 13, 29, 30, 1840, (draft), Southard to Isaac Southard, June 5, 1840, Southard Papers, PUL. In his letter of June 12, Isaac expressed his conviction that the Morris Company would refuse to "pay the money" it owed no matter what devices were tried. He also observed that he "should not be surprised" if the company "attempted secretly to get rid of you"—comments that would not have much relieved Southard's anxieties.

41. Although there is no evidence that Southard was pressed to pay any portion of the Morris Company's tax, his finances were nonetheless affected by the company's troubles. Despite his persistent proddings, the company was slow to pay expenses he had incurred while trying cases for them in various courts, and he never did receive his full recompense. See accounts in Box 112, Southard Papers, PUL.

42. William P. Sherman to Southard, February 14, 1840, Southard Papers, PUL.

43. Lewis Condict to Southard, April 11, 1840, Southard Papers, PUL.

44. There is an outline of Southard's standard stump speech in Box 81, Southard Papers, PUL. See also accounts in Newark *Daily Advertiser*, July 31, August 20, 1840. Quotes are from issue of August 20.

45. James Wilson to Southard, September 11, 1840, Southard Papers, PUL.

46. Newton *Sussex Register*, October 26, 1840.

47. Quoted in *A Gentleman of Much Promise: The Diary of Isaac Mickle, 1837–1845*, ed. Philip E. Mackey (Philadelphia: University of Pennsylvania Press, 1977), 1:92–93.

48. Trenton *Emporium and True American*, July 17, August 15, 22, 29, 1840; Paterson *Guar-*

dian, October 6, 1840.

49. William J. Chute, "The New Jersey Whig Campaign of 1840," *New Jersey History* 78 (1960):222–39, conveys the flavor of the Whigs' efforts.

50. McCormick, *Second American Party System,* p. 134.

51. Fallaw, "Whig Party," pp. 397–98.

52. My argument here contradicts that in Walter Fallaw's dissertation on the New Jersey Whigs. He believes that the Whigs abandoned their principles in the late 1830s because they were lured by the spoils of office. My own interpretation of the available evidence holds that issues remained important through the middle of the 1840s. On the subject of issues in the 1840 election and their relation to campaign spectacle, see the persuasive analysis of William R. Brock, *Parties and Political Conscience: American Dilemmas, 1840–1850* (Millwood, N.Y.: KTO press, 1979), pp. 4–5, 21–22, 73–74, 82.

53. Newark *Sentinel of Freedom,* October 13, 1840.

54. Charles Kinsey to Southard, December 30, 1840; Esther Felt Bentley, "Samuel L. Southard and Political Patronage," *Princeton University Library Chronicle* 23 (Autumn 1961): 1–15.

55. Quote is from Samuel L. Southard to Henry L. Southard, August 26, 1840, Southard Papers, PUL.

56. William A. Bradley to Southard, August 20, 1840. See also Lewis Condict to Southard, December 8, 1840, Henry L. Southard to Southard, December 20, 1840, Southard to Henry L. Southard, January 10, 1841, Southard Papers, PUL. See also William A. Graham to William Gaston, December 16, 1840, in J. G. de Roulhac Hamilton, ed., *The Papers of William Alexander Graham,* 4 vols. (Raleigh, N.C.: State Department of Archives and History, 1957–61), 2:131–132.

57. On the maneuvering for positions in a Harrison administration, see George R. Poage, *Henry Clay and the Whig Party* (Chapel Hill, N.C.: University of North Carolina Press, 1936), pp. 15–21; Albert D. Kirwan, *John J. Crittenden: The Struggle for the Union* (Lexington, Ky.: University of Kentucky Press, 1962), pp. 137–39; Seager, *And Tyler Too,* pp. 142–44; and Sydney Nathans, *Daniel Webster and Jacksonian Democracy* (Baltimore: The Johns Hopkins University Press, 1973), chap. 6.

58. Southard to Henry L. Southard, January 10, 1841, Southard Papers, PUL.

59. Isaac Southard to Southard, February 15, 1841, William B. Kinney to Southard, February 19,1841, Samuel Southard, Jr., to Henry L. Southard, February 4, 1841 (Box 160), Rebecca Southard to Southard, February 13, 1841 (Box 78), Southard Papers, PUL. See also E. Marsh to Southard, February 1, 1841, John J. Chetwood to Southard, February 3, 1841, and Virginia Southard Hoffman to Henry L. Southard, n.d., but March 1841 (Box 161), Southard Papers, PUL. Rebecca Southard told her son Henry on February 18 that his father's failure to be named to the cabinet "is Henry Clay's doings. He is the greatest enemy your father has. In fact, he is not the man he appears to be." (Box 160)

60. On Southard's low spirits in early 1841, see Samuel Southard, Jr., to Henry L. Southard, February 4, 1841, Box 160, Southard Papers, PUL.

61. William C. Preston to Willie P. Mangum, May 3, 1841, in Henry Thomas Shanks, ed., *The Papers of Willie Person Mangum,* 5 vols (Raleigh: State Department of Archives and History, 1950–56), 3:156.

62. Poage, *Henry Clay,* pp. 30–32. In his one public rebuke to Clay, Southard spoke out against holding a special session of the Congress. See John J. Chetwood to Southard, February 3, 1841, Southard Papers, PUL.

63. Henry Clay to John Lawrence, April 13, 1841, Manuscripts Division, University of Virginia. See also Clay to H. Bascom, April 17, 1841, Clay to John M. Berrien, April 20, 1841, Clay to Peter B. Porter, April 24, 1841, Clay to John Quincy Adams, April 29, 1841, typescripts of which are available in the Henry Clay Papers Project, Margaret I. King Library, University of Kentucky.

64. John Tyler to Henry Clay, April 20, 1841, typescript in King Library, University of Kentucky. See also Seager, *And Tyler Too,* pp. 150–52, and Robert Morgan, *A Whig Embattled* (Lincoln, Neb.: University of Nebraska Press, 1954), p. 31.

65. Seager, *And Tyler Too,* pp. 151–52, offers the telling judgment that in 1841, the issues at stake were less economic than political. They "turned fundamentally," he writes, "on Clay's attempt to seize control of the Whig leadership and drive Tyler back into the political exile from which he had unexpectedly reemerged in 1839. In this sense, the bank crisis was a test of strength, prestige, and personality between two strong and wilful men, each loathe to lose face in the struggle as it developed and waxed hotter." A more recent analysis of the political crisis of 1841, W. R. Brock's *Parties and Political Conscience,* pp. 88–100, offers a much less sympathetic analysis of President Tyler than does Seager.

66. (Draft), Southard to Lewis Condict, September 3, 1841, Southard Papers, PUL.

67. Accordingly to Tyler's biographer, Robert Seager, the cabinet walkout on September 11 was "planned, calculated, and coordinated by Henry Clay to wreck the Executive branch, punish John Tyler for his bank vetoes, and force his resignation." This is certainly a plausible reconstruction of Clay's mind-set at the time, but unfortunately no documentary evidence sustains the notion that Clay seriously expected Tyler to resign the presidency and have Samuel Southard replace him. See *And Tyler Too,* p. 160.

68. Isaac Gibson to Southard, July 19, August 1, September 30, November 5, 25, December 6, 1841, (drafts), Southard to Gibson, July 27, November 12, 1841, Isaac Southard to Southard, February 18, 26, 1842, Southard Papers, PUL.

69. (Draft), Southard to Samuel L. Gouverneur, November 12, 1841, Southard Papers, PUL. Gouverneur responded that he lacked the means to pay Southard what he demanded, and believed that Southard's letter had done him a "very great injustice. It is apparent on the face of your letter & breathes in every line of it." Gouverneur to Southard, November 17, 1841.

70. (Draft), Southard to P. R. Fendall, n.d., but ca. 1841–1842, Southard Papers, PUL.

71. (Draft), Southard to Isaac Williamson, November 25, 1841, and (draft), Southard to Isaac Gibson, November 12, 1841, Southard Papers, PUL.

72. Ogden Hoffman to Southard, February 5, March 3, 1842, James D. Harrow to Southard, February 5, 1842, (draft), Southard to General D'alvear, March 9, 1842, Southard Papers, PUL.

73. Southard to Rebecca Southard, February 17, 1842, Southard Papers, PUL. It is possible that Southard did not actually transmit this rebuke to his wife.

74. *Congressional Globe,* 27th Cong., 2nd sess., pp. 381, 382, 384, 385, 432.

75. The first official notice of Southard's "indisposition" is in *Congressional Globe,* 27th Cong., 2nd sess., p. 444 (April 27). See also (drafts), Southard to William Dayton, April 15, 1842 ("My health is slowly recovering") and Southard to Charles M. Dupuy, n.d., but May 10, 1842 ("I am entirely too unwell to discharge my official [duties]"). Southard Papers, PUL.

76. Samuel Southard, Jr., to Southard, May 10, 18, 1842, Southard papers, PUL.

77. *Congressional Globe,* 27 Cong., 2 Sess., p. 554. See also the draft letter from Southard to Jacob W. Miller, n.d., Box 76, Southard Papers, PUL, in which he explained "I am in great distress."

78. Henry Clay to Willie P. Mangum, June 7, 1842, in *Papers of Willie Person Mangum,* 3:356.

79. Isaac Southard to Southard, May 22, 26, 1842, Samuel Southard, Jr., to Southard, May 23, 26, 1842, Southard Papers, PUL. Henry Southard's obituary in the Trenton *State Gazette* noted that "he had enjoyed good health, and the full possession of his mental faculties, up to within a few days of his death, which occurred after only four or five days of illness induced by fatigue from walking." May 28, 1842.

80. Quote is from Henry Southard, Sr., to Southard, February 28, 1834, Southard Papers, PUL.

81. See Newark *Daily Advertiser,* May 27, 31, June 6, 10, 15, 16, 17, 18, 20, 24, 25, 28, 29, 1842; Trenton *State Gazette,* June 2, 7, 9, 11, 14, 16, 18, 21, 25, 28, 30, 1842.

82. *Congressional Globe,* 27th Cong., 2nd sess., p. 689; Newark *Daily Advertiser,* June 30, 1842. Adams related in his diary that his eulogy on Southard was one that Southard "had well deserved at my hands." Adams, ed., *Memoirs,* 11:190 (entry of June 28, 1842).

83. Plans were made by Southard's son Henry, in collaboration with John Taliaferro, to collect and publish these eulogies and various reminiscences of Southard in a memorial volume, but the effort came to naught.

Bibliography

Although this study is the product of six years' labor in many archives and academic libraries and the examination of a widely dispersed array of published and unpublished sources, its foundation remains the Samuel L. Southard Collection in Firestone Library, Princeton University. The approximately 20,000 items there pertaining to Southard, superbly organized by the Princeton University Library staff in the early 1960s and opened to researchers in 1964, document virtually every aspect of Samuel Southard's life, from his most controversial political operations to his mundane chores and accounts. (For details on the substance of the collection, consult Alexander P. Clark, "The Samuel L. Southard Papers," *Princeton University Library Chronicle* 20 (Autumn 1958): 45–47.)

Throughout his life Southard maintained a large personal archive of correspondence, legal briefs, contemporary documents and newspapers, speech drafts, expense accounts, and so forth. He threw virtually nothing away. Because of this, and because the integrity of his papers has remained largely intact since his death in 1842, any biographer has a wealth of materials with which to work in shaping a coherent narrative of Southard's life and career. Helpful as this mass of documents is, one crucial element of the Southard file is missing: his letterbooks. Southard wrote drafts and kept letterbook copies of much of his consequential correspondence. Unfortunately the letterbooks have disappeared. Equally regrettably, only a tiny fraction of Southard's letters to his contemporaries, prominent and obscure, survive. Southard's letters to his wife, Rebecca, for example, which would likely have offered signal insights into his often troubled domestic life, were as a rule destroyed by Rebecca Southard in order to keep them from the hands of their children. (On this matter see Rebecca's letter to her husband, ca. 1830, in Box 78 of the Southard Papers.)

Given this situation I have relied heavily on the notes and drafts Southard wrote on the back of incoming letters. Many of the draft letters cited in this biography are not separate missives but rough and hastily scrawled versions of letters that Southard ultimately sent. I have quoted from these drafts with confidence because where I have had the opportunity to compare drafts with actual letters, the concordance between the two has been nearly exact.

The Southard Collection at Princeton, then, is the essential source for this biography. My work could not have been completed, however, without access to literally thousands of other documents in three other major repositories of New Jerseyana—Rutgers University's department of special collections, the archives at the New Jersey State Library in Trenton, and The New Jersey Historical Society in Newark—as well as the New York Public Library and the Library of Congress manuscript collections. My debt to other scholars is great and, I trust, it is amply acknowledged in the notes accompanying the text. The bibliography that follows is a compilation of these citations, not an exhaustive listing of sources consulted.

Primary Sources

Manuscript Collections

Historical Society of Pennsylvania
  Roswell L. Colt Papers
  Gratz Autograph Collection

Hunterdon County Historical Society
  Charles Bartles mss.

Library of Congress
  Henry Clary Papers (microfilm)
  William Darlington Papers
  Maxcy-Markoe Papers
  James Monroe Papers (microfilm)
  David Porter Papers
  Samuel L. Southard Papers

Lilly Library, Indiana University
  Henry Clay Papers (photocopies)

Margaret I. King Library, University of Kentucky
  Henry Clay Papers (typescripts)

Massachusetts Historical Society
  Adams Family Papers (microfilm)

The New Jersey Historical Society
  Canfield Genealogical Papers
  Mahlon Dickerson Papers
  Philemon Dickerson Papers
  Edwin A. Ely Collection
  John P. Jackson Papers
  William Nelson Collection
  New Jersey Boundary Papers

New Jersey State Library
  Minutes of the Morris Canal and Banking Company, 1836–42
  Stacy G. Potts Autobiography
  Ratables, Bernard Township, N.J., 1778–1818
  Revolutionary War Card Index
  Isaac Williamson Papers

New York Public Library
  James Barbour Papers
  James Monroe Papers
  Samuel L. Southard Papers
  Robert Swartwout Papers
  United States Navy Department Mss., 1823–25

Princeton University Library
  Letters of James Iredell, Jr. (typescript)
  Memoirs of George Strawbridge
  Samuel L. Southard Papers
  Stockton Family Papers
  Smith Thompson Papers
  Garret D. Wall Papers

Rutgers University Library
  New Jersey Letters
  James Parker Papers
  Charles Philhower Collection
  Ferdinand S. Schenck Papers
  Isaac Southard Papers
  Samuel L. Southard Papers
  Peter D. Vroom Papers
  Garrett D. Wall Papers

Seeley G. Mudd Library, Princeton University
  College of New Jersey, Faculty Minutes, 1800–5
  College of New Jersey, Trustee Minutes, 1800–6
  Laws of the College of New Jersey
  John Maclean Papers
  Henry L. Southard file
  Samuel L. Southard file

University of Virginia
  Argosy Collection
  C. P. Gooch Papers

Virginia Historical Society
  Mercer Family Papers
  Census of King George County, 1800

Public Documents

Acts of the General Assembly of the State of New Jersey. Published in various places after each sitting, 1813–40.

American State Papers: Documents, Legislative and Executive, of the Congress of the United States. . . . 38 vols. Washington, D.C.: Gales and Seaton, 1832–61.

Congressional Globe. . . . 46 vols. in 111. Washington, D.C.: Globe Office, 1834–73.

Debates and Proceedings in the Congress of the United States. (Annals of Congress.) 42 vols. Washington: Gales and Seaton, 1834–56.

Journals of the Proceedings of the Legislative Council of the State of New Jersey. Published at various places after each sitting, 1828–41.

Letters Received by the Secretary of the Navy: Captain's Letters, 1805–85 (M-125). Records of the Navy Department (RG-45), National Archives, microfilm.

Letters Sent by the Secretary of the Navy to Officers, 1798–1866 (M-149). Records of the Navy Department (RG-45), National Archives, microfilm.

Register of Debates in Congress. . . . 14 vols. in 29. Washington, D.C.: Gales and Seaton, 1825–37.

Report of the Commissioners on the Controversy with the State of New York Respecting the Eastern Boundary of the State of New Jersey. Trenton, N.J.: Wilson and Halsey, 1807.

Report of the [New Jersey] Committee on the Correspondence Between Governor Clinton and Governor Williamson Touching the Arrest of a Ministerial Officer, &c. Trenton: William L. Prall, 1826.

Reports of Cases Argued and Determined in the Supreme Court . . . of New Jersey. 47 vols. Various places and publishers, 1819–86.

Reports of Cases Decided in the Court of Chancery of the State of New Jersey. 46 vols. Various places and publishers, 1877–90.

Richardson, James D., comp. *A Compilation of the Messages and Papers of the President, 1789–1897.* 10 vols. Washington, D.C.: Government Printing Office, 1896–99.

Votes and Proceedings . . . of the General Assembly of the State of New Jersey. . . , 1815–1840. Published at various places after each sitting, 1815–40.

Published Reminiscences, Diaries, and Papers

Adams, Charles Francis, ed. *Memoirs of John Quincy Adams, Comprising Portions of His Diary from 1795 to 1848.* 12 vols. Philadelphia: J. B. Lippincott and Co., 1874–77.

Bassett, John Spencer, ed. *Correspondence of Andrew Jackson.* 7 vols. Washington, D.C.: Carnegie Institution of Washington, 1926–35.

Elmer, Lucius Q. C. *The Constitution and Government of the Province and State of New Jersey, With Biographical Sketches of the Governors from 1776 to 1845, and Reminiscences of the Bench and Bar During More Than Half a Century.* (Collections of the New Jersey Historical Society, vol. 7.) Newark, N.J.: Martin R. Dennis & Co., 1872.

Fitzpatrick, John C., ed. *The Autobiography of Martin Van Buren.* Washington, D.C.: United States Government Printing Office, 1918.

Hall, John D., ed. *Forty Years of Familiar Letters of James W. Alexander.* 2 vols. New York: Charles Scribner, 1860.

Hamilton, J. F. DeRoulhac, ed. *The Papers of William Alexander Graham.* 4 vols. Raleigh, N.C.: State Department of Archives and History, 1957–61.

Hopkins, James F. and Hargreaves, Mary W., eds. *The Papers of Henry Clay.* 6 vols. in progress. Lexington, Ky.: University Press of Kentucky, 1959—.

Hunt, Gaillard, ed. *The First Forty Years of Washington Society in the Family Letters of Margaret Bayard Smith.* Reprint ed. New York: Frederick Ungar Publishing Co., 1965.

Mackey, Philip E., ed. *A Gentleman of Much Promise: The Diary of Isaac Mickle, 1837–1845.* 2 vols. Philadelphia: The University of Pennsylvania Press, 1977.

McGrane, Reginald C., ed. *The Correspondence of Nicholas Biddle Dealing with National Affairs, 1807–1844.* Boston: Houghton Mifflin Company, 1919.

Ogden, Aaron. *Autobiography of Aaron Ogden of Elizabethtown.* Paterson, N.J.: n.p., 1893.

Quincy, Josiah. *Figures of the Past: From the Leaves of Old Journals.* Boston: Roberts Brothers, 1883.

Reingold, Nathan, ed. *The Papers of Joseph Henry.* 2 vols. in progress. Washington, D.C.: The Smithsonian Institution Press, 1972—.

Sargent, Nathan. *Public Men and Events From the Commencement of Mr. Monroe's Administration in 1817, to the Close of Mr. Fillmore's Administration, in 1853.* 2 vols. Philadelphia: J. B. Lippincott and Co., 1875.

Shanks, Henry T., ed. *The Papers of Willie Person Mangum.* 5 vols. Raleigh, N.C.: State Department of Archives and History, 1950–56.

Williams, Amelia W., and Barker, Eugene C., eds. *The Writings of Sam Houson.* 8 vols. Austin, Texas: University of Texas Press, 1938.

Wilson, Clyde N., and Hemphill, W. Edwin, eds. *The Papers of John C. Calhoun.* 12 vols. in progress. Columbia, S.C.: University of Southard Carolina Press, 1959—.

Wiltse, Charles M., ed. *The Papers of Daniel Webster: Correspondence.* 5 vols. in progress. Hanover, N.H.: University Press of New England, 1972—.

Contemporary Broadsides, Pamphlets, and Books

An Answer to Mr. John L. Sullivan's Report to the Manufacturing Society in New Jersey in a Letter to the Directors of the Morris Canal Company by the President of that Company. New York: William A. Davis, 1828.

Argument of Samuel L. Southard in the Case of Stacy DeCow and Joseph Hendrickson versus Thomas L. Shotwell. . . . Philadelphia: Elijah Weaver, 1834.

Gordon, Thomas F. *A Gazeteer of the State of New Jersey, Comprehending a General View of its Physical and Moral Condition.* Trenton, N.J.: Daniel Fenton, 1834.

Law Opinion in the Case of the Paterson Manufacturing Society Against the Morris Canal and Banking Company. Paterson, N.J.: B. Burnett, 1829.

Minutes of Proceedings of the Courts of Enquiry and Court Martial in Relation to Captain David Porter. Washington: Davis and Force, 1825.

Porter, David. *An Exposition of the Facts and Circumstances Which Justified the Expedition to Foxardo.* Washington: Davis and Force, 1825.

Reasons for Granting to the Morris Canal and Banking Company an Increase of Banking Capital and the Loan of State Bonds. New York: James Van Norden, n.d.

Remarks on Reasons Why Mr. Southard Ought Not to Be Elected by the Legislature to Supply the Vacancy in the Senate, Created by the Resignation of Dr. Bateman. N.p., n.d.

Sketches of United States Senators of the Session of 1837–8, by "A Looker on Here in Verona." Washington, D.C.: William M. Morrison, 1839.

[Southard, Samuel L.] *A Short Statement of Facts, Connected with the Conduct of Mr. Southard, on what is usually called the Missouri Question.* N.p., n.d.

[Stockton, Lucius H.] *A History of the Steamboat Case, Lately Discussed by Counsel Before the Legislature of New Jersey, Comprised in a Letter to a Gentleman at Washington.* Trenton, N.J.: Privately Printed, 1815.

[.] *Reasons Why Mr. Southard ought not to be elected by the Legislature to supply the Vacancy in the Senate, created by the Resignation of Dr. Bateman,* n.p., n.d.

[.] *A Reply to Sundry Pretexts and Remarks of the friends of Mr. Southard to the six reasons offered why he should not be elected Senator. By a native and Real Inhabitant of New-Jersey.* Trenton, N.J.: George Sherman, 1829.

Title Papers of the Clamorgan Grant, or 536,904 Arpents of Alluvial Land in Missouri and Arkansas. New York: T. Snowden, 1837.

Newspapers

Bridgeton, N.J.
  Washington Whig, 1816–26

Newark, N.J.
  Daily Advertiser, 1836–42
  New Jersey Eagle, 1824–32
  Sentinel of Freedom, 1815–40

New Brunswick, N.J.
  Fredonian, 1811–25

Newton, N.J.
  Sussex Register, 1829–40

Paterson, N.J.
  Passaic Guardian and Paterson Advertiser, 1840–42
  Paterson Intelligencer, 1825–42

Salem, N.J.
  Salem Messenger and Public Advertiser, 1828–30

Trenton, N.J.
  Emporium, 1821–27
  Emporium and True American, 1829–39
  Federalist, 1814–25
  National Union, 1831–32
  New Jersey State Gazette, 1832–42
  True American, 1815–28

Washington, D.C.
  Globe, 1831–38
  Daily Telegraph, 1826–29
  National Intelligencer, 1823–29
  National Journal, 1827–29

Woodbury, N.J.
  Columbian Herald, 1819–20

Secondary Sources

Books

Ammon, Harry. *James Monroe: The Quest for National Identity*. New York: McGraw-Hill Book Company, 1971.

Banning, Lance. *The Jeffersonian Persuasion: Evolution of a Party Ideology*. Ithaca, N.Y.: Cornell University Press, 1978.

Bartlett, Irving. *Daniel Webster*. New York: W. W. Norton and Company, 1978.

Basset, John Spencer. *The Life of Andrew Jackson*. 2 vols. Garden City, N.Y.: Doubleday, Page and Company, 1911.

Baxter, Maurice. *The Steamboat Monopoly: Gibbons v. Ogden, 1824*. New York: Alfred A. Knopf, 1972.

Bemis, Samuel Flagg. *John Quincy Adams*. 2 vols. New York: Alfred A. Knopf, 1950, 1956.

Benjamin, Park. *The United States Naval Academy.* New York: G. P. Putnam's Sons, 1900.

Bill, Alfred Hoyt. *A House Called Morven.* Edited by Constance M. Grieff. Revised ed. Princeton, N.J.: Princeton University Press, 1978.

Billingsley, Edward B. *In Defense of Neutral Rights: The United States Navy and the Wars of Independence in Chile and Peru.* Chapel Hill, N.C.: University of North Carolina Press, 1967.

Brinton, Howard H. *Friends for 300 Years: The History and Beliefs of the Society of Friends Since George Fox Started the Quaker Movement.* New York: Harper and Brothers, 1952.

Brock, William R. *Parties and Political Conscience: American Dilemmas, 1840–1850.* Millwood, N.Y.: KTO Press, 1979.

Brown, Everett Somerville, ed. *The Missouri Compromises and Presidential Politics, 1820–1825: From the Letters of William Plumer, Junior.* St. Louis, Mo.: Missouri Historical Society, 1926.

Brown, Isaac V. *Memoirs of the Rev. Robert Finley, D. D.* New Brunswick, N.J.: Terhune and Letson, 1819.

Brown, Norman D. *Daniel Webster and the Politics of Availability.* Athens, Ga.: University of Georgia Press, 1969.

Brugger, Robert. *Beverly Tucker: Head Over Heart in the Old South.* Baltimore: Johns Hopkins University Press, 1978.

Burr, Nelson R. *Education in New Jersey, 1630–1871.* Princeton, N.J.: Princeton University Press, 1942.

Cadman, John W. *The Corporation in New Jersey: Business and Politics, 1791–1875.* Cambridge, Mass.: Harvard University Press, 1949.

Chambers, William Nisbet. *Old Bullion Benton: Senator from the New West.* Boston: Little, Brown, and Co., 1956.

Chase, James S. *Emergence of the Presidential Nominating Convention, 1789–1832.* Urbana, Ill.: University of Illinois Press, 1973.

Coit, Margaret. *John C. Calhoun: American Portrait.* Boston: Houghton Mifflin Company, 1950.

Coleman, Peter J. *Debtors and Creditors in America: Insolvency, Imprisonment for Debt, and Bankruptcy, 1607–1900.* Madison: The State Historical Society of Wisconsin, 1974.

Craven, Avery O. *Soil Exhaustion as a Factor in the Agricultural History of Virginia and Maryland, 1606–1860.* Urbana, Ill.: University of Illinois Press, 1926.

Cunningham, John T. *New Jersey: America's Main Road.* Garden City, N.Y.: Doubleday and Company, Inc., 1966.

Current, Richard M. *Daniel Webster and the Rise of National Conservatism.* Boston: Little, Brown and Company, 1955.

Curtis, James M. *Andrew Jackson and the Search for Vindication.* Boston: Little, Brown and Company, 1976.

———. *The Fox at Bay: Martin Van Buren and the Presidency, 1837–1841.* Lexington, Ky.: University Press of Kentucky, 1970.

Dictionary of American Biography. Edited by Allan Johnson and Dumas Malone. 20 vols. New York: Charles Scribner's Sons, 1928–37.

Dangerfield, George. *The Awakening of American Nationalism, 1815–1828*. New York: Harper and Row, 1965.

———. *Chancellor Robert R. Livingston of New York, 1746–1813*. New York: Harcourt Brace, 1960.

———. *The Era of Good Feelings*. New York: Harcourt, Brace, and World, Inc., 1952.

Eaton, Clement. *Henry Clay and the Art of American Politics*. Boston: Little, Brown and Company, 1957.

Ellis, Richard E. *The Jeffersonian Crisis: Courts and Politics in the Young Republic*. New York: Oxford University Press, 1971

Fee, Walter R. *The Transition from Aristocracy to Democracy in New Jersey, 1789–1829*. Somerville, N.J.: The Somerset Press, 1933.

Field, James A., Jr. *America and the Mediterranean World, 1776–1882*. Princeton, N.J.: Princeton University Press, 1969.

Foner, Eric. *Free Soil, Free Labor, Free Men: The Ideology of the Republican Party Before the Civil War*. New York: Oxford University Press, 1970.

Forbush, Bliss, *Elias Hicks, Quaker Liberal*. New York: Columbia University Press, 1956.

Forgie, George B. *Patricide and the House Divided: A Psychological Interpretation of Lincoln and His Age*. New York: W. W. Norton & Co., 1979.

Freehling, William W. *Prelude to Civil War: The Nullification Controversy in South Carolina, 1816–1836*. New York: Harper and Row, 1966.

Friedman, Lawrence M. *A History of American Law*. New York: Simon and Schuster, 1973.

Friend, Llrena. *Sam Houston: The Great Designer*. Austin, Tex.: University of Texas Press, 1954.

Goldberg, Isaac. *Major Noah: American Jewish Pioneer*. New York: The Jewish Publications Society, 1936.

Goldman, Perry M., and Young, James S., eds. *The United States Congressional Directories, 1789–1840*. New York: Columbia University Press, 1973.

Grundy, J. Owen. *The History of Jersey City, 1609–1976*. Jersey City, N.J.: Chamber of Commerce, 1976.

Gunderson, Robert G. *The Log-Cabin Campaign*. Lexington, Ky.: University of Kentucky Press, 1957.

Haines, Charles G. and Sherwood, Foster H. *The Role of the Supreme Court in American Government and Politics*. Los Angeles: University of California Press, 1957.

Hammond, Bray. *Banks and Politics in America: From the Revolution to the Civil War*. Princeton, N.J.: Princeton University Press, 1957.

Harlow, Alvin F. *Old Towpaths: The Story of the American Canal Era*. New York: D. Appleton and Co., 1926.

Hirsch, Susan E. *Roots of the American Working Class: The Industrialization of Crafts in Newark, 1800–1860*. Philadelphia: University of Pennsylvania Press, 1978.

Holt, Michael F. *The Political Crisis of the 1850s*. New York: John Wiley & Sons, 1978.

Horwitz, Morton J. *The Transformation of American Law, 1780–1860*. Cambridge, Mass.: Harvard University Press, 1977.

Howe, Daniel Walker. *The Political Culture of the American Whigs*. Chicago: University of Chicago Press, 1979.

Hurst, James Willard. *The Legitimacy of the Business Corporation in the Law of the United States*. Charlottesville, Va.: University of Virginia Press, 1970.

Johnson, Robert E. *Thence Round Cape Horn: The Story of the United States Naval Forces in the Pacific Station, 1818–1923*. Annapolis, Md.: U.S. Naval Institute Press, 1969.

Ketcham, Ralph. *James Madison: A Biography*. New York: The Macmillan Company, 1971.

Kett, Joseph F. *Rites of Passage: Adolescence in America, 1790 to the Present*. New York: Basic Books, 1977.

Kirwan, Albert D. *John J. Crittenden: The Struggle for the Union*. Lexington, Ky.: University of Kentucky Press, 1962.

Klamkin, Marian. *The Return of Lafayette: 1824–1825*. New York: Charles Scribner's Sons, 1975.

Lane, Wheaton J. *From Indian Trail to Iron Horse: Travel and Transportation in New Jersey, 1620–1860*. Princeton, N.J.: Princeton University Press, 1939.

Langley, Harold D. *Social Reform in the United States Navy, 1798–1862*. Urbana, Ill.: University of Illinois Press, 1967.

Latner, Richard B. *The Presidency of Andrew Jackson: White House Politics, 1829–1837*. Athens, Ga.: University of Georgia Press, 1979.

Levine, Peter D. *The Behavior of State Legislative Parties: New Jersey, 1829–1844*. Rutherford, N.J.: Fairleigh Dickinson University Press, 1977.

Livermore, Shaw Jr. *The Twilight of Federalism: The Disintegration of the Federalist Party, 1815–1830*. Princeton, N.J.: Princeton University Press, 1962.

Long, David F. *Nothing Too Daring: A Biography of Commodore David Porter, 1780–1843*. Annapolis, Md.: United States Naval Institute Press, 1970.

Maclean, John. *History of the College of New Jersey From its Origin in 1746 to the Commencement of 1854*. 2 vols. Philadelphia: J. B. Lippincott & Co., 1877.

Macleod, Duncan J. *Slavery, Race, and the American Revolution*. Cambridge, England: Cambridge University Press, 1974.

McCormick, Richard P. *The Second American Party System: Party Formation in the Jacksonian Era*. Chapel Hill, N.C.: University of North Carolina Press, 1966.

McCoy, Drew R. *The Elusive Republic: Political Economy in Jeffersonian America*. Chapel Hill, N.C.: University of North Carolina Press, 1980.

McGrane, Reginald C. *Foreign Bondholders and American State Debts*. New York: The Macmillan Company, 1935.

Maier, Pauline. *The Old Revolutionaries: Political Lives in the Age of Samuel Adams*. New York: Alfred A. Knopf, 1980.

Mark, Irving. *Agrarian Conflicts in Colonial New York, 1711–1775*. New York: Columbia University Press, 1940.

May, Ernest R. *The Making of the Monroe Doctrine*. Cambridge, Mass.: Harvard University Press, 1975.

Messler, Abraham A. *First Things in Old Somerset*. Somerville, N.J.: The Somerville Publishing Company, 1899.

Minutes of the Meetings of the Justices and Chosen Freeholders for the County of Somerset, May 13, 1772, to September 2, 1822. Somerville, N.J.: Somerset County Historical Society, 1978.

Mooney, Chase C. *William H. Crawford, 1772–1834*. Lexington, Ky.: University Press of Kentucky, 1974.

Moore, Glover. *The Missouri Controversy: 1819–1821.* Lexington, Ky.: University of Kentucky Press, 1953.

Morgan, Robert J. *A Whig Embattled.* Lincoln, Neb.: University of Nebraska Press, 1954.

Mullin, Gerald W. *Flight and Rebellion: Slave Resistance in Eighteenth-Century Virginia.* New York: Oxford University Press, 1972.

Munroe, John A. *Louis McLane: Federalist and Jacksonian.* New Brunswick, N.J.: Rutgers University Press, 1973.

Nathans, Sydney. *Daniel Webster and Jacksonian Democracy.* Baltimore: The Johns Hopkins University Press, 1973.

Newmyer, R. Kent. *The Supreme Court Under Marshall and Taney.* New York: Thomas Y. Crowell Co., 1968.

O'Connor, John E. *William Paterson: Lawyer and Statesman, 1745–1806.* New Brunswick, N.J.: Rutgers University Press, 1979.

Pasler, Rudolph J., and Pasler, Margaret C. *The New Jersey Federalists.* Rutherford, N.J.: Fairleigh Dickinson University Press, 1975.

Paullin, Charles O. *Paullin's History of Naval Administration, 1775–1911. . . .* Annapolis, Md.: U.S. Naval Institute, 1968.

Perkins, Bradford, *Castlereagh and Adams: England and the United States, 1812–1823.* Berkeley, Calif.: University of California Press, 1964.

Pessen, Edward. *Jacksonian America: Society, Personality, and Politics.* Homewood, Ill.: The Dorsey Press, 1969.

———.*Riches, Class, and Power Before the Civil War.* Lexington, Mass.: D.C. Heath and Company, 1973.

Poage, George R. *Henry Clay and the Whig Party.* Chapel Hill, N.C.: University of North Carolina Press, 1936.

Pocock, J. G. A. *The Machiavellian Moment: Florentine Political Thought and the Atlantic Republican Tradition.* Princeton, N.J.: Princeton University Press, 1975.

Prince, Carl M. *New Jersey's Jeffersonian Republicans: The Genesis of an Early Party Machine, 1789–1817.* Chapel Hill, N.C.: University of North Carolina Press, 1964.

Remini, Robert V. *Andrew Jackson.* 2 vols. to date. New York: Harper & Row, 1977–.

———. *Andrew Jackson and the Bank War.* New York: W. W. Norton and Co., 1967.

———. *The Election of Andrew Jackson.* Philadelphia: J. B. Lippincott Company, 1963.

———. *Martin Van Buren and the Making of the Democratic Party.* New York: Columbia University Press, 1959.

———. *The Revolutionary Age of Andrew Jackson.* New York: Harper and Row, 1976.

Risjord, Norman K. *The Old Republicans: Southern Conservatism in the Age of Jefferson.* New York: Columbia University Press, 1965.

Rogin, Michael Paul. *Fathers and Children: Andrew Jackson and the Subjugation of the American Indian.* New York: Alfred A. Knopf, 1975.

Sarna, Jonathan D. *Jacksonian Jew: The Two Worlds of Mordecai Noah.* New York: Holmes & Meier Publishers, Inc., 1981.

Schlesinger, Arthur M., Jr. *The Age of Jackson.* Boston: Little, Brown and Company, 1945.

Schumacher, Ludwig. *The Somerset Hills.* New York: New Amsterdam Book Co., ca. 1900.

Schwarz, Philip J. *The Jarring Interests: New York's Boundary Makers, 1664–1776.* Albany, N.Y.: State University of New York Press, 1979.

Seager, Robert, II. *And Tyler Too: A Biography of John and Julia Gardiner Tyler.* New York: McGraw-Hill Book Company, Inc., 1963.

Shy, John. *A People Numerous and Armed: Reflections on the Military Struggle for American Independence.* New York: Oxford Univeristy Press, 1976.

Smith, Daniel Blake. *Inside the Great House: Planter Family Life in Eighteenth-Century Chesapeake Society.* Ithaca, N.Y.: Cornell University Press, 1980.

Snell, John P., comp. *History of Hunterdon and Somerset Counties.* New York: Evarts and Peck, 1881.

Somkin, Fred. *Unquiet Eagle: Memory and Desire in the Idea of American Freedom, 1815–1860.* Ithaca, N.Y.: Cornell University Press, 1967.

Sprout, Harold, and Sprout, Margaret. *The Rise of American Naval Power, 1776–1918.* Princeton, N.J.: Princeton University Press, 1939.

Stanton, William. *The Great United States Exploring Expedition of 1838–1842.* Berkeley, Calif.: University of California Press, 1975.

Staudenraus, Peter J. *The African Colonization Movement, 1816–1865.* New York: Columbia University Press, 1961.

Swisher, Carl B. *The Oliver Wendall Holmes Devise History of the Supreme Court of the United States: The Taney Period, 1836–1864.* New York: The Macmillan Publishing Co., Inc., 1974.

———. *Roger B. Taney.* New York: The Macmillan Company, 1935.

Symonds, Craig L. *Navalists and Antinavalists: The Naval Policy Debate in the United States, 1785–1827.* Newark, Del.: University of Delaware Press, 1980.

Thayer, Theodore. *As We Were: The Story of Old Elizabethtown.* Elizabeth, N.J.: Grassman Publishing Company, 1964.

Tyler, David. *The Wilkes Expedition: The First United States Exploring Expedition, 1838–1842.* Philadelphia: American Philosophical Society, 1968.

Van Deusen, Glyndon G. *The Life of Henry Clay.* Boston: Little, Brown and Company, 1937.

———. *The Jacksonian Era: 1828–1848.* New York: Harper and Row, 1959.

Varg, Paul A. *United States Foreign Relations, 1820–1860.* N.p.: Michigan State University Press, 1979.

Vaughn, William Preston. *The Antimasonic Party in the United States, 1826–1843.* Lexington, Ky.: University Press of Kentucky, 1983.

Vecoli, Rudolph J. *The People of New Jersey.* Princeton, N.J.: D. Van Nostrand Company, 1965.

Wacker, Peter O. *Land and People: A Cultural Geography of Preindustrial New Jersey: Origins and Settlement Patterns.* New Brunswick, N.J.: Rutgers University Press, 1975.

———. *The Musconetcong Valley of New Jersey: A Historical Geography.* New Brunswick, N.J.: Rutgers University Press, 1968.

Welter, Rush. *The Mind of America, 1820–1860.* New York: Columbia University Press, 1975.

Wertenbaker, Thomas J. *Princeton: 1746–1896.* Princeton, N.J.: Princeton University Press, 1946.

Wheeler, Richard. *In Pirate Waters.* New York: Thomas Y. Crowell Company, 1969.

White, Leonard D. *The Jeffersonians: A Study in Administrative History, 1801–1829.* New York: The Free Press, 1951.

Williams, Frances Leigh. *Matthew Fontaine Maury: Scientist of the Sea.* New Brunswick, N.J.: Rutgers University Press, 1963.

Wilmerding, Lucius, Jr. *James Monroe: Public Claimant.* New Brunswick, N.J.: Rutgers University Press, 1960.

Wiltse, Charles M. *John C. Calhoun: Nationalist, 1782–1828.* Indianapolis, Ind.: Bobbs-Merrill Co., Inc., 1944.

———. *John C. Calhoun: Nullifier, 1829–1839.* Indianapolis, Ind.: Bobbs-Merrill Co., Inc., 1949.

Wood, Gordon S., ed. *The Rising Glory of America, 1760–1820.* New York: George Braziller, 1971.

Young, James Sterling. *The Washington Community, 1800–1828.* New York: Harcourt, Brace & World, Inc., 1966.

Articles

Banning, Lance. "The Moderate as Revolutionary: An Introduction to Madison's Life." *The Quarterly Journal of the Library of Congress* 37 (Spring 1980): 162–75.

Bentley, Esther F. "Samuel L. Southard and Political Patronage." *Princeton University Library Chronicle* 23 (Autumn 1961): 1–15.

Berthoff, Rowland. "Independence and Attachment, Virtue and Interest: From Republican Citizen to Free Enterpriser, 1787–1837." In *Uprooted Americans: Essays to Honor Oscar Handlin,* pp. 97–124. Edited by Richard L. Bushman et al. Boston: Little, Brown and Company, 1979.

Berthoff, Rowland, and Murrin, John M. "Feudalism, Communalism, and the Yeoman Freeholder: The American Revolution as a Social Accident." In *Essays on the American Revolution,* pp. 256–88. Edited by Stephen G. Kurtz and James H. Hutson. Chapel Hill, N.C.: University of North Carolina Press, 1973.

Birkner, Michael J. "Elias P. Seeley." In *The Governors of New Jersey, 1664–1974: Biographical Essays,* pp. 105–8. Edited by Paul A. Stellhorn and Michael J. Birkner. Trenton, N.J.: New Jersey Historical Commission, 1982.

———. "The 'Foxardo Affair' Revisited: Porter, Pirates and the Problem of Civilian Authority in the Early Republic." *The American Neptune* 42 (July 1982): 165–178.

———. "Journalism and Politics in Jacksonian New Jersey: The Career of Stacy G. Potts." *New Jersey History* 97 (Autumn 1979): 159–78.

———. "Peter Vroom and the Politics of Democracy." In *Jacksonian New Jersey,* pp. 11–38. Edited by Paul A. Stellhorn. Trenton, N.J.: New Jersey Historical Commission, 1979.

———. "Samuel L. Southard and the Origins of *Gibbons* v. *Ogden.*" *Princeton University Library Chronicle* 40 (Winter 1979): 171–82.

Cain, Marvin R. "William Wirt Against Andrew Jackson: Reflections on an Era." *Mid-America* 47 (April 1965): 113–38.

Chandler, Alfred D. "Anthracite Coal and the Beginnings of the Industrial Revolution in the United States." *Business History Review* 46 (Summer 1972): 141–81.

Chute, William J. "The New Jersey Whig Campaign of 1840." *New Jersey History* 78 (1960): 222–39.

Cranmer, H. Jerome. "Improvements Without Public Funds; The New Jersey Canals." In *Canals and American Economic Development*, pp. 126–46. Edited by Carter Goodrich. New York: Columbia University Press, 1961.

Dangerfield, George. "The Steamboat Case." In *Quarrels That Have Shaped the Constitution*, pp. 49–61. Edited by John A. Garraty. New York: Harper & Row, 1962.

"Earliest Ancestors of Somerset Families." *Somerset County Historical Quarterly* 5 (1916): 277–79.

Eichert, Magdalen. "Daniel Webster's Western Land Investments." *Historical New Hampshire* 26 (Fall 1971): 29–35.

Ellis, Richard E. "The Political Economy of Thomas Jefferson." In *Thomas Jefferson: The Man, His World, His Influence*, pp. 81–95. Edited by Lally Weymouth. New York: G. P. Putnam's Sons, 1973.

Ershkowitz, Herbert. "The Election of 1824 in New Jersey." *Proceedings of the New Jersey Historical Society* 84 (April 1966): 113–32.

————. "Peter D. Vroom." In *The Governors of New Jersey*. Edited by Paul A. Stellhorn and Michael J. Birkner. Trenton, N.J.: New Jersey Historical Commission, 1982.

————. "Samuel L. Southard: A Case Study of Whig Leadership in the Age of Jackson." *New Jersey History* 88 (Spring 1970): 5–24.

Ershkowitz, Herbert, and Shade, William G. "Consensus or Conflict? Political Behavior in the State Legislatures During the Jacksonian Era." *Journal of American History* 68 (December 1971): 591–621.

Hailperin, Herman. "Pro-Jackson Sentiment in Pennsylvania, 1820–1828." *Pennsylvania Magazine of History and Biography* 50 (July 1926): 193–240.

Hall, Edward M. "Samuel L. Southard." In *The American Secretaries of the Navy*. Edited by Paolo E. Coletta. Annapolis, Md.: U.S. Naval Institute, 1980.

Hay, Thomas Robson. "John C. Calhoun and the Presidential Campaign of 1824." *North Carolina Historical Review* 12 (January, 1935): 20–44.

Herrmann, Frederick M. "Anti-Masonry in New Jersey." *New Jersey History* 91 (Autumn 1973): 149–65.

Johnson, Herbert A. "*Gibbons* v. *Ogden* before Marshall." In *Courts and Law in Early New York: Selected Essays*, pp. 105–13. Edited by Leo Hershkowitz and Milton M. Klein. Port Washington, N.Y.: Kennikat Press, 1978.

Keller, Morton. "Reflections on Politics and Generations in America." *Daedalus* (Fall 1978): 123–36.

Langley, Harold D. "The Grass Roots Harvest of 1828." *United States Naval Institute Proceedings* 90 (1964): 51–59.

Latner, Richard B., and Levine, Peter D. "Perspectives in Antebellum Pietistic Politics: The Salience of Ethno-Cultural Issues." *Reviews in American History* 4 (March 1976): 15–24.

Lutzker, Michael A. "Abolition of Imprisonment for Debt in New Jersey." *Proceedings of the New Jersey Historical Society* 84 (October 1966): 1–29.

McCormick, Richard P. "Party Formation in New Jersey in the Jackson Era." *Proceedings of the New Jersey Historical Society* 83 (July 1965): 161–73.

McLachlan, James. "The Choice of Hercules: American Student Societies in the Early 19th Century." In *The University in Society: Europe, Scotland, and the United States from the 16th to the 20th Century*, vol. 2, pp. 449–94. Edited by Lawrence Stone. Princeton, N.J.: Princeton University Press, 1974.

Main, Jackson T. "The Distribution of Property in Post Revolutionary Virginia." *Mississippi Valley Historical Review* 41 (September 1954): 241–58.

————. "Sections and Politics in Virginia, 1781–1787." *William and Mary Quarterly*, 3rd ser., 12 (January 1955): 96–112.

Miles, Edwin A. "The Whig Party and the Menace of Caesar." *Tennessee Historical Quarterly* 27 (Winter 1968): 361–79.

Nagel, Paul C. "The Election of 1824: A Reconsideration Based on Newspaper Opinion." *Journal of Southern History* 21 (August 1960): 315–29.

Pease, William H., and Pease, Jane H. "Paternal Dilemmas: Education, Property and Patrician Persistence in Jacksonian Boston." *New England Quarterly* 53 (June 1980): 147–67.

Phillips, Kim T. "The Pennsylvania Origins of the Jackson Movement." *Political Science Quarterly* 91 (Fall 1976): 489–508.

Prince, Carl E. "James J. Wilson: Party Leader, 1801–1824." *Proceedings of the New Jersey Historical Society* 83 (January 1965): 24–39.

Shalhope, Robert E. "Thomas Jefferson's Republicanism and Antebellum Southern Thought." *Journal of Southern History* 42 (November 1976): 529–56.

Smith, Carlton B. "John C. Calhoun, Secretary of War, 1817–1825: The Cast Iron Man as an Administrator." In *America, the Middle Period: Essays in Honor of Bernard Mayo*, pp. 132–44. Edited by John B. Boles. Charlottesville, Va.: University of Virginia Press, 1973.

Smith, Culver R. "Propaganda Technique in the Jackson Campaign of 1828." *East Tennessee Historical Society Publications* 6 (1934): 44–66.

Thompson, Robert T. "Transportation Combines and Pressure Politics in New Jersey, 1833–1836." *Proceedings of the New Jersey Historical Society* 57 (January 1939): 1–15, 71–86.

Thomson, David W. "The Great Steamboat Monopolies, Part 2: The Hudson." *The American Neptune* 16 (October 1956): 270–80.

Van Deusen, Glyndon G. "Some Aspects of Whig Thought and Theory in the Jacksonian Period." *American Historical Review* 63 (January 1958): 305–22.

Unpublished Studies

Adair, Douglass Greybill. "The Intellectual Origins of Jeffersonian Democracy: Republicanism, The Class Struggle, and the Virtuous Farmer." Ph.D. dissertation, Yale University, 1943.

Andrews, Archie D. "Agriculture in Virginia, 1789–1820." M.A. thesis, University of Virginia, 1950.

Beckwith, Robert R. "Mahlon Dickerson of New Jersey, 1770–1853." Ph.D. dissertation, Columbia University (Horace Mann Teacher's College), 1964.

Ershkowitz, Herbert. "New Jersey Politics During the Era of Andrew Jackson, 1820–1837." Ph.D. dissertation, New York University, 1965.

———. "The Origin of the Whig and Democratic Parties: New Jersey Politics, 1820–1837." Unpublished MS.

Fallaw, Walter R. "The Rise of the Whig Party in New Jersey." Ph.D. dissertation, Princeton University, 1967.

Hargreaves, Mary W. "The Presidency of John Quincy Adams." Forthcoming in University of Kansas Presidency series.

Lorish, Robert. "William H. Crawford and the Presidential Election of 1824." M.A. thesis, University of Virginia, 1966.

Lowery, Charles D. "James Barbour, A Politician and Planter of Antebellum Virginia." Ph.D. dissertation, University of Virginia, 1966.

Perry, Perceval. "The Attitudes of the New Jersey Delegations in Congress on the Slavery Question, 1815–1861." M.A. thesis, Rutgers University, 1939.

Potter, Ralph K. "Early Southards of New York and New Jersey." Typescript in New Jersey State Library, Trenton.

Index

263